H9/86

Industrial Electronics *and Control*

2 nd edition

Industrial

Royce Gerald Kloeffler

Professor of Electrical Engineering
Kansas State University

Electronics *and* *Control*

New York · *John Wiley & Sons, Inc.* · *London*

SECOND EDITION

Second Printing, July, 1961

Library of Congress Catalog Card Number: 60–5600

Printed in the United States of America

Preface

This book has been written to give the college engineering student a survey of the theory and applications of electronics in industry. It has been designed to meet the requirements of students in mechanical, chemical, and industrial engineering plus power majors in electrical engineering who desire a knowledge in industrial-electronic applications. No attempt has been made to provide a quantitive approach to the design of circuits since such calculations require several credit hours of basic studies in the electronic field. The early chapters of this textbook are prepared for the student whose training has not included the basic theory of semiconductors and electron tubes. Some teachers may find the first eight chapters suitable for use as an introductory course for all electrical engineering students.

The last decade has seen the development and refinement of the junction transistor, several large capacity semiconductor rectifiers, several semiconductor photo devices, and the self-excited magnetic amplifier. These devices are rapidly replacing the vacuum and gaseous tubes in both the communication and the industrial electronic field. This emphasis on the semiconductor suggests a more simple approach to the theory of electronics. Accordingly, this book begins with the theory of solid state conduction and leads to the theory of rectification and amplification via semiconductor devices. The theory of the vacuum and gaseous tube follows logically and leads to a parallel approach to industrial electronic applications via semiconductor and tube devices.

v

The ASA standard symbols have been used throughout. The direction of conventional current has been adopted as standard, but the direction of both conventional and electron current is shown for the convenience of the student. Simple basic circuits have been employed rather than specialized ones whenever possible.

The book covers the latest (1959) developments, such as solid-state thyratrons, cryotrons, and cold cathode vacuum tubes. Additional chapters have been presented on the subjects of electronic instruments and computers.

I am grateful to my friends in industry who have reviewed portions of the text and have given permission for quotation from their articles and books.

R. G. KLOEFFLER

October 1959

Contents

ELECTRICAL GRAPHICAL SYMBOLS
(ASA)

Tube Components		Circuit Components	
Cathode Directly heated		Capacitor	fixed variable
Indirectly heated		Contact	open closed
Cold		Resistor Fixed	simple detailed
Photoelectric		Variable	simple detailed
Pool		Variable	simple detailed
Grid		Inductor Fixed	or iron core
Ignitor	ignitor	Inductor	variable tapped
Anode or plate		Transformer	
Target, X-ray			
Envelopes, High vacuum		Source	battery a-c
Gas filled		Circuit	junction ground
Rectifier Diode			
Transistor			

*   This symbol must always be used with an
identifying legend within or adjacent to
the rectangle.

chapter 1

Introduction

Electronics is a magic word covering a series of discoveries and inventions which have revolutionized the life of man in this twentieth century. In 1883, Thomas A. Edison discovered current conduction through gas in an incandescent lamp. This phenomenon, known as the Edison effect, marked the birth of electronic science. In 1887, Hertz discovered the electromagnetic waves predicted by Maxwell some years before. In 1895, Roentgen discovered X rays. About 1899, Marconi demonstrated the possibilities of wireless communication. In 1902, Fleming invented the "valve" or two-electrode detector. In 1906, DeForest invented the audion, or three-electrode tube. These basic discoveries gave an impetus to the work of hundreds of other scientists whose cumulative inventions and developments have produced what is known as electronics. The layman thinks of electronics as a combination of radio, television, telephone repeaters, and guided missile control. He may be unaware of the important applications in the industrial field such as high-frequency heating, power rectification, resistance welding, and electronic control. This book *will* treat those applications of electronics and control that lie outside the field of communication. A reliable source has predicted that the value of electronic industrial equipment produced in the year 1960 will be 10 billion dollars.

Electronics is that branch of science and engineering which relates to the conduction of electricity through a vacuum, gas, or semiconductor. The term also covers the action taking place in all circuits associated with electron devices. Thus, in a broader sense, electronics may be considered to include nearly all electrical phenomena.

The movement of electrons and other carriers in electron devices involves certain physical phenomena not considered in the study of electrical machinery. These phenomena include (1) the movement of carriers in semiconductors, (2) the removal of electrons from solids, (3) the production of ions in gases, (4) the movement of electrons and ions between electrodes, and (5) the control of the movement of electrons and ions by electrostatic and magnetic fields. An understanding of these processes requires a knowledge of several chemical, physical, and electrical concepts.

Atomic Structure

The electron theory of electricity and matter is a product of our twentieth century thinking and research. At the beginning of the century Thompson suggested the electron as a part of the normal atom. In 1913, Robert Millikan published the result of his work on isolating and measuring the charge on the ion. Thus the electron, a fundamental indivisible particle carrying a negative charge, was discovered. The counterpart or mate of the electron was named the proton, and consists of a particle having a mass approximately 1840 times that of the electron and a positive charge equal in magnitude to the charge on the electron. With these two particles as the building blocks of nature, Bohr suggested the structure of the atom as consisting of a small dense core or nucleus about which one or more electrons revolve. This structure is analogous to our solar system: the nucleus corresponds to the sun, and the revolving electrons correspond to the earth and the planets. The nucleus of the atom contains all the protons and, when present, all the neutrons. For the simple hydrogen atom the single proton constitutes the nucleus and a single electron the lone planet. For helium the nucleus consists of two protons and two neutrons with two electrons serving as the planets of the system. The attraction of the positive nucleus for the revolving electrons is counterbalanced by the centrifugal force of their motion about the nucleus. Bohr assumed the paths or orbits of the electrons to be circles and ellipses. The electrons moving in orbits close to the nucleus are subject to large forces of attraction, whereas those in outer orbits are acted upon by progressively smaller forces. The amount of energy possessed by an electron revolving in any orbit is definite and characteristic of that orbit. To explain the property of radiation due to electrons, it was necessary to assume that an electron may have several orbits and that it is capable of jumping from one to another of these orbits under suitable excitation. The change from one orbit to another is accompanied by the absorption or radiation of a definite amount of energy. This radiated energy may be in the form of light, heat, or other wave energy. Because of this energy exchange, science has developed later theories of energy levels and band theories in the realm of quantum mechanics.

The scientific world is constantly evolving newer and more advanced theories on the structure of matter. Since the Bohr model of the atom was proposed, the neutron, the positron, the neutrino, the meson, and other units have been added to the knowledge of the structure of matter. The theory of the structure of the nucleus of the atom and the changes that take place in it are of paramount importance in nuclear science and developments. However, electronic conduction is effected basically by transfers of electrons, and hence nuclear theory is not needed for an understanding of the operation of electronic devices. The electron has a dual type of behavior. It may have the characteristics of a charged particle or it may act like wave energy. In the simple structure of the Bohr atom and when moving in a vacuum (free space), the electron acts like a particle. As a particle its motion may be predicted by using the laws of mechanics and electrostatics. For the purpose of this chapter the particle theory is sufficient. In future chapters, additional theory covering the behavior of the electron within the structure of matter are given in the appropriate sections.

A molecule is usually a combination of two or more atoms. The normal molecule contains an equal number of electrons and protons and hence the same magnitude of negative and positive charge. If an electron is removed from a molecule, the remaining unit has an unbalanced positive charge and is called a *positive ion*. If an extra electron joins a molecule, the new unit carries a negative charge and is called a *negative ion*. The subtraction and addition of electron charges in forming ions does not change the chemical nature of the molecule since the restoration or addition of an electron will bring the molecule back to its normal neutral state. It is possible for a molecule to suffer the loss or the addition of two or more electrons. In such units the particle is called a multiple charged ion of appropriate sign. A single isolated electron is sometimes called a *negative ion*, but this terminology will not be used in this book.

Electricity

Electron theory offers a simple explanation of the phenomenon and the properties of electricity. Such explanations may be made in terms of a displacement of electrons. Thus if one or more electrons is removed from a normal (neutral) object, a *positive charge* is created on that object. Similarly, if extra electrons are added to a neutral body, a *negative charge* is created. The magnitude of the charge is measured by the deficiency or excess of electrons from the neutral state. A common unit of charge, the coulomb, consists of 6.3×10^{18} electrons. Electric charge is represented by the symbol Q.

Electric charges may be stored in capacitors (condensers). A capacitor usually consists of two parallel conducting surfaces separated by a nonconductor. A displacement of electrons from one surface to the other causes the capacitor to be charged and energy to be stored. If the two charged surfaces are later connected by a conductor, the displaced electrons return to their former positions, the capacitor is discharged, and the stored energy is released.

Electric charges may exist in gases or in a near vacuum as well as on metallic surfaces. In nature, clouds are often charged negatively or positively as a result of air currents and condensation of water vapor. The charges thus acquired may be great enough to result in destructive strokes of lightning. In electron tubes either negatively or positively charged ions may become concentrated in certain regions and thus constitute a charge known as *space charge*. Space charges are important considerations in the operation of electron tubes and are covered in later discussions.

Electrons (negative charges) and protons (positive charges) attract each other. Electrons (negative charges) repel each other. Positive ions repel each other. This basic law of attraction and repulsion of electric charges is fundamental in the operation of electronic devices.

Electric potential differences are created by a displacement of electrons. If some of the electrons in a straight metal bar are moved to one end of that bar (by any means), then that end is negative and the other end is positive. A difference of potential now exists between the ends, and the magnitude of that difference depends on the density of the excess (or deficiency) of the electrons at the ends. It may also be said that electric charges exist at the ends of this rod. The magnitude of these charges depends upon the total number of electrons displaced, whereas the difference of potential depends not on the number of electrons displaced but upon the *concentration or density* of the displaced electrons. The electric charge depends on the area of the region considered, whereas the potential difference is entirely independent of the area. Potential difference is measured by the work done in carrying a unit charge from one point to another and is independent of the path followed.

Electric conduction is the process of transferring electrons in an electric circuit. *Electric current is the coordinated movement of electrons along a conductor.* The movement may be continuous, as in direct current, or periodically changing in character, as in alternating, oscillating, or pulsating currents. The magnitude of the electric current is measured by the number of electrons that move past a point in the circuit per second. An ampere of current exists when transfer takes place at the rate of 1 coulomb (charge) or 6.3×10^{18} electrons per second. Individual electrons may drift (average) at a snail's pace in a copper conductor or at a speed approaching that of light in vacuum under a very high potential. The movement of individual electrons should not be confused with the propagation of an electric wave along a conductor, which takes place at a rate approaching the speed of light. The movement of electrons called *electron current* is opposite to the conventional direction of current adopted long before the electron theory was evolved. In the past many scientists and engineers have suggested that the conventional direction of current should be changed to coincide with the direction of electron movement. Although the suggestion has merit, it is unlikely to find adoption because of established practice and the fact that positive ions and other positive current carriers do move in the direction of conventional current. This book will indicate the direction of electron movement but will otherwise adhere to the conventional direction of current (direction positive charges are urged).

Electric conduction takes place in solids, in liquids, in gases, and in a vacuum. The theory of conduction in these media (except liquids) is given in future chapters. In liquids, conduction is through the medium of ions. If salt (NaCl), for example, is added to distilled water, it will dissolve and dissociate into fragments or ions. The sodium atom becomes the positive ion, and the chlorine atom the negative ion. If two electrodes are placed in the electrolyte and connected to a source of potential, the ions migrate to the electrode of opposite polarity. When the positive sodium ion reaches the negative electrode, it acquires an electron and becomes a neutral sodium atom. Likewise, the negative chlorine ion gives up one electron to the positive electrode and becomes a neutral chlorine atom.

Electron Ballistics

The theory of the movements of charged particles in electrostatic and magnetic fields is known as electron ballistics. The movements

Table 1

Name	Charge	Mass
Electron	$-e$	m_0
Positron	$+e$	m_0
Proton (H ion)	$+e$	$1{,}840m_0$
Neutron	0	$1{,}840m_0$
Alpha particle (He^{++})	$+2e$	$7{,}360m_0$
Neon (ion)	$+e$	$37{,}200m_0$
Argon (ion)	$+e$	$73{,}600m_0$
Mercury (ion)	$+e$	$372{,}000m_0$

of such particles depend upon the charges and masses of the particles, the strength of the fields, and the laws of motion.

The particle of major interest in electron tubes is the electron itself. In gaseous and vapor tubes, positive ions as well as electrons are of interest. The monotomic elements of the group of inert gases (helium, neon, argon, krypton, xenon, and radon) and of mercury vapor are commonly used in electron tubes. In each of these, the molecule consists of one atom. Hence either the term atom or molecule may be used in discussing the theory of the formation and movement of ions.

Calculations for the movement of charged particles in electric and magnetic fields are conveniently made by using the mks (meter-kilogram-second) system. In this system the units employed are: (1) volts for potential, (2) coulombs for charge, (3) newtons for force, and (4) webers for magnetic flux.

The relative electric charges and masses for several particles to be found in electron tubes are given in Table 1.

The symbol for the charge on the electron is e and for its mass m_0. Close values for the magnitude of these symbols in mks units are as follows:

$$e = 1.6 \times 10^{-19} \text{ coulomb} \tag{1}*$$

$$m_0 = 9.1 \times 10^{-31} \text{ kilogram} \tag{2}$$

$$\frac{e}{m_0} = 1.76 \times 10^{11} \text{ coulombs per kilogram} \tag{3}$$

* For more precise values of m_0 and e, see R. T. Birge, "A New Table of Values of General Physical Constants," *Rev. Modern Phys.* **13** (October, 1941).

The value given here for m_0 is for the electron moving with speeds small compared with the speed of light. For higher speeds (above 15 per cent of the velocity of light), the following expression by Lorentz should be used:

$$m_v = \frac{m_0}{\sqrt{1 - \left(\frac{v}{c}\right)^2}} \tag{4}$$

where m_v = mass of the electron in motion (relativity mass).
m_0 = mass of the electron at rest.
v = speed of the electron.
c = speed of light (3×10^8 meters per second).

Electrostatic Field

This is a region that exerts a force upon an electric charge. The direction of the field is that in which a positive charge is urged. An electrostatic field is produced by a change of potential E with distance. The strength of an electrostatic (electric) field is called *electric field intensity* and is represented by the symbol $\mathcal{E}$ (a vector). Electric field intensity $\mathcal{E}$ is measured by the potential gradient which is the change of potential with distance.

$$\mathcal{E} = -\frac{dE}{ds}^* \tag{5}$$

In an electric field the potential *falls* in the direction that a positive charge is urged. Therefore $\mathcal{E}$ and potential gradient are opposite in sign. The strength of an electrostatic field is also defined as the force exerted upon a unit charge. Hence, for a charge Q, the force will be:

$$F = \mathcal{E}Q \tag{6}$$

From the well-known laws of mechanics the following series of equations result:

$$F = ma \qquad \mathcal{E}Q = ma \qquad a = \frac{\mathcal{E}Q}{m} \tag{7}$$

where F is the force and a is the linear acceleration.

Since electric potential is measured by the work W done in moving a unit charge, it follows that for a charge Q

* By definition, the sign of the potential gradient is negative In the discussion and problems that follow, the negative sign will be dropped because the interest will be in magnitude only.

$$E = \frac{W}{Q} \quad \text{and} \quad W = EQ$$

Also,

Potential energy (stored) = work = EQ

Kinetic energy = $\frac{1}{2}mv^2$

Kinetic energy gained = potential energy lost

$$\tfrac{1}{2}mv^2 = EQ \tag{8}$$

$$v = \sqrt{2\frac{Q}{m}E} \tag{9}$$

Equation 9 shows that *both the speed and the kinetic energy acquired by a charged particle moving in an electric field is determined solely by the total potential* E *through which the particle has moved.* This fact gives the basis for a useful unit (electron volt) for measuring the energies involved in particle motion in electric fields. The *electron volt* is the energy acquired by an electron starting from rest and moving in a vacuum through a potential difference of 1 volt. The abbreviation for electron volt is ev. The energy involved in electron volts follows from equation 8.

1 electron falling through 1 volt   = 1 ev (energy)

1 electron falling through E volts = E ev (energy)
$$\tag{10}$$

Also

$$1 \text{ ev} = 1.6 \times 10^{-19} \text{ joule}$$

A uniform electric field may be produced between parallel surfaces. Let A and B represent two parallel plates separated by the distance s in Fig. 1. A potential difference E applied to the plates will set up a uniform field along the line xy and also in most of the region between the plates if the dimension of the plates is large compared to the separation s. The potential distribution along the line xy is shown in the right-hand view of Fig. 1. The potential rises uniformly (linearly) from 0 to E between the plates A and B so that the potential gradient and the electric-field intensity is constant in magnitude and equal to E/s. An electron (negative charge) released at x will be urged toward y with a constant force equal to εe and accelerated

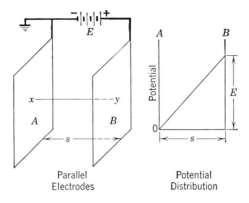

Fig. 1. Potential distribution between two planes.

uniformly until it reaches plate B at y. If E is made 500 volts and $s = 2.5$ cm, the following values of motion will result (mks system).

$$\text{Potential gradient} = \varepsilon = \frac{E}{s} = \frac{500}{2.5 \times 10^{-2}} = 20,000 \; \frac{\text{volts}}{\text{meter}}$$

$$\text{Acceleration} = a = \varepsilon \frac{Q}{m} = \frac{E}{s} \times \frac{e}{m_0} = 20,000 \times 1.76 \times 10^{11}$$
(equation 7)

$$= 3.52 \times 10^{15} \text{ meters per second per second}$$

$$\text{Speed at } y = \sqrt{2 \frac{Q}{m} E} = \sqrt{2 \frac{e}{m_0} E}$$
(equation 9)

$$= \sqrt{2 \times 1.76 \times 10^{11} \times 500} = \sqrt{1.76 \times 10^{14}}$$

$$= 1.325 \times 10^7 \; \frac{\text{meters}}{\text{second}} = 4.4 \text{ per cent velocity of light}$$

An electron beam (a pencil of flying electrons) is controlled and deflected by electric fields in cathode-ray tubes. To analyze such action, assume in Fig. 2 that an electron e moving with a horizontal speed of v_0 along the line aeb enters a uniform electric field (vertical) between two parallel plates at point e. Assuming the polarities indicated, it is evident that the electron will be deflected upward by the electric field and travel along the full line as shown. The speed of translation v_0 to the right will remain unchanged during the electron flight between the plates because the deflecting field is at right angles to that motion. The electric field between the plates (assumed uniform) will give the electron an accelerated motion upward, reaching an upward speed of v_y at the time the electron has emerged from the right-hand edge of the plates. From this point the electron will move on a straight line with a resultant speed determined by the two components v_0 and v_y. The angle θ of the resultant deflection will be determined by the component velocities v_0 and v_y.

The direction and magnitude of the resulting motion can be readily calculated as follows. Assume that the initial velocity of the electron is the same as that of the previous problem (1.325×10^7 meters per second), the plates are 1 cm apart with 100 volts applied, and the length of the plates l is 2.5 cm. The transit time for the electron having an initial horizontal component speed of v_0 is derived from

$$\underset{\text{(distance)}}{l} \quad = \quad \underset{\text{(speed)}}{v_0} \quad \times \quad \underset{\text{(time)}}{t}$$

$$t = \frac{l}{v_0} = \frac{2.5 \times 10^{-2}}{1.325 \times 10^7} = 1.885 \times 10^{-9} \text{ second}$$

$$\text{Acceleration upwards} = a = \frac{E}{s} \frac{e}{m_0}$$

$$= \frac{100}{1 \times 10^{-2}} \times 1.76 \times 10^{11}$$

$$= 1.76 \times 10^{15} \frac{\text{meters}}{\text{second}^2}$$

$$v_y = at = 1.76 \times 10^{15} \times 1.885 \times 10^{-9}$$

$$= 3.32 \times 10^6 \frac{\text{meters}}{\text{second}}$$

$$\text{Angle of deflection } \theta = \tan^{-1}\frac{v_y}{v_0} = \tan^{-1}\frac{3.32 \times 10^6}{1.325 \times 10^7}$$

$$= \tan^{-1} 0.25$$

$$= 14°$$

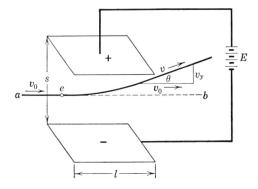

Fig. 2. Deflection of an electron in an electric field.

Final speed $v = \sqrt{v_0{}^2 + v_y{}^2}$

$$= \sqrt{1.325^2 \times 10^{14} + 0.332^2 \times 10^{14}}$$

$$= 1.368 \times 10^7 \frac{\text{meters}}{\text{second}}$$

The upward deflection of the electron while it is passing between the plates may be computed by using the formula

$$s = \tfrac{1}{2}at^2$$

$$s = \tfrac{1}{2}(1.76 \times 10^{15})(1.885 \times 10^{-9})^2$$

$$= 3.12 \times 10^{-3} \text{ meter} = 0.312 \text{ cm}$$

Magnetic Fields

These are often used for controlling the motion of charged particles. The action of a magnetic field upon charged particles follows from the theory of the force acting upon a current-bearing conductor placed in a magnetic field.

$$F = Bi \sin \theta$$

where F represents force in newtons per unit length, B the flux density in webers per square meter, i the current, and θ the angle the conductor makes with the magnetic field. A current consists of electrons or other charged particles in motion. Hence

$$i = Qnv$$

where Q is the charge on the particle in coulombs, v is the speed of the particle in meters per second, and n is the number of particles per unit length. Since the force on the individual particle is under consideration, n becomes unity and

$$F = BQv \sin \theta$$

In Fig. 3, let it be assumed that an electron e is projected at right angles ($\theta = 90°$) into a uniform magnetic field with an initial velocity of v_0. Since the field is directed in (toward the paper), the application of any convenient rule for the force upon a conductor will show that the electron will be deflected downward as it enters the field. With a uniform field and a constant speed v_0, the electron will be given a constant angular change or acceleration and will move in the arc of a circle. From the laws of mechanics this acceleration is v^2/r, where r is the radius of curvature of the path. Thus

$$F = ma = BQv = m\,\frac{v^2}{r}$$

and

$$r = \frac{mv}{BQ} \tag{11}$$

and for an electron where $Q = e$

$$r = \frac{v}{B} \times \frac{1}{e/m} = 5.69 \times 10^{-12}\,\frac{v}{B}\ \text{meters} \tag{12}$$

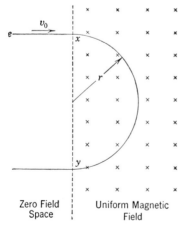

Fig. 3.   Circular deflection of an electron in a uniform magnetic field.

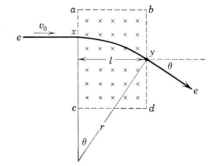

Fig. 4. Angle of deflection of an electron traversing a magnetic field.

Assume in Fig. 3 that v_0 is 2×10^9 cm per second and the field strength B is 10 gauss.

$$r = 5.69 \times 10^{-12} \frac{\overset{\text{(meters per second)}}{2 \times 10^7}}{\underset{\text{(webers* per square meter)}}{10 \times 10^4 \times 10^{-8}}}$$

$$= 11.38 \times 10^{-2} \text{ meter} = 11.38 \text{ cm}$$

The theory of the magnetic field at right angles to the moving electron (illustrated in Fig. 3) is applied in the deflection of a beam of electrons and is analogous to the use of the electric field as illustrated in Fig. 2.

The angle of deflection of an electron beam in a uniform magnetic field may be computed from the relations shown in Fig. 4. Here a magnetic field within the rectangle *abcd* is created by two parallel coils, one in front of and one in back of the page. An electron entering the field from the left with a velocity v_0 at point x will be deflected along the arc of a circle *xy* having some radius r. After emerging from the field at y, the electron will continue its velocity v_0 along a linear path. The angle of the arc *xy* is θ (lower angle) and by plane geometry is equal to the angle of deflection θ (at the right). Obviously, the sine of the angle θ is l/r. The length of field l is known and r can be calculated from equation 12 as in the preceding example.

Work Function

Work function is the energy in electron volts required to remove an electron completely from a substance. If two different metals are brought in contact, an inherent difference of potential exists between

* One weber equals 10^8 maxwells.

them. This potential is called contact emf and is equal to the difference between the work functions of the materials. A more complete explanation of these terms is given in later chapters.

The examples of electric and magnetic fields given in this chapter are the simplest type. More complex applications are given in Chapter 17.

PROBLEMS

1. Two large parallel planes in a high vacuum separated by a distance of 1.5 in. carry a difference of potential of 1500 volts. An electron is freed at the negative plane (near center) with zero velocity. Calculate (a) the potential gradient between the planes, (b) the velocity of the electron when it hits the positive plane, (c) the time the electron is in transit, and (d) the energy acquired by the electron in electron volts and joules (use mks system).

2. Increase the distance between the planes of Problem 1 to 10.16 cm, and recalculate.

3. (a) In Problem 1 substitute a + hydrogen ion (at positive plate) for the electron and solve. Repeat for (b) a neon ion, and (c) a mercury ion.

4. In Fig. 2, an electron enters the space between the two planes with an initial velocity of 10^9 cm per second. If the electric field between the planes is 5 volts per millimeter, what will be the angle of flight and the resultant velocity after the electron has traveled 2 cm to the right?

5. In Fig. 3, an electron is hurled with a velocity of 10^9 cm per second into a magnetic field of 15 gauss. Calculate the radius of the path of the electron. What will be the resultant velocity 1/1,000,000 of a second after the electron enters the magnetic field?

chapter 2

Electrical
Conduction in Solids

Wave Character of Electrons

The dual character of electrons acting as particles or as waves was suggested in Chapter 1. In that chapter the motion of electrons as particles in a vacuum under the influence of electric and magnetic fields was treated in accordance with the laws of mechanics. The wavelike behavior of electrons was postulated early in the twentieth century and was verified experimentally by Davisson and Germer. These men projected a stream of electrons upon a grating (atomic dimensions) and discovered a diffraction pattern that is characteristic of wave motion.

Wave motion is periodic and the velocity v of such motion is represented by the formula $v = f\lambda$, where f is the number of waves per second and λ is the length of the wave.

Initially, it is difficult to conceive of an electron revolving in an orbit about the nucleus of an atom and simultaneously having the property of a wave. A concept of this dual behavior, which has no physical reality, is suggested in Fig. 1. Here the electron e in completing a circular orbit covers four wavelengths (distance from a to b) in each revolution. Thus

$$\text{arc } ab = 1 \text{ wavelength} = \lambda$$

and

$$n\lambda = 2\pi r$$

For a given value of wavelength λ, n *must be an integer* because fractional wavelengths cannot exist without interference for the normal

15

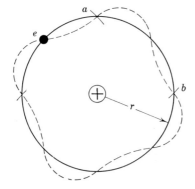

Fig. 1. Fictitious electron-wave orbit.

state of equilibrium in the atom. The integer n is called the quantum number, and theoretically can have a series of values as 1, 2, 3, etc. Atoms may have some electrons moving in elliptical orbits that require a double quantum number to specify each orbit. The important point in considering all orbital motion of electrons is to note that only a *definite set of orbits* (or shells) *is permitted* to exist for a given isolated atom.

Energy of Electrons

An electron revolving in an orbit surrounding the nucleus of an atom possesses three kinds of energy. First, it has potential energy determined by the integral or summation of the work required to carry the electron away from the attraction of its positive nucleus to its orbit of radius r (Fig. 2). Second, it has kinetic energy determined by its motion about the nucleus. This energy is equal to $\frac{1}{2} mv^2$, where m is the mass and v the velocity of the electron. Third,

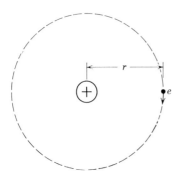

Fig. 2.

the electron has rotational energy arising from its electron spin on its axis.

Each electron is attracted toward the nucleus by a force equal to $-\mathcal{E}e$, where $\mathcal{E}$ is the electric field produced by the positive charge on the nucleus. This force is counteracted by the centrifugal force of the revolving electron. If an electron is to be moved from one orbit to the next one farther from the nucleus, a definite quantum of energy is required to produce this jump. In like manner, if an electron falls from one orbit to the next permissible inner one, a definite quantum of energy is released. Thus the position of an electron in an atom may be specified either by naming its shell or its orbit or by stating its energy level. The energy levels for electrons within an atom may be depicted by a series of horizontal lines, as indicated in Fig. 3. Here the vertical position of a line indicates the energy in electron volts, ev, which is possessed by the electron in a particular energy level. The distance between the horizontal lines indicates the amount of energy which must be added or released for the electron to jump up or down in the energy scale. The lowest energy level is called the first state of the electron and it corresponds to the inner orbit or shell of the atom. The higher levels or states are termed the second, third, etc. In accord with an earlier statement, an electron for an isolated atom can exist only in one of the energy levels or states, and the intervening spaces are forbidden zones.

The concept of energy levels provides a convenient method for depicting and explaining electronic phenomena of conduction, emission, and ionization in gases and solids. A complete understanding

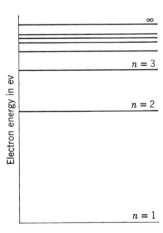

Fig. 3.   Atomic energy levels.

of this concept requires a knowledge of atomic physics, wave mechanics, and solid-state theory which lies beyond the scope of this text. Some of the simple aspects of this theory are employed in the studies which follow.

Multiple Electron Atoms

All atoms except hydrogen have more than one electron. The electrons fill the orbits or shells in a manner determined by the atomic number of the particular element. The distribution of the electrons at the various energy levels may appear as shown in Fig. 4. In the normal atom all the levels except the outer one will be filled. Those electrons in the outer or upper level are known as the valence electrons. They are the ones which participate in the joining of atoms to form molecules. They are also the ones which require a minimum of energy for removal to higher levels, and they are the ones which participate in conduction. Whenever a valence electron of an atom is removed from its normal energy level to a higher permitted level, the atom is said to be *excited*. If a valence electron is given sufficient added energy to remove it completely from its parent atom, the process is called *ionization*. After ionization takes place, the atom carries a positive charge and is called a *positive ion*. The concepts of excitation and ionization are important and are employed frequently in later sections of this text.

The energy to excite or ionize an atom must come from some external source such as light, heat, an electric field, or a flying particle.

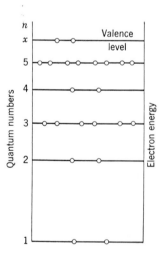

Fig. 4. Electrons in energy levels.

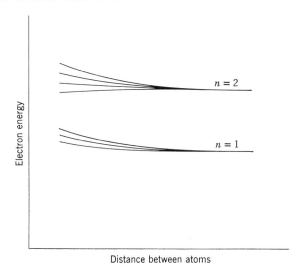

Fig. 5. Splitting of energy levels in atoms.

Multiple Atomic Structures

The crowding of individual atoms in space changes the energy concept developed for the single atom. In general, a low concentration of atoms constitutes a gas, a higher concentration produces a liquid structure, whereas a very high concentration results in a solid. Any concentration produces interactions between the electrons and nuclei of the adjacent atoms. These interactions result in an apparent splitting of the energy levels. The separation between the split energy levels increases as the atomic nuclei approach each other (see Fig. 5). Thus, as the orbits of valence electrons interpenetrate each other, the outer energy levels may be split or new sublevels formed. This splitting and reformation change the fixed energy levels into energy bands (instead of lines), and simultaneously narrow the width of the forbidden energy zones. The resulting energy band concept is illustrated in Fig. 6 and is widely used in later considerations.

The spacing between two adjacent atoms is limited by the Pauli exclusion principle, which may be partially explained as follows. On the one hand, the valence electrons of each adjacent atom are attracted by the positive charge on the nucleus of the other atom. This creates a force tending to pull the atoms together. On the other hand, each of the adjacent atoms normally has all its energy levels, except

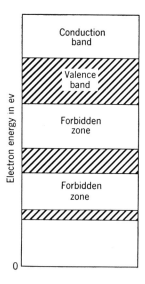

Electron energy in ev

0

Fig. 6.   Energy bands in atoms.

the outer one, filled with its full quota of electrons. Since no more electrons can be added at these levels, interpenetrations into the filled levels (or shells) are excluded. This exclusion is effected by a force of repulsion. Thus, when the force of attraction between positive nuclei and electrons of adjacent atoms equalizes the force of repulsion created by the Pauli exclusion principle, the spacing of the atoms becomes stable. It may be more helpful for the reader to say that the Pauli exclusion principle means that no two electrons may occupy the same quantum state.

Conduction in Metals

The ability of a solid to conduct electric current is determined by its physical structure. All metals and semiconductor solids, which are important in electronics, have a crystal type of structure. Metals are aggregations of crystals. Crystals are orderly arrangements of atoms of an element that form a solid. The arrangement of the atoms in a unit cell of a crystal for good metallic conductors such as copper, silver, and aluminum is illustrated in Fig. 7. Here an atom is located in each corner of the cube plus one at the center of each face of the cube. A two-dimensional crystal structure for copper is shown in Fig. 8. Here the copper atoms are held within the crystalline matrix by the bonding action of valence electrons which exist in the outer energy level of the atom. These bonds are called ionic

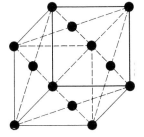

Fig. 7. Crystal cubic structure.

or electrostatic bonds. In metals, the valence electrons comprising these bonds are not definitely associated with any particular atom, but exist as a communal group. Accordingly, they are often referred to as *free* in the sense that they can move through the structure quite readily, and in the process, other like electrons take their place in maintaining the bonding structure of the crystal. This freedom of movement of valence electrons accounts for the ease of charge transfer and electric conduction in metallic crystal structures.

It may be helpful to note that the copper atom has 29 electrons surrounding the positive core or nucleus. The outer or valence shell of the copper atom contains only 1 electron; the other 28 are in shells closer to the nucleus, of which 2 are in the first shell, 8 in the second, and 18 in the third. The single valence electron is bound so loosely that it readily escapes and becomes a "free" electron.

The good conduction of copper is readily explainable on the energy band basis. The concentration of the copper atoms produces a split-

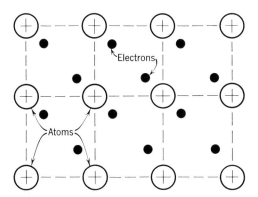

Fig. 8. Crystal structure in a metal.

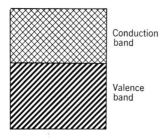

Conduction band

Valence band

Fig. 9.   Energy bands in metals.

ting of the permitted energy levels as previously described. The arrangement of atoms within the crystal entails an interpenetration of the electron energy levels from all sides, thus widening the energy level bands until the valence band overlaps the conduction band, as suggested in Fig. 9. Under these conditions the addition of a minute energy by an applied electric field raises some valence electrons into the conduction band and permits charge transfer (current).

In metals, the valence level is never filled, and hence it is always easy to raise electrons to the conduction band at all temperatures. At absolute zero temperature the nuclei of atoms are at rest and the valence electrons can move freely through the crystal structure with a wavelike motion so that the resistance of the metal is zero (unless impurities are present). As the temperature of the metal is raised, the atoms in the crystal partake of a thermal vibration which offers some opposition to the free movement of electrons. This explains the usual increase of resistance with rise in temperature for metals. (For further information on effect of temperature, see the section on superconductivity and cryotron, page 530.)

Fermi Level

The instantaneous energy of any electron within a solid is represented by its deviation from some reference point or level. This reference energy level for a particular solid is called the Fermi level. It is determined by the chemical elements and the structure of the solid. The Fermi level for metals is the maximum energy possessed by an electron in the valence band at absolute zero. For some solids this level lies at the top of the valence energy band; in others which contain *impurities* it may be located within a forbidden energy band. *In all cases, the difference between the Fermi level and the lower side of the conduction band represents the minimum energy required to produce conduction within that material.*

Insulators

An insulator is a substance that does not conduct electricity in the usual sense of the term. The resistivity of good practical insulators such as glass, mica, and Teflon, is of the order of 10^{15} ohms per cubic centimeter. This compares to a value of 10^{-6} ohm per cubic centimeter for a good metallic conductor. The high resistivity of the insulator results from an absence of any free electron or other charge carrier within the substance. Obviously, the electron bond structure of the insulator prevents any loosening of the electrons except through a disintegration of the material. On the basis of the energy band structure it means that the width of the forbidden energy zone between the valence band and the conduction band is too large to be mounted by the usual external forces. This is illustrated in the energy band diagram of Fig. 10. In this figure and others given later, only the upper energy bands are shown.

The reader may experience an initial difficulty in understanding energy diagrams like that of Fig. 10. Let it be understood that these diagrams represent pictorial not factual concepts. They are designed for discussing conduction in solids. Once accepted for what they are, they become a convenient media for treating semiconductor phenomena. *The energy bands should not be interpreted as channels through which electrons or holes move, but as energy levels in which conduction is or is not permissible.* For example, an electron raised to the conduction band level is free to be transported within the solid; or an electron in a filled valence band is not free to move. And last, electrons cannot have stable energies of the magnitudes represented anywhere in the forbidden zone.

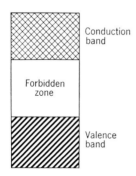

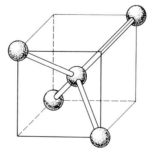

Fig. 10. Energy bands in insulators.

Fig. 11. Crystal structure of a covalent solid.

Semiconductors are a class of materials that lie between metals and insulators in conducting ability. They are not poor conductors or poor insulators or a mixture of good conductors and insulators. Their ability to conduct electricity may be controlled by the application of external energy in the form of heat, light, electric fields, or flying particles. Two semiconducting solids of special interest in electronics are germanium (atomic number 32) and silicon 14. Both these elements are formed of crystals wherein the atoms are held together by covalent bonds. Purified germanium and silicon are usually in the polycrystalline form but for greatest usefulness in semiconductor devices they are prepared in a single crystal form. In this form, the atoms arrange themselves in a regular pattern or lattice structure, as suggested in Fig. 11. The theory of conduction in these solids is treated in the sections which follow.

Intrinsic Semiconductors

An intrinsic semiconductor is a covalent solid that is free of any crystal imperfections. With germanium as an example, the crystal structure of a covalent solid is illustrated in Figs. 11 and 12. Each

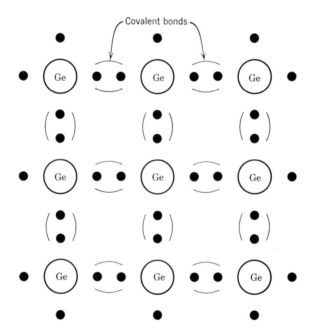

Fig. 12. Crystal structure of intrinsic germanium.

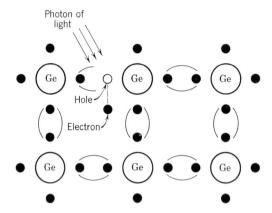

Fig. 13.   Electron-hole pair created by incident light energy.

atom of the crystal has four valence electrons. These four electrons
join with like electrons from adjacent atoms to form electron-pair or
covalent bonds. These bonds are so strong that each electron is
bound to the two atoms sharing it. Hence there are no free electrons
as found in metals. At absolute zero the valence bands are completely filled and conduction cannot take place. Thus at this temperature the germanium intrinsic semiconductor acts as an insulator.

If a sufficient amount of external energy in the form of heat or light
is properly applied to the crystal, an electron covalent bond may be
broken as shown in Fig. 13. An electron has now been set free and
conduction is possible. The conduction process is quite interesting.
First, the release of the electron leaves a vacant space, a "hole," in
the crystal structure, which acts like a positive charge. Also the
release of the electron *has created an electron-hole pair*. Now two
charge carriers are available for electric conduction—a negative
electron and a positive hole. The removal of the electron leaves an
unfilled valence energy band and conduction is possible within this
band. The electron energy band levels now exist as illustrated in
Fig. 14. If an electric field is present (left positive to right negative),
the electrons in the conduction band will move to the left and "hole"
conduction will move to the right in the valence band. *Actually a
hole cannot move*, but an electron from a covalent bond moves left
(one atom) to fill one hole and leaves a second hole (vacancy) on the
right. This is equivalent to saying that holes migrate to the right
in the direction of the field. This concept of the hole is a fiction

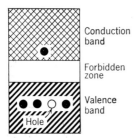

Conduction band

Forbidden zone

Valence band

Hole

Fig. 14. Energy relationship in intrinsic germanium after an electron-hole pair is formed.

which has been accorded respectability in the field of science and the reader should be prepared to embrace it. The Hall effect, described later in this chapter, will aid the reader in accepting this concept.

The current in the intrinsic semiconductor consists of two parts—electronic current arising from electron movement in the conduction band level, and hole movement in the valence band. The number of electrons and holes generated is the same, but the mobility of the electrons is higher, resulting in a larger component of current from the electron carriers. This gives rise to the statement that the electrons are the *majority* carriers in the intrinsic semiconductor.

The creation of electron-hole pairs by thermal or light energy results in a temporary separation unless an electric field is present to cause conduction. Once generated, an electron-hole pair will remain in the crystal for a finite lifetime before recombining. The generation and recombination are a continuing process. In germanium the lifetime of an electron-hole pair is about 10^{-4} sec. The process reaches an equilibrium quickly, wherein the rate at which they are formed just equals the rate at which they are captured by ionized atoms. It should be noted that in this process the number of negative and positive charges within the atoms plus the electron-hole pairs remains constant. Thus the semiconductor is electrically neutral and no space charge exists.

Perhaps the reader finds some gaps in his understanding of electron and hole conduction as discussed in the two preceding paragraphs. By referring again to Figs. 13 and 14, we see that external light or thermal energy generates electron-hole pairs. For each pair the electron is raised to the conduction energy level and is free to be moved by an electric field. The hole remains at the valence level band. In this position it could be filled by (1) any electron that has been raised to the conduction band level or (2) an electron from a covalent bond of a nearby germanium atom (valence band level). Generally, the electron from the adjacent atom (case 2) will fill the hole and a consecutive series of such "jumps" constitutes the hole movement as a carrier. Since the electrons at the conduction band level have a continuous free movement as carriers, compared to the step-by-step jumps for holes, it is to be expected that the rate of travel or mobility of the electron carriers will be higher than that for holes.

The majority of semiconductor devices in use today have characteristics of conduction which arise from the presence of impurities, and hence imperfections within the crystal. Accordingly, they are not classed as intrinsic semiconductors.

n-Type Semiconductors

The addition of a minute trace of an impurity of valence 5, such as arsenic or antimony to a crystallized structure of pure germanium or silicon, has a pronounced effect upon the conducting property of the combination. As these impurities enter in the crystal lattice of germanium, only four of the valence 5 electrons can serve as covalent bonds. This formation leaves one extra valence electron, as shown in Fig. 15. This extra electron is unattached and free as a charge to

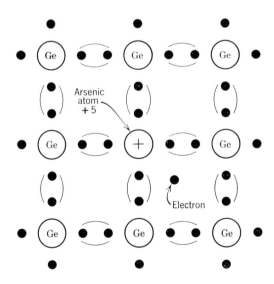

Fig. 15. Crystal lattice of germanium containing an arsenic impurity (valence 5).

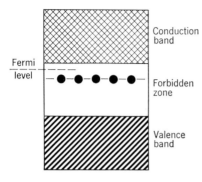

Fermi level

Fig. 16.   Energy levels in n-type germanium.

be transported within the crystal. Since the arsenic contributes free electrons to the crystal structure, it is referred to as a *donor* impurity. Also, since the resulting crystal structure has only negative (electron) charges available for transfer, it is known as an n-type semiconductor, where n stands for negative.

It should be noted that in this n-type of crystal structure, the arsenic atom becomes a positive ion. This $+$ion is "locked in" and is not free to move. Only the electron is free to move as a charge carrier. The crystal as a whole is neutral because the negative charge of each free electron is equalized by a like charge on the positive arsenic ion.

The energy band diagram for the n-type semiconductor is shown in Fig. 16. The presence of the arsenic impurity atoms has created a new energy level which lies in the normal forbidden zone for germanium. This new level lies in the upper part of the forbidden zone for germanium, and the resulting Fermi reference level for arsenic impurity lies halfway between this new level and the lower part of the conduction band. This indicates that a relatively small magnitude of external energy is necessary to raise the extra electrons into the conduction band.

p-Type Semiconductors

The addition of minute amounts of elements of valence three, such as boron, aluminum, indium, and gallium, to a germanium or silicon crystal structure affects the conducting property of the resulting combination. Each atom of the valence three impurity has only three valence electrons to join with the four valence electrons of the germanium atom. The missing valence electron leaves an incomplete covalent bond or "hole" in the resulting crystal structure, as shown in Fig. 17. The indium atom has robbed some nearby germanium atom of one covalent electron, leaving a vacant space, which acts like a positive charge. The vacant space may be filled by a covalent electron from an adjoining germanium atom, thus moving the hole to a new position. In this manner, a free positive space charge (hole) is created and becomes free to be transported within the crystal. Since germanium "doped" with indium has extra positive charges, it is called a p-type (p for positive) semiconductor. Also, since the indium atom steals an electron, it is called an *acceptor* impurity.

The indium impurity in the p-type semiconductor crystal exists as negative ions which are bound to the crystal lattice so they cannot take part in conduction. Hence any conduction within the crystal results from the movement of positively charged holes acting as carriers. The positive charges of the holes are neutralized by the negative charge on the impurity atoms so that no space charge exists within the crystal.

The energy band diagram for a p-type semiconductor is suggested in Fig. 18. The small open circles in the lower part of the forbidden zone represent a new energy level introduced by the p-type impurity atoms. At absolute zero this level is empty. It requires a small amount of energy to raise electrons from the Fermi level to the level

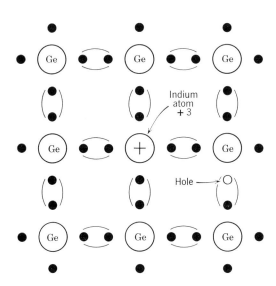

Fig. 17. Crystal lattice of germanium containing an indium impurity (valence 3).

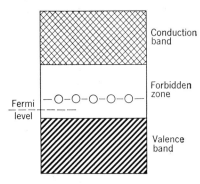

Fig. 18. Energy levels in p-type germanium.

created by the impurity atoms (ions). These electrons come from the germanium atoms at the valence level. The removal of these electrons leaves holes in the germanium atoms at this level. Now hole conduction takes place at the valence energy level as previously explained.

Junctions between Solids

Most semiconductor devices contain one or more junctions between solids. These junctions may be metal to semiconductor or semiconductor to semiconductor. The action taking place at the junctions follows the preceding theory plus some additional junction theory. This theory is treated in the next chapter.

Impurity Control in Semiconductors

Modern research has demonstrated that the properties of semiconducting solids are very sensitive to the amount and kind of impurity present. This knowledge has led to new techniques for controlling the impurity content in semiconductors, which, in turn, has resulted in great improvement in the properties and uniformity of crystals employed in commercial devices. A minute trace of impurity in the amount of one part in 10^8 will have considerable effect upon the conducting property of germanium. Germanium never exists in the pure state. It is refined commercially in an electric furnace. A seed of germanium crystal is placed in the molten mass which is cooled slowly. The crystal grows in size and the impurities present settle to one end and solidify last. The purity of the germanium may be improved further by repeating the melting and recrystallizing process until only one impurity atom exists in each billion or more germanium atoms.

After the germanium has been purified, it is remelted and processed into n-type or p-type. N-type conductivity (preponderance of negative carriers) is obtained by the addition of a small quantity (one part in 100 million) of either arsenic or antimony to the pure germanium. Similarly, the addition of an equally small quantity of boron, gallium, or indium produces the p-type (positive carrier) germanium.

The addition of these impurities to a melt of germanium permits the formation of grown crystals by the slow withdrawing of a seed crystal from the melt. Junction crystals may be produced by the addition of first one type of impurity and permitting the seed crystal to form partially, then adding the other type of impurity in a quantity to cancel the first and create an excess. Further addition of the first type of impurity in a suitable amount will cancel the second. In this manner, n-p-n or p-n-p junctions are formed. After solidification, the crystals are cut into many sections (slices) to provide tiny crystal junctions of the desired type for use in semiconductor devices.

Hall Effect

A conductor bearing an electric current is acted upon by a force when placed at right angles to a magnetic field. Since an electric current consists of moving charges of electricity, such charges will likewise be acted upon by a force and deflected by a transverse magnetic field. This phenomenon is employed in an experiment known as the Hall effect and is illustrated in Fig. 19. Here a magnetic field is directed perpendicularly (front to back) to the conductor AB. The applied potential difference across AB will cause a conventional current to flow to the right from A to B. An application of the rule for force on current in a magnetic field indicates that the conductor AB and any charge carriers present will be pushed upward. If the carriers consist of electrons (as in n-type) moving to the left, they will rise to the top of the conductor and create a − potential on the upper side (Fig. 19a). Again, if the charge carriers are holes (p-type), they will move to the right and be deflected to the upper side of the conductor (Fig. 19b), thereby creating a + potential on the top. Accordingly, the polarity of the potential created between the top and bottom of the conductor AB is a conclusive indication of the sign of the majority of the charges constituting the current. This experiment, or Hall effect, has been employed to prove the presence of holes in p-type semiconductors.

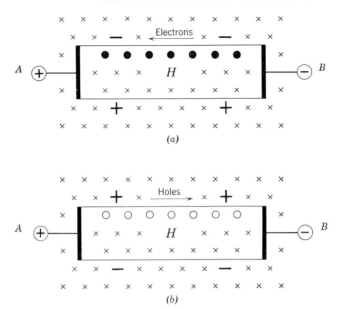

Fig. 19. Hall effect.

Summary of Energy-Level Bands

A brief summary of energy band theory, as suggested in Fig. 20, may be helpful before proceeding to a discussion of semiconductor devices.   In metals, the valence band rises to the conduction band, thus permitting excellent conduction.   In the insulator there is a very wide forbidden zone between the valence band and conduction band which bars conduction.   The narrow forbidden band in the intrinsic semiconductor permits some electrons to be raised to the conduction band through the formation of electron-hole pairs.   In the n-type semiconductor, the donor impurity atoms have created

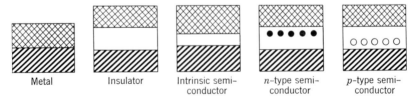

Fig. 20. Comparison of energy-level bands for solids.

some near-free electrons and an energy level near the top of the forbidden zone. Lastly, in the p-type semiconductor, the acceptor impurity has created an energy level near the bottom of the forbidden zone. Here electrons in the valence band may rise to the new level, leaving holes in the valence band and thus permit conduction to take place via holes within the valence band.

PROBLEMS

1. A rectangular wafer of p-type semiconductor is standing on edge (vertical). If the majority of the carriers present are moving from bottom to top, (a) what is the direction of the conventional current and (b) what is the polarity of the applied potential?

2. Substitute a wafer of n-type semiconductor in Problem 1 and solve.

3. A flat wafer of a semiconductor is placed on this page with the long edge vertical. A magnetic field rises normally (back to front) from the paper. A difference in potential is applied between the bottom $(+)$ and the top $(-)$. A sensitive measurement shows that the right side of the wafer is positive $(+)$ with respect to the left side. Is the semiconductor n-type or p-type? Explain.

REFERENCES

1. Martin, Thomas L., Jr., *Physical Basis for Electrical Engineering,* Prentice-Hall, Englewood Cliffs, New Jersey, 1957.
2. Kittel, Charles, *Solid State Physics,* John Wiley and Sons, New York, 1956.

chapter 3

Semiconductor
Devices

The phenomenon of nonlinear voltage-current relations in some substances and at the junctions of dissimilar substances has been known for a long time. As early as 1834, Faraday discovered the highly negative temperature coefficient of resistivity exhibited by silver sulfide. Early in this century many materials were employed in "wireless" reception which displayed nonlinear characteristics. These materials consisted of a lump of some mineral such as galena, silicon, iron or copper pyrites, zincite, bornite, or silicon carbide. In the process of signal detection these materials made up one side of a junction, whereas a feeler wire called a "catwhisker" bearing upon the material constituted the other terminal. This combination known as a crystal detector had a unilateral current characteristic in which electrons moved from the crystal to the metal point bearing upon them.

The disadvantages of this early device were that the crystal had "sensitive spots" which were destroyed by overload and heat and the sensitivity could be lost by slight displacements of the catwhisker. This form of crystal detector or rectifier was widely used in the amateur period of wireless telegraphy and the early days of voice radio. The more stable operation of the vacuum-diode detector caused the crystal detector to be displaced shortly after 1920. Experimentation on the construction and use of crystals as rectifiers was resumed during the 1930's, and two new crystal rectifiers, silicon and germanium, that were developed during this period were put into effective use during World War II. Later research on the crystal rectifier led to the invention of the transistor by J. Bardeen and W. H. Brattain in 1948.

The unilateral current-carrying characteristic of a junction of selenium and a metal was discovered in 1883, although commercial application of the combination was not made until 1930. A similar discovery of the unilateral characteristic of copper oxide on copper was made about 1920 and resulted in an early application of this combination.

Metal to Semiconductor Rectifiers

An ideal rectifier is any device which is capable of transforming an alternating (two-directional) current into a unidirectional conduction. Such a device would also offer zero resistance to the conduction of current in one direction while presenting an infinite resistance to a reverse flow. None of our electronic rectifiers is ideal. Most of them permit some reverse current to flow and all offer some resistance to the rectified current in the forward direction.

One important class of rectifying devices consists of a metal in contact with a semiconductor. In one type of rectifiers of this class (Fig. 1a), a metal point (small area) is held under mechanical pressure against a semiconductor crystal surface. In a second type, a metal plate (large area) is covered on one side by a semiconductor which usually has some form of bond with the metal (Fig. 1b). Obviously, the magnitude of the rectified current will vary with the area of contact between the metal and semiconductor. Surprisingly, however, the theory of current conduction across the metal semiconductor

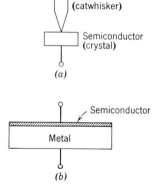

Fig. 1. Two types of metal to semiconductor rectifiers.

boundary may be quite different, and even the direction of current flow may be opposite in the two different area groups. These types of rectifiers are treated in the sections which follow.

Crystal Diodes

A crystal diode is a two-element device consisting of a sharp-pointed metal wire bearing upon a small section of an n-type germanium or silicon crystal, as illustrated in Fig. 2. These two elements are soldered to lead-in terminals and hermetically sealed in a

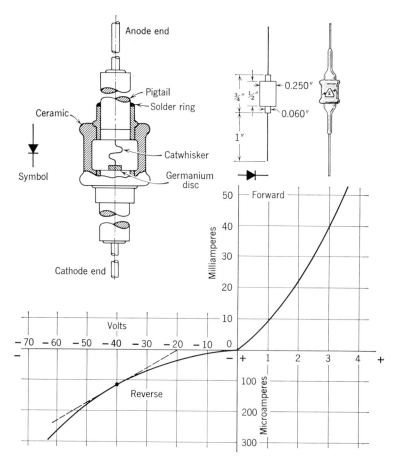

Fig. 2. Construction and characteristics of a typical germanium crystal diode (Courtesy Sylvania Electric Products Inc.)

ceramic or glass-enclosing cartridge. Plastic cases have been employed, but are subject to moisture penetration under high humidity conditions which lowers the sensitivity of the diode. The thin spring wire or "catwhisker" is usually made of tungsten but may be platinum, a platinum alloy, or phosphor-bronze. It may vary 1 to 5 mils in diameter and may have a point area of only one-half of 1 mil in diameter. It is usually formed into an S or C shape to provide the desired contact pressure. The crystal electrode is a thin (15 to 20 mils) square wafer or n-type germanium (or silicon). The surface of the wafer is polished, but should be etched to produce a surface of pure, clean, undistorted material. It is important that the cartridge of the diode have and maintain high insulation between terminals because any leakage of current will mask the sensitivity of the rectifying process.

The crystal diode is small in physical size, as shown by the dimensioned view in Fig. 2. This figure covers a typical commercial diode. However, miniature types of approximately half this size are also available.

The operating characteristic of a typical commercial crystal diode is given by the graph of Fig. 2. When the metal point is made positive with respect to the crystal base, electrons from the n-type germanium move readily from the semiconductor into the metal. This is the *forward* or easy flow path for the diode, and the current conduction is relatively large, as shown in the upper right-hand corner of the graph. When the polarity of the applied voltage is reversed, only a small current is permitted to flow (note negative current is given in microamperes). Thus the device restricts conduction in the reverse direction, and rectifying action results. The reverse current increases rather rapidly for higher negative voltages, reduces the effectiveness of the rectifying process, and also introduces losses that will result in heating at the contact. This last factor limits the peak reverse or *peak inverse voltage* which may be applied to a crystal diode. Incidentally, all rectifying devices have peak inverse voltage ratings which must not be exceeded if damage or breakdown is to be avoided.

A rise in the temperature of the diode will increase the current in both the forward and the reverse direction. This characteristic results from the negative temperature coefficient of resistance for most semiconductors. The characteristic curves for commercial diodes usually show a family of curves covering several operating temperatures.

The forward and the reverse current characteristic curves of the crystal diode shown in Fig. 2 are nonlinear. They are nonlinear because the volts per amperes ratio is changing. Also, the entire characteristic is nonlinear because the magnitude of the reverse current differs widely from the forward current for the same magnitude of applied voltage. The divergence from a linear relationship is shown by the calculation of a few volts per amperes values (resistance). In the forward direction

$$\text{Resistance to direct current at 1 volt} = \frac{1}{9.5 \times 10^{-3}} = 105 \text{ ohms}$$

$$\text{Resistance to direct current at 3 volts} = \frac{3}{40 \times 10^{-3}} = 75 \text{ ohms}$$

In reverse direction

$$\text{Resistance to direct current at} -40 \text{ volts} = \frac{40}{120 \times 10^{-6}} = 333,333 \text{ ohms}$$

Resistance to alternating current at

$$-40 \text{ volts} = \frac{40 - 20}{120 \times 10^{-6}} = 166,666 \text{ ohms}$$

The last calculation covers the a-c or incremental resistance which is the ratio of the incremental voltage change to the incremental current change as measured on the tangent to the curve at the point being considered (see line at −40 volts). This incremental resistance is the important one in all electronic devices where changing values are encountered and is the one employed in the design of electronic circuits.

An important characteristic of rectifiers, frequently used for comparison, is the rectification ratio. Rectification ratio is defined as the ratio of the current in the forward direction to the reverse current at a specified voltage. Using the numerical values given in the preceding paragraph, the rectification ratio would be 9.5×10^{-3} divided by 120×10^{-6}, or 79.2. Obviously, the calculated rectification ratio will vary with the peak inverse voltage applied and would be much higher for lower inverse peaks.

The conventional direction of current flow in the n-type germanium crystal diode is from the metal point contact into the crystal (opposite electron movement). The symbol for current direction is a bold face arrow as shown in Fig. 3. Commercial diodes usually have this

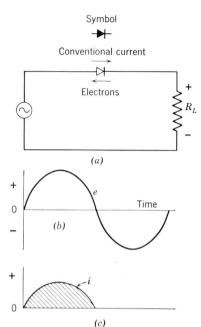

Symbol

Conventional current

Electrons

R_L

(a)

Fig. 3. Simple half-wave rectification.

(b)

Time

(c)

symbol stamped conspicuously on the device. The crystal terminal is the *cathode* and the point terminal the *anode*, with the conventional forward current flow from the *anode* to the *cathode*.

One example of the utility of any rectifier is shown in Fig. 3. A crystal diode is connected in series with a source of alternating current and a load resistance R_L, as suggested in Fig. 3a. The a-c source supplies a sine wave of voltage which varies instantaneously with time, as given in Fig. 3b. If the plus (+) value of voltage corresponds to the forward direction of current in the diode, the resulting current will be a varying pulse of unidirectional current, as given in Fig. 3c (small reverse current neglected). This circuit and process are known as half-wave rectification since only one-half of each cycle is rectified. A modification of the preceding circuit employing four crystal diodes is illustrated in Fig. 4. A similar process of reasoning shows that this circuit will rectify both halves of the a-c waves and this method is called full-wave rectification. The preceding circuits give a pulsing form of rectified output which may be unsuitable for some applications. Devices known as smoothing filters may be used to level out the pulses into a smooth d-c output. These devices are

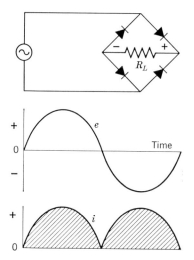

Fig. 4. Full-wave rectification.

covered in a later chapter. Crystal diodes also find wide application as detectors, wherein they have a rectifying action, but by virtue of associated circuits serve to detect or filter out component signals from a complicated wave form.

Many theories have been offered to explain the rectifying action taking place in an n-type germanium diode. Several of them, however, have been disproved by experimental evidence, and others are disputed, so that there is no universally accepted theory today. However, there are some basic concepts covered in the preceding chapter which may guide the reader to some plausible understanding of the rectifying action.

Let us begin with a general statement that the characteristics of all rectifying semiconductor devices in this chapter depend (1) on the impurity content of the semiconductor, (2) the nature of the surface (semiconductor) treatment, and (3) the detailed structure established by some forming process. Previous discussion has shown that the conductivity of n-type germanium arises from negative carriers released by the impurity present. This conductivity will depend on the amount of impurity doping and the resulting concentration of negative carriers. Thus the resistivity of the crystal can be controlled during the production of the crystal. Within the body of the crystal the resistivity will be constant. Hence if identical contact electrodes are placed on opposite faces of the crystal, the conduction should be the same in either direction and no rectification will result.

Since the rectification cannot take place within the body of the crystal, it must occur at the crystal surface junction with a second electrode. Now if the electrodes at the opposite faces of the crystal are of the same material but of different areas, some asymmetrical conduction may occur under reversed applied fields. This follows because the resistance at the junction under the small area electrode may differ for the two directions of current.

Next, let us consider the case of the germanium crystal diode previously described. Assume that a sharp tungsten point rests upon a clean crystal surface which has not been formed in any manner. When a positive (+) potential is applied at the point, the free electrons in the nearby surface of the crystal are drawn into the point and conduction results. Since the area of the point is so small, a high potential gradient will be produced in the surface of the crystal immediately surrounding the point. This gradient breaks the covalent bonds of the germanium atoms in the surface near the point and generates electron-hole pairs. Immediately the additional electrons pass to the positive point electrode, and the holes migrate into the crystal in search of electrons coming from the crystal base electrode. The new condition and phenomenon are pictured in Fig. 5. This new type of action is called *hole injection* and it appears to account for the major portion, or nearly all, of the forward conduction at the rectifying area. When the applied voltage is reversed, the point becomes negative and in a sense tends to inject electrons into the crystal, but the crystal already contains negative carriers. The positive potential at the crystal base attracts the negative carriers normally in the n-type germanium and thus causes a small reverse current. At high negative potentials, the potential gradient of the electric field within the crystal induces generation of some electron-hole pairs with a resulting rise in reverse current.

Experiments show that for a given germanium n-type crystal wafer, the conduction characteristic will be the same for pure tungsten,

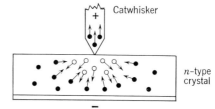

Fig. 5. Hole injection.

platinum, or nickel point contacts of the same size, pressure, etc. These results indicate that the conduction from the metal whisker is independent of the work function and contact potential of the junction materials. This deduction tends to confirm the hole injection theory covered in the preceding paragraph.

Many types of crystal diodes differ from the one of the preceding discussion in an important respect. Although the basic construction is the same, the crystal wafer is subjected to various types of forming treatment. Those treatments serve to change the crystal surface underneath the point contact from an n-type to a p-type of germanium (or silicon). The treatment may be effected by the application of some material or solution to the crystal surface followed by the passage of a relatively large current in the reverse direction for a short period (such as one second). A second method is the use of a point electrode plated with indium plus the short current injection. A third method is to keep the crystal at a high temperature in a vapor of an impurity for a long time (diffusion). All these treatments serve to inject a small amount of p-type impurity into the surface of crystal. *This injection produces a new* p-n *junction in the surface beneath the point.* Now the theory of rectification is changed to that of a p-n junction which differs from the preceding case, as suggested in Fig. 6. Holes exist above the p-n junction because of the injected p-type impurity. A positive potential on the point will repel the holes to the p-n junction beyond which they will migrate toward the negative base electrode and recombine with electrons. Electrons from the n-type portion likewise migrate under the influence of the electric field to the p-n junction, and thence to the point electrode. Thus the conduction consists of both positive and negative carriers. The inherent tendency toward a neutral charge equilibrium in both the p-type and n-type regions will continue to maintain the supply of electrons and holes.

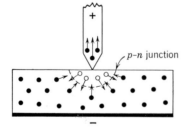

Fig. 6. Rectification at a p-n junction in a crystal diode.

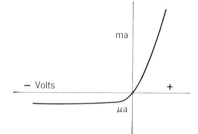

Fig. 7. Characteristic curve of a crystal diode having a *p-n* junction.

When the polarity of the applied potential is reversed, the negative point electrode will attract the +holes in the *p*-region away from the *p-n* junction. In like manner, the +base electrode will attract the negative carriers away from the *p-n* junction. Under these conditions the reverse current will be very small and also practically constant in magnitude for a wide range of negative or reverse applied voltage, as indicated in Fig. 7. A more complete analysis of action at a *p-n* junction is given later in this chapter.

Silicon Crystal Diodes

Silicon crystal diodes have a similar construction and the same theory of operation as germanium diodes. They possess the advantages of lower reverse currents, higher rectification ratios, and the ability to operate at higher ambient temperatures. These advantages have been offset by difficulties in producing silicon with a high degree of purity. However, the silicon crystal diode has long been the standard ultra-high-frequency detector because of its efficiency, small size, and low noise level. The theoretical reason for the superiority of silicon lies in the wider forbidden zone between the valence energy band and the conduction band. For silicon this forbidden zone corresponds to 1.1 ev of energy, whereas for germanium the band width is 0.7 ev. This difference means that silicon is less sensitive to thermal agitation over a certain band of temperatures. This permits satisfactory operation at higher ambient temperatures and also reduces noise arising from thermal action.

Zener Diode

A Zener diode is a type of silicon crystal diode having an unusual reverse current characteristic as illustrated in Fig. 8. The reverse current is called a Zener current and it and the inverse voltage point of breakdown can be controlled by the amount of impurity in the

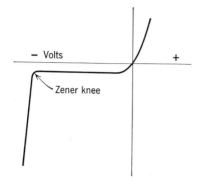

Fig. 8. Characteristic of a Zener diode.

semiconductor, the nature of the electrodes, and the forming treatment employed. The form of the Zener current characteristic may be very useful if diodes can be reproduced to give this shape consistently. After the reverse current passes the Zener knee, it increases rapidly with little change in reverse voltage. This is a constant-voltage variable-current characteristic. For many automatic operations in industrial control it is necessary to employ a constant d-c voltage as a reference. Previously, a gaseous diode (to be described later) has served to furnish a constant reference voltage. The Zener diode offers a simple, light, and efficient reference source.

Crystal Diode Ratings and Characteristics

Crystal diodes are available in a wide range of ratings. Forward current may vary from 1 ma to 200 ma and higher. Peak inverse voltages vary from 15 to 1000 and higher. Forward resistances and permissible temperatures cover a wide range. To find the proper diode for his particular need, the design engineer uses the characteristics and rating sheets of the manufacturer.

Crystal diodes are employed in a host of applications as rectifiers and detectors.

Metallic Rectifier Cells

Several combinations of substances have been discovered which, when assembled in the form of a sandwich, show the property of unilateral conductivity. These assemblies usually consist of a metal plate, a blocking layer, and a semiconductor, as shown in Fig. 9. The blocking layer or rectifying layer is a very thin section of material which is located at the surface junction between the metal and the semiconductor. This layer is formed by some electrochemical or heat-treating process. It permits electrons to move readily from the metal to the semiconductor, but offers a high resistance to conduction in the reverse direction. A metal electrode, called a counter electrode, is placed in contact with the semiconductor to collect the rectified current. Rectifying units of this class are metal-semiconductor, broad-area type, and the devices employing them are called metallic rectifiers, blocking-layer rectifiers, or barrier-layer rectifiers.

Copper Oxide Rectifiers

The copper oxide rectifier cell is a sandwich consisting of a layer of cuprous oxide on copper. One method of producing the cell is by heating a pure copper disk or plate in a furnace to a temperature of approximately 1000° F and then quenching it in water. This treatment produces a thin film of cuprous oxide with an outer layer of cupric oxide. The cupric oxide is then removed, leaving a thin layer (about 3 mils or 1000 molecules thick) of cuprous oxide on one side. Contact with the cuprous oxide is made by electroplating a nickel coating on the surface. The cells are circular or square and have a hole in the center so that they can be assembled on an insulated rod and clamped together in stacks as shown in Fig. 10.

The current-voltage characteristic of a copper oxide cell per square inch of area is given in Fig. 11. The resistance-voltage characteristic

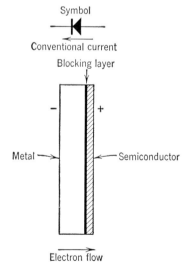

Fig. 9. Elements of a blocking-layer metallic rectifier and its symbol.

Fig. 10. Copper oxide rectifiers. (Courtesy General Electric Company.)

is illustrated in Fig. 12. These curves show that the inverse voltage per cell should be limited to the order of 8 to 10 volts. They also show that the resistance decreases with rise in temperature for both forward and reverse conduction. The number of cells needed in series is determined by the applied voltage (inverse voltage limit), and the area of the cells is calculated from the desired value of rectified current (d-c average) The copper oxide rectifier is subject to aging (increase of contact resistance) with time, with service, and when operated at temperatures in excess of 45° C. In service the

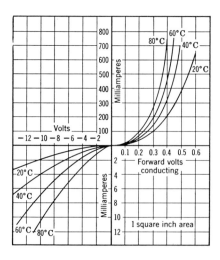

Fig. 11. Current-voltage characteristics of copper oxide rectifier cell. (Courtesy General Electric Company.)

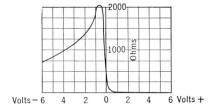

Fig. 12. Resistance-voltage characteristic curve of a copper oxide rectifier element. (Courtesy General Electric Company.)

resistance increases to approximately twice the initial value and then becomes fairly stable. The rating given the rectifier is based on the final expected value, so that initial performance exceeds the rating.

The copper oxide rectifier has been widely used since its discovery in 1920 for battery charging, electroplating, motion picture arcs, corrosion protection, rectification for instruments, and so forth. It has the ability to withstand momentary voltage and current overloads and also has a long life. Its blocking layer is permanent and not subject to unforming. Hence it may remain in a blocking circuit for years like a silent sentinel ready for action at an instant's notice. Its disadvantages are its weight and relatively low peak inverse voltage (PIV). Competitive rectifiers have replaced it for most applications. For low voltage applications (up to 10 volts) where ruggedness is important and for replacements, it should continue to serve.

The theory of action in the copper oxide cell stems from the fact that the cuprous oxide is a p-type semiconductor layer. The copper as a metal contains an abundance of free electrons. When an electric field is applied to the cell, as suggested in Fig. 13, the holes are repelled toward the blocking layer by the positive potential, and electrons move across the barrier. The result is that the potential barrier at the blocking layer is lowered and both electrons and holes

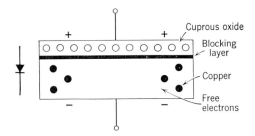

Fig. 13. Illustration of action in copper oxide cell.

serve as carriers through the cell. If the electric field is reversed, the holes are attracted away from the blocking layer and only a few electrons cross the boundary.

Selenium Rectifiers

A selenium rectifier cell is a sandwich made up of four layers, as shown in Fig. 14. An aluminum plate constitutes the base plate, serves as the current collector, and gives rigidity to the cell. This plate is covered by a layer of selenium which is subsequently reduced to the crystalline form. Next a metal is sprayed on top of the selenium to serve as a counter electrode. Last, the sandwich is given an electrochemical forming treatment which develops a blocking layer between the selenium (semiconductor) and the counter electrode. Commercial selenium cells are produced by different methods, some of which are trade secrets. In one process, the selenium is evaporated upon the aluminum plate in a vacuum. After the counter electrode is applied, the blocking layer is formed by applying a relatively high inverse voltage for a long period of time. The completed selenium cells are then assembled in stacks in a manner similar to that employed for copper oxide cells. The current-voltage characteristic of the selenium rectifier parallels that of the preceding rectifier types, as shown in Fig. 15. Any specification for the peak inverse voltage or the amperes per unit area is rather difficult. This follows because the cells are subject to aging or the increase of resistance across the blocking layer with time. This aging, in turn, is a function of temperature. Thus, if we increase either the peak inverse voltage or the current output, the temperature rises, aging increases, and the life of the cell is decreased. If a low cost rectifier is desired at the sacrifice of long life, a peak inverse voltage of 45 volts may be used.

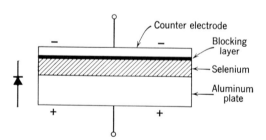

Fig. 14.   Selenium rectifying cell.

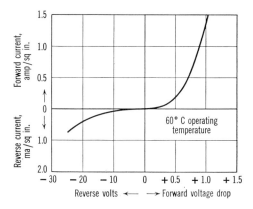

Fig. 15. Typical d-c characteristics of selenium rectifiers.

Conversely, if long life is desired, an inverse peak of 18 to 26 volts will be employed. Incidentally, processed cells vary in their resistance characteristics, and hence are graded and assigned suitable inverse voltage ratings.

In comparison with the copper oxide rectifier, the selenium type has the advantage of lightweight, higher peak inverse voltage, and satisfactory operation at temperatures up to 75° C. The corresponding disadvantages of the selenium rectifier are (1) its susceptibility to corrosion from acid fumes, moisture, and alkalis and (2) the unforming nature of its blocking layer. To protect against corrosion, various finishes of varnish or paint are applied to the rectifier surfaces. The paints and varnishes give a varying degree of protection against corrosion. For absolute protection against the most severe corrosive conditions, the selenium rectifier can be immersed in oil and hermetically sealed in a metal container. For miniature type rectifiers small circular disks are assembled in a tubular enclosure such as glass, Bakelite, and phenolic tubes (see Fig. 16). This construction likewise gives suitable protection against corrosion and physical abuse.

When the selenium rectifier is unused for a period of time, its blocking layer unforms or partially loses its high blocking resistance in the reverse direction. In general, this characteristic is not serious because the blocking layer will reform to its original value within a few cycles whenever an alternating voltage is applied across the cells. Obviously, this unforming characteristic makes the selenium rectifier unsuited to certain types of blocking applications.

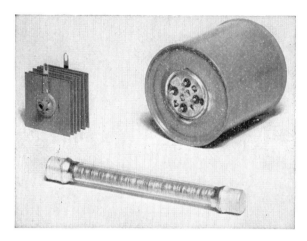

Fig. 16. Selenium rectifiers. (Courtesy General Electric Company.)

The selenium rectifier enjoys a wide application in the rectifier field. Its cells can be placed in series to rectify high voltages (up to 50,000 volts) for X-ray machines or electrostatic precipitation. In like manner, cells can be placed in parallel to give current of considerable magnitude for electric power applications. Millions of small selenium rectifier stacks are employed for electric power supplies in radios, television sets, and all kinds of electronic devices.

Trade secrets covering the forming processes employed in the production of selenium cells have partially masked the theory underlying the rectifying action within the cell. Hence no plausible theory has ever been offered. The cell functions well and there we shall let it rest.

Magnesium-Copper Sulfide Rectifier

This rectifier was invented in Austria and has been manufactured in the United States under basic patents issued to Samuel Ruben in 1925. This blocking-layer metallic rectifier uses a magnesium plate for the metallic electrode and copper sulfide for the semiconductor. A counter electrode is placed in contact with the copper sulfide for collecting the current. The cells are assembled in stacks on a stud with intervening radiator plates and held under pressure. The active blocking layer is formed between the magnesium plate, which becomes oxidized, and the copper sulfide by an electrochemical forming process. The forward direction of the current (conventional) is from the semiconductor-copper sulfide to the metal magnesium. It is possible that holes are formed in the oxide or copper sulfide giving a theory of conduction similar to the copper oxide unit. This rectifier unit must be carefully protected from absorption of moisture to assure long life. It has a relatively large reverse current which results in a lower rectification ratio (75 to 1) and a reduced efficiency.

The magnesium-copper sulfide rectifier has the advantage of high current density (25 to 50 amp per square inch) and the ability to operate over a wide range of temperatures (from −70 to 135° C). It has the disadvantage of a low inverse peak of 5 volts, which tends to limit its application to relatively low voltages. This rectifier may be employed for the same general applications as the metallic rectifiers previously discussed.

p-n Junction Rectifiers

The discovery, research, and development surrounding the junction between a *p*-type and an *n*-type semiconductor have brought about revolutionary advances in rectifiers and control in both the electric power and communication fields. The *p-n* junction is a relatively thin boundary layer between a *p*-type and an *n*-type semiconductor material within a single crystal structure. The thickness of the boundary layer depends on the mode of production of the *p-n* junction. A seed of a germanium crystal may be withdrawn for a distance within a germanium melt containing *p*-type impurity, then suddenly an *n*-type of impurity may be added to the melt to cause the *n*-type to predominate. As the seed continues to be withdrawn, a junction is formed between the *p*-type and *n*-type germanium. In a second process, a section of *n*-type germanium surface is covered with a *p*-type impurity or exposed to a vapor of *p*-type impurity. A subsequent forming process (diffusion at high temperature) will cause some of the *p* impurity to penetrate the surface, leaving a *p-n* junction. Again, a *p*-type material like indium may be placed on one side of a thin wafer of pure germanium and an *n*-type impurity, such as arsenic, on the other side. Then pressure and high current may be applied to cause the impurities to penetrate from each side and produce a *fused* or *alloyed* product with a *p-n* junction.

An analysis of the rectifying action at a *p-n* junction may be of interest. First, let us consider two separated sections of *n*-type and *p*-type crystal, as shown in Fig. 17*a*. Within the *n*-type section there are many electrons set free by the donor impurity and these have a random motion within the section. The entire *n*-section is neutral (same number of − and + charges). If the impurity atoms are uni-

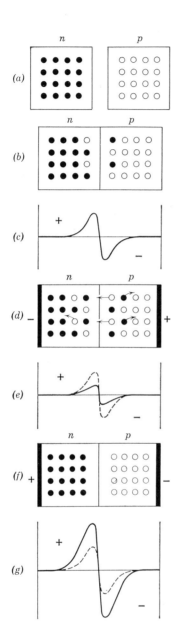

Fig. 17. n-p junction rectifier.

formly distributed throughout the crystal lattice structure, there will
be no differences in potential (space charge) between the parts of the
unit.   In the *p*-type section the holes will likewise have a uniform
distribution and, following the same line of reasoning, there are no
differences of potential or space charge within this unit.   If these
n-type and *p*-type sections are brought together physically, nothing
will happen because (1) there is no contact emf (basic material is the
same) and (2) energy equal to the work function of the basic material would be necessary to cause any movement of electrons across
the boundary.

Next assume that an *n-p* junction *has been formed* between the
n-type and *p*-type material, as shown in Fig. 17*b*.   Under this situation, the material exists as a single unit crystal and the lattice structure is perfectly matched throughout the junction area.   Now electrons in the *n*-section can drift across the junction into the *p*-section,
and in like manner holes can drift across the junction into the *n*-sec-
tion.   At first thought it might appear that this procedure would continue until the drifting electrons annihilated the holes, and vice versa.
However, this *does not happen* because the presence of the electrons
and holes is an essential part of any *n*-type or *p*-type structure—their
number remains constant, but their *distribution may change*.   Actually, the drift of electrons and holes continues only momentarily
until an equilibrium is established.   To understand this, note that
when an electron leaves the *n*-section, that section tends to become
positive.   Also note that when a hole enters the *n*-section, it also
causes the *n*-section to become positive.   Therefore, the drift of carriers across the *n-p* junction causes a rise of + charge and potential
on the *n* side of the junction, and, similarly, a fall of potential on the
p side.   This change of potential quickly brings the carrier drift to
an equilibrium.   Furthermore, the + and − carriers which cross the
n-p junction will remain relatively close to the junction, and the
charge distribution on the left for the *n*-section and on the right for
the *p*-section does not change.   The result of the preceding considerations is that two potential hills are built up at the junction, as shown
in Fig. 17*c*.   These potential hills oppose any further movement of
carriers across the junction and the carrier movement is in equilibrium.

Next, let us consider the rectifying action at the *n-p* junction.   If a
difference of potential is applied across the outside faces of the crystal, as shown in Fig. 17*d*, the added potential will attract electrons
to the right and holes to the left, giving a new charge carrier distri-

bution. The applied potential is in such a direction as to oppose the natural potential hills shown in Fig. 17c. Hence this applied potential lowers the resulting potential hills across the junction to some new value, as suggested in Fig. 17e. This is the condition for the forward flow of rectified current which now assumes a large magnitude.

Last, assume that the polarity of the applied potential is reversed, as shown in Fig. 17f. Now the + potential on the left attracts the electrons away from the n-p junction, whereas the − potential on the right attracts the holes away from the junction. Hence very few of the carriers freed by the impurities can drift across the junction. The applied voltage is now added to that of Fig. 17c to produce the very high potential blocking hills depicted in Fig. 17g. Thus this is the blocking direction of the rectifier. The only carriers available for transfer are those freed from the germanium atoms by thermal action. Therefore the reverse current is *very* small and usually is of constant value until the peak inverse voltage passes safe limits.

Germanium Power Rectifiers

Germanium power rectifiers use p-n junctions for rectifying large magnitudes of current for electric power applications. They differ from those point contact rectifiers, which may have p-n junctions, in possessing broader areas of contact and in the methods of processing and assembly, but not in the basic theory of operation. The heart of the germanium power rectifier is the rectifying cell. In one typical assembly, a pure germanium wafer 0.020 in. thick and the size of a dime has an antimony impurity on one side and indium on the other (Fig. 18). A forming process fuses and alloys the impurities into the wafer and produces a p-n junction. Next, thin metal electrodes (disks) are soldered to the faces of the resulting crystal structure. Last, the unit is covered with a plastic varnish to seal out moisture and other contaminating agents.

The characteristics of the germanium rectifying cell are marvelous. It conducts forward current up to 100 amp per square centimeter over the active area of the p-n junction. This is 1000 times the rating for copper oxide and selenium cells. The permissible peak inverse voltage varies with the results of the forming process. Cells are tested and graded into groups rated for peak inverse ratings (PIV) of 15, 30, 50, and 65 volts. Small area cells have been rated at higher values up to 125 volts. These ratings are a-c rms values, and hence the equivalent d-c value would be approximately 40 per cent higher. The rms values are used for PIV because these recti-

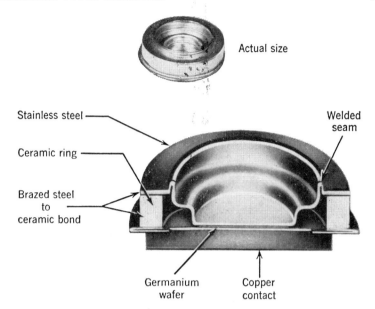

Actual size

Stainless steel

Welded seam

Ceramic ring

Brazed steel to ceramic bond

Germanium wafer

Copper contact

Fig. 18. Germanium power rectifier. (Courtesy General Electric Company.)

fiers are usually employed in the electric power field where all personnel are accustomed to the a-c and rms terminology. The I^2R losses at the p-n junction are very low so that the efficiency of the germanium rectifier is very high (up to 94 per cent in some multiple circuits). The maximum safe operating temperature at the p-n junction is 100° C.

The assembly of one type of germanium rectifier cell is shown in Fig. 18. The enclosing unit seals out moisture and other contamination. The heavy copper base serves as a heat sink to store and carry away the heat generated at the p-n junction. If air cooling is planned for the rectifier, the copper contact is expanded to a plate or fin of large dimensions, and cooling results from convection or forced air flow. If water cooling is desired, the germanium cell or cells may be attached (with electric insulation) to a tube or chamber through which water is circulated to carry away the generated heat.

The completed germanium cells may be connected in parallel to give large rectified current outputs. Again the cells may be connected in series to give higher voltage outputs. Since the characteristics of individual cells vary with the forming process, it is necessary to match carefully the forward and reverse resistances and the PIV of cells employed in either parallel or series combinations.

Complete germanium power rectifiers carry output voltage ratings of 65 volts, 125 volts, and 150 volts, and capacities of 25 and 50 kw. Completed units consist of germanium cells, transformers, cooling systems, and protective units.

The excellent characteristics of this rectifier suggest that it is an ideal unit with great possibilities. Unfortunately, these ideal characteristics present a few problems for the design engineer which are discussed in the following paragraph.

Germanium power rectifiers are used on electric power supply and load circuits that are subject to sudden load variation with resulting current and voltage transients. For example, a short circuit on the d-c rectified load is possible. This means that the forward current through the cell may rise to a tremendous value limited only by the resistance and the reactance of transformer windings and circuit elements outside of the rectifier. Although the resistance of the germanium cell is very low, the heat produced varies as the square of the short-circuit current. Since the thermal storage capacity of the tiny cell is very low, the temperature may rise to the point of melting the parts and destroying the cell. In like manner, a transient voltage rise from the power source or from an inductive load on the load circuit may cause the PIV to exceed safe limits and destroy the germanium cell. The period of time required for cell destruction arising from either of the preceding faulty conditions is exceedingly short (perhaps 1 cycle of 60-cycle current). Accordingly, the usual protective devices employed in electric power circuits are too slow to give adequate protection to a germanium cell and special protective means are necessary on applications where heavy transients may occur.

Silicon Power Rectifiers

Silicon power rectifiers employ large area p-n junctions like germanium. Their theory of operation, the general methods of production, and their operating characteristics parallel those of the germanium rectifier. Their rectifying cells are superior to germanium because they will operate satisfactorily at temperatures up to 190° C at the p-n junction and because they will withstand a higher peak inverse voltage. Since silicon is produced from sand, the supply is unlimited and the cost low. However, it is more difficult to produce silicon having a high degree of purity.

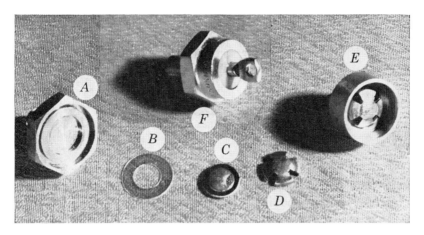

Fig. 19. Silicon power rectifier. (*A*) Base with stem. (*B*) Mica washer for centering. (*C*) Basic silicon diode. (*D*) Contact spring. (*E*) Assembled "header" with seal. (*F*) Assembled rectifier cell. (Courtesy Westinghouse Electric Company.)

The assembly and parts of a typical silicon rectifying unit are shown in Fig. 19. This hermetically sealed unit may be used to provide d-c forward currents up to 22 amp with a PIV up to 400 volts. The rectifier case is the cathode terminal. These units may be assembled on copper structures designed to remove the generated heat by convection, forced air cooling, or water cooling. They are adaptable for mounting and connections in various forms of bridge circuits for rectification of a-c power.

Point-Contact Transistor

Research on semiconductors and developmental work on the germanium crystal diodes led to the invention of the point-contact transistor by J. Bardeen and W. H. Brattain. This transistor consists of the addition of one catwhisker and a second circuit to the point-contact diode. The new construction is shown in Fig. 20. The point contact on the left is called the emitter, and the second contact placed a few thousandths of an inch from the first is termed the collector. In operation the emitter point is biased + by a source of low potential, whereas the collector point is connected to the negative (−) side of a higher potential source. If a varying potential (signal) is applied in series with the emitter, it will cause relatively large changes in electric power in the collector circuit. The reasons for

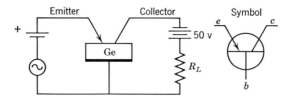

Fig. 20.   Point-contact transistor circuit.

this action may be deduced from preceding discussions. First assume that the collector point is removed or its circuit is opened.
Then the emitter and its circuit become a simple diode rectifier.
A rising positive potential on the emitter injects holes into the crystal, and carrier (holes and electrons) conduction results. Similarly,
if the emitter point is removed or its circuit opened, the collector
point and its circuit become a crystal diode rectifier. However, for
the negative potential normally applied to the collector point, only
a small reverse electron current results.

Now, if both the emitter and collector circuits are restored, the
theory of operation of the transistor unfolds, as suggested in Fig. 21.
First, a positive potential on the emitter point injects holes into the
surrounding germanium crystal surface. Since the collector point is
very close and has a strong negative potential, it attracts and collects

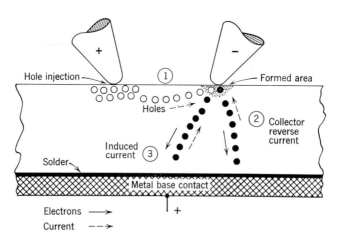

Fig. 21.   Action in point-contact transistor. (Courtesy *Bell Laboratories
Record,* January 1956.)

these holes which serve as one component of the collector current (labeled No. 1). Second, the negative potential on the collector point repels free electrons in the n-type germanium and creates the reverse electron current from the base of the crystal. This component of current is labeled No. 2 in Fig. 21. A third component of collector current (No. 3) arises from a more complicated phenomenon. Here the association of the collector point and the germanium plus a forming process results in a change in the surface state of the crystal that permits an induced and increased electron current between the collector and the crystal base. Obviously, the forming process at the collector point is responsible for the induced component of current, but no universally acceptable explanation has come to light. One suggestion which has been offered is that the forming process injects some impurities from the collector point into the crystal surface. If these impurity atoms serve as "hole traps," they could influence the components of electron current from collector to base in a manner similar to a p-n junction. It should be noted that the variations of potential on the emitter serve to control all components of the collector current.

The preceding theory suggests that the current in the output or collector circuit is larger than in the emitter or input circuit. The current multiplication lies in the range of two to three times and is indicated in the curves of Fig. 22. These curves show the magnitude of the collector current with change of collector voltage for a series

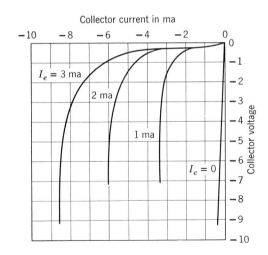

Fig. 22. Characteristic of a point-contact transistor.

Fig. 23. Point-contact transistor. (Courtesy Western Electric Company.)

of constant emitter current values. For zero current or open circuit in the emitter, the collector current is very small—the reverse diode current. For 1 ma emitter current, the collector current shows a value approximately three times as large. Also the differences in collector current for higher values of emitter currents show consecutively a multiplication of two to three times. It should be stressed that the current multiplication in the point-contact transistor is not of major importance as far as resultant amplification and gain are concerned. The important factor is the power gain.

The power gain of the point-contact transistor is expressed in terms of the input and output (load) resistances. This follows since power may be expressed in terms of I^2R. If for a given cell, the emitter contact resistance is 200 ohms and the corresponding resistance for the output or load is 10,000, the power gain is approximately fifty times for the same current in emitter and collector. If the device has a current multiplication, the resultant gain will be correspondingly higher. A commercial point-contact transistor is shown in Fig. 23.

Junction Transistors

A junction transistor is a multielement device consisting of a series of p-n junctions. This device, like the point-contact transistor, provides power amplification for small input signals. The structure and circuit of an n-p-n junction transistor are illustrated in Fig. 24. The n-section input on the left is called the emitter, the middle p-section is the base, and the n-section on the right is the collector. The term emitter is applied to the section which injects carriers (in this case electrons) into the device, and the term collector applies to the end element that collects the carriers. In the n-p-n transistor, a low magnitude of negative potential is applied to the emitter and a much higher positive potential is applied to the collector. The physical size of a commercial transistor is very small, as shown on the right of Fig. 24. The p, or base, section is approximately 0.001 in. thick and the n-sections are proportionately small.

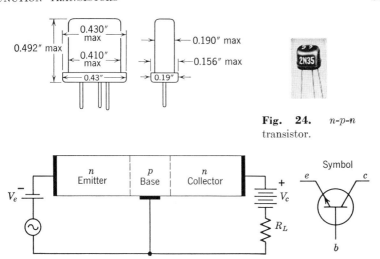

Fig. 24. *n-p-n* transistor.

The theory of the *n-p-n* transistor may be deduced by thinking of the device as two independent junction rectifiers, and then considering the performance of the recombined element. To do this the reader should be familiar with the theory of action for junction rectifiers given earlier in this chapter (see Fig. 17). Let us consider the action at junction J_e across the left *n-p* sections of Fig. 25. Holes and electrons diffuse across this junction and result in a potential hill for electrons (negative carriers) from the emitter. The negative potential applied to the emitter lowers the potential hill so that carriers should pass readily across the junction (holes left and electrons right). This represents the forward flow of current for the emitter

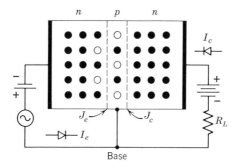

Fig. 25. *N-p-n* transistor.

n and base p considered as a junction rectifier, and the forward resistance is low. Turning to the junction J_c between the p and n sections on the right, one finds that the $+$ potential on the collector-base circuit represents the reverse bias for a rectifier. Hence only a small reverse current results and the resistance across the junction J_c is very high.

New factors enter the picture when we combine the preceding actions into a composite result. These factors arise from the extreme thinness of the p (base) section. As electrons drift or diffuse into the base region, very few have the opportunity for recombination with the holes present and nearly all pass into the n collector region and are collected by the positive electrode on the collector. Also, few of the electrons, which drift into the p base region, move to the base electrode because of the long thin path (vertical). As a result of these factors, the emitter current, which crosses the J_e junction, divides, with the larger part (0.9 to 0.985) moving to the collector and the remainder passing to the base. Thus there is no multiplication of emitter current in the collector circuit as with the point-contact transistor, but an actual ratio of less than one. However, the collector current is many times the magnitude of the base electrode current. If α represents the collector to emitter current ratio, then the collector to base current ratio becomes

$$\frac{I_c}{I_b} = \frac{\alpha}{1 - \alpha} \tag{1}$$

and for an α of 0.95

$$\frac{I_c}{I_b} = \frac{0.95}{1 - 0.95} = 19$$

The current multiplication from base to collector is useful in an amplifier circuit where the input signal is fed into the base instead of the emitter. This circuit is treated later in the book.

The theory of action taking place in an n-p-n transistor may be depicted also by energy level diagrams, as illustrated in Fig. 26. With no applied external potentials (Fig. 26a), some free electrons exist in the conduction bands for the n-type sections. Likewise, some holes appear in the forbidden zone for the p-type base region. The characteristic potential hill, described earlier, exists in the p-type base section. With normal polarity and potentials applied to the emitter and collector, the energy level diagrams shift to that of Fig.

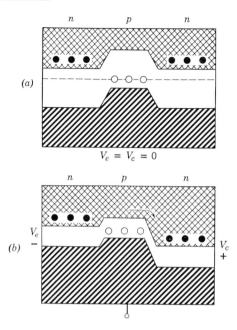

Fig. 26. Energy diagrams for n-p-n transistor.

26b. The potential hill is now lowered and the electrons pass over the reduced hump and fall to a lower level where they are attracted by the positive potential on the collector.

Many junction transistors employ a p-n-p structure and circuit, as illustrated in Fig. 27. Here the charge carriers in the emitter, base, and collector sections are respectively opposite to those in the n-p-n

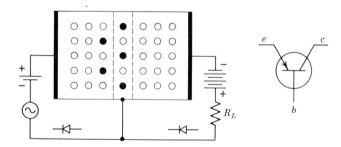

Fig. 27. P-n-p transistor.

transistor. Also the polarity of the applied potentials has been reversed so that holes move from the emitter over a small potential hill into the collector section and are attracted to the collector electrode where they recombine with electrons. Characteristics of the p-n-p transistor parallel those of the n-p-n type. The resistance at the junction from emitter to base is low and from base to collector high, and power amplification results. The differences between the two types lie in the polarity of the applied potentials, the direction of current, and the majority carriers—electrons in n-p-n and holes in p-n-p. Manufacturers often produce n-p-n and p-n-p transistors having identical ratings except for polarity and direction of current. The circuit designer chooses the type that uses polarities which fit the circuitry needed for his problem.

The characteristic curves for a typical commercial n-p-n transistor are given in Fig. 28. The rating for this cell is as follows:

> Description: germanium n-p-n junction transistor
> Maximum ratings
>> Collector voltage (collector to base) $+40\ V$
>>   (collector to emitter) $+25\ V$
>> Collector current, direct $+10\ ma$
>> Total dissipation $50\ mw$
> Characteristics
>> Alpha   0.975
>> Emitter resistance r_e 26 ohms
>> Base resistance r_b 800 ohms
>> Collector resistance r_c 2 meg
>> Alpha cutoff frequency   800 kc/s

Transistors are constructed of germanium or silicon with the germanium predominating in number. A wide range of ratings is available. Collector voltage varies from 10 to 65, and collector currents from 10 ma to 15 amp and higher. Power output varies from 50 mw to 35 watts and higher.

The characteristics of junction transistors can be improved and controlled by design and production. One basic method of control is to vary the density of the impurities and charge carriers across a given region such as the base region. This gives a form of "built-in" electric field which will hasten the drift of electrons across the region. The maximum operating temperature of germanium transistors is approximately 75° C. This limitation arises for two reasons: (1) to permit the heat dissipation from units of small surface area and

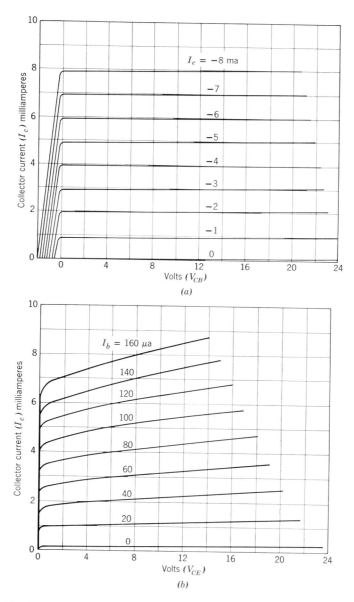

Fig. 28. Characteristic curves of *n-p-n* transistor. (*a*) Collector to base voltage. (*b*) Collector to emitter voltage. (Courtesy Sylvania Electric Products Inc.)

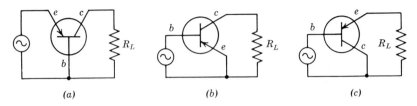

Fig. 29. Basic circuits for p-n-p transistor amplifier. (a) Common grounded base. (b) Common or grounded emitter. (c) Common or grounded collector.

(2) to prevent the change of operating characteristics which results from higher temperatures.

Junction transistors may be employed as amplifiers in three different basic circuits as shown in Fig. 29. Part (a) of this figure illustrates the common or grounded base connection used in preceding figures. Part (b) shows the common or grounded emitter connection which enjoys wider use than the others. The circuit of part (c) is termed the common or grounded collector. All these basic circuits are covered in control applications in later chapters.

The three resistances previously listed under characteristics (r_e, r_b, and r_c) are useful in understanding the operation of the transistor, in establishing equivalent circuits, and in making calculations. These resistances are dynamic or a-c resistances and are those associated respectively with the emitter, the base, and the collector. These resistances are three of the basic parameters of transistors. Unfortunately, there are many other parameters needed to cover the three basic transistor amplifier circuits depicted in Fig. 29. The reader will find an extensive treatment of these parameters and their application to various equivalent circuits in Ref. 15 at the end of this chapter.

Power Gain in Transistor Amplifiers

The concept of the amplifying action within a junction transistor is sometimes difficult to attain. One helpful approach to an understanding is through the medium of an equivalent circuit. Such a circuit is given in Fig. 30. This circuit has been inserted into a transistor block and the resistances are assigned the values given for a typical transistor on a preceding page. Three factors are important in analyzing this equivalent circuit. First, the output of the collector-base circuit is utilized in a load R_L (assumed as 100,000 ohms). Second, the action within the transistor (previously described) is equivalent to inserting a current generator (G_c) between the collector and base as indicated. Third, the collector resistance is the value which applies to an inverse current (not the forward current).

The power gain in the transistor amplifier is the ratio of power output to the power input. Power in terms of current and resistance is approximately equal to the current squared times resistance. Thus the power input to the emitter is approximately $i_e{}^2 r_e$ and power output from the collector is $i_c{}^2 R_L[(\alpha i_e)^2 R_L]$.

$$\text{Power gain} = \frac{\text{power output}}{\text{power input}} = \frac{(\alpha i_e)^2 R_L}{i_e{}^2 r_e} = \frac{\alpha^2 R_L}{r_e} \text{ (approx.)} \quad (2)$$

Applying the resistance values given in Fig. 30,

$$\text{Power gain} = \frac{(0.975)^2 (100{,}000)}{27} = 3800$$

Power gain is usually expressed in decibels (db) where

$$\text{Decibels} = 10 \log \frac{P_{\text{out}}}{P_{\text{in}}}$$

which applied to this example gives

$$\text{Decibels} = 10 \log \frac{3800}{1} = 35.8$$

Point-Contact versus Junction Transistors

The point-contact transistor differs from the junction type in two ways. First, the point-contact type produces a collector current two to three times the emitter current. Second, the direction of the col-

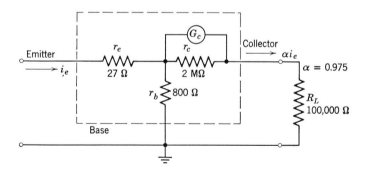

Fig. 30. Equivalent circuit of a junction transistor. (All resistances are a-c values.)

lector current in the point-contact type is such that a portion of it may be returned to the emitter through simple circuit elements to produce positive feedback. Positive feedback can be used to make the transistor oscillate, or to build regenerative computer-type circuits. To produce positive feedback, two junction type transistors must be connected back to back. It should be noted that junction transistors have almost completely replaced point-contact types because of the greater uniformity and better over-all characteristics of the junction type.

The Hook Collector Transistor

In the n-p-n and p-n-p junction transistors previously described, the current in the collector was slightly less than that in the emitter. In other words, the current gain, or α, was less than one. The addition of another n or p section and a third junction, as suggested in Fig. 31a makes possible current multiplication greater than one. Such transistors (n-p-n-p or p-n-p-n) are called hook collector transistors. In these devices the p or n section adjacent to the normal collector section has a floating potential since it does not have any external connection. Here the floating section and the normal collector section constitute the hook collector. The theory of action of this combination follows from previous discussion covering junction devices. The electron energy levels (without external applied potentials) are shown in Fig. 31b.

When external potentials are applied as shown in Fig. 31a, the energy levels shift to those shown in Fig. 31c. The plus bias applied to the emitter serves to inject holes into the first p section from where they diffuse rapidly across the thin n section into the floating section. In this floating section the holes are trapped in the hook. In this position the holes have a low potential energy, but they produce a high positive potential which aids the electrons from the collector to move to the left in the conduction band. Now the collector current consists of holes and many electrons, whereas the emitter current is basically hole current. As a result of the hook, the collector current may exceed the emitter current many times. The hook collector transistor has found little application as an amplifier.

Semiconductor Controlled Rectifier

The semiconductor controlled rectifier (also known as the solid-state thyratron) is a new four-unit three-junction device which holds great promise as a *controlled rectifier*. Although its physical make-up

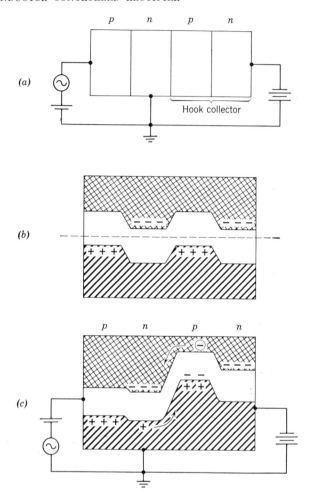

Fig. 31. Hook collector transistor and electron energy diagrams.

is similar to the hook collector, its function and mode of operation are quite different. As these lines are written (1958), it appears that this new device is destined to revolutionize our future electronic designs in the power control field.

The theory of action of the semiconductor controlled rectifier follows from the theory of the p-n junction rectifier covered earlier. Figure 32a shows a single p-n junction rectifier and two identical p-n junction rectifiers in series. At the right of the figure the character-

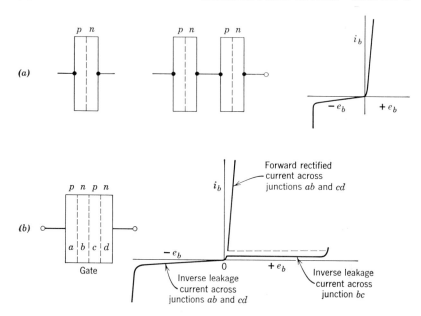

Fig. 32. Semiconductor controlled rectifier.

istic of a single unit is shown. The characteristic for the two in series follows that of the single unit except that all voltage values will be doubled because the voltage drops are in series. If we bring the two series p-n units of Fig. 32a together and form an intimate n-p junction between them, the four-unit, three-junction semiconductor rectifier results (Fig. 32b).

The new combination p-n-p-n will have a different i_b–e_b characteristic from that just considered because the central n-p junction is reversed with respect to the two end p-n junctions. Accordingly, if a potential forward-biased for the end p-n section is applied, these units would offer a very low resistance. However, this applied potential would be in the blocking direction for the central n-p junction. The resulting characteristic for the combined unit is shown in Fig. 32b (right). A forward potential for end p-n sections results in a very low inverse current through the central n-p section until the Zener knee is reached. At this point the normal electron avalanche effect takes place. Now the voltage drop falls to a low value and the rectified current flows, which is limited primarily by the load resistance. When the applied a-c potential reverses, the end p-n

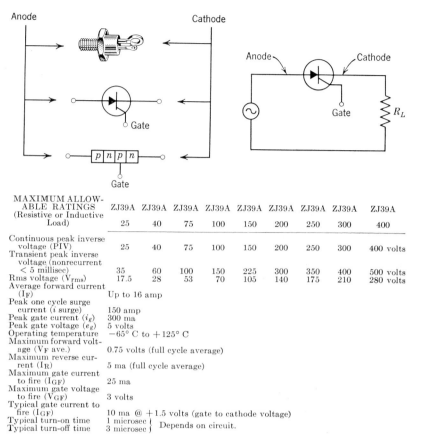

MAXIMUM ALLOW- ABLE RATINGS (Resistive or Inductive Load)	ZJ39A 25	ZJ39A 40	ZJ39A 75	ZJ39A 100	ZJ39A 150	ZJ39A 200	ZJ39A 250	ZJ39A 300	ZJ39A 400
Continuous peak inverse voltage (PIV)	25	40	75	100	150	200	250	300	400 volts
Transient peak inverse voltage (nonrecurrent < 5 millisec)	35	60	100	150	225	300	350	400	500 volts
Rms voltage (V_{rms})	17.5	28	53	70	105	140	175	210	280 volts
Average forward current (I_F)	Up to 16 amp								
Peak one cycle surge current (i surge)	150 amp								
Peak gate current (i_g)	300 ma								
Peak gate voltage (e_g)	5 volts								
Operating temperature	$-65°$ C to $+125°$ C								
Maximum forward voltage (V_F ave.)	0.75 volts (full cycle average)								
Maximum reverse current (I_R)	5 ma (full cycle average)								
Maximum gate current to fire (I_{GF})	25 ma								
Maximum gate voltage to fire (V_{GF})	3 volts								
Typical gate current to fire (I_{GF})	10 ma @ $+1.5$ volts (gate to cathode voltage)								
Typical turn-on time	1 microsec								
Typical turn-off time	3 microsec	Depends on circuit.							

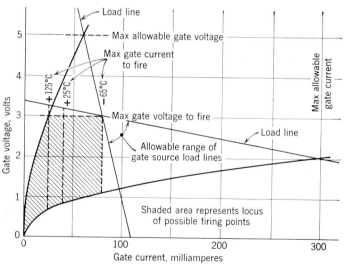

Fig. 33. Characteristics of silicon-controlled rectifier. (Courtesy General Electric Company.)

sections are blocking and reduce current to very low values until the
Zener knee and avalanche point are reached. These conditions are
depicted in Fig. 32b.

The silicon-controlled rectifier is a three-junction semiconductor
device for use in power control and power switching applications requiring blocking voltages up to 400 volts and load currents up to 50
amp. Series and parallel circuits may be used for higher power applications. A new developmental type and its characteristics are
shown in Fig. 33.

The importance of the silicon-controlled rectifier lies in the ease
with which its conduction (rectification) can be initiated and timed.
This property is not indicated in either Fig. 32 or 33. The simplest
circuit for control of the silicon unit is given in Fig. 34a. Here conduction is initiated by applying a positive potential to the "gate"
section. The positive potential may be continuous from a battery as
shown, it may be derived from the a-c source, or it may be a pulse
of very short duration. Only 1 or 2 volts and a peak current of 300
ma are required at the gate for initiating (firing) the conduction.
These low values are sufficient since the potential is applied in the
forward direction for the p-n junction. The firing is considered to
be a current phenomenon rather than one arising from a potential.
The theory of the initiation of conduction is indicated in Fig. 35.
This figure shows electron energy levels following the procedure used
earlier in Fig. 17 of this chapter. When forward rectifying potential
is applied, the natural drift of holes and electrons across the junction produces the potential hills shown by the dotted lines in Fig. 35b.
When a positive potential is applied to the gate, the electrons move
down out of the gate section and lower the potential hills at the cen-

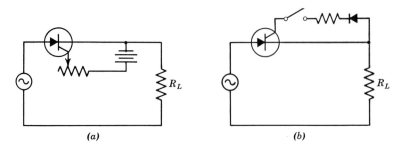

(a)   *(b)*

Fig. 34. Half-wave controlled rectifier circuit using (*a*) simple d-c gate circuit,
(*b*) simple a-c gate.

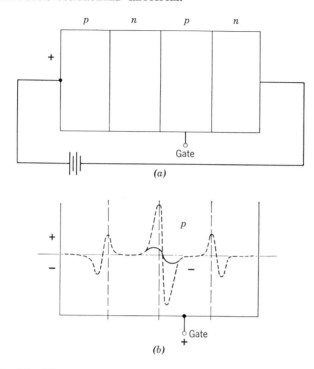

Fig. 35. Electron energy diagram in a *p-n-p-n* controlled rectifier.

tral *n-p* junction (solid lines Fig. 35*b*). This removes the blocking action, and current (conventional) flows readily through the entire unit left to right. Once rectification is initiated, current continues to flow until the voltage falls to zero. For the simple circuits of Fig. 34*a*, half-wave rectification will continue as long as the gate terminal is energized by the battery. If the gate circuit is energized by a synchronous timing circuit (applied voltage frequency), it is possible to initiate the conduction at any point in the forward voltage half cycle. Thus it is possible to control the magnitude of the rectified current by a time control of the instant of firing. Suitable circuits for this type of operation are covered in a later chapter. Initiation of gate firing by application of alternating current (plus directional crystal diode) is illustrated in Fig. 34*b*.

The application of the silicon-controlled rectifier for high-speed switching of a-c and d-c power loads is illustrated in Figs. 36 and 37. In Fig. 36, two silicon-controlled rectifiers are employed to con-

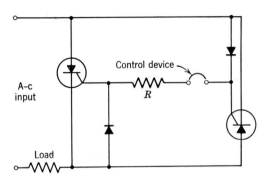

Fig. 36. A-c static switch provides high-speed switching of power loads. (Courtesy General Electric Company.)

duct the a-c power through the load (one for each direction). These units are fired by two gate circuits, each of which contains one semiconductor diode (crystal), a common resistor, and control switch. It will be noted that the directional diodes serve to apply the potentials to both the rectifier and diode circuits with the correct polarity and proper sequence. The control device closes and opens the a-c power circuit as required.

The d-c static control switch of Fig. 37 employs only one silicon-controlled rectifier. With the start and stop switches open, all the upper parts of the circuit are at + potential (the anode, R_L, r, and both terminals of capacitor C). When the start switch is closed, the positive charge residing on all the upper parts is connected to the

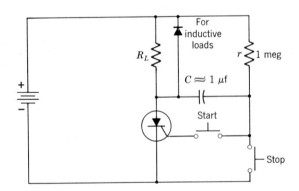

Fig. 37. D-c static switch circuit. (Courtesy General Electric Company.)

gate terminal and a transient current (discharge) flows in the correct direction to fire the rectifier. The magnitude of this discharge is limited by the 1 meg resistor and the capacity of the capacitor, but is sufficient to initiate conduction. When the start switch is opened, the capacitor charges up to near full-line potential since the RI drop across the rectifier is less than 1 volt. Now when the "stop" switch is closed, the right-hand side of the capacitor (carrying a plus charge) is connected to a minus terminal. The positive charge on the right is canceled instantly, permitting the electrons on the left side of C to rush to the anode and lower its potential to below zero. This transient drop of voltage at the anode stops conduction.

The advantages of the silicon-controlled rectifier are (1) high switching speed, (2) low forward voltage drop (high efficiency), (3) instant availability (no warm-up time), (4) a rugged static device, and (5) small size and weight. This rectifier looks much like the silicon power diode described earlier, and it is mounted and cooled in the same manner. The probable future application and circuits for this new device are treated in subsequent chapters.

Photoelectronics

The term photoelectronics may be applied to the action of photons (energy in light) upon atoms. In this chapter we are interested in three types of effects produced in solids by light and other forms of electromagnetic waves. First, light falling upon a solid may change its resistance and this is termed *photoconductive action*. Second, incident light energy may move carriers (charges) across a barrier layer and create an electric field. This is called *photovoltaic action*. A third effect of the energy of incident light is the removal of electrons from the surface of a solid. This phenomenon is known as *photoemission*. The first and second effects are covered in succeeding sections, and the third is treated in the next chapter.

Photoconductive Devices

In 1873, Willoughby Smith observed that high-resistance elements consisting of tiny rods of selenium became better conductors when exposed to daylight or to any artificial illumination. A large number of different forms of selenium cells have been devised to take advantage of this property of selenium. Many of these cells are old in the art, so that this device antedates all other photoelectric cells in time of practical use. One basic construction and circuit for a selenium light cell is illustrated in Fig. 38. Two comblike grids *A* and B are intermeshed to form a plate structure and are covered with selenium by evaporation. The thin coat of selenium is reduced to the gray crystalline form by heating. The circuit between terminals A and B consists of a thin bridge of selenium which covers the grid-like division line. This bridge is thin, has a short length, and a relatively large cross-sectional area, all of which serves to lower its resistance to impinging light. The ratio of light to dark current for this device may be four to one or higher. The theory of action is to be found in the formation of electron-hole pairs by the energy contained in the photons of light which penetrate the thin selenium. Thus the rise of current conduction stems from the added presence of both positive and negative carriers.

Since World War II, great strides have been made in research and development on semiconductors for photoconductive applications. Cadmium sulfide, cadmium selenide, lead sulfide, and germanium have been added to selenium for commercial usage. Other materials having some application are lead sulfide, silver sulfide, and silicon. The new photoconductive devices use semiconductors in three different forms or subtypes. These forms are labeled (1) thin films

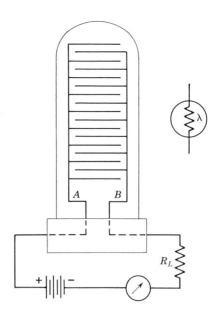

Fig. 38. Construction and circuit of a photoconductive cell.

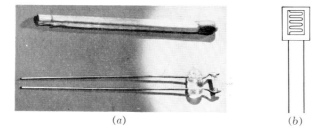

(a)   (b)

Fig. 39. Cadmium sulfide cells. (*a*) (Courtesy General Electric Company.) (*b*) (Courtesy Hupp Electronics Company.)

(described previously), (2) bulk, and (3) *p-n* junctions. All forms exist as a single crystal or as a crystal conglomerate.

The *cadmium sulfide photoconductive cell* currently enjoys the widest application among photoconductive devices. This device is produced in several commercial forms, two of which are illustrated in Fig. 39. The heart of the device is either a tiny CdS crystal (a few millimeters) or a layer of chemically deposited CdS. The CdS crystal may be pure, but usually contains a small amount of impurity (called an activator in this device) which usually adds to the sensitivity of the cell. The activator employed may be silver, antimony, or indium.

The dark resistance of a CdS crystal may be 10,000 to 100,000 times greater than its resistance when illuminated with 100 foot-candles of light.* This represents the maximum range, whereas the effective range after allowing for absorption of the enclosure may be of the order of 600 to 1. The tiny cells show a usable resistance change with light intensities as low as 0.0001 foot-candle. The relative response of the CdS cell to radiation of different wavelength is shown in Fig. 40. Although the resistivity is especially sensitive to blue and ultraviolet radiation, it also has pronounced sensitivity to X rays, gamma rays, and nuclear radiations such as beta rays and alpha particles.

The superiority of the CdS cell over competitive light-sensitive devices lies in the fact that it can control directly (without amplifiers) sufficient power to operate relays (see Fig. 41). It is small, rugged, light, and relatively inexpensive. It will operate on either

* A foot-candle is the illumination on a surface at a distance of 1 foot from a source of 1 candle.

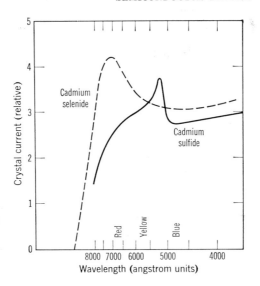

Fig. 40. Spectral response of cadmium sulfide crystals (solid curve) and cadmium selenide crystals (dotted curve) to visible portion of the spectrum runs from about 3800 to 7600 A. (Courtesy General Electric Company.)

direct or alternating current using circuits shown in Fig. 41.   In conjunction with a small relay it may play a vital part for (1) door openers, (2) burglar alarms, (3) flame failure detectors, (4) smoke detectors, or (5) lighting control for street lamps, homes, or factory. Tiny CdS cells may be assembled in multiple (straight line) to read holes on cards or punched tape for automatic business machines. Cadmium sulfide cells have a long record of service for X-ray measurements.

A suggested energy band structure for CdS is shown in Fig. 42. For this material the forbidden band is rather wide (2.4 ev).   It is assumed that the impurity atoms in the crystal structure are responsible for the "hole traps."   It is further assumed that these impurity atoms have energy levels near the middle of the forbidden band and that as stationary atoms they are able to trap the holes (prevent recombination by electrons) for a period of time.   The result of this trapping or delay of hole recombination is that 10,000 times as many electrons can pass through the crystal as there are photons absorbed.

The *cadmium selenide cell* parallels the CdS cell in its construction and general theory of operation.   In specific characteristics the

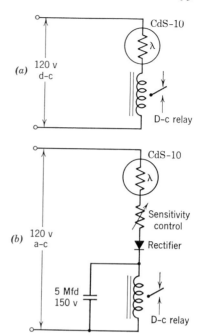

Fig. 41. Circuits for applying cadmium sulfide cells.

change of resistance from dark to light is one hundred times greater in CdS, whereas the time response of the CdS cell is one hundred times as long as the cadmium selenide. Thus the CdS cell is used where a large current change for a given variation of light is important, and the cadmium selenide is used where fast action (short time

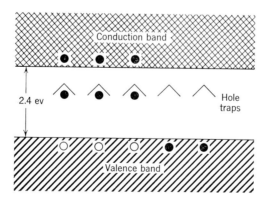

Fig. 42. Probable energy bands in cadmium sulfide crystal.

constant) is necessary. The high sensitivity of cadmium selenide in the red region of the light spectrum (see Fig. 40) makes this type of unit desirable for operation under illumination produced by tungsten incandescent lamps. The response of cadmium selenide decreases with rise in temperature. The cadmium selenide cell has been used successfully in automatic dimmers for automobile headlights.

The *lead sulfide photoconductive cell* has a maximum sensitivity at a wavelength of about 2 μ in the infrared region. It also has high signal-to-noise ratio and a fast time response in the range of 100 to 1000 microseconds. This cell can detect very fine differences in the chemical composition of many gases, liquids, and solids by measuring their characteristic infrared absorption (heat rays). Thus a cell can continuously monitor the exact composition of fluids flowing through pipes or plastic sheets moving along rollers. Similarly, it can evaluate the constituents of smoke for smoke control, or ascertain fluid or gaseous turbidity. The acute sensitivity to invisible heat waves of the near-infrared makes the lead sulfide cell a valuable contrivance for detecting warm objects without physical contact and over long distances.

Germanium Photodiode

Any of the germanium diodes previously covered may be modified to serve as a photoconductive device. This modification requires (1) a provision for light to fall on the germanium crystal in the immediate region of the point contact or at the *p-n* junction and (2) a connection of the electrodes in series with a load resistor and a d-c potential biased in the reverse direction. For the point-contact diode, provision is made for the light to fall on the thin crystal base and penetrate to the region of the point. For the *p-n* junction diode, the encapsulation should contain a transparent window to permit light to fall on the *p-n* junction. When light falls on the junction area, electron-hole pairs are formed and the resulting diffusion and movement of these carriers cause the cell current to increase in proportion to the light intensity. Since germanium has no hole traps, the change in current is small relative to that in the CdS cell. Accordingly, these devices require an amplifier in their output circuit to produce the power necessary for many control applications.

A miniature germanium junction photodiode and its characteristic curves are shown in Fig. 43. The tube is normally operated in series

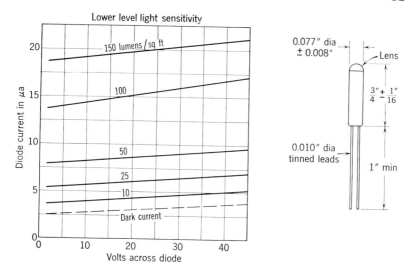

Fig. 43. Characteristic of photodiode. (Courtesy Sylvania Electric Products, Inc.)

with a load resistance of 100,000 ohms. It is designed for rapid, high-speed scanning and reading punched cards and tapes. It may be used for motion picture sound pickup applications. Its high output impedance permits coupling to vacuum tubes and grounded collector transistor circuits.

Photovoltaic Devices

In 1839, Edmond Becquerel discovered that when one of two electrodes immersed in an electrolyte is illuminated, a difference in potential appears between the electrodes. This principle was employed in an early commercial device which consisted of a sensitive electrode of cuprous oxide and an anode of lead immersed in an electrolyte of lead nitrate. In 1876, while experimenting with the conductivity of amorphous selenium rods embedded in iron, Adams and Day discovered that a difference of potential was created when light fell on their apparatus. This phenomenon of the creation of a potential difference by light falling on a junction of selenium and iron was rediscovered by Charles Fritts in 1884 and by B. Lange in 1930. The first commercial application of this phenomenon was announced in 1931 by the Weston Electrical Instrument Corporation, and was known as the Photronic Cell.

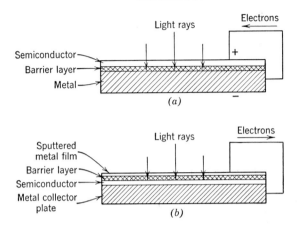

Fig. 44. Construction of photovoltaic cells. (*a*) Back plate type. (*b*) Front plate type.

Photovoltaic devices consist of a sandwich of elements similar to those used in the broad-area barrier-layer type of rectifiers—copper oxide on copper and selenium on iron. Curiously, when the device is used as a photovoltaic device, the direction of electron flow may be opposite to that observed when it is used as a rectifier. The construction of a simple back plate photovoltaic cell is illustrated in Fig. 44a. Light falling upon a thin semiconductor layer causes electrons to move to the metal, where they build up a negative potential. In the meantime, the semiconductor has lost electrons and assumes a positive potential, and a difference of potential is built up between the two electrodes. This difference of potential does not become very high (about 0.3 to 0.5 volt) because the electrons can leak back to the semiconductor through the barrier layer.

The theory of photovoltaic action follows from the preceding discussion. When photons of light energy are absorbed by semiconductor atoms, electron-hole pairs are formed. For those actions at or close to the barrier layer (boundary between semiconductor and metal), the electrons move into the metal and the holes are trapped in the semiconductor. Some electrons do leak back and a state of equilibrium is soon produced for a given light intensity. Actually, the direction by which the electrons leak back is the normal direction of electron movement when the same device is used as a rectifier. However, the resistance for this direction of electron flow is high (a few hundred ohms at low voltages) as shown by rectifier characteristics (see Fig. 12). Hence the device works satisfactorily for the low potentials generated by photovoltaic action.

Commercial photovoltaic cells use selenium as the semiconductor since it gives more stable characteristics covering magnitude of voltage, temperature changes, and effects of age. Modern cells use the front plate type of construction illustrated in part (*b*) of Fig. 44. Here the selenium is placed on an iron collector plate and after being given a suitable forming treatment is covered with a thin transparent sputtered film of metal (gold, etc.). With this construction the barrier layer is between the transparent film and the selenium. This construction reverses the polarity of the cell and has the decided advantage that less light is lost in reaching the barrier layer. It is probable that some light energy penetrates the semiconductor to the rear junction and produces a small counter emf action, but this is of minor magnitude.

Selenium photovoltaic cells are utilized by connecting a load such as an indicating meter or a sensitive relay between its electrodes (Fig. 45). The current output in microamperes is practically linear for near zero values of load resistance, as shown in Fig. 46. As the load resistance rises, the linearity falls off rapidly because of the increase of internal leakage across the barrier. The linearity may be improved by the use of a shunt resistor shown by a dotted line in Fig. 45. The color sensitivity of the selenium photovoltaic cell compares favorably with that of the human eye in the range of visible light, and can be closely matched by the use of appropriate filters. The characteristic of the selenium changes somewhat with temperature and these cells should not be subjected to temperatures higher than 50 degrees C. These cells are also subject to fatigue and aging, but they may be given artificial aging during manufacture so as to show little change in the hands of the user.

The principal applications of photovoltaic cells are in the fields

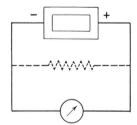

Fig. 45. Circuit for photovoltaic cell.

of (1) photographic exposure meters, (2) foot-candle meters, (3) lighting control, and (4) automatic iris control on cameras. A commercial foot-candle meter and an exposure meter are illustrated in Fig. 47. They are used by lighting engineers to measure the resultant illumination in schools, homes, and commercial buildings. Both instruments consist of a photovoltaic cell and a microammeter in series enclosed in a compact case. The meters are calibrated to measure appropriate light units. The energy efficiency of selenium photovoltaic cells is approximately 1 per cent.

The *solar battery* (announced by Bell Telephone Laboratories in 1954) is a type of photovoltaic cell that uses wafer-thin silicon strips about the size of razor blades. These units consist of carefully refined strips of silicon, into the faces of which an impurity has been diffused in the form of a microscopic layer near the surface. These formed strips constitute a *p-n* junction, and the energy in the sunlight moves electrons to one face and holes to the other, thus giving polarity to the battery. Among the advantages of the solar battery are (1) long life, (2) relatively high efficiency (6 per cent), and (3) more power developed than in other photovoltaic devices. Silicon strips covering an area of one square yard will develop 50 watts of power. Solar batteries have been employed as a source of

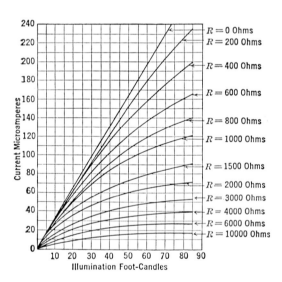

Fig. 46. Current-illumination characteristic of a photovoltaic cell for various load resistances. (Courtesy General Electric Company.)

(a)   (b)

Fig. 47. Photovoltaic cells. (*a*) Foot-candle meter. (*Courtesy* General Electric Company.) (*b*) Photoexposure meter. (*Courtesy* Weston Electric Company.)

energy on remote repeater stations, on wire communication circuits, and on space satellites.

The *atomic cell* (Radio Corporation of America Laboratories, 1954), like the solar battery, consists of a wafer of semiconductor containing a *p-n* junction, but utilizes the energy from the beta rays of radioactive material instead of the energy in light. One side of the semiconductor is coated with strontium-90 which gives off beta particles (electrons) at high velocity for twenty years before the better half of its radioactivity is dissipated. Each beta ray releases 200,000 electrons at the *p-n* junction. The cell develops 0.25 volt and has a small power output sufficient for transistor circuits.

Thermistors

The term Thermistor is applied to a line of fabricated semiconductors which have a negative coefficient of resistance with a rise in temperature. The word Thermistors is a contraction of "thermal resistors." The most common ones are made of mixtures of metallic oxides, including those of nickel, copper, zinc, and manganese. In some types the resistances may be doubled with a temperature decrease of as little as 30° F. The temperature-resistance characteris-

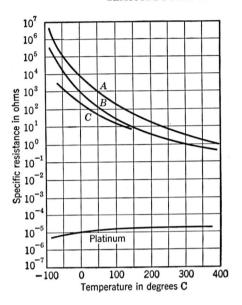

Fig. 48.   Temperature-resistance characteristics of thermistors compared to platinum.

tics of three Thermistors are illustrated in Fig. 48.   A commercial unit is shown in Fig. 49.

Thermistors may be used wherever temperature variations exist or can be produced.   The variations in temperature may be brought about in three ways: (1) externally, by changes in surrounding air,

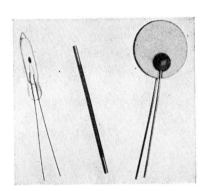

Fig. 49.   Thermistors.   (Courtesy Bell Telephone Laboratories.)

water, etc., (2) internally, where the current through the Thermistor changes its temperature, and (3) indirectly, by means of a heating coil surrounding the Thermistor element. Thermistors have numerous applications in telephone and broadcasting service and in the industrial control field.

The theory of action within the Thermistor follows discussions from the preceding chapter. As the temperature of the semiconductor rises, the thermal generation of electron-hole pairs increases and lowers the resistance. It is well to note that the Thermistor is an *ohmic* device, that is, its resistance, as calculated by volts impressed divided by amperes resulting, remains constant for both directions of current flow as long as the temperature remains constant.

Silicon Carbide Devices

Crystals of silicon carbide act as a nonlinear semiconductor in which the current varies as a power of the applied voltage. The material is nonohmic and differs from other nonlinear semiconductors in that it conducts current equally well in both directions. Silicon carbide devices are usually processed by mixing large numbers of small crystals with a ceramic binder (usually clay) and then molding the mixture into various shapes under high pressure. The molded forms are then fired at a high temperature (approximately 1200° C). Several forms of commercial silicon carbide devices are shown in Fig. 50 along with the characteristic conduction curve for this

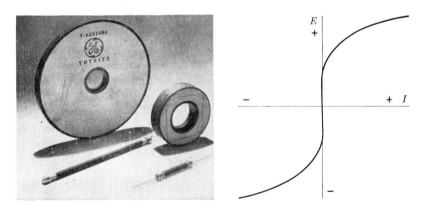

Fig. 50. Thyrite resistors and their characteristic. (Courtesy General Electric Company.)

material. In the trade, silicon carbide is often referred to as Thyrite, which is a registered trademark for this product.

The formula that approximates the voltampere characteristic of a silicon carbide resistor is:

$$i = Ke^n \tag{3}$$

where i = instantaneous alternating or direct current.

$\quad K$ = a constant (amperes at 1 volt).

$\quad e$ = instantaneous applied voltage.

$\quad n$ = an exponent.

The constant K depends on the resistivity and the dimension of the particular resistor under consideration. The exponent n depends upon various factors in the manufacturing process, and has a value within the range of 3.5 to 7. (For an ordinary linear resistor, $n = 1$.)

Equation 3 and the characteristic curve of Fig. 50 show the important usefulness of silicon carbide devices. Thus at low voltages the resistance is very high, but when the applied voltage rises to what may be a dangerous value for equipment, the silicon carbide produces a near short circuit and protects this equipment.

The theory of current conduction in the silicon carbide semiconductor is not well understood. One theory, which is somewhat plausible, is that the resistor has a large number of very thin barrier layers. Perhaps these layers exist as films upon the surface of the crystals. Under low potentials very little electron movement results, but under a rising potential electrons tunnel through these exceedingly thin films and produce the rapid rise in current.

The basic reason for using silicon carbide devices is to protect equipment from destruction by overvoltage and resulting overcurrent. Hence these devices are used in parallel with the equipment to be protected. The oldest and widest application is that of lightning arresters to protect electrical power lines and other electrical equipment from direct and indirect strokes of lightning. A second use of silicon carbide devices is to guard against voltage surges (inductive kicks) across iron-cored coils when the circuit is opened. These devices are also used as a stabilizing influence on rectifier and other electronic circuits where voltage surges may occur. Millions of tiny silicon carbide units (called varistors) are used in telephone circuits and handsets to prevent audio "pops" (in receivers) arising from minute voltage surges.

PROBLEMS

1. The crystal diode of Fig. 2 is connected in series with a 1000 ohm resistor for half-wave rectification. If an applied sine wave of emf produces a peak forward current of 22 ma, what is the peak value of the reverse current? What is the average value of the rectified current? (Average value equals 0.318 of the peak current.)

2. A single copper oxide cell of Fig. 11, having an area of 3 sq in., is connected in series with a resistor to a sine wave emf having a peak value of 10 volts. If the peak voltage drop across the cell is 0.4 volt at 40° C, calculate (a) the peak forward current, (b) the peak reverse current, (c) the rectification ratio, and (d) the ohmic value of the resistor.

3. In an n-p-n junction transistor, the collector current is 0.9 of the emitter current. What is the ratio of the collector current to the base current?

4. If the transistor of Problem 3 has an emitter resistance of 35 ohms and is connected to a load resistor of 125,000 ohms, what is the approximate power gain expressed as a ratio? expressed in decibels?

5. A certain silicon carbide resistor carries a current of 1 ma when 1.1 volt is impressed across it. What current does it pass under the following voltages and for differing values of exponent n?

Volts	n_1	n_2	n_3
10	1	3	5
100	1	3	5
1000	1	3	5

REFERENCES

1. Henish, H. K., *Rectifying Semiconductor Contacts*, Oxford University Press, 1957.
2. Dunlap, W. C., Jr., W. Crawford, *An Introduction to Semiconductors*, John Wiley and Sons, New York, 1957.
3. Hamann, C. E., and E. A. Harty, "Fundamental Characteristics and Applications of Copper-Oxide Rectifiers," *Gen. Elec. Rev.*, August 1933.
4. Clark, Carole A., "Selenium Rectifier Characteristics, Applications, and Design Factors," *Elec. Commun.*, 20, 1941.
5. Cornelius, E. C., "Germanium Crystal Diodes," *Electronics*, February 1946, p. 118.
6. Shockley, W., "Transistor Physics," *American Scientist*, January 1954.
7. Shockley, W., "Holes and Electrons," *Physics Today*, October 1950.
8. Shockley, W., M. Sparks, and G. K. Teal, "Properties of p-n Junction Transistors," *Phys. Rev.*, July 1951.

9. Roka, E. G., R. E. Buck, and G. W. Reiland, "Developmental Germanium Power Transistors," *Proc. IRE,* August 1954.

10. Jacobs, John E., "The Photoconductivity Cell," *Gen. Elec. Rev.,* July 1951.

11. Jacobs, John E., "The Use of Semiconductors as Detectors of X Radiation," *Proc. Nat. Electronics Conf.,* February 1952.

12. Middlebrook, R. D., *An Introduction to Junction Transistor Theory,* John Wiley and Sons, New York, 1957.

13. Kodak Electron Detector, Pamphlet No. U-2.

14. Frenzel, R. P., and F. W. Gutzwiller, "Solid-State Thyratron Switches Kilowatts," *Electronics,* March 28, 1958.

15. Hunter, L. P., *Handbook of Semiconductor Electronics,* McGraw-Hill Book Company, New York, 1956.

chapter 4

Electron Emission

Electron Emission

Electron emission is the liberation of electrons from the surface of solids. This liberation requires energy to overcome two separate forces. One force results from the atomic and other structural bonds which hold electrons within the surface boundary of the solid. The second force arises from the attraction of the positive charge within the solid for the electron as it leaves the surface. The total energy required to perform this double task is called the work function of the material.

In Chapter 2 we discussed the bonds which limit electron movement within solids and the energies involved in producing electric conduction. In this chapter we shall discuss similar factors as they affect the *removal of electrons (external) from a solid*.

Electron emission is usually concerned with metals. In metals, electrons are loosely bound and they participate in a large random movement within the body of a solid. However, as electrons approach the surface of a metallic solid they meet a strong potential barrier to an exit. The cause of this barrier is shown in Fig. 1. This figure represents a single row of atoms lying in any plane within the solid. As an electron *e* moves from left to right along this row, it experiences moderate changes in energy level as it passes the atomic nuclei within the body of the solid. However, as it approaches the surface of the solid, the energy required to move it against the force of its parent atoms and those behind it rises rapidly. If this single row and single plane picture were to be expanded to a three-dimensional concept, it would be obvious that a large potential energy barrier is present at the surface.

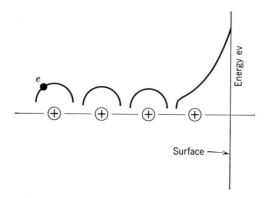

Fig. 1

An electron breaking through the surface of a metal leaves behind a positive charge of $+e$, which is called the *image charge*. As suggested in Fig. 2, the emitted electron is subject to a force of attraction in accordance with Coulomb's law.   In theory it is assumed that the positive charge resides within the surface at a distance x equal to the advance of the electrons from the surface.   Thus, to move the electron away from the surface requires work that is equal to the summation or integral of force times the distance moved ($\int f\,dx$).

The total work or energy required to overcome the potential energy barrier at the surface plus the energy required to remove the electron to infinity against the coulomb force is called the *work function*. Work function is generally represented by the symbol ϕ and is expressed in electron volts (ev).   The work function of several materials employed in electronic devices is given in Table 1.   The magnitude of work function depends upon the atomic and the crystal structure of a given material.

The concept of work function may be represented by a simple energy level diagram as indicated in Fig. 3.   Here the lower band

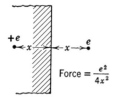

Fig. 2.   Image charge and force.

Table 1

Material	Work Function ϕ (electron volts)	Material	Work Function ϕ (electron volts)
Platinum	5.0	Thorium on tungsten	2.63
Tungsten	4.52	Calcium	2.5
Carbon	4.5	Barium	2.0
Mercury	4.4	Sodium	1.9
Molybdenum	4.3	Calcium oxide	1.9
Tantalum	4.1	Potassium	1.55
Nickel	4.0	Strontium oxide	1.4
Copper	4.0	Cesium	1.36
Thorium	3.0	Barium oxide	1.1
Magnesium	2.7		

represented by μ shows the range of energy values in electron volts which are normally possessed by electrons within the metal. These energy values may vary from near zero up to that of the Fermi level at the top of the valence band. The additional energy required to remove the electron completely from the metal is the work function ϕ represented by the upper band. A more complete picture of the change in energy level for an electron during the complete cycle of emission is suggested in Fig. 4. From some interior position x the potential energy level rises rapidly as the surface is approached, then after emerging the energy continues to rise with distance to overcome the attraction of the image charge.

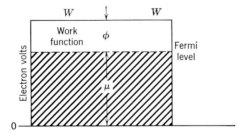

Fig. 3. Energy diagram illustrating work function.

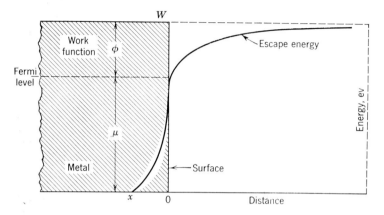

Fig. 4. Energy level diagram for electron emission from inside to outside of a metal.

Emission Phenomenon

Electrons may be liberated from metals in these five different ways: (1) thermionic emission, (2) high field emission, (3) secondary emission, (4) photoelectric emission, and (5) radioactive disintegration. Some radioactive materials eject electrons (beta rays) during their slow process of disintegration. This phenomenon is important in many scientific studies. In some electron tubes which contain gas and which start with cold cathodes, it is probable that radioactive materials within or near the tube and sometimes photoelectric emission provide the initial electron emission for exciting or starting the functioning of the device. The other methods for producing electron emission are discussed in the following sections.

Thermionic Emission

This is the liberation of electrons from a metal produced by the thermal agitation of its atoms. The phenomenon is analogous to the evaporation of liquids. At normal temperature, the molecules of a liquid have some thermal agitation, but few of those at the surface "jump out" far enough to remain as vapor. With a rise in temperature, the individual motions of the molecules become more violent and an increasing number do overcome the attraction of the liquid and do evaporate or "boil out." In like manner, the electrons in a metal are closely held by electron affinity, and a relatively small number have sufficient thermal energy to break away from the surface at ordinary temperatures. With a rising temperature the thermal movement of the atoms and the kinetic energy of the electrons increase so that more and more succeed in breaking through the potential energy barrier at the surface of the metal. As the electrons break out in space, the force of attraction of the positive image charge remaining on the metal soon overcomes the initial velocity of emission, and the electrons drop back into the metal. Thus, when operating in a zero electric field, the electrons never get very far from the surface of the heated metal.

The phenomenon of thermionic emission may be conceived as illustrated in Fig. 5. Let it be assumed that a filament or cylindrical conductor of tungsten is placed in a vacuum or in a space filled with inert gas at low pressure. At a certain temperature of the filament the thermal motion of the molecules and electrons becomes great enough so that a number of electrons are thrown out as shown in part (a) of Fig. 5. A further rise in temperature of the filament will be accompanied by an increase in the kinetic energy of the electrons and an increase in the number and initial velocity of those emitted (part b of Fig. 5). A still higher temperature of the filament will result in a greater agitation and velocity of electrons so that a cloud or atmosphere of electrons will be formed as depicted in part (c) of Fig. 5. It should be understood that Fig. 5 represents an isolated filament and the surrounding space magnified many times. Many electrons emitted from the filament never travel over 0.01 mm before returning, and few go farther than 1.5 mm. It is obvious that the initial velocity of emission will vary over wide limits, a large number having a relatively low velocity and a few having a velocity sufficient to carry them into the outer region of the electron cloud.

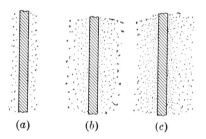

Fig. 5. Changes of thermionic emission with temperature.

(a)   (b)   (c)

The initial velocity of emission that an electron must have in order to break away from a tungsten filament can be readily calculated from equation 9, page 8, where E represents the work function of tungsten in volts (Table 1).

$$v = \sqrt{2\,\frac{e}{m}\,E} = \sqrt{2 \times 1.76 \times 10^{11} \times 4.52}$$

$$= 1.26 \times 10^6 \text{ meters per second}$$

$$= 2{,}820{,}000 \text{ miles per hour}$$

The purity of an emitting material and the cleanliness of its surface have a considerable bearing upon the amount of thermionic emission. Wilson found that the emission of a hot platinum filament may be reduced to 1/250,000 of its normal value by first heating it in oxygen or boiling it in nitric acid. A small amount of hydrogen around a heated filament overcomes the effects of oxygen and nitric acid. The presence of a small amount of water vapor in a tube will greatly reduce the thermionic emission. Special care is used in the preparation of emitters to eliminate or neutralize the harmful effects of occluded gases and water vapors. Thermionic emission may be greatly increased by a surface layer (usually one atom thick) of thorium, barium, strontium, or calcium on a base of tungsten, nickel, and some other metals.

Equation of Thermionic Emission

Early in the twentieth century O. W. Richardson reasoned that electron emission from hot solids bore a similarity to the evaporation from liquids. Using the classic kinetic theory, he developed an equation representing electron emission and performed experiments that checked the correctness of his theory to his own satisfaction. Some

Table 2

	A	b_0
Tungsten	60.2	52,400
Thoriated tungsten	3.0	30,500
Barium oxide	0.01	12,000

contemporary scientists did not obtain equally satisfactory experimental results, which led Langmuir to refine the experiment by eliminating errors resulting from the presence of gas in the tube and impurities in the filament and thus to verify the form of Richardson's equation. Richardson suggested a second equation for emission which was formulated by S. Dushman and checked experimentally. The latter equation, which holds general acceptance today, is as follows:

$$I = AT^2\epsilon^{-b_0/T} \tag{1}$$

where I = the emission current in amperes per square centimeter of emitting surface (saturation current density).

T = the absolute temperature (degrees C + 273) = Kelvin.

ϵ = the natural base of logarithms.

A = a constant.

$$b_0 = \frac{\phi}{k} = \frac{\text{Work function}}{\text{Boltzmann's constant } (0.863 \times 10^{-4} \text{ volt per degree K})}.$$

The various factors that control electron emission from hot bodies have made it difficult to correlate the values of constants derived from scientific deductions with those determined experimentally. Accordingly, the constants are determined by experiment and calculations, and the equation is treated as empirical.

For pure metals A is a universal constant, but for coated metal cathodes both A and b_0 vary because of the degree of coverage of coated material, temperature, and other factors. Experimental values of the constants for some cathode materials are given in Table 2.

The curve representing the trend of Richardson's equation is given in Fig. 6. It should be noted that this curve and equation 1 give the emission current (saturation current density) from a hot body or cathode and do *not* represent the current that may pass to a plate or anode in an electron tube.

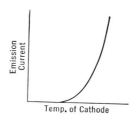

Fig. 6. Curve of thermionic emission.

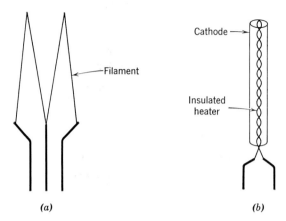

(a)   *(b)*

Fig. 7. Thermionic cathodes: (*a*) directly heated type, (*b*) indirectly heated type. (Courtesy Radio Corporation of America.)

Construction of Cathodes

The electrode from which electrons pass into the vacuum or gas in an electron tube is called the *cathode*. Cathodes may be classified as hot or cold. Hot cathodes may be either directly or indirectly heated. The directly heated type uses a filament construction as illustrated in part (*a*) of Fig. 7. The filament may be pure tungsten, thoriated-tungsten, or an oxide-coated alloy of nickel. Directly heated filament-cathodes require comparatively little heating power and are used in tubes designed for use with dry batteries. The indirectly heated cathode, shown in Fig. 7*b*, consists of a thin metal sleeve coated with an oxide emitter coating. Within the sleeve is a heater made of tungsten or tungsten-alloy wire encased in aluminum oxide for insulation. The cathode-heater sleeve is usually made of nickel or some nickel alloy such as Konal—an alloy of nickel, cobalt, iron, and titanium.

The heater-cathode construction is well adapted for use in electron tubes intended for operation from a-c power lines and from storage batteries. The use of separate parts for the emitter and heater offers three advantages. First, the insulation of these parts permits the cathode to be operated at almost any potential regardless of heater potential. Second, the separation of parts and of the thermal inertia of the cathode proper prevent a-c hum from affecting other parts of the circuit. Third, the heater-cathode construction permits a very close spacing between the cathode and other electrodes in a tube. This close spacing gives a lower voltage drop in rectifiers and a higher gain in amplifiers.

Tungsten Cathode

The desirable properties of a material for a thermionic emitter of electrons are a high melting point, a low work function, and a long life. Tungsten has been used as an emitter for many years. It melts at 3600° K and is generally operated at temperatures 2450° K to 2600° K. At these temperatures it can be operated for several thousand hours to furnish an excellent supply of electrons. Tungsten has a relatively large work function so that its efficiency as measured in amperes of emission per watt of heating power is rather low. Pure tungsten was used in early electron tubes of all kinds and is still used in tubes that have a high plate voltage (above 10,000) and wherever severe positive ion bombardment of the cathode is likely to occur. The characteristics of pure tungsten as an emitter are shown graphically in Figs. 8 and 9.

Thoriated-Tungsten Cathode

The thoriated-tungsten cathode was developed by Langmuir and his co-workers. This cathode is made of pure tungsten impregnated

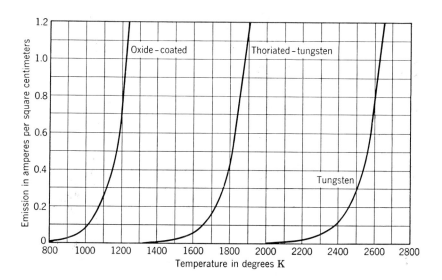

Fig. 8. Emission of typical hot-cathode emitters.

with approximately one per cent of thorium oxide (thoria). At its normal operating temperature of 2000° K, the uncarbonized thoriated-tungsten cathode has an emission per unit of surface more than 10,000 times that of a pure tungsten filament. And its emission (at 2000° K) is more than ninety times that of tungsten at the temperature of 2400° K.

The thoriated-tungsten cathode is prepared for service by being mounted in a tube and heated to 2700 or 2800° K for a few minutes. It is then operated at the normal operating temperature of 1900 to 2000° K. The first heating at the higher temperature reduces part of the thorium oxide to pure thorium. The thorium atoms thus formed diffuse through the body of the cathode and slowly come to the surface where they form a skin or layer one molecule thick. Thus the emission of electrons comes from the thin layer of thorium atoms which have a low work function and hence give a copious emission. At the normal operating temperature, the thorium atoms are evaporated slowly from the cathode, but others from the inside diffuse to the surface to take their place.

After thousands of hours of service, all the thorium atoms within the cathode may be used for replacements and then the emission of the cathode will fall off. In general, the filament or cathode may be rejuvenated by heating it for a short time to 2800° K and then by restoring the temperature to 2000° K. The first step reduces more thorium oxide to thorium and probably drives from the filament certain impurities, such as gas atoms, which have become occluded in it during the period of operation. This step is sometimes called deactivation since it stops the emission of the thorium for the time being. The second step is known as activation. Under activation the normal diffusion of thorium restores the thorium atomic layer on the surface and within a few minutes the emission returns to its full value.

The thoriated-tungsten cathode is sensitive to bombardment by positive gas ions which knock off the thorium surface atoms and reduce the emission. This sensitivity has been reduced by a carbonizing treatment which is given to all thoriated-tungsten cathodes manufactured today.

Although 4000 volts has often been suggested as an upper limit for plate voltage for thoriated tungsten, successful operation up to 10,000 and even 15,000 volts has been secured in carefully evacuated transmitting tubes.

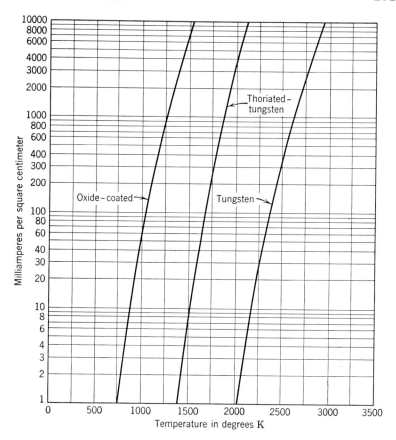

Fig. 9. Thermionic emission of cathodes.

The emission characteristic of the thoriated-tungsten cathode is illustrated in the curves of Figs. 8 and 9. This emitting material (uncarbonized) was widely used in the construction of tubes for radio receiving sets during the period 1925 to 1930. The general adoption of the heater type of cathode after that period has confined the application of the thoriated-tungsten cathode to power amplifier and rectifier tubes operating in the range of 750 to 5000 volts.

Oxide-Coated Cathode

In 1904, Wehnelt discovered that a small amount of calcium oxide on platinum greatly increased the electron emission. This discovery led to many experiments using various alkaline earth oxides placed on metallic cores and to the development of excellent cathodes. Barium and strontium oxide were found to be excellent materials; a mixture of approximately 50 per cent barium oxide and 50 per cent strontium oxide provides a coating with satisfactory mechanical properties and a copious emission.

The oxide-coated cathode is analogous to the thoriated-tungsten cathode in a number of ways. First, the addition of the oxide increases the emission as does the thorium coating. Second, the oxide-coated cathode has a high emitting efficiency like the thoriated-tungsten cathode. Third, any overheating of the oxide-coated filament above a critical temperature greatly reduces the emission. Fourth, the oxide-coated filament must be activated before it is ready for service.

The base or core for the oxide-coated cathode is generally made of nickel because of its good physical properties and low cost. Several alloys have been developed for the cathode base, among which Konal offers a speedy chemical reduction of the oxide, giving a supply of the free alkaline earth metal for activation. The alkaline earth oxides are not stable in ordinary air; hence it is necessary to coat the core with their carbonates, nitrates, or hydroxides and subsequently to reduce these to oxides. The barium and strontium carbonates or nitrates may be applied by spraying the base with a suspension in any acetate with a little nitrocellulose for a binder.

The prepared filament is now mounted in the tube in which it is to be used. The tube is evacuated and kept on the pumps while the cathode is heated to a temperature of about 1400° K to reduce the coating to oxide. Activation is now brought about by (1) prolonged heating, (2) applying a potential of several hundred volts to the anode, or (3) both. When the electron emission becomes about 300 ma per square centimeter for a temperature of 1100° K, there will be no further increase and the filament is ready for use.

After several thousand hours of normal use, the emission from the oxide-coated cathode declines rather rapidly. When this point is reached, the tube should be discarded since little can be done to restore its emitting property. Tubes using oxide-coated cathodes are frequently guaranteed for a life of 8000 hours and commonly operate for 20,000 hours and longer. The temperature emission characteristics of oxide-coated cathodes are shown in Figs. 8 and 9.

Oxide-coated cathodes are made in both the filament and heater types illustrated in Fig. 7. The operating temperatures for these cathodes vary from about 800 to 1100 degrees, depending upon the emission required, the expected life, and the application.

Effect of Gas upon Emission

The presence of gases has a harmful effect upon the emission and operation of *vacuum* tubes. It has been pointed out that oxygen and water vapor greatly reduce the emission from some materials and that the bombardment by positive ions may destroy the emitting surface layer of coated cathodes. Thus it is imperative that harmful gases be removed and, in the case of vacuum tubes, that all gases be removed as far as feasible. The gas that is present in a tube comes from two sources. First, there is the gas that occupies the open space in the tube, and, second, the gas that is occluded or adsorbed in the surface of the metal, glass, and other materials inside the tube. The occluded or adsorbed gas can be removed by heating the parts where it resides. This heating may be accomplished by passing current through the material as in emitters, by placing the tube in a high-frequency induction field, or by electron bombardment of electrodes. Oxygen may be removed by using hydrogen gas or by exhausting the tube and then refilling the space with an inert gas. The final evacuation is accomplished in two ways. First, a vacuum pump removes a large part of the gas, and then a material known as a "getter" completes the operation. The getter is a chemical substance, such as barium, magnesium, aluminum, and tantalum, that has the property of combining with gases when they are vaporized. In glass tubes a small amount of getter is mounted in a position where it will be heated and vaporized by the induction field.

Comparison of Emitter Materials

The characteristics of emitters vary so widely with the temperature and other factors that it is difficult to make comparisons. An approximate comparison of emitting efficiency is given in Table 3. A slight increase in operating temperature will increase the efficiency of emission at the expense of the expected life. At the optimum condition of operation a thoriated-tungsten emitter will give approximately 1 amp of useful emitted current per square centimeter of surface. Under similar conditions the oxide-coated emitter may give only 0.1 amp or less of useful current. It might be concluded from

Table 3

Cathode Material	Temperature (degrees K)	Amperes Per Square Centimeter	Milliamperes Per Watt	Watts Required Per Ampere
Tungsten	2450–2600	0.2–0.65	3–8	333–125
Thoriated-tungsten	1900	1.15	100	10
Oxide-coated	800–1100	0.01–0.22	50–300	20–3.3

this comparison that the thoriated-tungsten was more desirable; this would be true if the volume of emitted current per unit area were the important factor. On the other hand, an oxide-coated emitter will require approximately one-tenth as many watts energy per square centimeter for operation as a tungsten cathode. This comparison points to the use of oxide coating for low exciting watts and small emission currents. It should be remembered that only tungsten will withstand positive ion bombardment where very high voltages are involved.

Applications of Emitter Materials

The oxide-coated cathode must always be used for the indirectly heated type because the other cathodes require too high a temperature for satisfactory operation. This application covers nearly all the millions of tubes in use in a-c receiving sets. The oxide-coated filament type is best suited wherever quick "heat up" is necessary, and it is essential where a low heating energy drain is necessary because of long hours of operation.

Thoriated-tungsten and tungsten cathodes find their application in the power tubes used in radio, telephone, and carrier-current transmitters.

In general, it may be said that (1) oxide-coated cathodes are used for tubes up to 100 watts with plate ratings up to 750 volts,* (2) thoriated-tungsten cathodes are used for tube capacities from 100 to 1000 watts with plate voltages up to 4000 and 5000 volts, and (3)

---

* High plate-voltage ratings up to 20,000 volts have been used in gaseous tubes and large vacuum tubes having sufficient cathode-anode spacing.

tungsten is used for cathodes in tubes with ratings from 1 kw up and plate potentials of 5000 volts and higher.

Schottky Effect

The emission from hot cathodes does not follow Richardson's equation when an electric field is applied in the surrounding region. Schottky showed that a rising electric field increased the electron emission and the phenomenon bears his name. The action of the external field is depicted in Fig. 10 which follows from Fig. 4. The external field OF aids the electrons to escape from the hot cathode. If the electron volts of energy provided by the external field are subtracted point by point from the normal energy required, there remains a new curve showing the reduced escape energy. The highest point on this new curve is represented by a value of W'. Thus the maximum energy required for escape has been reduced by the amount of $W - W'$. Obviously, the thermionic emission will be increased above its normal value without an external field. Schottky derived the following equation:

$$I = I_0 \epsilon^{e^{3/2} \mathcal{E}^{1/2}/KT} \tag{2}$$

where I_0 = current, from Richardson's equation with zero field.

This equation agrees with experiment to within a few per cent for fields up to 10^6 volts per centimeter for smooth pure metal surfaces. Under normal operating conditions where the applied field is of the

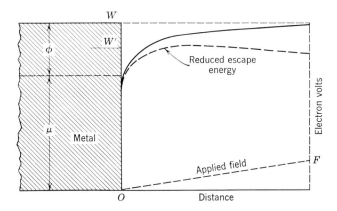

Fig. 10. Reduction in escape energy by an external electric field.

order of 2000 volts per centimeter, the increase in emission arising from an external field is about 10 per cent at 2000° K.

High-Field Emission

This is the liberation of electrons from cold metals by virtue of a very high potential gradient at the surface of the metal. At normal temperatures relatively few electrons in a metal attain a velocity at the surface sufficient to overcome the surface potential energy barrier. However, some of them do so, but upon emerging from the surface they leave behind a positive image charge which attracts them back into the surface. Accordingly, the electrons that do emerge move only an infinitesimal distance from the surface before returning. A very powerful electric field having a magnitude of over one million volts per centimeter is required to pull such electrons from the surface after this transient release. Such fields are difficult to attain, and this method finds little application in electronic devices. The student should remember the extreme difficulty of extracting electrons from cold electrodes, since this fact forms the basis of unilateral conductivity in electron tubes.

The theory of high-field emission is illustrated in Fig. 11 and follows the discussion covering Figs. 4 and 10. Here a powerful applied field lowers the resulting escape energy curve so far that the peak energy W'' required for emission is below that normally possessed by many electrons (μ). Accordingly, tremendous quantities of electrons pour

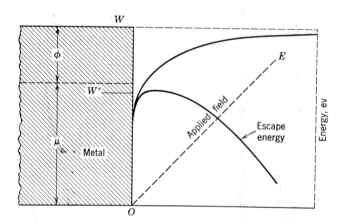

Fig. 11.   High-field emission produced by an external applied field.

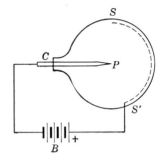

Fig. 12. An electron microscope employing high-field emission.

forth and the metal surface will disintegrate if the applied field is maintained.

High-field emission may take place in a vacuum tube at a relatively low anode potential when the field is concentrated at sharp points.

One excellent example of high-field emission has been demonstrated by J. A. Becker of the Bell Telephone Laboratories in the form of an electron microscope illustrated in Fig. 12. A spherical glass tube exhausted to a high vacuum contains a metal electrode C and a conducting fluorescent screen SS'. The electrode C is swaged to give a very fine point and is further treated by repeated dippings in an acid solution to remove any impurities and to attain a point P of nearly infinitesimal size. A potential of 230 volts applied at B was capable of producing a potential gradient of over one million volts per centimeter at point P because of the sharpness of the point. The electrons attracted to the fluorescent screen gave a beautiful picture of the structure of the metal point P.

Another example of the use of high-field emission occurs in mercury-pool tubes where a positive space charge created by positive mercury ions produces a high field at the surface of the metallic mercury. This application receives subsequent treatment.

Secondary Emission

This is the ejection or "splashing-out" of electrons from a solid due to bombardment by electrons, positive ions, or other flying particles (Fig. 13). Usually this emission is the result of electrons attracted to an electrode having a positive potential. A single primary impinging electron may eject from one to ten secondary electrons from the electrode, depending upon the work function of the material, the condition of its surface, and the velocity of the primary electron. Obviously, the kinetic energy of the primary electron is imparted

Fig. 13. Secondary emission.

to the secondary electrons and added to their normal energy in such a way that they are able to overcome the potential barrier or work function of the surface. The energy of the impinging electron must be greater than the work function of the electrode surface. Generally, secondary emission requires energy of incident electrons of the order of 20 ev. The presence of adsorbed gas in the surface of the electrode increases the secondary emission. Here the presence of the gas molecules under the surface molecules weakens the potential energy barrier and permits the kinetic energy of the impinging electron to become more effective. Secondary emission may be reduced by coating the surface of a metal with carbon.

Secondary emission occurs at some electrodes in nearly all electron tubes. Sometimes its presence has no adverse effect upon operation, sometimes it is a disturbing factor, and in other tubes it is employed for a useful purpose. Several cases of its effect are treated in appropriate future sections. One insidious adverse effect occasionally occurs in glass tubes having high plate voltages. Here, stray high-speed electrons may concentrate on a small area on the glass enclosure, inducing a positive charge because of secondary emission, and produce a temperature rise sufficient to soften the glass and permit a "blown in" which destroys the tube.

Photoemission

Photoemission is the ejection of electrons from the surface of a solid by the energy of incident light or electromagnetic radiation. In 1888, William Hallwachs found that if he charged a zinc plate to a negative potential and then exposed it to ultraviolet light, it gradually lost its charge. However, the plate did not lose its charge when exposed to ultraviolet light after being raised to a positive potential. This phenomenon wherein the electric charge upon a body may be changed by light is known as the Hallwachs effect. Later experiments have shown that other metals and many substances exhibit the property of photoemission. Among the desirable materials for photoemissive emitters are sodium, potassium, cesium, rubidium, and the alkali earths strontium and barium.

The theory of photoelectric emission involves a brief review of the theory of light. In 1905, Einstein suggested that light consists of closely packed bundles of energy termed light quanta. These light quanta, or darts of light, could travel long distances and still maintain the same quantity of energy, enough to emit electrons from a solid. This theory has come to be accepted as the quantum theory of light and of radiant energy. The energy bound up in the light quantum is called the "photon." Einstein reasoned that incident radiant energy was transferred to surface electrons in a quantum of magnitude hf, wherein a portion of this energy was used for removal of the electrons and the remainder appeared as kinetic energy. In mathematical form the relationship is as follows:

$$hf = \phi + \tfrac{1}{2}mv^2 \tag{3}$$

where h is Planck's constant, f is the frequency of the incident light, and ϕ is the work function of the emitter in equivalent electron volts. The term hf is the energy of the impinging electrons (photons) which overcomes the work function ϕ and gives a velocity v to the emitted electrons. Inspection of equation 3 shows that if hf equals ϕ, the electron will have zero velocity and will not be emitted. Thus there is a minimum or *threshold frequency* for the incident radiation below which photoelectric emission will not result. In this connection, the maximum value of the work function ϕ for appreciable photoemission by *visible light* is 1.63 ev.

There are two laws of photoelectric emission. The first states: *The number of electrons released per unit of time at a photoelectric surface is directly proportional to the intensity of the incident light.* This law makes the principle of photoemission very valuable for light measurement and many other applications. The second law states: *The maximum energy of electrons released at a photoelectric surface is independent of the intensity of the incident light but is directly proportional to the frequency of the light.* This law implies that the energy imparted to the electron by electromagnetic radiations is directly proportional to the frequency of these radiations.

The reason for the first law of photoemission is rather obvious and the second law of photoemission follows from equation 3 because h

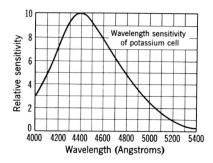

Fig. 14. Photoemissive color sensitivity of potassium. (Courtesy General Electric Company.)

and ϕ are constants for a given emitter, making $\frac{1}{2} mv^2$ proportional to f.

Color sensitivity is the relative response of photoemissive materials to various light radiations. A curve of the sensitivity of potassium is given in Fig. 14. This curve covers the green-blue-violet part of the visible spectrum with the peak occurring in the violet range. Photosensitive materials having a peak in the red range of the spectrum are very desirable for use under the light from incandescent lamps which radiate their maximum energy in the near infrared.

Photosensitive films generally show a much greater emission than a pure metal or substance. In this respect and several others, photo-electric emission parallels thermionic emission. Thus thermionic emission from tungsten is greatly increased by a film of thorium one molecule thick, and emission from a metal covered by barium oxide with a monomolecular layer of barium on the outside is still greater. The surface treatment of thermionic emitters also greatly affects the resulting emission. These various factors control the work function of the emitting surface. In a similar manner the photoelectric emission may be improved by a thin (molecular) layer of cesium on magnesium, whereas a much greater emission may be attained by a thin deposit of cesium upon a sub-base of cesium oxide covering a base of pure silver. Again, the treatment of potassium in hydrogen will change the color sensitivity and will improve the emission of that light-sensitive material.

PROBLEMS

1. What must be the initial velocity of an electron in centimeters per second in order to be emitted from (*a*) thorium? (*b*) thoriated tungsten? (*c*) barium? (*d*) barium oxide?

2. Calculate and plot the curve of emission of a tungsten cathode through points 1800, 2000, 2200, 2400, 2600, and 2800° K, using Richardson's equation.

3. A certain tungsten cathode is operated by an applied potential of 5.0 volts and 1.0 amp and supplies a saturation emission current of 50 ma. What percentage of the input is transformed into effective energy of emission?

4. A tungsten filament has a diameter of 0.025 in. and operates at 2500° K. What must be the length of the filament to give a saturation current of 0.5 amp? (Use curves.)

5. A barium oxide-coated cathode consists of a cylinder 0.1 in. in diameter and 1.0 in. long. What will be the saturation current when the cathode operates at 1000° K? (Use curves.)

6. Calculate the ratios of the saturation emission currents from tungsten, thoriated-tungsten, and barium oxide-coated cathodes for normal operating temperatures of 2400, 1900, and 1000° K. (Use curves.)

REFERENCES

1. Richardson, O. W., *Emission of Electricity from Hot Bodies,* second edition, Longmans, Green and Co., New York, 1921.
2. Langmuir, I., "The Electron Emission from Thoriated-Tungsten Filaments," *Phys. Rev.,* **22**, 357 (1923).
3. Dushman, S., "Thermionic Emission," *Rev. Modern Phys.,* **2**, 381 (1930).

chapter 5

Vacuum Tubes

Unilateral Conductivity

In 1883, Thomas Edison observed that electrons would pass from a hot filament or cathode to a cold plate whenever the plate was at a positive potential with respect to the filament, but that no electrons would pass in either direction if the plate was at a lower potential (negative) with respect to the filament. This property of a device which permits electrons to flow in one direction only is called *unilateral conductivity*. The unilateral conductivity of a tube having two electrodes, one hot and the other cold, was utilized by Fleming for the detection of high-frequency radio waves. This device, known as the Fleming valve, was patented by him in 1905. The Fleming valve was important in the early application of radio telegraphy, and it was one of the leading discoveries in the history of electronics.

Contact Electromotive Force

Volta discovered that when two different metals were placed in contact and then separated, they acquired electric charges. This phenomenon arises from the difference in work function of the metals. It may be explained by reference to the blocks of tungsten and nickel shown in Figs. 1 and 2. If the two blocks are placed as in Fig. 1a and are in an uncharged state, there is no difference of potential between them. Now if they are brought together as in part (b) of Figs. 1 and 2, their contact surfaces must come to the same potential. Under these conditions, the Fermi levels of the energy diagrams for the two metals must be on the same straight line. Here the outer faces of the blocks are at a difference of potential equal to the difference of

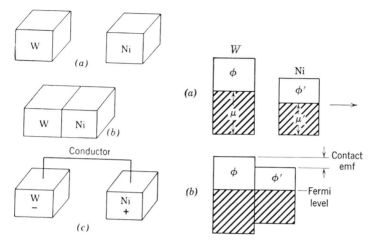

Fig. 1. Configurations illustrating contact electromotive force.

Fig. 2. Energy diagrams illustrating contact emf.

the work functions. This difference in work function $(4.52 - 4.0 = 0.52$ volt) is the *contact electromotive force*.

Contact electromotive force may be understood by thinking of the electron activity at the contact surfaces of the two blocks. Some electrons in each block have sufficient energy to move a few atomic diameters beyond the surface barrier to enter the adjoining block. Obviously, more electrons leave the block having the lower work function. This movement of electrons reaches a state of equilibrium quickly because of the attraction of the image charges. Since more electrons leave the nickel block, it will have a positive charge (electropositive) and the tungsten a corresponding negative charge and potential.

If two separated blocks of tungsten and nickel are joined by a conductor, the same inherent difference of potential of 0.52 volt will exist between them. Here the potential difference is the resultant of two different contact emf's. If the conductor is magnesium $(\phi = 2.7)$, the resultant potential difference is found by the following equation.

$$\begin{matrix} \text{W} & \text{Mg} & \text{Mg} & \text{Ni} \\ (4.52 - 2.7) & + & (2.7 - 4.0) & = 0.52 \text{ volt} \end{matrix}$$

Contact electromotive forces are rather small in magnitude, but do exert some influence on the operation of electron tubes.

Theory of Rectification in Vacuum

The theory of unilateral conductivity is simple and follows directly from the principles covered in previous chapters. It will be assumed first that a hot electrode (cathode) and a cold electrode (anode) are placed in a tube where a good vacuum exists. The anode will be free (not connected to anything), as shown in Fig. 3. The battery A supplies current for heating the cathode, and when the optimum temperature is reached a cloud of electrons will surround the cathode. Each of the individual electrons in the cloud is thrown off with some initial velocity, and it moves out toward the anode against an attraction from its image positive charge on the filament. Since the anode is of neutral potential, it does not influence the electron. In all probability the kinetic energy of the electron due to initial velocity of emission will be overcome before it reaches the anode, and it will drop back to the filament. Now as point x is moved from a towards b, the current in the filament rises, which raises the temperature of the cathode, increases the rate of emission, and increases the initial velocity of emission of electrons. As this process is continued, a point will be reached where a few electrons will have a sufficient initial velocity to carry them over to the anode where they will "stick." The presence of these electrons on the anode will give it a negative charge, and this charge will now repel those electrons that approach the anode. Obviously, a point of equilibrium will soon be reached where no more electrons will become attached to the anode for the given temperature of the filament. If, now, point x is moved nearer to b, the initial velocity of some electrons will be raised so that they can overcome the small repulsion of the anode and land on it. Again, the negative potential on the anode will rise and a new

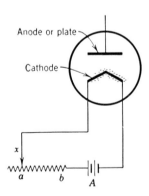

Fig. 3

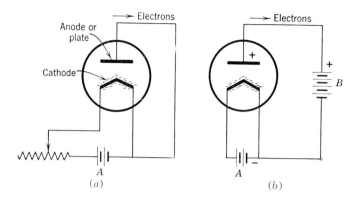

Fig. 4

condition of equilibrium will be reached. Since the anode is free and insulated electrically, the electrons that land on it have no avenue of escape.

If the circuit of Fig. 3 is changed by connecting the anode electrically to the filament as shown in Fig. 4a, the action of the device is altered considerably.

The joining of the electrodes introduces a contact emf if different metals are involved. Assuming that the filament of the cathode is tungsten and the anode is nickel, a contact emf of 0.52 volt will exist with the anode positive with respect to the cathode. When the temperature of the cathode becomes sufficiently high, the initial velocity of emission of some electrons will carry them to the anode as in the preceding case. This movement of electrons to the anode will be affected by the contact emf now present, and for the metals assumed the positive value on the anode will aid (attract) the passage of the electrons. Thus the electron transfer will be larger than in the preceding case. The electrons that land on the anode will not accumulate as before, since they are free to return to the cathode via the external conductor. Thus a very small continuous electron current will be produced by the electrons passing through the vacuum from cathode to anode and returning via the external path.

The addition of a battery in series with the anode circuit, as shown in Fig. 4b, gives one common circuit for the use of the two-electrode tube. The theory of action becomes an extension of the preceding discussion. The hot cathode emits a cloud of electrons. Each electron that leaves the cathode is subject to a number of forces and factors that determine whether it moves over to the anode. The first factor is the initial velocity of emission determined by the temperature of the cathode. A second factor is the positive image charge on the cathode. A third and new factor is the attraction of the positive charge on the anode for the electron. A fourth factor is the negative space charge, which is explained in the next section. The contact emf, if present, is a minor factor. The initial velocity of emission and the attraction of the anode are positive factors tending to carry the electron over to the anode. The attraction of the cathode is a negative factor and the negative space charge in general is also negative or opposing in its action. If the polarity of the B battery in Fig. 4b is reversed so that the anode becomes negative with respect to the filament, the anode will repel the electrons that approach it and, except for a very low negative potential (fraction of a volt), no electrons will ever be able to land on the anode. Here the negative anode becomes the controlling factor and accounts for the unilateral conductivity of this type of vacuum tube. It should be noted that the positive potential placed on the hot cathode will not secure electrons from the negative anode because the anode is cold and is not a source of electron emission.

The circuit of Fig. 4a has been employed experimentally for converting heat energy directly into electricity. In the experiment, heat energy (nonelectrical source) was applied to an efficient cathode emitter. Electrons of high-emission velocity aided by contact electromotive force land on a nearby anode and return through the closed circuit, thus generating electric energy. The efficiency of heat to electric conversion was 6 per cent.

Negative Space Charge

The individual electrons emitted from a cathode are negative charges and as such they exert a force of attraction or repulsion upon surrounding charged bodies and particles. The cloud of electrons emitted from a filament thus acts as a charge or field in the region surrounding the cathode (Fig. 5). This cloud is very dense close to the filament and grows thinner rapidly as the distance from the filament is increased. The action of this space charge on an individually emitted electron is easy to analyze. As the electron breaks through the surface of the filament, it is repelled by the millions of other emitted electrons lying close to the filament as well as by those farther away. Thus at this point the space charge exerts a very powerful opposing effect upon this electron. As the electron moves

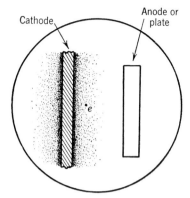

Fig. 5. Negative space charge surrounding a hot cathode.

out farther, as illustrated in Fig. 5, it is repelled toward the filament by all electrons in space between it and the anode and is repelled (aided) toward the anode by all electrons in space between it and the cathode.

The influence of negative space upon the operation of a diode may be explained by means of potential distribution curves. The actual distribution of potential in the region between the cathode and the anode is determined by (1) the distribution of the electrons emitted by the cathode and (2) by the electric field created by any potential applied between the cathode and anode. Three possible conditions for the interaction between these factors are shown in the nine parts of Fig. 6.

The first column of three illustrations (*adg*) depicts the negative space charge from a hot cathode between the cathode and anode for three different conditions. The middle column of illustrations shows the potential distribution between two parallel electrodes (both cold) created by potential differences of zero, +20 volts, and +100 volts. The last column of illustrations in Fig. 6 gives the potential distribution, which results from the simultaneous action of the negative space charge and the electric field. The reader should study these views of Fig. 6 carefully in order to understand how negative space charge influences conduction between the cathode and anode in the vacuum diode and in other multielectrode vacuum tubes. In the top horizontal row of views, a hot cathode produces a negative space charge surrounding the cathode. With zero applied field the potential distribution is negative near the cathode, as shown by cross-sectional area beneath the 00 line in parts (*a*) and (*c*). In the parts

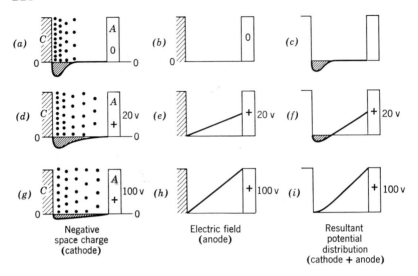

| Negative space charge (cathode) | Electric field (anode) | Resultant potential distribution (cathode + anode) |

Fig. 6. Diagram illustrating space charge, electric field, and potential distribution in a vacuum diode with parallel electrodes.

(d), (e), and (f), a low electric field of 20 volts serves to attract many electrons to the anode, thus reducing the density of electrons and the space charge near the cathode. Here the negative space charge (part f) limits considerably the number of electrons reaching the anode. Finally, a study of parts (g), (h), and (i) illustrates how a stronger electric field nearly overpowers the negative space charge and gives a resulting potential distribution which assures that nearly all electrons of emission pass to the anode. Obviously, a much higher electric field will attract all electrons to the anode.

Construction of Anodes

The anode is always the *electron-collecting electrode* in an electron tube. In the first tubes built, the anode was constructed in the form of a little plate or sometimes two little plates connected in parallel and placed on each side of the filament type of cathode. The name plate has persisted down to the present time for the anodes of tubes used in communication circuits. For tubes used in power circuits and photoelectric devices, the term anode is more generally used.

The anode or plate is usually constructed so that it surrounds the cathode in the vacuum type of electron tube. This construction reduces the length of electron path and the resultant potential drop from cathode to plate. The typical plate structure is a hollow tube of circular or oval cross section, as illustrated in Fig. 7.

Many different materials have been used for constructing anodes. The desirable mechanical properties for this service are easy workability, mechanical strength at high temperatures, high thermal radiation, and low vapor pressure. Tungsten has desirable properties, but it is hard to form and hence has little use for anode construction. Molybdenum has all desired properties except high heat emissivity. This weakness is overcome by use of radiating fins and a roughening of its surface and coating with materials such as zirconium powder (sintered).

Graphite has considerable use as an anode material. Its principal weakness is that it absorbs more gas than other materials. Nickel has a low melting point but can be used for low-power tubes. It is usually carbonized by a process wherein a well-adhering layer of amorphous carbon is deposited on the nickel. This process provides a heat emissivity approaching that of a black body and serves to reduce secondary emission. Tantalum is a satisfactory material for anode construction and is finding an increasing application in this field. Like molybdenum, it usually requires fins on the anode and a roughened surface to increase the heat-radiating area.

The principal limitation in the design of an anode is its heat-radiating ability. The anode receives heat from two principal sources: (1) the heat radiated from the cathode and (2) the heat generated by the impact of the impinging electrons from the cathode.

If an electron is not intercepted in its flight from the cathode to anode, it strikes the anode with a kinetic energy equal to $\frac{1}{2}mv^2$. In

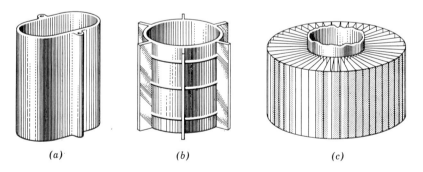

(a)   (b)   (c)

Fig. 7. Typical plate structures. (Courtesy Radio Corporation of America.)

high-vacuum tubes this kinetic energy is equal to the anode potential times the charge on the electron, or

$$e_b e = \tfrac{1}{2}mv^2$$

All this energy must be transformed into heat. Thus the power represented by anode voltage times the anode current is transformed into heat energy at the anode, and this energy must be dissipated by radiation, convection, and conduction to the outside medium. The bombardment of the anode by the electrons does eject numerous electrons from the anode through secondary emission. The electrons of secondary emission fall back into the anode and do not affect the magnitude of the anode current in the diode.

Characteristics of a Vacuum Diode

A two-electrode tube having a gas pressure of about 10^{-8} atmosphere or less is called a high-vacuum diode. A vacuum diode has two characteristics that are fundamental in understanding the operation of two-electrode tubes and the multielectrode tubes to be covered later. The two variables in the diode are the electron emission of the cathode and the potential applied between the cathode and the plate. If one is held constant and the other is changed, the two characteristics can be observed.

The plate-voltage characteristic of a diode can be determined by connecting the tube in the circuit of Fig. 8. The filament or heater current should be held at rated value to give normal electron emission, and then the potential between the plate and cathode e_b can be varied from zero up to a high value. The resulting change of plate current i_b with the variation in applied plate voltage is given in Fig. 9 for two different values of filament voltage. The lower portion of these curves rises rather slowly at first, then more rapidly for a time, and ultimately bends over and tends to become horizontal. The slow rise of the plate current from 0 to a is caused by the strong *retarding influence of negative space charge*. Then as the rising electric field overcomes the negative space charge (Fig. 6), the plate current increases linearly. Finally, when the plate voltage becomes sufficiently high, it attracts nearly all the emitted electrons and the curve tends to become horizontal in the region of b to c. Here the plate current is *limited by emission*. For a higher filament voltage and higher cathode emission, the plate current will rise higher along the line bd before it bends over.

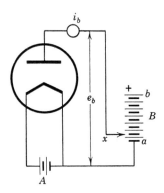
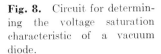

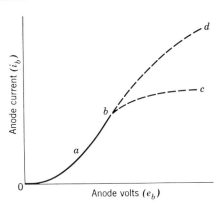

Fig. 8. Circuit for determining the voltage saturation characteristic of a vacuum diode.

Fig. 9. Plate-voltage characteristic of a vacuum diode.

The term "saturation" is sometimes applied to the phenomenon taking place in the region of bc (Fig. 9), but this is an unfortunate choice of word. Actually the plate is capable of accepting an infinite increase of electrons, but is limited by the available supply of electrons emitted from the cathode.

The portion of vacuum diode characteristic that is used in application is the full line region from 0 to b of Fig. 9. This portion of the i_b–e_b characteristic may be represented by the following equation credited to Child.

$$i_b = A \frac{e_b^{3/2}}{x^2} \tag{1}$$

where i_b = total plate current.

   e_b = total plate voltage.

   x = distance between electrodes.

   A = constant which depends on the geometry of the electrodes.

For a given tube where x is constant, the equation reduces to

$$i_b = k e_b^{3/2} \tag{2}$$

It should be noted that Child's equation holds where all points of the cathode are at the same potential and at the same distance from the plate as in the heater type of cathode. This condition does not exist where the cathode is a filament having a varying potential along its length. Child's equation also does not hold after saturation is approached or if electrons are emitted with an initial velocity.

The current covered by Child's equation and the preceding discussion should never be confused with emission current. After saturation the plate current does represent the total emission current but not before.

A second characteristic of the diode is determined from the circuit of Fig. 10 by holding the plate supply potential E_{bb} constant and varying the filament current from zero up to the maximum permissible. The variation of plate current for a series of plate supply potentials is illustrated in Fig. 11. The trend of these curves is approximately the same as those of Fig. 9, but the cause of the trends is reversed. The initial plate current is limited by emission, since the plate is attracting all the electrons being emitted. The trend of this part of the curve is similar to the curve that follows Richardson's equation. The i_b curve tends to flatten out at the higher filament currents because of the negative space-charge effect. Thus at low filament currents and temperatures the space charge is negligible and the plate attracts all the electrons emitted, but as the cathode emission rises the space-charge effect becomes stronger and stronger and finally prevents the plate from attracting additional electrons even though more are available in the expanding electron cloud. The curves of Fig. 11 are sometimes called temperature saturation curves. In these the plate attraction is constant with the negative space charge growing stronger, whereas in Fig. 9 the negative space-charge effect is constant and the plate attraction is growing stronger. In Fig. 11, the plate-current curve for $E_{bb} = 100$ volts rises more rapidly from zero because of the Schottky effect (page 105).

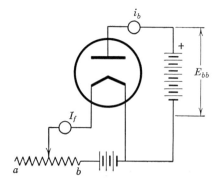

Fig. 10. Circuit for determining the temperature saturation characteristic of a vacuum diode.

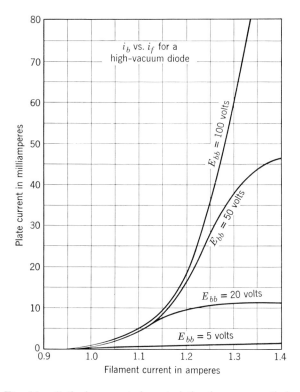

Fig. 11. Cathode-current characteristic of a vacuum diode.

Rectification of Alternating Currents

The unilateral property of the two-electrode tube suggests a simple method of rectifying alternating current or transforming it to a uni-directional current. A two-electrode vacuum tube is connected in a circuit of Fig. 12 with an alternating voltage impressed between the cathode and plate and a low voltage a-c supply for the cathode heater. On the top half of the alternating-voltage cycle (part b) the plate is positive and electrons will pass to it. The electron flow will produce a current loop as indicated in part (c). When the voltage drops to zero, the current drops to zero, and when the plate becomes negative it repels the electrons emitted and no current results. Thus the alternating voltage results in a pulsating direct current which is termed half-wave rectification. If it is desired to utilize the idle portions of the alternating-voltage loops, a second anode may be added as shown in Fig. 13. An analysis of the operation of this cir-

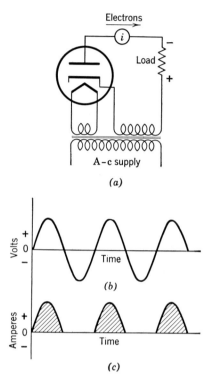

Fig. 12. Circuit and curves showing half-wave rectification of alternating current.

cuit will show that, when the alternating-current supply main L_1 on the left is positive, the electrons move in the direction shown by the full-line arrows. Conversely, when the supply main L_2 on the right is positive, the electrons move as indicated by the dotted-line arrows. This action gives a full-wave rectification of current in the d-c load circuit as illustrated by part (c) of Fig. 13. The conventional current is indicated by the bold-faced arrow on the right of part (a). This pulsating form of direct current is satisfactory for charging storage batteries and for electroplating. Whenever a steady direct voltage or current is necessary, the pulsations can be smoothed out by filters as explained later.

A simple circuit of a rectifier, a filter, and a potential divider is given in Fig. 14. This complete unit is called a power pack and is widely used in radio receivers, radio transmitters, and other electronic assemblies as the source of direct voltage. The resistor at the right of the circuit with its numerous taps serves as a potential divider for furnishing a selection of voltages.

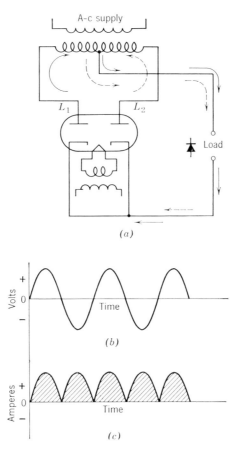

Fig. 13. Circuit and curves showing full-wave rectification of alternating current.

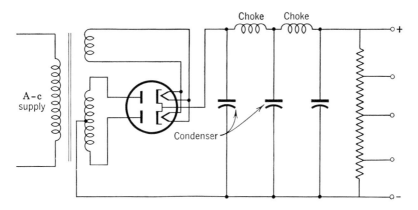

Fig. 14. Circuit for a power pack.

Applications of High-Vacuum Diodes

The applications of the vacuum diode are determined by its inherent properties. It is essentially a rectifier. Its plate current is limited by the negative space charge, so it has a small current rating. The potential drop from cathode to plate is rather high and varies with the plate current. This large voltage drop results in a low efficiency of rectification unless high voltages are used. In the low voltage field the vacuum diode is used as a detector of radio signals and in power packs for radio receivers requiring currents of low magnitude. The characteristics of a tube for this type of service are illustrated

FULL-WAVE HIGH-VACUUM RECTIFIER

Filament—coated	
Voltage	5.0 a-c volts
Current	2.0 amp
Peak inverse voltage, max	1400 volts
Peak plate current per plate, max	375 ma
With Condenser-Input Filter	
A-c plate voltage per plate (rms), max	350 volts
Total effective plate-supply impedance per plate, min	50 ohms
D-c output current, max	125 ma
With Choke-Input Filter	
A-c plate voltage per plate (rms), max	500 volts
Input-choke inductance, min	5 henries
D-c output current, max	125 ma

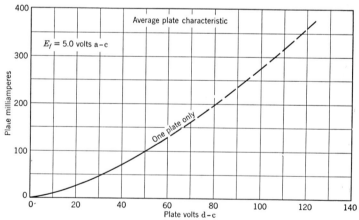

Fig. 15. Vacuum rectifier tube rating and characteristic. (Courtesy Radio Corporation of America.)

KENOTRON
GL-5625
HIGH VOLTAGE VACUUM RECTIFIER

General Characteristics

Filament voltage	20 volts
Filament current	25 amp
Tube voltage drop (1 amp)	4000 volts
Peak inverse voltage	150,000 volts
Peak plate current	1 amp
Average plate dissipation	750 watts

X-Ray Warning Notice

If tube is operated at anode voltage in excess of 16 kv, X-ray radiation shielding may be necessary to protect the user against possible danger of personal injury from prolonged exposure at close range.

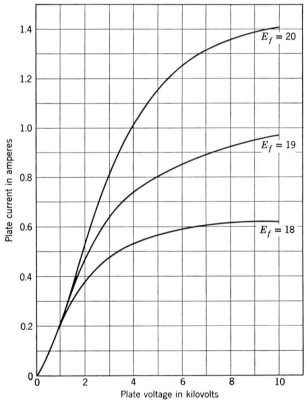

Fig. 16. Rating and characteristic of a high-voltage vacuum diode. (Courtesy General Electric Company.)

in Fig. 15. The vacuum diode will withstand a high inverse voltage, that is, a high negative potential on the plate, without an arc-back. This makes it very desirable for high voltage, low current rectification. Thus it is widely used for furnishing direct current of the order of 1000 to 100,000 volts for X-ray machines, radio transmitting tubes, smoke precipitators, and dust eliminators. Vacuum diodes for the latter class of service are known as *kenotrons*. A typical kenotron and its rating and characteristics are illustrated in Fig. 16.

Three-Electrode Vacuum Tube

In 1907, DeForest added a third electrode to the Fleming valve and called the new device the audion. The third electrode, which

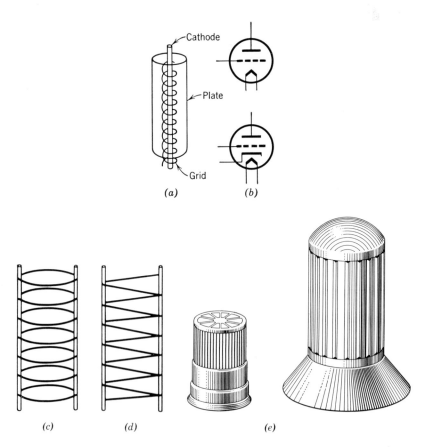

Fig. 17. (*a*) Schematic triode. (*b*) Triode symbols. (*c*), (*d*), (*e*) Typical grids. (Courtesy Radio Corporation of America.)

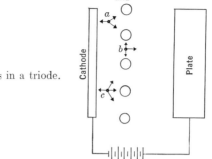

Fig. 18. Forces acting upon electrons in a triode.

he called a grid, consisted of a zigzag wire which was placed between a heated filament and a flat plate (anode). The value of the grid lay in its ability to control the electron current between the cathode and the plate, and this invention constituted one of the most important developments of the twentieth century. It has extended the field of communication by wire across continents, it has made possible radio communication around the world, and it has revolutionized the use and control of electric power in the industrial world.

The modern three-electrode vacuum tube, known by the family name of triode, uses cathodes and plates like those described in the preceding pages. The grid is usually a coil of fine wire wound in the form of a helix and interposed between the cathode and plate. The construction may consist of circular concentric cylinders as shown schematically in Fig. 17a. Other grid types are shown in parts (c), (d), and (e) of Fig. 17. The standard symbols for the triode are given in part (b) of Fig. 17; the upper symbol represents the filament type of cathode and the lower the heater type. The cathode heater is not an electrode.

Theory of Grid Action

The three-electrode vacuum tube functions by a change of the charge residing upon the grid. This change in charge (and potential) serves to control the electron stream between the cathode and the plate. The process of control can be visualized in a number of different ways. One simple visualization follows from Fig. 18, which is a schematic diagram of a cross section taken through the axis of a three-electrode tube. Here the helical wire grid appears as circles. When the cathode is heated, it will emit a cloud of electrons, part of which will be attracted over to the plate by its positive charge. The electrons that go to the plate must pass through the meshes of the grid and hence will be affected by the potential residing on the grid. Assuming that the grid is positively charged with respect to the cathode, an electron in position a will be subject to several forces acting on it: first, the initial velocity of emission; second, the attraction back to the cathode due to the image positive charge left on the cathode; third, the influence of negative space charge; fourth, the attraction due to the plate; and, last, the attraction of the charge on the grid wires. The attraction of the grid wires will be in the directions indicated, but the resultant of all these forces will be toward the plate. Thus the grid aids (controls) the passage of electrons to the plate. If an electron progresses to the point shown at b, it will be subject primarily to three influences: (1) its instantaneous velocity, (2) the attraction of the plate, and (3) the resultant attraction of the grid wires. The resultant force of the grid wires is zero, and hence the grid is now ineffective, but it has accomplished its task in helping the electron to escape from the cathode and the repulsion of negative space charge. An electron in the position c is subject to the same group of forces as any other electron, but the resultant of the attraction of the grid wires and the pull of the plate potential is directly toward the grid wire, and hence this electron will land on the grid.

If the potential of the grid is now made negative with respect to the cathode and a like process of reasoning is applied, it is evident that the action of the grid will always oppose the passage of the electrons to the plate. The degree of opposition offered will depend on the magnitude of the negative potential. It is apparent that a strong negative potential or negative bias may bar all electrons from passing to the plate or from passing to the grid itself.

A second method of analyzing grid action involves a study of the potential distribution in the three-electrode tube. If in Fig. 19, part (a), a plane kl is passed perpendicularly to the axis of the tube, it will show a potential distribution from cathode to plate as in part (b). Let it be assumed that the cathode is at zero or ground potential and that the plate is maintained at a potential of 100 volts above the cathode by the battery. If the grid were omitted and the cathode heated, the potential distribution would be given by curve g of Fig. 19, the depression of the curve being due to the negative space charge. Now, if the grid is added and raised to a small positive potential, the potential distribution will be raised to that of curve f with point X

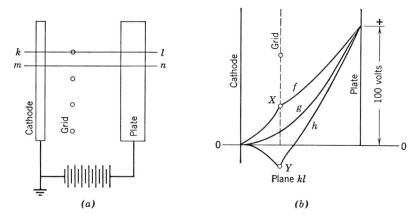

Fig. 19. Potential distribution in a triode (plane through grid.)

at the exact potential of the grid. Again, if a negative potential is applied to the grid, the potential distribution will fall to that of curve h, where Y is the negative potential applied to the grid. The change in the potential distribution will not be so pronounced for other planes in the three-electrode tube. Thus if a plane is passed through mn of Fig. 19, part (a), the potential distribution will be represented by curves f' and h' of Fig. 20. Planes passed through intermediate points would show potential distribution curves varying between the limiting cases illustrated in Figs. 19 and 20. In any case, the effect of the potential on the grid is obvious. When the grid potential is raised, it aids the electrons in breaking away from the cathode and moving to the plate, whereas a negative potential opposes the electron movement to the plate.

Fig. 20. Potential distribution in a triode (plane between grid wires).

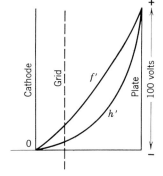

It is evident from the preceding paragraph that the closeness of the wires in the grid will affect the degree of the grid control of the electron stream. If a coarse mesh is used, electrons will pass midway between the wires with a relatively small influence from the grid. A fine or close mesh will give a more uniform and effective control. Some tubes have a coarse grid near the center and a fine mesh at the top and bottom. These are known as variable-mu tubes and their advantage will be pointed out later.

Triode Circuits

A conventional circuit for a triode using batteries for the source of power is shown in Fig. 21. This is an early type of circuit which is still standard for portable equipment. The input signal (a varying potential) is applied between the grid and cathode. The amplified output is delivered to the load represented by the resistance R_L. The power supply for the plate circuit is called the B battery and the grid-bias source is called the C battery. These letters b and c have become associated with the potentials and currents which occur respectively in the plate and grid circuits of vacuum tubes (see list of symbols in front of text).

For many applications of the triode and other multielectrode vacuum tubes the grids are operated at a negative potential with respect to the cathode (negative bias). This negative bias assures that the grid circuit does not absorb any appreciable amount of power and that operation is in the more desirable range of the operating characteristics of the tube. A negative grid bias may be provided by any of the three circuits given in Fig. 22. Circuit (a) employs a battery for producing a negative bias, whereas circuit (b) uses a

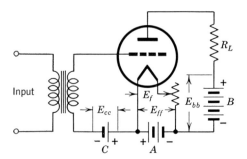

Fig. 21. Conventional circuit for a triode.

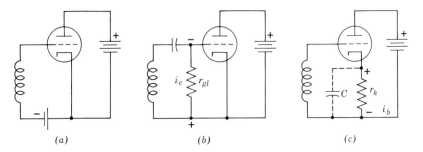

Fig. 22. Grid bias circuits. (*a*) Fixed bias. (*b*) Grid-resistor bias. (*c*) Cathode bias.

grid resistor to provide the bias. In normal tube operation many electrons land on the grid. If the grid is "free," that is, has no direct current return path to the cathode, it will build up a negative charge and potential. This potential may be sufficient to cut off the flow of electrons to the plate, or at least prevent the proper functioning of the tube. However, if a high resistance (0.25 to 10.0 megs) called a grid leak is connected from the grid to cathode as shown in Fig. 22*b*, it will permit the electrons to leak back to the cathode. With a suitable magnitude of grid-leak resistance, the fall of potential ($i_c r_{gl}$) can be maintained at a suitable negative value. (Negative bias attainable is limited to low-power tubes and low values.) In a similar manner, the plate-cathode current i_b may be employed to produce a desired voltage drop ($i_b r_k$) in the cathode resistor circuit of Fig. 22*c*. The cathode resistor r_k employs resistances within the range of a few thousand ohms. The capacitor C, frequently used across the cathode resistor, acts as a low-impedance shunt to alternating signal currents. This by-pass shunt prevents the signal currents from disturbing the normal bias on the grid.

Characteristics of a Three-Electrode Tube

The important characteristics of the three-electrode tube shows how the anode or plate current changes when either the grid voltage or the plate voltage is varied, with the other held constant. The transfer characteristic of a triode may be determined through the use of the circuit given in Fig. 23. The cathode is heated to its normal operating temperature and a voltage E_{bb} is applied to the plate. The grid is supplied by a circuit for varying the potential impressed upon it from a range of negative values up through a series of positive

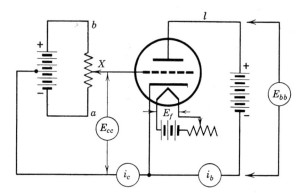

Fig. 23.   Circuit for determining a triode transfer characteristic.

values. This variation is secured by moving the point X along the
potentiometer from point a to point b. At point a the grid may be
made so strongly negative that no electrons can pass to the plate.
As the grid is made less negative, some electrons do pass to the plate,
and with the movement of X to b the plate current i_b rises along the
curve as shown in Fig. 24. After the grid becomes positive with
respect to the cathode, a small current i_c begins to pass to the grid
and follows the trend shown by the dotted curve on Fig. 24. It should
be understood that the magnitude of the grid current is generally
smaller than that indicated. The curve of Fig. 24 shows the operation of a tube for only one value of plate voltage, and, since a range
of positive potentials may be used on the plate, the complete picture

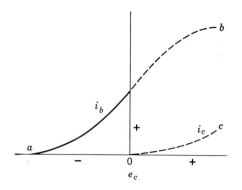

Fig. 24.   Transfer characteristic of a triode.

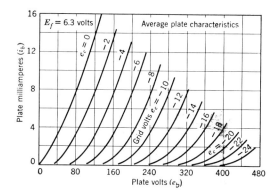

DETECTOR-AMPLIFIER TRIODE

Heater—coated unipotential cathode

Voltage	6.3 volts
Current	0.3 amp

Direct interelectrode capacitance

Grid to plate	3.4 $\mu\mu$f
Grid to cathode	3.4 $\mu\mu$f
Plate to cathode	3.6 $\mu\mu$f
Maximum overall length	2⅝ in.
Maximum seated height	2⅛₆ in.
Maximum diameter	1⁹⁄₁₆ in.

AMPLIFIER

Plate voltage, max	300 volts
Grid voltage, min	0 volts
Plate dissipation, max	2.5 watts
D-c heater-cathode potential, max	90 volts
Cathode current, max	20 ma

Typical Operation—Class A_1 Amplifier

Plate	90	250 volts
Grid	0	−8 volts
Amplification factor	20	20
Plate resistance	6700	7700 ohms
Transconductance	3000	2600 μmhos
Plate current	10	9 ma

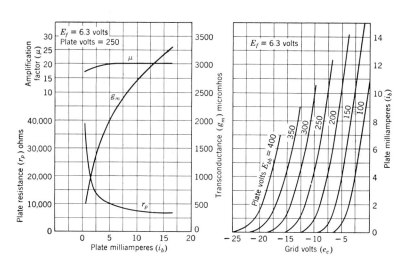

Fig. 25. Rating and characteristics of a detector-amplifier triode. (Courtesy Radio Corporation of America.)

of the characteristic of a tube must be obtained through a family of curves for different plate potentials, as shown in Fig. 25 (lower right). A second set of family curves given in the upper right view of the same figure shows how the plate current varies with changes in the plate voltage. These curves are known as the plate characteristic curves, and they are very useful in designing electronic circuits. The plate characteristic curves may be obtained directly by using a suitable test circuit, or they can be obtained by replotting the data given in the transfer characteristics.

Both sets of curves covered in the preceding paragraph are static characteristics, that is, they apply for a static or constant potential between the cathode and the plate. In the application of the three-electrode tube some form of load must be placed in the plate circuit. This load (Fig. 26a) will present a resistance R_L to the current and will give a fall of potential over itself. Thus the potential between the cathode and plate does not remain constant as E_{bb} but becomes e_b where $e_b = E_{bb} - i_b R_L$. This fall in plate potential will reduce the plate current below the values determined by the circuit of Fig. 23. The effect of this lowering of plate potential with the increase of grid potential is to give a lower curve as shown solid in Fig. 26b. This new curve is the *dynamic characteristic* for the given load resistance. Obviously, the dynamic characteristics for a known load resistance can be determined experimentally by inserting this load at point l on Fig. 23. However, since there are an infinite number of possible load resistances, it is not feasible to give all dynamic characteristic curves. Hence it is customary to determine the dynamic

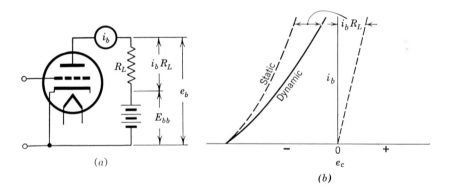

(a)

(b)

Fig. 26. Static and dynamic transfer characteristics of a triode.

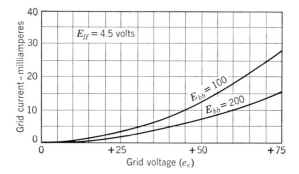

Fig. 27. Typical grid-current characteristics of a triode.

curve for a given load from a family of static curves by suitable calculations.

Two grid-current characteristics are given in Fig. 27. With a higher plate voltage E_{bb}, the plate attraction is relatively stronger and fewer electrons land on the grid, resulting in smaller values of grid current.

Amplification Factor

The chief value of the vacuum type of triode lies in its ability to amplify a relatively weak signal in the form of a change of potential or charge impressed across its grid. Such a change of potential will produce a rather large change of current in the plate circuit, and this change of current passing through a resistance or one winding of a transformer will produce a change of voltage of increased magnitude. It is possible for a mere change of charge on the grid (representing zero or nearly zero power input) to produce a large change of current and voltage in the plate circuit. Thus there would appear to be an infinite increase of power. In actual circuits some power is absorbed in the input circuits so that infinite amplification of power is not attained.

The amplifying power of a triode is the measure of the greater effectiveness of changes in the grid potential over those of the plate potential. The obvious way of stating such a measure is by means of a ratio of the voltages employed. Thus, mathematically, the amplification factor mu (μ) may be expressed as

$$\mu = -\frac{e_b - e_b'}{e_c - e_c'} \quad \text{(for } i_b = \text{constant)} \tag{3}$$

where $e_b - e_b'$ is the change in plate voltage required to compensate for a small change in grid voltage represented by $e_c - e_c'$. Since a decrease in plate voltage is necessary to compensate for an increase in grid voltage, the minus sign is necessary if mu is to be considered as a positive number. The factor mu may be determined from the transfer characteristics of the tube by substituting values in equation 3. Referring to Fig. 25 (lower right), it will be found that 11 ma of plate current will be produced by 100 volts on the plate and a 0.0 volt on the grid. This same current will be produced by 200 volts on the plate and -5 volts on the grid. Thus

$$\mu = -\frac{(100 - 200)}{0 - (-5)} = \frac{100}{5} = 20$$

Similar calculations for other values of constant current will give a like value for mu. If points are taken for low values of plate current where the curvature of the characteristic is high, the value calculated for mu will vary.

In terms of calculus, the amplification factor is expressed as follows:

$$\mu = -\frac{\partial e_b}{\partial e_c} = -\frac{de_b}{de_c} \quad (i_b = \text{constant}) \tag{4}$$

The amplification factor depends on the geometry of the tube. The closer the control grid can be placed to the cathode, the more effective it will be in controlling the electron stream to the plate, and hence the higher the amplification factor will be. This closeness is limited by the necessary insulation of parts as well as by mechanical strength and construction. The amplification factor of a triode varies from about 3 as a minimum to about 100 as a practical maximum, the exact value depending upon the purpose for which the tube was designed.

For some applications it is desired to have a variable mu. This is secured by a close spacing of the grid wires at the top and bottom of the grid and a coarse spacing at the center. This construction and the effect upon the plate-current characteristic are illustrated in Fig. 28. The characteristic curve of a triode and other multielectrode tubes near the cutoff point is broadened, and the tube can be used for amplification at lower levels of plate current. This type of construction is known by the terms supercontrol grid, remote cutoff, and variable mu. Tubes employing this type of grid are used for automatic volume control.

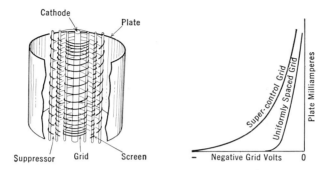

Fig. 28. Construction and curves of a variable-mu tube. (Courtesy Radio Corporation of America.)

Mutual Conductance and Transconductance

The mutual conductance of a triode is the rate at which the plate current changes with the grid voltage. Mathematically, it is the derivative of the plate current with respect to the grid voltage.

$$g_m = \frac{\partial i_b}{\partial e_c} = \frac{di_b}{de_c} \quad (e_b = \text{constant}) \tag{5}$$

Mutual conductance (g_m) is the slope of the transfer characteristic curve and is expressed in terms of microamperes per volt, or micromhos. The concept of mutual conductance may not be easy to grasp. It may help to think of the conductance of (one circuit) the plate-cathode circuit as being affected (mutually) by the voltage impressed across (a second circuit) the grid-to-cathode circuit.

For an example, take the point on the lower right-hand curves of Fig. 25 corresponding to 5 ma on the 100 volt plate curve. Assume a current swing from 4.0 to 6.0 ma which corresponds to a change of 1.0 volt on the grid. Hence

$$g_m = \frac{2 \times 10^3}{1} = 2000 \text{ micromhos}$$

Since the adoption of multigrids or electrodes for tubes, the term transconductance often displaces the expression mutual conductance. The mutual conductance referred to above becomes the control-grid-to-plate transconductance, and similar terms designate the electrodes involved in the transconductance in multielectrode tubes. The value of the transconductance varies because it depends on the varying curvature of the transfer characteristic of a tube.

Plate Resistance

The plate resistance of a triode is the rate of change of plate voltage with respect to the rate of change of plate current at constant grid potential. Mathematically, it is the derivative of the plate voltage with respect to the plate current.

$$r_p = \frac{\partial e_b}{\partial i_b} = \frac{de_b}{di_b} \quad (e_c = \text{constant}) \tag{6}$$

Plate resistance is the reciprocal of the slope of the plate characteristic curves (Fig. 25, upper right). This plate resistance is frequently referred to as the *a-c resistance* or the dynamic resistance to distinguish it from the d-c plate resistance. The d-c plate resistance is the quotient of the static plate to cathode voltage E_{bo} divided by the static or quiescent plate current I_{bo}. This resistance is of little importance in tube operation. For a sample calculation of a-c plate resistance r_p, use the curve $e_c = -4.0$ and $i_b = 10$ ma for the upper right curves of Fig. 25. Here a swing of 40 volts on the plate will give a current change of 5.3 ma. Thus

$$r_p = \frac{40}{5.3 \times 10^{-3}} = 7500 \text{ ohms} \quad (\text{approx.})$$

Parameters of Multielectrode Vacuum Tubes

The three factors of amplification—amplification factor μ, control-grid-to-plate transconductance g_m, and plate resistance r_p—are termed the parameters of multielectrode vacuum tubes. These factors are related to each other as follows:

$$r_p \times g_m = \mu \tag{7}$$

The magnitude of the parameters depends on the geometry of the tube, such as the spacing of the cathode, grid, and plate, the diameter of the grid wires, the spacing of the grid wires, and the area of the plate. The parameters of a tube are important in the design of vacuum-tube circuits.

The parameters of a triode vary with plate current as illustrated in Fig. 25 (lower left) for a 6J5 triode. The amplification factor is usually constant throughout a wide range of plate current, but the transconductance and plate resistance usually show much variation.

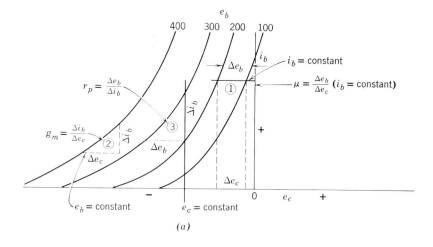

(a)

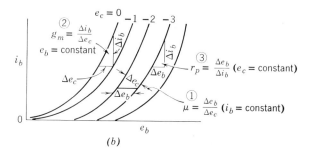

(b)

Fig. 29. Determination of tube parameters from curves by using increments. (a) Transfer characteristics. (b) Plate characteristics.

In the design of circuits the values of the parameters are obtained from data furnished in the tube manuals of the manufacturers, or they may be calculated from the curves for the tube:

The parameters of a triode may be determined from either the static transfer characteristics or the plate characteristics of the tube. The method of solution is indicated in Fig. 29. Here increments are selected between adjacent curves of a family and applied in the form of the preceding equations 4, 5, and 6. The student should find the equations, the curves, and the increments self-explanatory and useful in solving problems in this chapter.

The circuit and the action of a simple triode amplifier are suggested in the two views of Fig. 30. A varying signal voltage is ap-

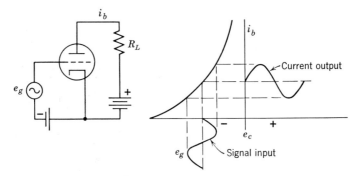

Fig. 30. Amplifier circuit.

plied between a negatively biased grid and cathode. This potential variation produces an amplified current variation in the output or plate-cathode circuit. The resulting action is shown on the right-hand view where a sine-wave signal e_g is applied to the dynamic transfer characteristic of the tube. The output is a sine wave of current superimposed on a direct-current component. However, the output wave departs somewhat from the signal wave form because of the curvature of the dynamic characteristic. When this current passes through the load resistance R_L, it produces an amplified voltage drop $i_b R_L$.

The significance of the tube parameters in the amplifying process is best shown by reducing the amplifying circuit of Fig. 30 to an equivalent circuit illustrated in Fig. 31. In this equivalent circuit where we are interested in varying voltage and current only, the sources of power are omitted and the triode is conceived as an alternating voltage generator. In accord with the definition of μ, any

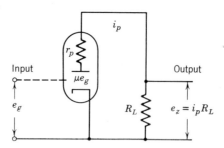

Fig. 31. Equivalent circuit of a triode.

voltage change on the grid such as e_g is equivalent to a voltage change of μe_g on the plate ($\mu = \Delta e_b / \Delta e_c$). Thus the tube acts as a generator having an emf of μe_g. This generator has an internal resistance (a-c) which has been defined as r_p. When this generated voltage is applied to the load resistor R_L, the resulting current is

$$i_p = \frac{\mu e_g}{r_p + R_L} \qquad (8)*$$

and the voltage drop e_z across the load is

$$e_z = i_p R_L = \frac{\mu e_g}{r_p + R_L} R_L \qquad (9)$$

The voltage gain in this equivalent amplifier circuit is:

$$\text{Gain (voltage)} = \frac{e_z}{e_g} = \frac{\mu e_g R_L}{r_p + R_L}\left(\frac{1}{e_g}\right) = \mu \frac{R_L}{r_p + R_L} \qquad (10)$$

The gain may be computed from the transconductance g_m thus:

$$g_m = \frac{\Delta i_p}{\Delta e_c} = \frac{i_p}{e_g}$$

and

$$i_p = g_m e_g \qquad (11)$$

Following the steps given in equation 10 (where $R_L \gg r_p$),

$$\text{Gain} = g_m R_L$$

Load Lines

The operation of a vacuum-tube amplifier may be determined graphically also. In this method, a "load line" for a given load is drawn on the family of plate-voltage plate-current curves. These curves can be obtained from the tube manufacturer, or they may be determined by experiment in the laboratory. The load line is the locus of the i_b-e_b points for any given value of load R_L and has a slope equal to $-1/R_L$. In a triode operated with a pure resistive load (Fig. 30), the load line is determined as follows (see Fig. 32).

(1) Locate point A at the power supply voltage E_{bb} *and* at $i_b = 0$.

(2) Determine point B by taking E_{bb}/R_L. This is the current that would flow if there were no drop through the tube and the entire supply voltage appeared across the load resistor.

(3) Connect points A and B with a straight line.

* See standard symbols in front of text.

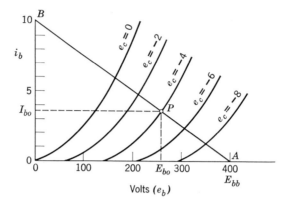

Fig. 32. Determination of amplifier performance with the load line.

The quiescent point P is the intersection of the load line and the particular grid-bias curve being considered. Thus, in Fig. 32 with no signal applied and a grid bias of -4 volts, the plate current will be 3.6 ma and the voltage 260. The total power drawn from the $B+$ supply will be $0.0036 \times 400 = 1.44$ watts, of which $0.0036 \times 260 = 0.94$ watt will be dissipated by the plate of the tube and the remainder by the load resistance.

Upon the application of signal to the grid, the instantaneous *operating point* will move along the load line in accordance with the instantaneous grid voltage. When we assume that the grid signal swings from the quiescent point of -4 volts to -2 volts and then to -6 volts, the maximum swing or peak-to-peak value is 4 volts. Vertical and horizontal projections from the intercepts of these grid voltages on the load line will show that, for this peak-to-peak swing on the grid, the plate voltage e_b has changed from 210 to 305 volts and the plate current i_b has varied from 4.8 to 2.3 ma. This concept may be stated in equation form and applied where nothing higher than the second harmonic is present, as follows.

	Plate Voltage	Plate Current
Peak-to-peak value	$E_{b\ max} - E_{b\ min}$	$I_{b\ max} - I_{b\ min}$
Peak value	$\dfrac{E_{b\ max} - E_{b\ min}}{2}$	$\dfrac{I_{b\ max} - I_{b\ min}}{2}$
Rms value	$\dfrac{E_{b\ max} - E_{b\ min}}{2\sqrt{2}} = E_p$	$\dfrac{I_{b\ max} - I_{b\ min}}{2\sqrt{2}} = I_p$

Thus

$$\text{Peak power} = \frac{(E_{b\,max} - E_{b\,min})(I_{b\,max} - I_{b\,min})}{4} \tag{12}$$

$$\text{Rms power} = \frac{(E_{b\,max} - E_{b\,min})(I_{b\,max} - I_{b\,min})}{8} \tag{13}$$

or

$$\text{Rms power} = I_p{}^2 R_L = I_p E_p$$

$$\text{Gain} = G = \frac{E_{b\,max} - E_{b\,min}}{E_{g\,max} - E_{g\,min}} \tag{14}$$

If distortion is not present, the average plate current remains constant with and without signal. The total power drawn from the plate supply averaged over a complete cycle is a constant, and any a-c power which is delivered to the load must be subtracted from the steady-state plate dissipation. In other words, less power is wasted in heating the plate of the tube when a signal is applied to the grid.

Plate Current in a Triode

Child's equation for the two-electrode tube can be modified slightly for application to the triode. The modified equation becomes

$$i_b = K \left(\frac{e_b}{\mu} + e_c \right)^{3/2} \tag{15}$$

where K is a constant depending on the tube dimensions. Obviously, the expression in the parenthesis refers to the grid potential and not to the plate potential of Child's equation. This equation does not hold for low values where mu is not constant nor for high values where saturation effects are present; also, for positive values of grid potential, i_b represents the sum of plate and grid currents.

Types of Triodes

Triodes may be classified on the basis of (1) their construction, (2) their use, or (3) their power rating. Under the first classification triodes are built with all glass enclosures, in metal envelopes with air cooling, and in metal tubes with water cooling. Most tubes use glass enclosures. Glass construction gives a lower cost because it utilizes the manufacturing technique developed through years in producing electric light bulbs. Glass has a low heat-dissipating ability and is limited to use in tubes having a maximum plate dis-

POWER TRIODE (GROUNDED GRID)
Filament (thoriated-tungsten)

Filament voltage	11.0
Filament current	285 amp
D-c plate volts, max	15,000
Grid volts	−220
Amplification factor	40
Plate dissipation, max	50 kw

Fig. 33. Water-cooled power triode. (Courtesy Radio Corporation of America.)

sipation of approximately 1000 watts. Two kinds of glass are used in forming glass tubes—an ordinary soft glass for small tubes and for tubes of low rated capacity, and a hard glass having a higher softening and melting temperature for power tubes, which must dissipate considerable heat and operate at a high temperature.

The metal receiving tube is small in physical size and its metal case serves as a shield from external fields. The active parts of the tube are of normal size, but a large saving in space is made in the stem and in the metal envelope which fits the electrode assembly closely.

The amount of heat energy that can be dissipated by radiation and convection in air from glass and metal tubes is rather limited because the volume of the tube increases more rapidly than the surface area. It is possible to obtain a greater output by operating glass tubes in parallel. A more direct solution is the use of water cooling or forced air cooling for tubes. Pure copper is used extensively in so-called external plate designs for tubes in various power ranges and physical sizes. In tubes of this type, the copper plate forms part of the envelope, and forced air or water cooling is used to maintain the temperature and the copper-to-glass seal at safe temperatures. With the aid of these cooling methods, tubes of relatively small physical size can handle very large amounts of power.

POWER TRIODE
Filament (thoriated-tungsten)

Filament voltage	12.6
Filament current	29.0 amp
D-c plate voltage	6200 max
Plate dissipation	3 kw
D-c grid volts	−200
Amplification factor	29

Fig. 34. Air-cooled power triode, (Courtesy Radio Corporation of America.)

A typical water-cooled triode of 50 kw capacity is illustrated in Fig. 33. Water cooling of tubes involves some construction and maintenance problems, which has led to the development and extensive use of forced air cooling. A typical forced air-cooled triode of 4.2 to 8.8 kw capacity is shown in Fig. 34.

The three-electrode vacuum tube may be classified as amplifier and relay, oscillator or a-c generator, modulator, and detector or demodulator. The particular function performed by the tube depends not upon its construction but upon the external circuits with which it is associated. Thus a single tube might be connected into circuits for serving as amplifier, oscillator, modulator, or detector. The theory of amplification is illustrated in Fig. 30 (right). In practice certain types of tubes are chosen for the different applications, but this selection is not determined by any difference in their inherent theory of operation. The circuits and applications of triodes are covered in succeeding chapters.

Limitations of a Triode

There are two properties of a triode and its circuit which limit its range of operation as an amplifier. The first limitation arises from the capacitance coupling between the grid and plate circuit as suggested in Fig. 35. The grid and plate are two conductors sep-

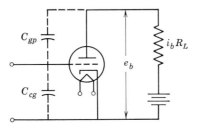

Fig. 35. Interelectrode capacitances in triodes.

arated by a dielectric (vacuum), and thus constitute a capacitor C_{gp}. A capacitor is an open circuit to a direct current but is a conductor for alternating current. Thus, although the cathode-grid (input) and cathode-plate (output) circuits of Fig. 35 appear to be separated, the interelectrode capacities result in a coupling between them. Through this coupling a feedback may occur from plate-to-grid circuit caused by changes of potential (alternating) on the plate. The reader may wish to visualize this phenomenon as a potential divider effect of a varying voltage impressed across the interelectrode capacitances C_{gp} and C_{cg} in series. This feedback will interfere with the normal control by the grid, or it may even start oscillations (at high frequencies) and cause the tube to act as an oscillator.

The second limitation in the triode amplifier circuit results from the normal changes in the cathode-plate potential e_b with changes in the plate load current. Since the amplification within the tube depends on both the grid and the plate potentials, it is obvious that wide changes in the plate voltage e_b may introduce variations in the amplification of the tube. This factor may limit the use of the triode to small voltage input signals.

The Tetrode

The tetrode contains a fourth electrode, a grid, placed between the control grid and the plate. This fourth electrode, called a screen grid, overcomes the two limitations of the triode but adds a disadvantage of its own. The construction and circuit of a screen-grid tube are shown schematically in Fig. 36. The presence of the screen grid places two capacitances in series between the plate and control grid. The resultant capacitance of two capacitances in series is much lower in magnitude than either one. Accordingly, the reduction of control grid to plate capacitance largely overcomes the feedback which occurs in triodes.

The screen grid is held at a constant or nearly constant potential,

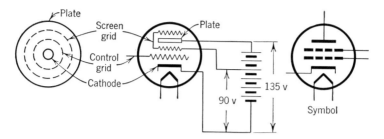

Fig. 36. Schematic diagram of a tetrode and its circuit.

as shown in the circuit of Fig. 36 and the potential distribution diagram of Fig. 37. Thus the screen grid sets up in the space surrounding itself a constant potential which normally approaches that of the plate. This space potential supplies a constant accelerating force (attraction) for any electrons that pass the meshes of the control grid. Normally nearly all electrons that reach the position of the screen grid pass through the meshes of the grid and land on the plate. *Moderate changes in the plate potential will not influence the number of electrons reaching the plate.* Thus the screen grid has served to overcome the second limitation of the triode. Naturally, the screen grid attracts those electrons which are traveling directly toward its mesh wires, and these electrons constitute a small screen-grid current.

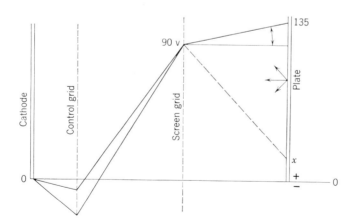

Fig. 37. Potential distribution in a screen-grid tube.

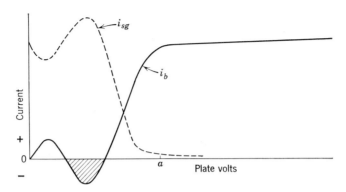

Fig. 38. Plate-voltage characteristic of a screen-grid tube.

The screen-grid tube gives an unexpected performance when the plate voltage falls to low values because of large output current. This action is shown by the plate-voltage characteristic of Fig. 38. Obviously the plate-current characteristic is undesirable at low plate potentials from zero to a. The reason for this action may be understood by studying Fig. 37. When the plate voltage falls to some low value such as x, the potential distribution from screen grid to plate drops to that shown by the dotted line. Now the electrons arising from secondary emission on the plate are delivered into a field which rises toward the screen grid. Accordingly, these electrons move to the screen grid and constitute a screen-grid current. Under certain conditions it is possible for the number of electrons of secondary emission to exceed the primary impinging electrons so that the plate current may reverse its direction as suggested in Fig. 38. Screen-grid tubes of later manufacture have been improved by special treatment of the plate (carbonizing) which reduces their tendency toward secondary emission.

Many tetrodes have been manufactured and many are currently in use. The present trend is to produce screen-grid tubes for replacement only.

The Pentode

The pentode is a tube having five electrodes. The fifth electrode, called the suppressor grid, was added to overcome the harmful effect of the secondary emission in the screen-grid tube. The suppressor

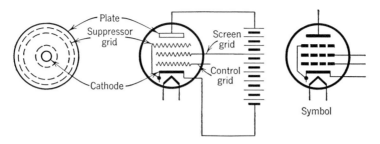

Fig. 39. Schematic diagram and circuit of a pentode.

grid is a mesh placed between the plate and screen grid as shown in
Fig. 39. It is usually connected directly to the cathode inside the
tube, though it may be brought outside for other connections. When
connected to the cathode the suppressor grid serves as a shield or
suppressor to prevent the electrons of secondary emission from passing to the screen grid. The suppressor grid performs this function
by creating a field of near zero potential through which electrons
(secondary emission) must pass before coming under the influence
of screen grid. This explanation may become more clear from a study
of Fig. 40, which gives a schematic potential distribution for a
pentode. Here point P represents the constant zero potential on
the suppressor grid. Electrons splashed out of the plate must move
away from it against the attraction of its positive potential and past
point P before they come under the influence of the potential on the
screen grid.

The pentode permits wide swings of plate potential without affecting the fidelity of amplification. The action of the suppressor permits
large power output for low input voltage on the control grid and it

Fig. 40. Potential distribution in
a pentode.

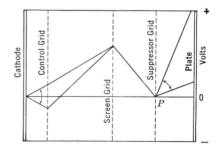

REMOTE CUTOFF PENTODE

Heater voltage	6.3 volts
Heater current	0.3 amp
Plate voltage	250 volts
Screen voltage	100 volts
Plate resistance	1 meg
Plate current	11.0 ma
Grid—No. 1—bias (approx.) for transconductance of 40 μmhos	−20.0 volts

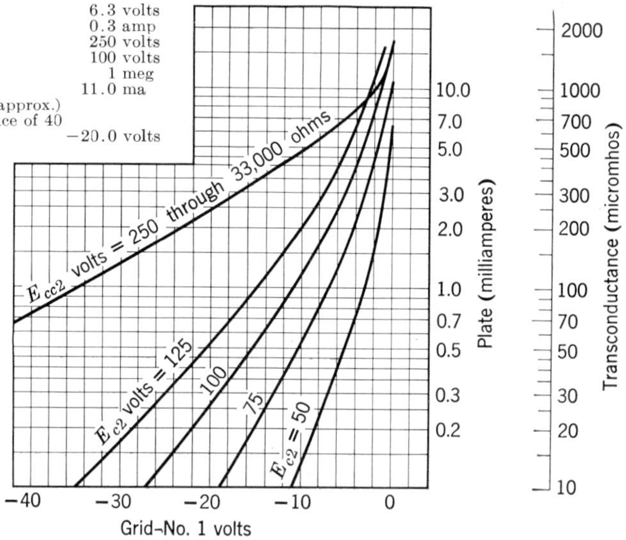

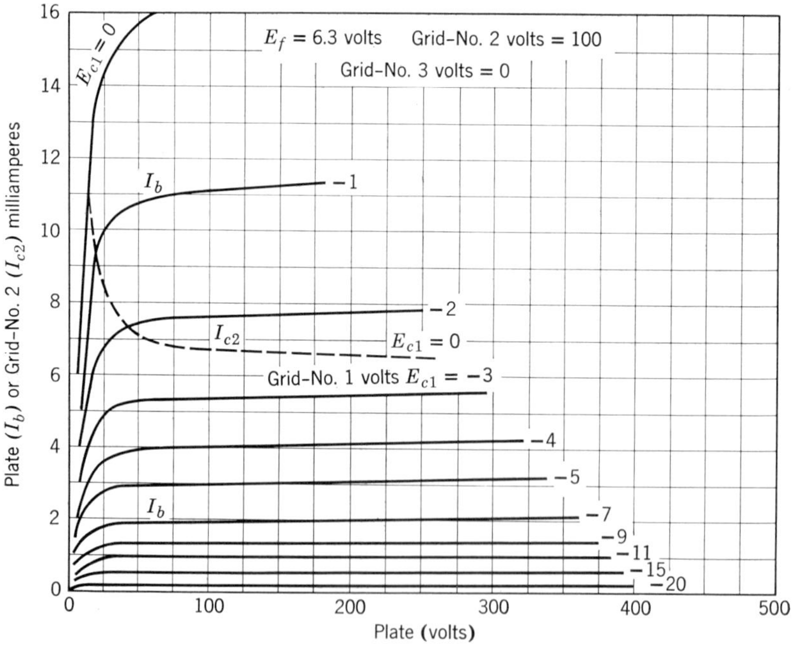

Fig. 41. Characteristics of a pentode.

permits high-voltage amplification at moderate values of plate voltage. Accordingly, some pentodes have a large power output and are used in the final stage of audio amplification for supplying the current to the loudspeaker. Other types of pentodes are used as voltage amplifiers.

Some pentodes are designed to give a variable mu. This is secured by a close spacing of the grid wires at the top and bottom of the grid and a coarse spacing in the center. This construction widens the transfer characteristic near the cutoff point and permits grid-bias volume control in radio-frequency amplifiers.

The construction of a typical pentode, its rating, and plate characteristics are given in Fig. 41.

Beam Power Tube

A beam power tube is a multielectrode device in which directed electron beams increase the power capacity and operating characteristics of the tube. This tube has three special features in its construction. First, the screen and control grid are composed of wires wound in helices so that each turn of the screen is shaded from the cathode by a turn of the control grid. This careful alignment tends to pass the electrons to the plate in beams and serves to reduce the magnitude of the screen-grid current. The second feature in the construction of the beam power tube is the use of beam-forming plates which are connected to the cathode (Fig. 42). These plates serve to prevent any electrons from leaving the grid near its end supports and serve to give a sharp cutoff for the beams. The third feature of

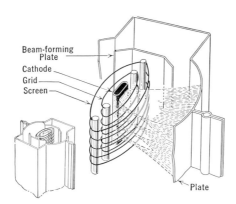

Fig. 42. Construction of a beam power tube.

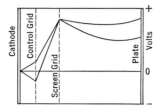

Fig. 43. Potential distribution in a beam power tube.

construction of the beam power tube is that the screen grid and plate are spaced relatively far apart (Figs. 42 and 43) and that these electrodes are operated at approximately the same potential. This construction results in a suppressor action between the screen and plate. To understand this action, assume that screen and plate are at the same potential and that the cathode is cold (zero emission). Under this condition the potential distribution between the screen and plate will be uniform and no potential gradient will exist. Next assume similar conditions with normal emission from the cathode and a control-grid potential that permits a normal plate current. Now moving electrons are present everywhere between screen and plate, and these electrons constitute a negative space charge which is strengthened by the action of the suppressor plates and by the fact that the electrons exist in concentrated beams. This negative space charge lowers the potential in the region between screen and plate and results in *a change of pace of the moving electrons*. This change of pace results in a variation of density of the electrons in the screen-plate space with a corresponding change of potential distribution. The net result of this action is the formation of a virtual suppressor between the screen and plate as shown in Fig. 43.

The rating and characteristics of a typical beam power tube are given in Fig. 44. It should be noted that wide changes of plate potential above 75 volts have little effect upon plate current. Also, the lower set of curves shows a sharp bend at the knee of plate-current plate-voltage curve. This means that little harmonic distortion occurs above the bend.

The advantages of tubes of the beam power type are high power output, high power sensitivity, and high efficiency. They are frequently used in the output stage of radio receivers and for other forms of load. The construction of a beam power tube of 100 watts plate dissipation is illustrated in Fig. 45. The reader will find the construction details of interest.

BEAM POWER AMPLIFIER

Heater—coated unipotential cathode
Voltage (a-c or d-c)   6.3 volts
Current   0.9 amp

SINGLE-TUBE AMPLIFIER—CLASS A₁

Plate voltage, max   360 volts
Screen voltage, max   270 volts
Plate dissipation, max   19 watts
Screen dissipation, max   2.5 watts

Typical Operation

	Fixed	Bias	Cathode	Bias	
Plate	250	350	250	300	volts
Screen	250	250	250	200	volts
Grid	−14	−18	.....	.....	volts
Cathode resistor	.....	.....	170	220	ohms
Peak a-f grid voltage	14	18	14	12.5	volts
Zero signal plate current	72	54	75	51	ma
Max signal plate current	79	66	78	54.5	ma
Zero signal screen current	5	2.5	5.4	3	ma
Max signal screen current	7.3	7	7.2	4.6	ma
Plate resistance	22,500	33,000	.....	.....	ohms
Transconductance	6,000	5,200	.....	.....	μmhos
Load resistance	2,500	4,200	2,500	4,500	ohms
Total harmonic dist.	10	15	10	11	%
Max signal power output	6.5	10.8	6.5	6.5	watts

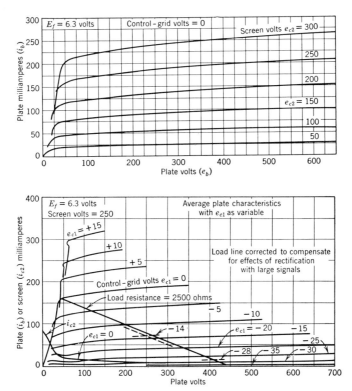

Fig. 44. Rating and characteristics of a beam power amplifier. (Courtesy Radio Corporation of America.)

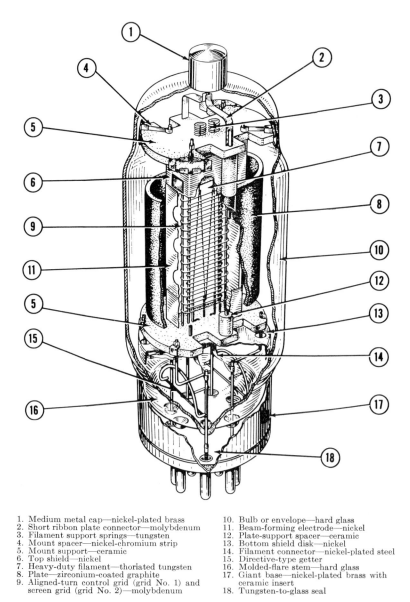

1. Medium metal cap—nickel-plated brass
2. Short ribbon plate connector—molybdenum
3. Filament support springs—tungsten
4. Mount spacer—nickel-chromium strip
5. Mount support—ceramic
6. Top shield—nickel
7. Heavy-duty filament—thoriated tungsten
8. Plate—zirconium-coated graphite
9. Aligned-turn control grid (grid No. 1) and screen grid (grid No. 2)—molybdenum

10. Bulb or envelope—hard glass
11. Beam-forming electrode—nickel
12. Plate-support spacer—ceramic
13. Bottom shield disk—nickel
14. Filament connector—nickel-plated steel
15. Directive-type getter
16. Molded-flare stem—hard glass
17. Giant base—nickel-plated brass with ceramic insert
18. Tungsten-to-glass seal

Fig. 45. Materials used in beam power tube. (Courtesy Radio Corporation of America.)

Pentagrid Converter

The pentagrid converter is a multielectrode tube having one cathode, one plate, and five grids. It is a dual-purpose tube which does not involve any new theory of action above that covered in preceding types. It is commonly used as a frequency converter, and the use of five grids gives rise to the name pentagrid converter. Frequency conversion involves the action of an oscillator and a modulator. The circuits for the pentagrid converter combine these two functions within a single tube, and the electron stream serves as the coupling.

Vacuum Phototube

The photoemissive tube consists of a cold cathode having a photosensitive surface and an anode placed in a glass envelope. These two electrodes are connected in series with a battery (anode positive) and a load consisting of a resistance as shown in Fig. 46. Light or other radiant energy falling upon the cathode emits electrons which are attracted to the positive anode and give rise to a current through the external circuit, including the load. In the vacuum phototube the space within the glass envelope is highly evacuated.

Commercial tubes are enclosed in cylindrical glass envelopes as shown in Fig. 47. The anode is usually a single straight wire; the cathode is a sheet in the form of a semicylinder. The light-sensitive material is deposited on the cathode either before or after the tube is assembled and evacuated. The alkali metals are the most effective photoelectric emitters because of their low work function. The emission from a cesium surface matches the characteristics of the human eye more closely than the other pure alkali metals. This

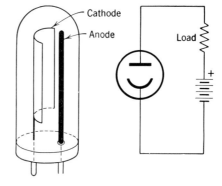

Fig. 46. Construction and circuit of a phototube.

Anode volts	250
Average cathode current	25 μa
Microampere/lumen	45
Max response	4000 A
Dark current	0.0125 μa
Spectral surface	S-4

Fig. 47. Vacuum phototube. (Courtesy Radio Corporation of America.)

property coupled with its very low work function (1.91 ev) is responsible for its wide use as a photoelectric emitter. Sodium or cadmium may be used for the measurement of ultraviolet light. Thin films of alkali metal on surfaces of other metals are found to have lower photoelectric work functions than either metal alone. This parallels the reduction of the thermionic work function obtained with a thin film of thorium on tungsten. A thin film of cesium on an oxidized surface of silver, or on a surface of antimony or bismuth, has been used commercially.

The sensitivity of a photoemissive surface depends upon the material and the frequency of the radiant energy. The sensitivity of a widely used photoemissive material is shown in Fig. 48. Sensitivity is frequently expressed in terms of visible radiation. When given in this way it is known as "luminous sensitivity" and is given *in terms of microamperes per lumen of light flux.* For many types of phototubes, sensitivity is measured with radiation provided by a tungsten lamp operated at a filament color temperature of 2870° K. This is the approximate operating temperature of exciter lamps used on sound-on-film equipment.

In total darkness a sensitive phototube will conduct a small current (dark current) because of leakage between the "lead-in" wires to the cathode and anode. The leakage current tends to introduce errors when the tube is employed for measurements under low intensities of light. It is reduced in some "special" tubes by bringing the anode lead out of the top of the tube, thus increasing the length and resistance of the leakage path between the anode and cathode.

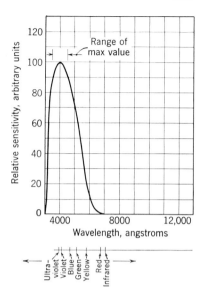

Fig. 48. Spectral sensitivity of a typical photoemissive surface.

The average anode characteristic of the vacuum phototube of Fig. 47 is given in Fig. 49. The voltage drop across the load resistor (Fig. 49) for various values of luminous flux and load resistance may be determined graphically by constructing load lines as indicated. The potential difference between the applied anode potential (250)

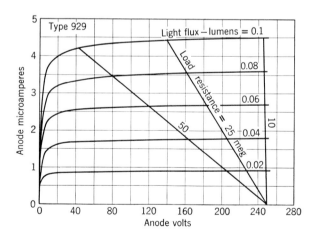

Fig. 49. Average anode characteristic of a typical vacuum phototube. (Courtesy Radio Corporation of America.)

and the intersection of the load line and the light flux curve gives the resulting voltage drop.

The vacuum phototube and its load circuit require an electronic amplifier to boost its signal for performing useful functions. The chief applications of phototubes are the measurement of light and the operation of relays. Circuits for such functions are covered in the application sections of this text. The advantages of the vacuum phototube are (1) that its output is *directly proportional to the intensity of the light flux* following the first law of photoemission and (2) that it responds satisfactorily to high frequencies of light changes.

Many commercial phototubes contain a small amount of inert gas. The presence of gas changes the theory of action and increases the sensitivity of the device. Gas phototubes are treated in Chapter 7.

Electron-Multiplier Tubes

The electron-multiplier tube utilizes both photoemission and secondary emission to produce a very sensitive device for detecting and amplifying radiant energy. The basic principle of this device is illustrated in Fig. 50. Photons of light falling upon the light sensitive electrode on the left eject electrons by photoemission. These electrons are attracted by a positive electric field to the next electrode or dynode where secondary emission takes place. The number of secondary electrons emitted may range from two to ten, depending on the work function of the surface and the potential through which the primary electrons have fallen. The secondary electrons then become primary electrons attracted to the next electrode, and so

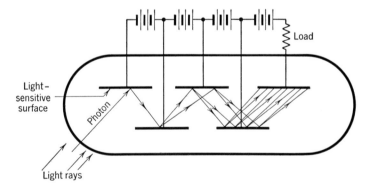

Fig. 50.   Principle of a photoelectric electron-multiplier tube

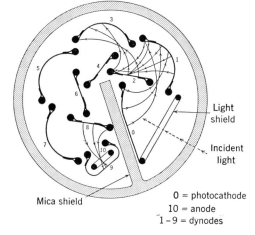

Light
shield

Incident
light

Mica shield

0 = photocathode
10 = anode
1 - 9 = dynodes

Fig. 51. Electron-multiplier tube. (Courtesy Radio Corporation of America.)

Fig. 52. Cross section of the electron-multiplier tube in Fig. 51.

forth, to the last stage or anode. Thus through a series of electrodes, each having a higher potential than the preceding one, any amount of amplification may be attained theoretically. A practical limit in multiplication arises through space-charge effects and power dissipation in the final stages.

A commercial electron-multiplier tube is shown in Fig. 51 and an enlarged cross section of the device in Fig. 52. In this device incident light entering the tube releases electrons from the light-sensitive cathode 0 from whence they are drawn to electrode 1 where secondary emission begins and continues at increasing values throughout nine successive stages. This tube is capable of multiplying feeble photoelectric current produced at the cathode by an average value of 1,000,000 times when operated at 100 volts per stage. The output current is a linear function of the exciting illumination under normal operating conditions. The frequency response of this tube is flat up to about 100 Mc per second, above which the variation in electron transit time becomes a limiting factor.

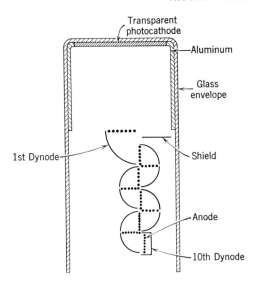

Fig. 53. Cross section of photomultiplier tube. (Courtesy Allen B. Dumont Laboratories.)

A third type of geometrical construction for the dynodes in an electron-multiplier tube is shown in the cross-sectional view of Fig. 53. Here the impinging light falls upon the end of the tube which is a transparent photocathode. The dynodes consist of quarter cylindrical shells nested together as shown to produce a series of secondary emission amplifiers. An advantage of this construction is that all stages, other than the first, are identical, and hence the total number of stages can be varied by the designer to provide the amplification desired.

The electron multiplier tube is applied in light-operated relays (auto headlight control), in sound reproduction from films, in facsimile transmission, in light-flux meters, in scintillation counters, and in scientific research involving low light levels. Some of its industrial applications will be covered later. For purposes of comparison it should be noted that the maximum anode current for the electron multiplier may be 10 ma, whereas the maximum anode current of a vacuum phototube is about 20 μa—a ratio of 500 to 1. Again, the output load resistance of a phototube must range from 1 to 25 meg whereas the electron multiplier may use low values of load resistance —a decided advantage.

Cold-Cathode Vacuum Tubes

The development of a cold cathode to perform the function of emission in vacuum tubes was announced early in 1959. This cold cathode was developed by the U. S. Army Signal Research and Development Laboratory and Tung-Sol Electric Inc. The cold-cathode tube differs physically from the standard hot-cathode tube in two ways. First, the nickel sleeve of the cathode is covered with a high-purity, porous magnesium oxide coating (35 microns thick). Second, the tube contains a tiny tungsten starter filament which starts emission with a single flash lasting less than a second. Once started, cold-cathode emission is sustained without the need of a heater. In operation a potential difference of approximately 180 volts exists across the magnesium coating. This potential is not sufficient to produce high-field emission, and this fact leads to one theory that the conduction through the oxide and the resulting emission is an avalanche effect (see page 173 for avalanche theory as applied to gaseous conduction).

The cold cathode operates with a cold blue luminescent glow which is proportional to the intensity of electron emission. Since the cathode is not heated, the over-all efficiency of the cold-cathode vacuum tube is much higher than its hot-cathode counterpart. Laboratory life tests indicate that the cold-cathode tube has an indefinite life. Since hot-cathode burnouts is one of the dominant causes of receiving tube failure, it appears that the cold-cathode device should have a wide application. It is expected that a line of cold-cathode vacuum tubes will be available for distribution early in 1960.

PROBLEMS

For the solution of problems requiring the use of characteristic curves of tubes, it is suggested that the curve sheet be covered with transparent paper held by short strips of masking tape. Light construction lines on this cover paper will not mar the original curves, and the overlay may be removed to serve as a part of the solution of the problem.

1. A certain vacuum diode has an emission of 10 ma for a plate potential of 50 volts. Assuming that Child's law holds for the tube, calculate and plot the saturation-emission current for 20 volt steps from zero to 100 volts on the plate.

2. Assume in Fig. 16 a cathode-anode separation of 2 cm and a peak applied potential of 20,000 volts. What will be the velocity of an electron

when it hits the anode if it left the cathode with zero initial velocity? What will be the energy of this electron on impact in (a) electron volts? (b) joules?

3. What is the d-c plate resistance of the vacuum diode shown in Fig. 15 when the plate current is 100 ma?

4. The kenotron of Fig. 16 is employed for half-wave rectification, feeding a load resistor of 10,000 ohms. What is the voltage across the load resistor when the drop across the tube is 1000 volts? What power is being dissipated at this instant in the load? within the tube (including filament power)?

5. Determine the amplification factor of the triode in Fig. 25 for i_b values of 4 and 6 ma, using the transfer characteristic.

6. Determine the amplification factor of the triode in Fig. 25 for i_b values of 8 and 10 ma, using the average plate characteristic curves.

7. Determine g_m for the triode in Fig. 25 for $e_b = 200$ volts and i_b near 6 ma; also for $e_b = 300$ with i_b near 3 ma.

8. Calculate r_p for the triode in Fig. 25 for values of e_c at 0, -10, and -24 volts.

9. A tube has an amplification factor μ of 8 and an r_p of 9500 volts for a certain condition of operation. What is g_m in micromhos?

10. From the following data find approximate values of μ, r_p, and g_m at the point $e_b = 180$ volts, $e_c = -12.5$ volts.

e_b(volts)	e_c(volts)	i_b(ma)
180	-12.5	7.5
160	-10.0	7.5
180	-12.3	7.84

11. The vacuum phototube of Fig. 47 is connected in the circuit of Fig. 46 with an applied d-c potential of 250 volts and a resistance of 10 meg. Let the light falling on the cathode of the tube change from zero to 0.1 lumen and 0.5 lumen. Calculate the voltage drop across the resistor for each case. (Use curves of Fig. 49 for this tube.) Does the answer check with law No. 1 for photoelectric emission?

12. A triode has an amplification factor of 8 and a plate resistance r_p of 1000 ohms. If a grid signal e_g of 10 volts is applied to the tube when connected to a load resistor of 5000 ohms, calculate (a) the plate current i_p, (b) the voltage drop e_z across the load resistor, and (c) the gain (voltage).

chapter 6

Electrical

Conduction in Gases

For a long time gases were supposed to be perfect insulators. Dry air and other gases seemed to offer a high opposition to the flow of electric current. About 1900 J. J. Thomson performed experiments which showed that gaseous ions serve as carriers for the electric current.

The conduction of electric current in gases is not easily predictable since it depends on many variables. The resulting conduction may vary with the gas employed, the gas pressure, the potential between electrodes, the electrode material, the shape of electrodes, the distance between electrodes, the shape of the enclosing medium, and other factors. Conduction in gases may be attained with either hot or cold cathodes, but the action will be different in each case. All this is in contrast with the theory of conduction of electricity in solids and in vacuums which has been considered in the preceding parts of this text.

Kinetic Theory of Gases

The molecules of a gas are in a constant state of motion similar to that of molecules in liquids and solids. Those in gases enjoy a greater freedom of movement so that what is termed gas pressure is really the result of multiple impacts of gas molecules upon the walls of the restraining enclosure. The simple kinetic theory of gases assumes the molecules to be small spheres which collide with each other in the course of their constant motion. The distance a molecule moves before it collides with another is called its free path. Obviously, the lengths of paths vary greatly, some being relatively short and others long. A study of the distribution of these paths will give a *mean length of free path* or average path which is of importance in the theory of electrical conduction in gases. The mean length of free path depends on the gas pressure and rises in magnitude as the pressure falls and the molecules are farther apart. The mean length of free path will also depend upon the size of the molecules. Mean length of free path of gaseous molecules is of the order of 0.02 to 0.2 mm for a pressure of 1 mm of mercury.

An electron projected in a gas will likewise collide with the molecules present. After its first collision it will bounce off in a new direction until it experiences a second collision, and then in a new direction for a third collision, and so on. In this manner it will travel in a zigzag path through the gas. The distance between collisions is the length of free path for the electron, and the average length of these paths is the *mean length of free path* for the electron. Since the electron has a smaller mass and a smaller size than the molecules of gas, it will experience fewer collisions and will have a longer length of free path (approximately six times that of the molecule).

The mean free length of path in a gas depends on the pressure, the molecular concentration, and the temperature. The relationship between these variables is covered by the following equation:

$$p = nKT \tag{1}$$

where p = pressure.

n = concentration, or the number of molecules per unit volume.

K = Boltzmann constant.

T = temperature in degrees Kelvin.

From this equation the concentration n is proportional to p/T. Since the mean free length of path is inversely proportional to the concentration n, it follows that the mean free length of path is directly proportional to the temperature T and inversely proportional to the pressure p.

The molecules of the noble gases and mercury vapor consist of one atom. These atoms possess kinetic energy because of their thermal agitation, as suggested. In addition to this kinetic energy, these atoms may be given potential energy by displacements of electrons in their atomic structure. In the normal state the electrons in the atom exist in certain orbits or energy levels. If one or more electrons in an outer orbit are disturbed by the addition of energy, they may be moved out of their normal orbit or energy level into a higher level or they may even be removed from the atom. In this process the atom acquires new energy. This new energy may be released or radiated very quickly with a return to a normal state, or it may be retained for a short time before release. *Thus a gas atom is capable of receiving, transporting, and releasing energy through rapid changes in its atomic structure.* This property combined with its kinetic energy plays a very important part in electrical conduction in gases.

Gaseous Conduction

The term gaseous conduction implies the conduction of current by a gas itself and within itself. Such conduction is simple to understand. The gas-filled tube of Fig. 1 contains two cold electrodes held at a difference of potential by a battery. Assume that one gas atom has been ionized to produce one positive ion and one electron through the action of X rays. The electron will be attracted to the positive electrode and will enter the circuit leading to the battery. The positive ion will be attracted to the negative electrode and upon arrival will seize an electron from the plate and unite with it to form a neutral atom of gas. This simple dual action has removed one electron from the negative electrode and supplied one electron to the positive electrode. This transfer constitutes an electric current. Multiply this single transfer by millions and simple gaseous conduction results.

The ions taking part in gaseous conduction must be produced by some secondary action. Often such secondary action involves one or more forms of electron emission. When this happens the emitted electrons join the ion movement, and the total current through the gas consists of the pure gaseous conduction plus an electron current.

Fig. 1. Simple gaseous conduction.

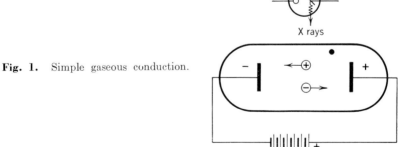

Thus the electric conduction in gases usually involves two or more processes of electron transfer.

Methods of Producing Ions

Gases may be ionized (1) by thermal action, (2) by electromagnetic radiation, and (3) by collision with particles. Gases in a flame become ionized by thermal action. X rays, gamma rays, cosmic rays, and other forms of electromagnetic radiation such as ultraviolet light have the power of ionizing a gas. Alpha particles and beta particles released from radioactive materials collide with gas particles and leave an ionized path. Much of our early and later scientific study has utilized the ionizing property of flying particles and the energy of radiation. In gaseous electronic devices, ionization by collision with electrons plays a very vital role.

Ionization by Collision

Ionization by collision with electrons is produced in gases by the accelerating force of an electric field. The primary electrons for the ionizing process are generally released by thermionic emission or photoemission. To get a concept of ionization by collision, assume for the gaseous tube of Fig. 2 that the gas pressure and the electric field are of suitable value for ionization to occur. Electrons emitted from the negative hot cathode will be accelerated by the electric field toward the positive anode, resulting in collisions with atoms of gas while in flight. A certain collision with a Bohr atom shown in the figure results in ionization of that atom. Here the approaching primary electron is aimed at an electron in the outer orbit of the atom. This orbital electron is moving to the right, and the collision with the primary electron also moving to the right will increase its speed so that it will break away from the atom. The orbital electron

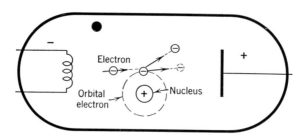

Fig. 2. Ionization by collision.

carries a negative charge $(-e)$ and the atom becomes a positive ion with a charge equal to $(+e)$ in magnitude. The primary impinging electron glances off at some angle as shown and continues its transit until it reaches the positive anode. During the ionizing collision the primary electron gives up a definite amount of energy to the atom. Hence *the resulting positive ion acquires and carries a unit of energy which will be released again whenever the ion reverts to a normal atom.*

Each electron passing between the electrodes of the tube of Fig. 2 under the influence of the electric field suffers many collisions with the atoms in the intervening space. Only a few (less than one per cent) of these collisions result in ionization. This follows because the electron may not possess sufficient energy to produce ionization or because the nature of the collision is not favorable for ionization.

The preceding discussion might lead one to assume that the collisions of molecules and the impacts between flying electrons and atoms were actual physical contacts like those of a baseball bat hitting a ball. Such is probably not true. According to the concept of atomic structure, collisions and impacts may become the interaction of the charges on electrons, atomic nuclei, and molecules. As one molecule of gas approaches another, the electrons in their outer orbits exert a repulsion for each other, and when they approach close enough this force of repulsion may become sufficient to cause the molecules to stop and then bound away from each other. In like manner, when a high-speed electron approaches an atom, if the electron in the outer orbit happens to be in the direct path of the projected electron, the force of repulsion between the two may carry the one free from the atom and produce ionization. If one recalls that the ratio of the charge on the electron to its mass for moderate velocities is 1.76×10^{11} (mks system), it is obvious that the force exerted by the charges vastly outweighs the importance of the insignificant mass. It should be noted that, since atoms are nebulous, electrons and even positive ions may pass through atoms provided they do not move on a line through the electrons or the nucleus.

Gases may be ionized by the collision of positive ions with atoms. However, the positive ions present in gaseous tubes are not very effective ionizing agents. Their large mass relative to the electron prevents rapid acceleration in an electric field and their larger size results in more collisions with molecules, so they have little opportunity to acquire velocities sufficient for ionizing collisions. It is well to remember that in the simplest gas, hydrogen, the positive ion (a proton) is 1840 times as heavy as the electron. In the more complex gaseous elements used in commercial tubes, the positive ion has a mass several thousand times as large as the electron (see Table 1, page 6).

Types of Electron Collisions

The collision of electrons with gas atoms can be divided into four classes. First, many collisions result in a mere "bouncing off" or change of direction of the electron where little or no energy is imparted to the atom. These are known as *elastic collisions* and constitute the majority of all impacts. Next, some collisions occur when the energy of the electron is insufficient to produce ionization but is great enough to move a valence electron out of its orbit or energy level. In this case, the atom has been given some energy and is said to be *excited*. This excited state of the atom is subdivided into two classes.

If the atom releases its energy immediately in the form of radiation as *visible light*, it belongs in the second class of collision. This class is the principle of gaseous light sources. However, if the energy from the electron impact is retained for a short period of time, the atom is said to be in a metastable state (third class). A metastable atom may receive additional energy from a second collision which is enough to produce ionization, and usually releases its energy in the form of heat. It should be noted that the excited atoms (both classes) retain all electrons, and hence do not carry a charge and are unaffected by an electric field. The fourth class of electron collision is the *ionizing collision*. If the conditions are favorable for ionization to occur, all four classes of collision take place.

Ionizing Potential

The term ionizing potential may have two different meanings. First, as often applied, it refers to that potential which must be applied between two electrodes to produce ionization for a given gas, pressure, temperature, and electrode spacing. Second, one may speak of the ionizing potential as the voltage through which an electron must fall to produce ionization. Following this concept, *each gaseous element requires a definite energy in electron volts to produce ionization*. The approximate excitation and ionizing energy for a few monatomic gases are given in Table 1.

Table 1

Gas	Excitation (electron volts)	Ionization (electron volts)
Neon (Ne)	16.6	21.5
Argon (A)	11.6	15.7
Xenon (Xe)	8.3	12.1
Mercury (Hg)	4.6	10.4

Deionization

Deionization is the reverse process of ionization. It is effected by a recombination of positive ions and electrons to form neutral normal atoms. Such recombinations are accompanied by a release of the energy required for ionization and imprisoned in the positive ion during its existence. Recombination may take place (1) inside the volume of gas, (2) along the walls of the gas-enclosing chamber, or (3) at an electrode under the attraction of an electric field. Recombinations do not take place readily inside the gas volume if an electric field is present because positive ions and electrons will have high relative velocities in opposite directions. If the conditions are favorable for the formation of negative ions (atom plus an electron), recombination may take place readily since the negative ion with larger mass moves more slowly than an electron, even in the presence of an electric field. Also the negative ion gives up its extra electron readily to a positive ion. Positive ions which diffuse to surface walls obtain electrons readily for deionization. Electrodes having negative potentials attract positive ions and supply electrons for recombinations. The energy released during deionization may be in the form of heat and may aid electron emission at the cathode. The preceding statements on recombinations apply to low-pressure discharge conditions but not to high-pressure discharges where mean free paths are negligible compared to electrode spacing.

Stages of Electrical Conduction in Gases

Electrical conduction in a gas between cold electrodes may pass through and exist in three successive stages. These stages are called the Townsend discharge, the glow discharge, and the arc. The term discharge arose from early experiments wherein gaseous conduction served to discharge electricity stored in condensers. The Townsend

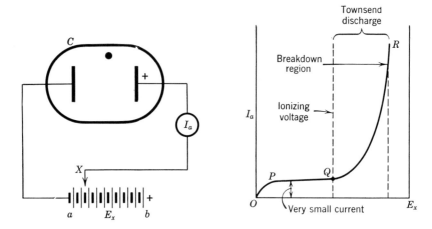

Fig. 3. Circuit and phenomena for Townsend discharge.

discharge can be explained by the circuit and curve of Fig. 3.   Two
cold plates are placed in the chamber C containing gas under reduced
pressure.   A variable voltage from source E_x is placed across the
plates.   Beginning with X at zero or a, the voltage is raised as X
moves to position b with a current flow in the circuit as shown by
the curve $OPQR$.   Although no ionizing agent is provided within the
chamber, a small number of ions are present because of cosmic rays
and other electromagnetic radiations which exist outside of the
chamber or because of radioactive substances which may be present
on the inside or outside.   The small number of ions present and
being formed constantly will be attracted to the electrodes and will
constitute a *very minute current* which will rise along the line OP
under the influence of a weak field.   The voltage at P is sufficient to
sweep all these ions out of space as rapidly as they are being formed,
and from point P to Q there will be no change of current.   At point
Q the ionizing potential for the pressure and gas used is reached.
Hence a few ions will be produced and their transfer will add to the
very minute current present.   Now, as the voltage is raised above
the ionizing potential, more primary electrons will produce ionization.
Furthermore, as the potential rises, two things may occur.   First,
an occasional primary electron may have more than one ionizing
collision while in transit, and second, the new electrons formed by
collisions may in turn effect one or more ionizing collisions while en
route to the anode.   These actions become accumulative with the

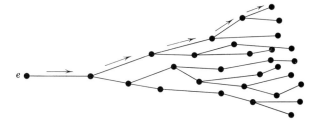

Fig. 4. Accumulative ionization via avalanche effect.

rise in anode potential and produce an avalanche effect, as depicted in Fig. 4. This accumulative process causes the gaseous conduction current to rise rapidly following an exponential form of curve shown in Fig. 3. Ultimately, as point x is moved to the right, the current tends to rise without apparent limit until a breakdown region is reached. The breakdown region is marked by two occurrences: (1) the operation of the tube becomes self-sustaining and (2) the discharge passes into the second stage—the glow discharge.

Up to this point the conduction has depended upon the production of some ions by some external agent such as electromagnetic radiations. If this external action had been stopped, the current would have dropped to zero. At the breakdown point a stage has been reached where the products of ionization (electrons and positive ions) will reproduce sufficient carriers to keep the conduction continuous (self-sustaining). This action is accomplished by secondary electron emission arising from bombardment by positive ions plus the energy released during recombination. The cause of this electron emission and self-sustaining action is to be found in the progressive change in the potential distribution between the electrodes in the tube. This phenomenon is shown in Fig. 5.

Fig. 5. Potential distribution during Townsend discharge.

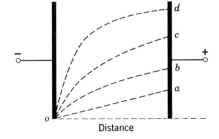

Initially, the potential distribution between the cold cathode and anode is linear, as shown by line oa. Then as the anode potential rises and as the number of heavy slow-moving positive ions increases, the potential distribution from cathode to anode shifts to the lines ob, oc, and finally od. For the final distribution, the potential gradient becomes very high near the cathode. This high gradient accelerates the positive ions and provides secondary electron emission from the cold cathode. After reaching the breakdown point, the Townsend discharge may pass into other types of discharge such as the corona, the glow, and the arc. The term breakdown potential is known also as sparking potential and ignition potential.

The Townsend discharge may occur in any cold-cathode gaseous tube. It is the type of conduction that occurs regularly in the gaseous phototube.

Paschen's Law

The breakdown voltage E_b in the Townsend discharge depends upon the geometry of the electrodes, their work function, the gas employed, the gas pressure, and the distance between the electrodes. Paschen's law states a relationship between the breakdown voltage and two of the preceding variables—gas pressure and the distance between the electrodes. To understand this relationship, a particular gas and electrode material may be chosen and the cold cathodes may be assumed to be parallel plates, thus giving a uniform electric field if space charge effects are ignored. If the electrodes are held at a fixed spacing d and the gas pressure is increased from 0 to X, the trend of the breakdown voltage E_b varies as shown in Fig. 6. Here the mean free path of the electron will control the intensity of ionization and, in turn, the breakdown voltage. At zero gas pressure, no gas atoms are present, and hence an infinite breakdown voltage would be required. For a low gas pressure some atoms are present, but their concentration is low and the mean length of path large. Hence a very high voltage would be necessary to produce the necessary intensity of ionization to result in breakdown. Now as the gas pressure rises, the concentration rises, the mean free path becomes less, and conditions are more favorable for breakdown. An optimum condition for breakdown occurs for the gas pressure represented by point b on the curve of Fig. 6. When the gas pressure exceeds the optimum point at b, the mean free length of path becomes too short and a higher potential gradient (and hence over-all potential) is

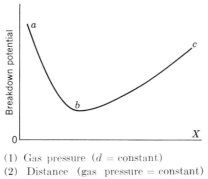

(1) Gas pressure $(d = \text{constant})$

(2) Distance (gas pressure = constant)

(3) $p \times d$

Fig. 6. Breakdown characteristic following Paschen's law.

necessary to produce sufficient ionization as shown by the region from b to c in Fig. 6.

Next, assume the gas pressure is held constant and the spacing (d) between the electrodes is varied from 0 to some point X in Fig. 6. The measured breakdown voltage will again follow the same general trend as before. Here, also, the length of free path of the electron determines the characteristic curve. At short spacings the electrons experience few collisions and the necessary breakdown voltage must be very high. For large spacing the distance may equal several lengths of free path, and again E_b must be high. The optimum condition for breakdown is likely to occur at a spacing approximating the mean free length of path for the conditions assumed. This characteristic variation of breakdown voltage with electrode spacing has been utilized in the design of cold-cathode rectifiers and grid-glow tubes to be covered in the following chapter. Thus a spacing corresponding to point b on Fig. 6 requires a relatively low breakdown voltage, whereas a short spacing such as point a will permit three times such potential before conduction occurs.

The preceding discussion discloses that the trend of change of breakdown voltage with variation of gas pressure for a constant electrode spacing is the same as for the inverse condition, namely, a variation of electrode spacing for a constant gas pressure. From this disclosure it is obvious that a similar trend will follow for a variation in the product of gas pressure times distance, or $p \times d$. This relationship is known as *Paschen's law*. Paschen's law states that, for parallel plane electrodes in a given gas at a given temperature, the breakdown voltage is a function of the product of the pressure and the electrode separation. To understand this law one should remember that under the conditions assumed the mean free path is inversely proportional to the pressure, so that the ratio between the spacing and the mean free path remains the same. Thus the number of free paths between the electrodes remains the same for a particular product of $p \times d$.

Glow Discharge

The glow discharge is a self-maintaining discharge (conduction) between cold electrodes which is marked by a luminous region, a low current density, and a relatively high voltage drop between electrodes. One important characteristic of this discharge is the *nearly constant voltage drop* which exists throughout a wide range of current, as suggested in Fig. 7. This discharge is inherently unstable and must be restrained by some form of load impedance (Chapter 7).

The glow discharge is the stage of conduction which succeeds the breakdown and termination of the Townsend discharge. This discharge gets its name from its soft luminous effect exemplified in the familiar neon sign. It is employed in several cold-cathode devices where the spacing between the electrodes is relatively short. However, all early and many current devices consist of long tubes. Some of the properties of the glow discharge for a long tubular chamber under an applied d-c potential are indicated in Fig. 8. Most of the light comes from the long positive column with supplementary bright areas at the cathode glow, the anode glow, and the negative glow points. The potential distribution shows a rapid rise of voltage close to cathode, then a gradual rise throughout the long positive column, with a final spurt or rise in potential near the anode. This form of potential distribution may be explained by the slow mobility of the positive ions in the long positive column. The ions form a positive

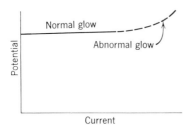

Fig. 7.   Characteristic of glow discharge.

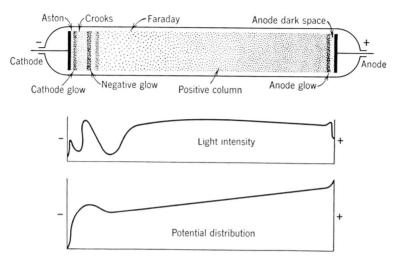

Fig. 8. Distribution of quantities in a long gaseous column with a cold cathode. (Reprinted with permission from L. B. Loeb, *Fundamental Processes of Electrical Discharge in Gases,* John Wiley & Sons, 1939, p. 566, Fig. 269.)

space charge which moves down to the cathode and gives a form of virtual anode close to the cathode. The rapid rise in voltage beginning at the cathode is equal to the glow voltage for the particular pressure and gas used. This voltage is several times the ionizing potential and it produces primary electrons and ions in sufficient numbers to make the discharge self-maintaining. This rise in voltage, often called the cathode fall of potential, depends upon the material used in the electrodes, upon the kind of gas, and upon the gas pressure in the tube. This voltage lies within the range of 50 to 300 volts. The positive ions are repelled by the positive potential at the anode so that only electrons exist in a narrow region called the anode dark space. In this region a more rapid rise of potential (stronger electric field) is needed to withdraw the electrons from the positive column.

When the current in the glow discharge is small the cathode glow covers a small area of the cathode. Then as the current through the tube rises, the area of the cathode glow increases in proportion until it covers the cathode completely. During this period the voltage drop across the tube remains nearly constant and this region of Fig. 7 is called the normal glow. If the current in the tube is permitted to rise beyond the point where the cathode glow has covered the cathode, the characteristic of the discharge changes rapidly. The increase of current will be accompanied by a rise of voltage drop between the cathode and anode and the glow of the tube column will rise in intensity. This new state is called the abnormal glow. A further increase of current causes an acceleration in the brightness of the glow and rise in voltage as the discharge passes through a transition region and changes to a new stage called the arc. Since the tube operation throughout the glow discharge is unstable, it is necessary to limit the current by external means. In neon signs this control is built into the transformer that supplies the power.

Arc

The arc is a discharge (conduction) in space between electrodes which is distinguished by a high current density, high temperature, bright source of light, and a negative resistance characteristic. This characteristic wherein the voltage across the arc varies inversely with the current is shown in Fig. 9. This inverse characteristic tends to damage any equipment associated with the arc and requires a stabilizing impedance in the external circuit which will limit the current.

The phenomenon of the electric arc depends on many factors such as the nature and temperature of the electrodes and the composition and pressure of the gas. The arc itself is composed of electrons, positive ions, and excited atoms (both light producing and metastable). Undoubtedly, many metastable atoms suffer second collisions that result in ionization, whereas others release their energy in the form of heat. The high temperature may influence the arc phenomenon in several ways. First, the high temperature may increase electron emission from the cathode and thus increase the current. Second, the temperature may be sufficient to produce ionization by thermal agitation. Third, the high temperature reduces the energy necessary to produce ionization by collision. All these processes may act accumulatively to produce intense electrical conduction. With this

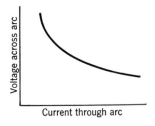

Fig. 9. Characteristic of the electric arc.

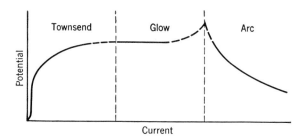

Fig. 10. Summary of the stages of discharge between cold electrodes in a low-pressure gas.

increase in current comes still higher temperatures, and thus the arc feeds on itself.

In the electric power field the arc may be a mighty destructive force, but when properly harnessed it is of great value in gaseous electronic devices which are covered in the next chapter.

Stages of Gaseous Conduction

The three stages of gaseous discharge with cold cathodes are briefly summarized in Fig. 10. In the Townsend discharge initial conduction is produced by some ionizing agent and a minute current exists under a rising potential until the ionizing potential is reached. After reaching this point the conduction current rises rapidly with voltage, and the potential distribution shifts to bring about a new stage wherein the discharge is self-sustaining. In the new stage (the glow discharge) the potential drop across the tube is constant while the current rises until the cathode glow covers the cathode surface. A further rise in current flow results in a rise in cathode-anode drop, a rise in luminous brightness, and a change to the arc discharge. The arc discharge is marked by an intense luminosity and a fall of potential with a rise in current. Thus the transitions in the three stages are marked by (1) *a rise of current and a rise in potential,* (2) *a rise of current and a constant potential,* and (3) *a rise of current and a fall of potential.*

In all forms of electrical conduction in gases the positive ions play the vital part. The large mass and slow mobility of these ions cause them to form a dense concentration in the space where conduction is taking place. Langmuir has termed such concentrations or positive space-charge regions the *plasma*. The plasma has boundaries on all sides. For example, in Fig. 8, the end boundaries occur at the negative glow and the anode glow. The other boundary is the outside of the column. This outer boundary may be the wall of the tube, but in general the outside boundary is a layer or sheath. This *sheath* is a region consisting of ions, metastable atoms, and normal atoms. The sheath differs from the plasma in that the ions are in a general state of diffusion and do not have a coordinated drift as a part of the current. The sheath can be likened to a thin layer of water on the inside of a pipe having a rough inner surface. This outer skin of water may be nearly stationary and yet serve as a boundary for the water flowing through the pipes. In gaseous conduction tubes, sheaths may represent the boundaries for electrodes as well as enclosing surfaces.

The preceding discussion of electric conduction in gases has assumed the use of a cold cathode, whereas most of the gaseous tubes in commercial use employ hot cathodes. The hot cathode furnishes a copious supply of electrons continuously. These electrons add greatly to the conduction of current (electron flow) and reduce the voltage drop required for producing simple ionization. The conduction of current is non-self-sustaining and the characteristics differ greatly from conduction in vacuum or self-sustaining conduction in gases. The characteristics of the hot-cathode gaseous tube will be covered in the following chapter.

Gaseous Lighting Units

Many lighting units operate on the principle of light production in either the glow or arc discharge as explained in the preceding sections. The neon light consists of a long glass tube about $\frac{1}{2}$ in. in diameter and is filled with neon gas under low pressure. It is a very efficient source of light, giving a reddish-yellow color. Its low cost and high efficiency have resulted in a widespread use for sign lighting all over the world. Argon gas and sometimes helium and mixtures of gases are used to give different colors in sign lighting.

Glow lamps consist of small bulbs filled with an inert gas such as neon under low pressure and containing two electrodes. The light production arises mainly from the cathode glow. These lamps are inefficient as light sources, but millions of them are used as night lights, pilot lights, and indicator lights for switches and electric appliances. Several neon glow lamps are illustrated in Fig. 11.

Mercury-vapor lamps are old in the lighting art. They consist of evacuated glass enclosures, either tubes or bulbs, containing a small quantity of mercury. They operate with the arc discharge and give

S-14
3-WATT   S-14
2-WATT   G-10
1-WATT   G-10
½WATT   T-4½
¼WATT   T-2
/25 WATT

Fig. 11. Neon glow lamps. (Courtesy General Electric Company.)

a bluish yellow light devoid of red rays. The color causes human faces to have a deathly pallor; hence these sources find little use to-day unless their light is modified in some manner.

The fluorescent lamp consists of a long glass tube coated on its inner surface with a fluorescent material known as phosphor and containing a small amount of mercury vapor. Emitter electrodes at the ends of the tube produce initial electrons for ionizing the mercury vapor and furnishing ultraviolet light. This light causes the phosphor to fluoresce and give forth visible light. The different phosphors available are capable of producing different colors of light, including white, at relatively high efficiencies compared to the heated-filament type of light source.

The gaseous conduction of mercury vapor has given rise to a number of important developments. Much of the electromagnetic radiation from the ionized mercury vapor is ultraviolet light. Ultraviolet rays have a high therapeutic and sterilizing value. Accordingly, one type of mercury-vapor lamp (called a sun lamp) is built to give healthful light for man and animals. A special form of this lamp (germicidal) is used for sterilization in refrigerators, in operating rooms, and in treatment of wounds.

The sodium-vapor lamp uses the vapor of sodium as the gaseous conducting medium. A small quantity of metallic sodium is contained in an inner chamber. It requires several minutes for the lamp to heat up, evaporate the sodium, and come to full normal brilliancy. The lamps give a yellow light at a very high luminous efficiency and find some use for highway lighting.

chapter 7

Gaseous and Vapor Electron Tubes

Gaseous versus Vacuum Tubes

Two criteria for distinguishing between vacuum and gaseous electron tubes are (1) the pressure of the gas and (2) the mean free path of the electrons. In a highly evacuated tube of 10^{-8} mm pressure at $0°$ C, there are more than ten billion molecules in each cubic centimeter. For the ordinary vacuum tube of 10^{-6} mm pressure, the mean free path of the electron is of the order of 42 meters. Since the electrode spacing in vacuum tubes never exceeds 2 or 3 cm (except in cathode-ray tubes), it is obvious that electrons move freely from cathode to anode with rare collisions with molecules of gas. In contrast with this picture, in gaseous tubes the normal spacing distances of electrodes is much greater (up to several inches), whereas the mean free path for common gas pressures of 10^{-2} to 10^{-1} mm is of the order of *a millimeter* or less. Thus in gaseous tubes the electrons suffer many collisions in transit and are likely to produce an intense ionization of the gas.

Neutralization of Negative Space Charge

Positive ions formed in an electron tube tend to neutralize the negative space charge surrounding a hot cathode. If a small amount of an inert gas is admitted to a high-vacuum diode, the gas molecules will be ionized by collisions with the emitted electrons in transit to the anode. The electrons formed by collision will be attracted to the positive anode and, because of their small mass, will reach it quickly. The positive ions formed by collision will move to the negative cathode rather slowly because of their large mass. Since the positive ions move slowly, they will remain in the cathode-anode space for a long time relative to the time of transit of electrons. Accordingly, a large number of positive ions may exist at a given instant within the region of the negative space charge surrounding the hot cathode. A single positive ion close to an electron will *neutralize the charge* of that electron at that instant. Thus the field produced by this pair is zero (neutral space charge). In an infinitesimal fraction of a second the electron of the pair is whisked away by the electric field and the positive ion moves a short distance toward the cathode. In its new position the positive ion will be close to a second electron and at that instant will serve to neutralize this electron. In this manner the slow mobility of the positive ion will permit it to neutralize many (perhaps hundreds) of electrons while passing through the negative space-charge region. It is readily conceivable that, if at every instant the region surrounding the cathode contains the same number and distribution of positive ions and electrons, the negative space charge will be completely neutralized. This ideal state may seldom exist, but any degree of neutralization will overcome partially the negative space charge and will increase the number of primary electrons that are attracted to the anode. In passing, it should be noted that, if the positive ions present close to the cathode exceed the number of electrons, they will act like a positive grid very close to the cathode and thereby will increase greatly the primary electron flow to the anode.

The conduction of electricity in the gaseous hot-cathode tube may be considered as consisting of the three following components:

1. The primary electron current existing in a high vacuum.
2. The gaseous conduction resulting from electron transfer by ions.
3. *The increased flow of electrons of thermionic emission resulting from the neutralization of negative space charge.*

The third component is the largest in magnitude and of the greatest importance. Component number two is usually small in magnitude. The addition of a small amount of gas or vapor greatly increases the current rectified by a diode. It also reduces the voltage required between the cathode and anode. This action is illustrated in the curves in Fig. 1a, giving a comparison of the anode-current anode-voltage characteristics of hot-cathode vacuum and gaseous tubes. In the

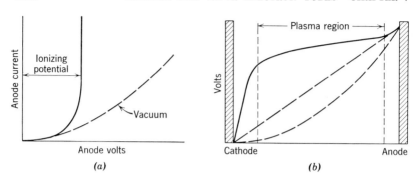

Fig. 1. Current and potential characteristics in a hot-cathode gaseous or vapor-rectifier tube.

gaseous tube with negative space charge neutralized, the anode current rises abruptly after the ionizing potential is reached, giving a constant anode-cathode drop with load. Thus for the gaseous tube the rectified power output is increased and at the same time the power loss within the tube is reduced. Both these changes increase the efficiency of rectification of alternating current.

Potential Distribution in Hot-Cathode Gaseous Tube

The presence of positive ions in gaseous and vapor tubes has a marked effect upon the potential distribution between the cathode and anode. In a high-vacuum tube the negative space charge depresses the voltage near the cathode, whereas in the gaseous tube the positive ions tend to neutralize this negative space-charge effect. Furthermore, if sufficient gas or vapor is present, an arc form of discharge takes place. The positive ions form a plasma for the arc which extends close to the cathode giving the potential distribution as shown in Fig. 1b. The trend of this curve is similar to that of the glow-discharge tube, but here the magnitude of the cathode drop from plasma to cathode is much lower. In the glow-discharge tube a high voltage is necessary to produce electrons from a cold cathode, whereas in the tube under consideration a copious supply of electrons is emitted thermionically. In the gaseous and vapor-arc tubes the total fall of potential from anode to cathode is of the order of 10 to 25 volts. The exact form of the potential distribution curve will vary with the gas or vapor and the pressure used and somewhat with the geometry of the tube. In general, there will be a rise of potential from the plasma of the arc to the anode for extracting the electrons out of the plasma. The potential distribution which would exist in vacuums because of negative space charge is indicated by the lower dotted line in Fig. 1b.

Cathode Sputtering

The positive ions produced in a gaseous tube bombard the hot cathode. When the ions hit the cathode they give up energy in two ways. First, the positive ions possess kinetic energy arising from the velocity acquired in the electric field. Second, the positive ion carries potential energy resulting from ionization. This latter energy is released when recombination takes place at the cathode. Both forms of energy given up when the positive ion hits the cathode may be transformed into heat, thus raising the temperature of the cathode and increasing the rate of thermionic emission. This process is utilized in the ionic-heated cathode and will be referred to later. If the electric field is too high, the bombardment of the positive ions may disintegrate the emitting surface. This action is known as *cathode sputtering,* and the removed active material such as thorium or barium may land on a nearby electrode such as a grid and result in emission from that electrode. The loss of active material from the sputtered cathode will reduce the emission from the cathode and may make the cathode inoperative, thus ruining the tube for further service. Cathode sputtering results from (1) insufficient cathode emission (underheating), (2) too large cathode-anode current (overload), or (3) too high cathode-anode voltage drop. Since these conditions have a direct interrelation, two of them occur simultaneously. Cathode sputtering can be prevented with a suitable resistor in the load circuit to limit the current output of the tube to the rated value and by having the cathode at normal emission temperature and the correct bulb temperature before anode voltage is applied.

The anode-cathode voltage drop at which cathode sputtering begins is called the *disintegration voltage.* The disintegration voltage for thermionic emitters is 22 for mercury vapor, 25 for argon gas, and 27 for neon gas.

Although cathode sputtering is very harmful in an electron tube, the sputtering process may be useful in some manufacturing processes. Thus a thin coating of a metal may be placed on a plate or an electrode by sputtering this metal from a second electrode serving as a cathode.

Peak Inverse Voltage

Peak inverse voltage (PIV) is the maximum inverse or reverse voltage which a tube having unilateral conductivity will withstand without a reverse current flow. The term PIV does *not* refer to the insulation or dielectric strength of the tube parts. In the high-vacuum tubes previously discussed it was pointed out that with a cold cathode, exceedingly high inverse voltage (anode negative and cathode positive) could be employed without any danger of a reverse current (called breakdown or arc-back). However, when gas is present in a tube, conduction may take place from a negative cold anode because of the Townsend discharge, the glow discharge, and the arc discharge. Also the breakdown potential follows the curve representing Paschen's law. Accordingly, in gaseous and vapor electron tubes the maximum inverse voltages must be held at much lower values.

The permissible peak inverse voltage for gaseous or vapor tubes decreases rapidly with a rise in pressure. As the gas pressure rises above zero, the ionization by collision increases. The tendency to arc-back depends on the number of positive ions present, and hence the permissible gas pressure will be determined by the PIV requirement. In tubes employing mercury vapor, the temperature of the tube becomes an important factor because of the amount of mercury evaporated, and hence the vapor pressure depends on the coolest place in the tube where the vapor condenses.

Gaseous Rectifier Diode

The first commercial gaseous diode known as the Tungar rectifier was placed on the market in 1916. It was filled with argon gas under a pressure of approximately two pounds (absolute). The argon gas furnished the positive ions for neutralizing negative space charge and the relatively high gas pressure reduced evaporation and thorium loss from the cathode. The anode was a graphite disk with its lead brought in from the top of the tube. The cathode was a helical coil of thoriated-tungsten wire connected through leads to a screw type of base, as illustrated in Fig. 2. In current tubes the cathode filament is operated at a low voltage of 1.8 to 2.2 volts and with currents of 6 to 27 amp, depending upon the output rating of the particular tube. The tube "fires" or conducts with a nearly instantaneous start. No harm results from impressing voltage on the anode before the cathode reaches operating temperature because the relatively high gas pressure limits the velocity (collisions) of the positive ions. The average d-c pickup voltage for the tube is 12 volts and the average arc drop (anode to cathode) is only 7 volts. A low PIV is necessary

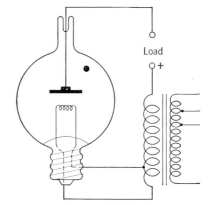

Fig. 2. Circuit for a half-wave Tungar rectifier.

Load

+

to prevent a glow discharge and arc from starting on the nonconducting half of the cycle of rectification.

Rectifiers employing xenon gas under low pressure are produced in a wide range of ratings. For a low gas pressure and low average direct current of 0.25 amp, the peak inverse voltage rating is 10,000 volts, whereas for somewhat higher gas pressure and an output rating of 16 amp, the PIV is 620 volts. A commercial gas diode and its rating are shown in Fig. 3.

RECTIFIER EL6B
(Half-wave)
TANTALUM ANODE AND XENON GAS

Cathode
Filament voltage	2.5 volts
Filament current	21 ± 2 amps
Heating time	1 min

Anode
Peak inverse voltage	920 volts
Arc drop (average)	9 volts
Starting voltage (average)	12 volts
D-c current (continuous)	6.4 amps
D-c current (10 sec)	12.8 amps
Max commutation factor (V/μsec	
$\times A/\mu$sec	0.66
Ambient temp. limits	−55 to 75° C

Note: The cathode should be heated before the load voltage is applied.

Fig. 3. Typical gaseous rectifier tube. (Courtesy Electrons Inc.)

The maximum commutation factor referred to in Fig. 3 is defined as the product of the rate of current decay in amperes per microsecond just prior to commutation (when applied voltage passes through zero) and the rate of inverse voltage rise in volts per microsecond just after commutation. The meaning and significance of this factor may be explained as follows. During the half of the rectification cycle when conduction is taking place, the cathode-anode space is filled with positive ions. As the applied voltage falls to zero and then reverses, we expect deionization to take place with all positive ions removed. However, under some conditions, especially those of an inductive load, the load current does not go to zero (at zero applied voltage) and positive ions remain in the cathode-anode space. When the applied voltage reverses and the anode becomes negative, these positive ions are attracted to the anode. If the accelerating potential is sufficient, the bombarding ions will become occluded in the surface of the anode. This phenomenon is known as "clean-up" and it reduces the amount of free gas within the tube and in consequence the gas pressure. Any reduction in gas pressure changes the operating characteristics of the tube and is objectionable.

Mercury-Vapor Rectifier Diode

The mercury-vapor rectifier diode uses a hot cathode and mercury vapor under a *low pressure*. It should not be confused with the pool type of tube which uses a pool of cold metallic mercury for a cathode. A small quantity of mercury is inserted in a hot-cathode evacuated tube. A part of or all the mercury vaporizes and the vapor atoms ionize and serve as the conducting medium in the tube. The conduction is of the arc type. In comparison with the vacuum diode, the mercury-vapor tube carries a much larger current, has a neutralized negative space charge, and has a nearly constant cathode-anode voltage drop (within the range of 10 to 20 volts) which is nearly independent of current. The absence of negative space charge and its accompanying losses allows a larger electrode spacing and smaller size electrodes for a given current-carrying capacity. It also permits the use of an electron-emitting cathode of higher efficiency and much larger current-carrying capacity. The anodes consist of disks made of metal or graphite which are mounted on leads brought out at the top of the tube. The hot cathodes are of the oxide-coated type and are generally placed within a hollow metal cylinder to reduce radiation losses. Various configurations have been used in the construction of these cathodes as illustrated in Fig. 4.

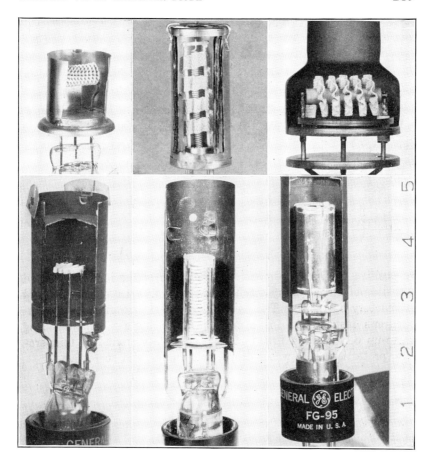

Fig. 4. Assemblies of oxide-coated cathodes used in gaseous and vapor tubes. (Courtesy General Electric Company.)

Glass-enclosing tubes are used for mercury-vapor units having small current-carrying capacities, and metal-enclosing tubes for the larger capacities.

The mercury-vapor rectifier is superior to the gaseous rectifier in that it will withstand much higher peak inverse voltages of the order of 5,000 to 10,000 volts. However, the mercury-vapor diode has the disadvantage that voltage should not be applied to the anode until the cathode and the entire tube reach normal operating temperature. Such application of voltage when the cathode is cold or partially heated will result in the destruction of the cathode-emitting surface

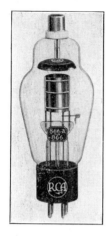

Fig. 5. Mercury-vapor rectifier tube (average anode current 0.25 amp). (Courtesy Radio Corporation of America.)

by positive ion bombardment. Special care in the installation and operation of mercury-vapor tubes is necessary to insure long life and satisfactory operation. The user should observe carefully the manufacturer's instructions for operation in an upright position, long warm-up period when first installed, suitable surrounding temperature, protection from water drops, acid fumes, and so forth.

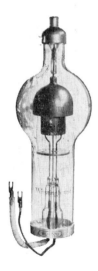

MERCURY-VAPOR RECTIFIER
WL-857B

Filament volts	5.0
Filament current	30.0 amp
Anode volts drop	15.0
Peak inverse volts	22,000
Average load current	10 amp
Condensed mercury temperature limits	30–40 °C

Fig. 6. Mercury-vapor rectifier. (Courtesy Westinghouse Electric Corporation.)

The accepted name for the mercury-vapor diode in the power industry is the *phanotron*. These tubes have average current output ratings of from 0.25 to 30 amp. A tube of low rating is shown in Fig. 5 and one of high current and voltage in Fig. 6. Phanotrons are used for supplying direct current for applications where medium values of voltage and current are required.

Thyratrons

The thyratron is a triode containing inert gas or mercury vapor under low pressure. It is a gaseous diode plus a control grid. The admission of gas or vapor into a three-electrode vacuum tube greatly changes the characteristics and operation of the device. The presence of gas renders the tube useless as a grid-controlled amplifier but makes it valuable as a grid-controlled arc rectifier. To perform this function the grid must act as an enclosure to control all passage of electrons and positive ions between the cathode and anode. This

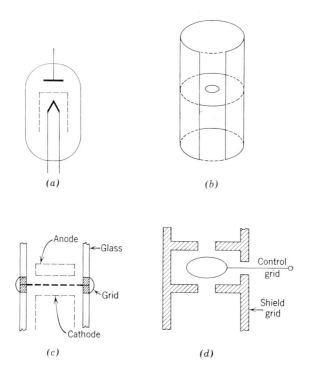

Fig. 7. Forms of thyratron grid structures.

means that the grid surrounds the cathode or it may enclose and separate both the anode and cathode as shown in Fig. 7. Passage through the grid may be through a wire mesh or via a single hole in a baffle, as shown in Fig. 7b.

The theory of action of the thyratron can be pictured by considering its behavior in a d-c circuit. Let the filamentary cathode of Fig. 8 be heated to normal temperature for emission and let switches S_p and S_c be open. Close S_p, placing a high positive potential on the anode with the grid free, and nothing will happen if the grid has a fine mesh. This follows because the free grid is made negative by the electrons from the cathode landing on it. This negative grid repels the electrons emitted by the cathode so that few get past the meshes of the grid to start ionization. Next, if switch S_c is connected to the positive side of the C battery, electrons pass through the grid readily, ionization starts, an arc develops, and the tube conducts an electric current which is limited by the magnitude of the load resistance. After the ionization has started, the opening of switch S_c, causing a free grid to exist, has no effect on the cathode-anode arc. Likewise, if the switch S_c is connected to the negative side of the C battery, the resulting negative charge on the grid has no appreciable effect on the arc. Thus *the grid has the power to start the arc but no power to control its magnitude or to stop it after it has started.* The reason for this unexpected action lies in the presence of the positive ions in the arc. These ions, which fill the cathode-anode space, constitute the plasma of the arc. When the grid is made negative, it attracts some of the positive ions from the plasma, and these positive ions fly to and cluster around the grid like bees coming to a hive

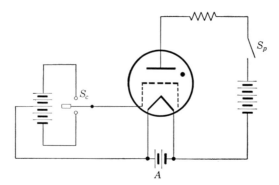

Fig. 8. Thyratron in a d-c circuit.

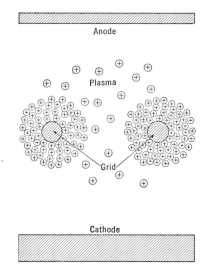

Fig. 9. Grid action in a thyratron.

(Fig. 9).   Each positive ion seizes an electron and becomes a neutral atom.   However, the process is continuous and the cluster or sheath of positive ions surrounding the grid creates a positive field (space charge) as far as the surrounding region is concerned.   If the grid is made more negative, a thicker sheath of positive ions surrounds it but without any effect on the cathode-anode arc, if the meshes of the grid are some distance apart.   However, if the grid wires are very close together (almost touching), the sheath of positive ions around the grid will serve to limit the cathode-anode arc.   Thus, theoretically, a closely spaced grid plus a high negative grid potential can be used to limit and even to stop an arc.   Such means are *not* employed in practice.   The simple and usual method for interrupting the arc when using direct current is to break the cathode-anode circuit by opening the switch S_p.   The arc will be interrupted also if the anode-cathode voltage is reduced below the ionizing potential.   The latter action may be produced by a voltage transient such as the discharge from a capacitor.

The potential required on the grid of a thyratron to permit the rectifying arc to start depends on several factors.   These factors are the size of the openings of the grid, the gas or vapor pressure within the tube, the general geometry of the tube, the grid current and circuit resistance, and the potential applied to the anode.   The voltage conditions for starting the arc depend to a large degree on the structure of the grid. Thus with a fine-mesh grid (small hole or holes) a positive potential must be applied to the grid to start gaseous conduction, whereas with a coarse grid (large hole or holes) the arc may start with a negative potential on the grid. For the range of gas pressures used on thyratrons the low pressures require a higher potential gradient to start the arc. The positive potential on the anode determines the electric field within the tube and hence the "pull" upon the electrons. Thus a high initial positive voltage on the anode will require a more negative potential on the grid to prevent the formation of an arc. For a given tube, there is a certain ratio of anode volts to grid volts at which the tube will "fire." This ratio is called the grid-control ratio. It can be expressed as

$$\rho = - \left(\frac{e_a}{e_c}\right) \qquad i_a = 0$$

and it bears a resemblance to the amplifying factor mu of the vacuum triode. The grid-control characteristics of thyratrons from which the grid-control ratio can be obtained are illustrated in Fig. 10. The grid-control ratio for a tube with the characteristic A is cy/dy at point y.

Thyratrons may be classified by the sign of the grid-control voltage that permits the starting of the tube. A negative-control tube is illustrated by curve A of Fig. 10 where a negative potential must be applied to the grid to prevent starting for all values of anode po-

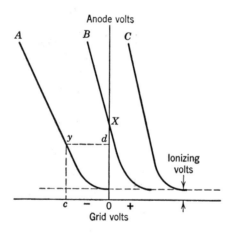

Fig. 10. Anode grid-voltage characteristic of thyratrons.

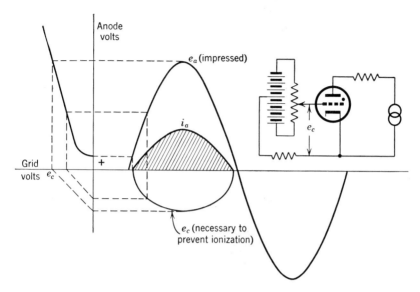

Fig. 11. Action of a thyratron on alternating current.

tential within the range of operation. For a similar reason, curve C represents a tube having a positive control. Curve B of Fig. 10 represents a tube of the intermediate-control class. This tube requires a positive grid for starting for anode voltages up to point X and a negative grid for higher values. This class of tube has a short deionization time and is used for inverter circuits.

The thyratron is a "natural" for use on a-c circuits. If the grid is given a potential sufficiently positive so that the tube will conduct for all values of anode potential (above ionizing potential), the tube will rectify all positive loops of a-c potential exactly like a gaseous diode. However, if the potential of the grid of the thyratron is controlled in a suitable manner the thyratron may be made to conduct current or to stop current at will. This follows because the alternating voltage passes through zero twice during each cycle and is negative for half of each cycle. Thus if the grid of the thyratron is brought to the critical value, as determined by the grid-control ratio, the arc is struck each time the anode voltage becomes positive, but, if the grid voltage is lowered (made more negative), the current will stop at the end of the positive-anode voltage loop. Then when the anode voltage becomes positive on the next and succeeding cycles, the tube does not "fire." This simple grid control for starting and stopping current rectification in the anode circuit has given rise to the term "trigger tube" for the thyratron. The operation of the thyratron on alternating current is illustrated in Fig. 11. The grid voltage necessary to stop conduction for any given anode potential is given by the grid-control characteristic on the left. The necessary restraining values can be referred to the impressed alternating-voltage cycle as shown by the graphical construction of Fig. 11. The curve e_c shows the necessary values of grid potential to prevent conduction for corresponding values of positive anode potentials. For a complete "stop" current, the grid must have a negative value greater than the maximum of the e_c curve.

Grid Firing Control

Nearly all commercial thyratrons are of the negative control type. The time of firing or triggering a thyratron may be controlled by the following methods.

1. Amplitude control. A variable negative d-c bias placed in the grid-cathode circuit.

2. Phase-shift control. An alternating voltage from the applied power source injected into the grid-cathode circuit. This voltage is subject to phase-shift variations for control purposes.

3. Combinations of methods 1 and 2 in series in the cathode grid circuit.

The application of these methods of control follows directly from the theory of action and curves of Fig. 10. Amplitude control is brought about by applying a negative bias to the grid as illustrated in Fig. 12. For the bias shown under a the thyratron conducts current beginning at point X and the area of the rectified current loop is reduced slightly. An increase in the bias to the value shown under b will permit the tube to fire at point Y so that the magnitude of the rectified current has been reduced to one-half the normal value. Values of negative bias between those shown will give other magnitudes of current. Obviously, this is a very simple method of controlling current values, but it has some limitations and disadvantages. First, the maximum reduction in magnitude is one-half value (one-fourth cycle). This maximum reduction is critical because the firing point depends on both the grid and anode potentials and a temporary decrease in anode voltage might cause the tube to skip some cycles. For like reasons changes in anode potential, thermionic emission from cathode, and changes in temperature will vary the fir-

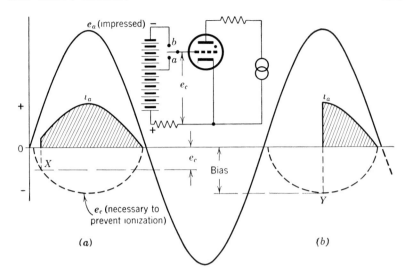

e_a (impressed)

b

a

e_c

$+$

ι_a

ι_a

0

X

e_c

Bias

Y

e_c (necessary to prevent ionization)

(a)   (b)

Fig. 12.   Amplitude grid control of a thyratron.

ing point, and hence the control of the current magnitude for a given grid-bias setting may not be sufficiently exact for some applications.

A more exact timing and firing of the thyratron can be secured by phase-shift control. In this method an alternating voltage derived from the anode supply line is applied to the grid. The phase of the grid voltage is shifted with respect to the anode voltage by suitable means, giving results as shown in Fig. 13. If the grid voltage e_g is "in phase" or ahead of the anode voltage as shown in part a, the tube fires as soon as the positive loop of the anode potential reaches the ionizing voltage and the complete loop is rectified. A delayed shift of the grid voltage e_g as shown in part (b) will cause the rectification to begin at the end of one-third of the positive loops. A further shift in the grid voltage will delay the firing to a point near the end of the positive loop, as illustrated in part (c). A shift of the grid potential from "in phase" to a lag of 180 degrees will permit a control from "full" to zero magnitude of current. Any change of anode voltage will be reflected in a change in grid voltage and in the value of the e_c curve so that the period in the cycle where the firing occurs will remain nearly constant.

For many applications of the thyratron a combination of the d-c bias and phase-shift control gives the best results. The combined methods are suggested in Fig. 14. Under one method the grid bias

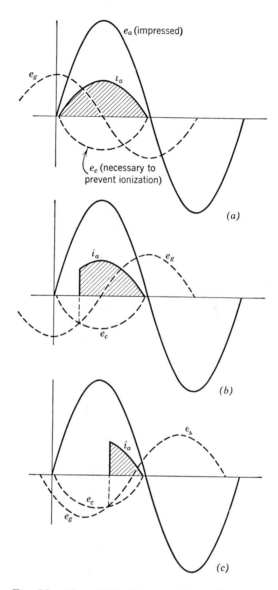

Fig. 13. Phase-shift grid control in a thyratron.

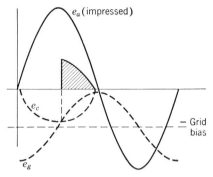

Fig. 14. Phase-shift control superimposed upon a normal grid bias
in a thyratron.

is made sufficiently negative to prevent the tube from firing if the a-c
grid potential is not applied. Then the phase of the a-c component
is shifted to give the desired firing point. Since the grid is always
negative, the power required for the grid input is reduced to a very
low value. The second useful combination of a-c and d-c grid voltage for firing thyratrons is the use of an alternating voltage component with a fixed phase shift (usually 90 degrees), and then the
firing time is controlled by a variation of the magnitude of the d-c
bias (Fig. 14).

The phase shift for the grid circuits of thyratrons and other electronic devices may be produced by mechanical devices or by simple
circuits, one of which is illustrated in Fig. 15. The theory of this
phase-shifting circuit is illustrated in the vector diagram of Fig. 15.
The alternating voltage impressed across the cathode-anode circuit
is in phase with that across points A and P. With a very high value
of resistance R, the point G on the vector diagram will show voltage

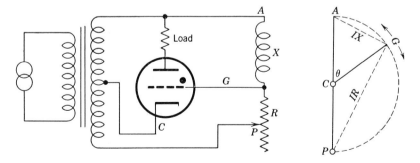

Fig. 15. Simple phase-shift circuit and vector diagram.

CG (cathode-to-grid) nearly in phase with that across the cathode-anode circuit. Now as R is reduced, the magnitude and phase of AP remains unchanged, but the position of G will swing clockwise on the arc of a circle, thus throwing the cathode-grid voltage out of phase with the cathode-anode voltage and making possible a 180 degree phase shift. For all positions of shift the magnitude of CG remains constant. A condenser may be substituted for the inductance of Fig. 15 to give another simple phase-shifting circuit. In making this change, the relative positions of R and C must be interchanged in order to retain a lagging phase shift.

Thyratron Construction and Problems

Thyratrons of small capacity have cathodes of the oxide-coated filament type as in vacuum tubes. Those of large capacity use heavy ribbon filaments to give copious emission but very low voltage drops between the ends of the filament. These cathodes are surrounded on the sides (open top) to reduce heat radiation and in turn reduce the energy required for emission. A few cathodes are indirectly heated. The grids are placed farther from cathodes than in vacuum tubes to reduce the grid temperature, reduce possible grid emission, and reduce the amount of emitting material which might be sputtered from the cathode. Anodes for thyratrons are disks of tantalum or graphite. Inert gas such as argon, xenon, or mercury vapor at pressures varying from one to 50 microns are employed in thyratrons.

Thyratrons are available in many sizes and ratings. A miniature thyratron together with its rating and characteristics is shown in Fig. 16. Those of small and medium size are generally filled with inert gas and use glass enclosures. It is possible to build thyratrons with current ratings as high as 100 amp and with voltages up to 100,000. Current designs show PIV voltages up to 25,000 with small average current (1.0 amp), and high current up to 18 amp average with a PIV of 1500.

A large capacity thyratron and its rating and characteristics are illustrated in Fig. 17. A special feature of this design is its high commutation factor rating. This rating is accomplished by two features of construction. First, there is a close spacing between the anode and grid which results in a minimum number of ions being affected by the anode field at the end of conduction. Second, the anode is thoroughly shielded from the cathode, leaving only a small portion of its area available for ion bombardment. The tube en-

MINIATURE THYRATRON
INERT GAS-FILLED, 4-ELECTRODE

Heater voltage	6.3 volts
Heater current	0.6 amp
Cathode heating time	20 sec
Peak inverse voltage	1300 volts
Peak forward voltage	650 volts
Negative control voltage	
Before conduction	100 volts
During conduction	10 volts
Anode voltage drop	8 volts

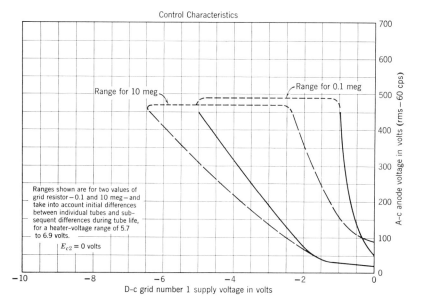

Ranges shown are for two values of grid resistor — 0.1 and 10 meg — and take into account initial differences between individual tubes and subsequent differences during tube life, for a heater-voltage range of 5.7 to 6.9 volts.

$E_{c2} = 0$ volts

Control Characteristics

Range for 10 meg

Range for 0.1 meg

A-c anode voltage in volts (rms — 60 cps)

D-c grid number 1 supply voltage in volts

Fig. 16. Miniature thyratron GL-5727. (Courtesy General Electric Company.)

closure is heat-resistant glass and the cathode is placed in a heat-conserving cylinder. (See Fig. 7c.)

One of the problems in the use of thyratrons is the control of the magnitude of the grid current. The grid of the vacuum triode is usually maintained negative and there is no grid current problem. However, in the gaseous triode the conduction via an arc consists of

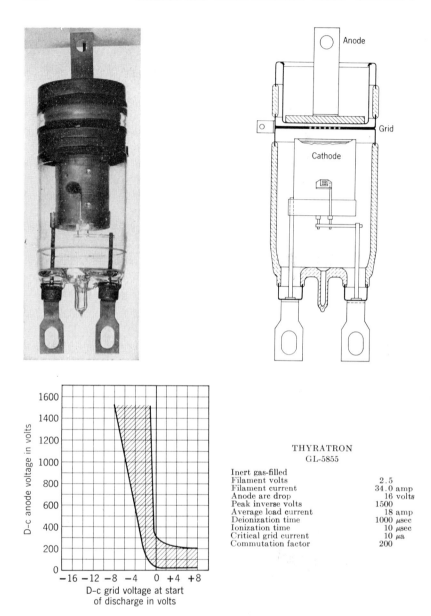

THYRATRON
GL-5855

Inert gas-filled
Filament volts	2.5
Filament current	34.0 amp
Anode arc drop	16 volts
Peak inverse volts	1500
Average load current	18 amp
Deionization time	1000 μsec
Ionization time	10 μsec
Critical grid current	10 μa
Commutation factor	200

Fig. 17. Construction, rating, and control characteristic of a thyratron. (Courtesy General Electric Company.)

both electrons and + ions. Here there is a relatively large grid current because positive ions land on the grid when it is maintained negative. This grid current produces heating, lowers the input impedance of the grid input circuit, and thus affects the external components and firing-control circuit for the thyratron. Accordingly, grid resistors having magnitudes in the range of ½ to 2 meg must be placed in series with all grids on thyratrons having three electrodes.

A second problem in the use of thyratrons may be the preciseness of the firing and the period required for ionization and deionization within the tube. Ionization time for commercial thyratrons varies from 10 to 20 microseconds and deionization time from 100 to 1000 microseconds. One method of assuring the instant of firing is to employ a *highly peaked* alternating voltage wave instead of a sine wave for the phase-shift control of firing. This peaked voltage wave gives more positive firing and tends to reduce the ionization time. When the thyratron is used for high-frequency pulsing, the deionization time becomes very important. The deionization time is reduced by the design of special thyratrons filled with hydrogen gas. Since the mass of the hydrogen ion is only a small fraction of that of other inert gases (see Table 1, Chapter 1), the time of ion transit is greatly reduced. Deionization time can also be controlled in a degree by the spacing between the anode and cathode.

Shield-Grid Thyratron

The thyratron with three electrodes has certain limitations somewhat similar to those of the vacuum triode which can be overcome through the use of a fourth electrode called a shield grid corresponding to the screen grid in the vacuum tetrode. The shield grid is usually a hollow metal cylinder containing two circular disk baffles as shown in Fig. 18. Each baffle contains a hole for the passage of electrons and ions. The control grid is a small ring placed in the conduction path midway between the baffles of the shield grid. (See Fig. 7d.) The shield grid is maintained at a constant direct voltage which tends to stabilize operation and to give the desired grid-control ratio.

The shield-grid construction serves to minimize grid current from a variety of causes and to permit satisfactory operation of the tube in a high-impedance grid circuit. These advantages are accomplished in three ways. First the shield grid reduces both the anode-to-control-grid and the control-grid-to-cathode interelectrode capacity. The former is important in thyratron circuits since the steep wave-front transients frequently encountered in these circuits may

GENERAL CHARACTERISTICS

Electrical Design

Number of electrodes		4
Cathode type—indirectly heated		
Voltage	5.5	5.0 volts
Current, approx	11.0	10.0 amp
Heating time, typical		5 min
Peak voltage drop, typical		16 volts
Approximate starting characteristics		
Anode voltage	100	2000 volts
Shield-grid voltage	0	0 volts
Control-grid voltage	+1.0	−14.0 volts
Anode to control-grid capacitance		0.07 μμf
Deionization time, approx		1000 μsec
Ionization time, approx		10 μsec

Maximum Ratings

Maximum peak anode voltage		
Inverse	750	2000 volts
Forward	750	2000 volts
Maximum negative control-grid voltage		
Before conduction		1000 volts
During conduction		10 volts
Maximum negative shield-grid voltage		
Before conduction		300 volts
During conduction		5 volts
Maximum anode current		
Instantaneous, 25 cycles and above	77	40 amp
Instantaneous, below 25 cycles		13.0 amp
Average	2.5	6.4 amp
Maximum control-grid current		
Instantaneous		1.0 amp
Average		0.25 amp
Maximum shield-grid current		
Instantaneous		2.0 amp
Average		0.50 amp
Maximum time of average current		15 sec
Temperature limits, condensed mercury	+30° to +95°	+40° to +80° C
Recommended temperature, condensed mercury		+40° C

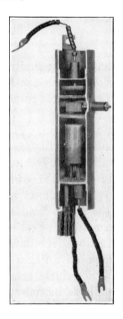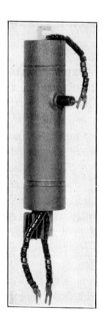

Fig. 18. Shield-grid thyratron FG-172. (Courtesy General Electric Company.)

be transmitted to the control grid through this capacity, causing premature firing. The reduction in the cathode-to-control-grid capacity is of lesser importance though it does reduce the grid current input where a-c potentials are applied. The second advantage of the shield grid is its action in shielding the control grid from contamination and temperature. The shielded position reduces the amount of material evaporated or sputtered from the cathode and anode which may become deposited on the control grid. Also the shielded position reduces the radiated heat and lowers the temperature of the control grid which, in turn, reduces grid emission. A third advantage of the shield grid is to permit the use of a small control grid which reduces both the emission current from cathode and any current arising from the interelectrode capacity. It should be noted that the shield-grid current does not pass through the control-grid circuit.

Application of Thyratrons

The thyratron is one of the most useful control devices invented in the twentieth century. Its applications are too numerous to mention. In one application it serves as a relay. A small change of potential on the grid starts or stops a rectified current which is performing some useful function. A constant temperature is maintained in an electric furnace or oven by a thermostat that controls the phase shift or the on-and-off potential on the grid of the thyratron which furnishes rectified current to the device. Lighting circuits may be dimmed or lighted slowly or turned on and off by thyratrons. Here the thyratron varies the flux (saturation) in an iron-core reactor that is in series with the lighting circuit. The armature of a d-c motor may be supplied with direct current rectified by a thyratron, and the starting, stopping, and speed control may be governed by the voltage phase shift on the grid of the tube. The grid circuits of thyratrons may be energized by light falling upon a photocell.

Mercury-Pool Tubes

A mercury-pool tube uses a pool of cold mercury for a cathode. The conducting medium consists of emitted electrons plus ions produced in the mercury vapor. The conduction due to the mercury vapor is of the arc-discharge type. Since electrons are not readily extracted from a cold metal, some special means must be employed (1) to initiate and (2) to maintain an emission of electrons from the mercury pool. Two general methods are used for initiating the electron emission, one mechanical and one electrical. In the application of mechanical methods an auxiliary anode is connected to the mercury pool for an instant. This may be accomplished (1) by tipping the tube so that the liquid mercury flows to a point where cathode and anode are brought in contact, (2) by moving the anode so as to dip into the mercury pool, or (3) by raising a plunger so that it contacts an auxiliary anode momentarily. In any of these processes the momentary contact between the mercury (cathode) and an auxiliary anode causes a transient current followed by a spark which immediately develops into an arc.

One electrical method for starting electron emission is to place an auxiliary anode (called an ignitor) so that its point dips into the mercury. A transient current from the point to mercury produces a spark for emission. A second electrical method follows a principle employed in early mercury-arc lamps wherein a high transient electric field was induced close to the mercury pool by an inductive voltage "kick." This transient field is sufficient to cause a breakdown and start of conduction on the Townsend and glow-discharge principle.

After the emission of electrons is initiated from the pool, it is maintained by the principle of high field emission. Following the initial emission, electrons are attracted to the main anode. En route, ionization starts, develops into an arc, and the resulting plasma fills the space between the anode and the pool. This plasma comes very close to the mercury and produces a sheath so thin that the electric field is sufficient to secure emission via high-field emission. The emission current originates at one or more cathode spots on the pool. These cathode spots look like little craters on the surface of the pool and they travel about over various paths or eddies.

One important advantage of all mercury-pool tubes is that the mercury cathode is capable of furnishing enormous emission temporarily without damage. Thus the tube will withstand temporary overload and even short circuit without destruction of the cathode. The mercury vapor condenses on the walls of the tube and returns to the pool.

One type of mercury-pool rectifier has been used since the early part of this century. This device and its circuit are shown in Fig. 19. The tube was built with two anodes for full-wave rectification. The glass enclosure had a large upper chamber to provide cooling area. The arc was started by tilting the tube so that the mercury could

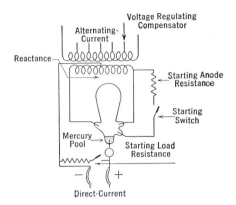

Fig. 19. Full-wave mercury-arc rectifier.

contact the auxiliary starting anode. These tubes had a maximum capacity of about 30 amp and were widely used for charging storage batteries. A few tubes of this type are still in service for rectifying alternating current for use on series d-c street-lighting systems of the luminous-arc type. These early pool-type rectifiers had four disadvantages: (1) They had a fragile glass envelope, (2) they were not suited to the dissipation of heat, (3) they were limited in current capacity, and (4) their rectified voltage and current waves had wide fluctuations and were not suitable where a smooth flow of d-c power was desired. These disadvantages led to the development of the water-cooled metal-tank multielectrode rectifier.

Multielectrode Metal-Tank Rectifier

The multielectrode rectifier was introduced into the electric-power field about 1925. This rectifier consists of a large cylindrical steel tank surrounded by a water-cooled jacket and evacuated to a pressure of one-millionth of an atmosphere. The cathode consists of a pool of mercury at the bottom (Fig. 20). There are from six to eighteen main anodes, like the one shown at the left of the figure. It consists of a graphite cylinder connected to the outside through an insulating bushing in the wall of the tank. The main anodes are placed in a cylindrical insulating shield. The value of using multielectrodes is twofold. First, electricity is transmitted most economically by multiphase circuits (usually three-phase), and, second, the multiphase rectifier gives a smoother output. The latter statement is illustrated by the rectified wave forms of Fig. 20. The

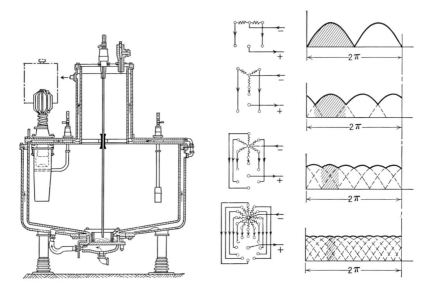

Fig. 20. Cross section of a steel-tank mercury-arc rectifier and rectified wave forms from single and multiphase rectifiers. (Courtesy Allis-Chalmers Manufacturing Company.)

half-wave, three-phase circuit gives a more desirable output wave, and the additions of more phases and anodes will increase the number of ripples but reduce their magnitude. A three-phase supply may be split into six, twelve, and eighteen phases by suitable transformer connections. The steel-tank, mercury-arc rectifier is a very rugged device, effectively cooled by water for any desired capacity and designed to give a smooth voltage, current, and power output.

The steel-tank rectifier is started by the small central starting anode (Fig. 20) which can be lowered into the mercury and then withdrawn by an electromagnet. The breaking of the mercury contact on withdrawal strikes the arc which is then "picked up" by one of the main or auxiliary anodes that has the highest positive potential at that instant. The various main anodes will pick up the arc in rotation as they become sufficiently positive and maintain it until the load is taken over by another of higher positive potential. The output current at any instant is the arithmetic sum of the current of all anodes. Theoretically, only one anode having the highest positive potential would be expected to carry the load current at a given instant. In practice the inductance in transformer windings in series with the anodes causes an anode to carry current for a time after a succeeding anode begins to conduct. Hence in practice, two or more of the multianodes may be carrying part of the load current simultaneously. In the use of the multielectrode rectifier, the rectified d-c load may go to zero, which would extinguish the arc and make it necessary to re-establish ionization whenever the load returns. To avoid this contingency, one or more auxiliary anodes (see right side of Fig. 20) are constantly energized through a circuit independent of the load and they serve to keep gas ions present in the tank continuously. The continuous presence of gas ions in the arc chamber introduces a problem in the operation of the multielectrode rectifier. When any one of the multianodes has a negative inverse voltage on it, it repels electrons and, theoretically, its current goes to zero, but positive ions may be present near it because of electrons en route to an adjacent anode. These positive ions will be attracted to the first anode and their bombardment may produce a hot spot on the anode which will emit electrons. Then this anode becomes a cathode and a reverse arc starts which will become a short circuit from anode to anode in the rectifier. Such a short circuit is called an "arc-back" or a "flash-back" and it will open the protective equipment and cause a shutdown.

The multielectrode steel-tank rectifier is widely used for large-power d-c applications. Over 3,000,000 kva of these rectifiers are in service. The important applications are electric railway service, electrolytic processes in industry, and motive power in steel mills. The advantages of these units over rotary types of conversion are (1) simple and rugged construction, (2) long life, (3) high over-all conversion efficiency, (4) high momentary overload capacity, and (5) quiet operation. Certain disadvantages of the multielectrode tank rectifier are causing it to be superseded by the single-anode type described on the following pages. These disadvantages are: (1) There is a greater possibility of arc-backs due to several anodes in the same arc chamber. (2) The multianodes require large spacing between cathodes and anodes with correspondingly higher arc drops and reduced efficiency. (3) The damage to any anode or part causes the entire unit to be taken out of service for repairs.

Excitron Single-Anode Rectifier

The excitron is a single-anode mercury-pool rectifier embodying the same general principles of construction as outlined for the multianode device. The cross section and control circuit for a sealed-type of excitron are shown in Fig. 21. The unit is enclosed in a permanently sealed steel tank and is cooled by an internal helical water cooling coil which carries away 92 to 95 per cent of the internal heat loss from the mercury-vapor arc. The heat extracted by the circulating water is removed in a heat exchanger so that raw water does not clog or corrode the unit cooling system. The excitron has two anodes. The main anode is a graphite cylinder which is closely surrounded by a control grid. The excitation or auxiliary anode is of metal and is placed at the bottom just above the mercury pool (cathode). An insulating baffle is placed as shown between the grid and cathode to diffuse the arc, assist in cooling, and reduce any tendency for arc-back.

The excitron rectifier is excited by a cathode spot which is maintained continuously by a small arc between the cathode and the excitation anode. This continuous excitation gives rise to the name excitron. The excitation arc is supplied by selenium rectifiers which furnish a current of 7 to 8 amp for an arc drop of 10 to 14 volts. (See circuit for excitation arc in lower part of Fig. 21.) The excitation or holding arc is initiated by an electromagnetic coil beneath the mercury pool. The de-energization of this coil causes an iron plunger to rise (float) and touch the excitation anode. This contact causes current which, in turn, energizes the electromagnetic coil and pulls the plunger down. The latter action produces a spark followed by an arc leading to the mercury-pool cathode. Continuous operation of the excitation arc is assured as long as power is available because if the excitation arc should become extinguished for any reason, the coil is de-energized and the plunger automatically rises and re-establishes the holding arc.

The output of the excitron is controlled by the grid in a manner similar to the action in a thyratron. When a negative potential, with respect to the cathode, is placed on the grid, the anode is prevented from carrying current although it becomes positive with respect to the cathode. If the grid is made positive by phase-shift control at any time during the positive interval of the anode, the main arc will be established and current conduction will continue until the anode goes negative. In addition to controlling the rectifier output, the grid decreases the deionization time at the end of the anode conduction period and aids in reduction of arc-backs at the commutation point.

Excitrons are assembled in groups of 6, 12, or more, and mounted on a common frame for giving multiphase rectification of electric

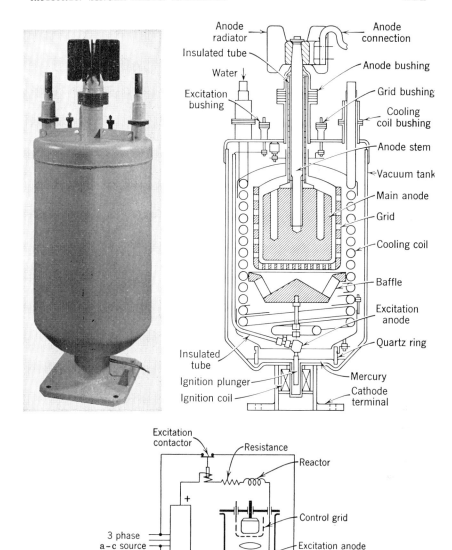

Fig. 21. Assembly, cross section, and circuit of an excitron. (Courtesy Allis-Chalmers Manufacturing Company.)

power. Assemblies are available in voltage ranges of 250 to 1000 volts direct current and all standard kilowatt capacities.

Excitrons have the advantages over the multianode single-tank type in (1) reduced likelihood of arc-backs since main anodes are in separate tanks, (2) higher efficiency because closer spacing between cathodes and anodes gives lower arc drop, and (3) easier maintenance and quicker repairs because in case of failure a spare unit excitron can be used to replace the defective unit.

Excitrons are commercially available as sealed units (that is, fully evacuated and welded), and as pumped type. In the latter, auxiliary pumping equipment is required to maintain the vacuum. The pumped type may be disassembled on the job for repairs.

Ignitron

The ignitron is a three-electrode mercury-pool rectifier developed by Slepian and Ludwig in 1932. Its name was derived from the method of igniting or starting the arc. The device has the same basic construction of graphite anode and mercury-pool cathode as employed in the excitron rectifier, but it differs in that the arc *is started on each positive cycle and no holding arc is used.* The third electrode, called the *ignitor,* terminates in a point which dips into the pool of mercury (Fig. 22). The ignitor is a short rod of ceramic material such as silicon carbide or one having a graphite center with a boron carbide coating.

The theory of operation of the ignitron is simple. With a voltage placed across the cathode-anode circuit (anode positive), nothing happens because there are no electrons emitted from the cold mer-

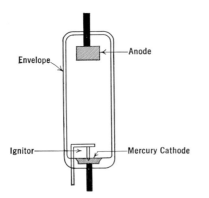

Fig. 22.   Basic ignitron structure.

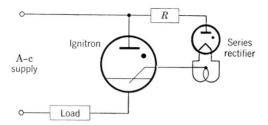

Fig. 23. Anode firing circuit for an ignitron.

cury cathode. However, if a flash of current is passed through a circuit connecting the ignitor and cathode a spark will be created at their contact. This spark will produce some emission, and ionization of the mercury vapor will result. The arc thus established will continue as long as a suitable potential is maintained in the anode-cathode path.

The phenomena accompanying the development of the arc in the ignitron consist of two parts. The mercury does not come into intimate contact with the rough surface of the ignitor which is composed (microscopically) of a number of sharp points. The flash of voltage across the ignitor-cathode circuit causes a potential gradient of approximately one million volts per centimeter across the point contacts, which is high enough to pull electrons out of the cold mercury. Simultaneous with this initiation of electron emission, the rise of current through the high resistance rod of the ignitor produces a potential gradient between the surface of the mercury and the top of the rod. This electric field accelerates the emitted electrons upward to ionization, and the development of an arc to the ignitor terminal which, in turn, is transferred upward to the anode (if positive).

The ignitron finds its application as a controlled rectifier for alternating currents. Since the rectified anode current will go to zero each time the negative voltage loop is applied, it is necessary to ignite the tube for each positive cycle. This result can be obtained by the circuit given in Fig. 23. The hot-cathode diode in the auxiliary circuit conducts current as soon as its anode reaches the ionizing potential. This current passes through the ignitor, causing it to fire the ignitron since its anode becomes positive at the same time. When the ignitron fires, its arc-drop or cathode-anode potential falls to a low value of about 12 volts. This lowers the voltage across the series auxiliary circuit, consisting of rectifier and resistance at ignitor, so that the current in this circuit becomes very low or falls to zero.

The output of the ignitron may be regulated by controlling the time phase of firing or igniting. One method for accomplishing this control substitutes a thyratron for the diodide rectifier in Fig. 23. The desired time of firing the ignitron is secured by either amplitude control or phase-shift control of the thyratron. Another method of firing and controlling the output of the ignition utilizes special electrical networks having "trigger" action.

Ignitrons are often fired by the discharge of a condenser using some form of trigger circuit for initiating the discharge. One reactor-excitation circuit of this type is shown in Fig. 24. This circuit consists of three main parts: the firing circuit proper, a voltage-compensating network, and a phase-shifting reactor. In the firing circuit a capacitor C is charged through a linear reactor (constant reactance throughout range of applied voltage). The capacitor voltage is impressed across the ignitor circuit through a saturable reactor and directional filters (copper oxide rectifiers, page 45). The saturable reactor becomes magnetically saturated when the impressed voltage (and resulting current) reaches a predetermined value. At this critical point the reactance of the saturable reactor decreases and the capacitor discharges a peak current through the ignitor-cathode circuit along the path shown by the arrows.

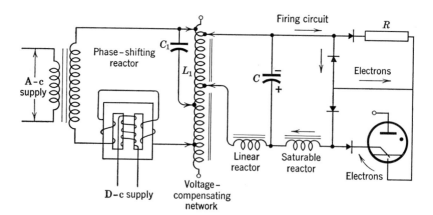

Fig. 24. Network for firing ignitrons (boldface arrows show direction of conventional current flow).

The function of the voltage-compensating network (C_1 and L_1 in parallel) is to furnish a nearly constant input voltage to the firing circuit regardless of fluctuation in the a-c supply. L_1 is a saturating reactor so designed that at normal line voltage its lagging circuit is just balanced by the leading current of capacitor C_1. If the line voltage is too high, the reactor L_1 begins to saturate and draws an excess magnetizing current. This lagging current passing through the phase-shifting reactor (left) produces a quadrature voltage drop and reduces the firing-circuit voltage. If the line voltage is low, L_1 draws a small magnetizing current and the stronger leading capacitor-charging current in passing through the phase-shifting reactor increases the firing-circuit voltage. This voltage-compensating action is so effective that the supply-line voltage can vary 50 per cent without ignition failure.

The phase-shifting transformer (see saturable reactor, page 292) has a three-legged iron core with series additive windings on the outer legs. With the d-c coil unexcited, the series coils are highly inductive and will shift the phase of the voltage applied to the firing circuit. If sufficient direct current is passed through the coil on the central leg to saturate the entire core, the reactance of series windings falls to a low value and the phase of the voltage applied to the firing circuit is advanced. Intermediate values of direct current will give a corresponding degree of phase shift that will determine the time of firing the ignitron.

The a-c supply for this reactor excitation must be the same as that applied to the anode-cathode circuit of the ignitron. The circuit of Fig. 24 will control single-phase, half-wave rectification. Full-wave rectification can be attained by substituting the ignitor-cathode circuit of a second ignitron for resistor R.

Early ignitrons were encased in glass tubes as shown in Fig. 22, but current practice employs metal envelopes in order to (1) facilitate the dissipation of heat, (2) increase physical sturdiness, and (3) improve the psychological reaction of industry toward the use of these tubes. The metal-encased ignitrons are water cooled via helical copper coils on the inside or outside of the enclosure. All small and medium capacity ignitrons are evacuated and given a permanent seal, as shown in Fig. 25. Today all large capacity ignitrons for power rectification are available in both the pumped and sealed type. The permanently sealed unit has been made feasible by new techniques in (1) extracting the gas from all metal parts inside of the tank and (2) producing better seals between the insulators and metal enclosure

W
555I-A

Thermostat

Fig. 25. Ignitron and thermostat used in spot welding. (Courtesy Westinghouse Electric Corporation.)

of the ignitron. A sealed-type ignitron used for resistance welding
is shown in Fig. 25. In service the ignitron must be protected from
overheating and operated at a minimum cost. The cost of operating
the unit involves both that of electricity and of the water cooling
supply. Accordingly, two thermostatic controls are involved in the
protection of the ignitron. One thermostat (shown in Fig. 25) controls a magnetic valve (on and off) to regulate the water temperature within close limits for minimum water consumption. A second
thermostat not shown disconnects the electric power circuit if the
maximum safe temperature of the tube is reached because of water
supply failure.

A large capacity ignitron of the pumped type for power rectification is shown in Fig. 26. In this unit the vacuum is maintained by

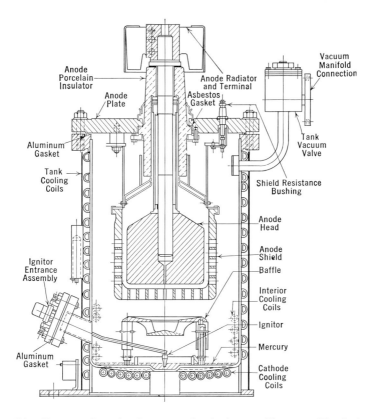

Fig. 26. Cross section of a large-capacity ignitron. (Courtesy Westinghouse
Electric Corporation.)

a mercury condensation pump. Large capacity sealed ignitrons have the same construction as the pumped type except that they are permanently welded and sealed. In addition, the sealed type is equipped with one or more spare ignitors because this electrode is more sensitive to failure than any other part of the device.

On rare occasions arc-backs do occur in ignitrons though they are not damaging to the units. These arc-backs may result from tiny hot spots (craters) which develop on the graphite anode and serve temporarily as emitters. In order to improve the arc-back characteristic, baffles are placed in the ignitron, as illustrated in Fig. 26. A further precautionary measure is the placing of an anode shield or grid around the anode with a suitably timed potential to reduce any tendency to arc-back.

There are two important applications of the ignitron in industry. The first is the control of resistance welding—spot, butt, and line welding. The second is for rectification for d-c power applications. The use of the ignitron has been rather revolutionary in making possible new applications of welding because it assures a uniformity of results never attained previously. In this field a combination of two ignitrons serves as an electronic switch for controlling the period of application of alternating current in making resistance welds. A circuit for performing this function is given in Fig. 27. Two ignitrons are connected with reversed polarity in parallel with each other and in series with the primary of a welding transformer. One ignitor conducts one-half of a cycle, the other on the other half cycle as in full-wave rectification. However, the circuit employed gives alternating current, not a unidirectional current. The electronic switch action

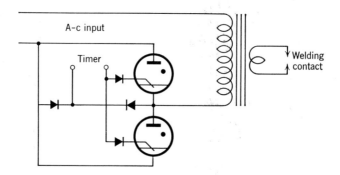

Fig. 27. Circuit for an electronic control switch consisting of two ignitrons.

of these two ignitors is controlled by opening and closing the timer gap of Fig. 27. The ignitors will be fired on alternate half cycles by firing current flowing through the ignitors and the directional copper-oxide rectifiers. These directional rectifiers are necessary because *an ignitor will be destroyed if more than 5 amp flows through it in the reverse direction.* The complete analysis of the operation of the circuit in Fig. 27 is left to the reader.

Ignitron versus Thyratron

Although ignitrons and thyratrons have many characteristics in common, they are not competitive in their applications. The thyratron is essentially a low current and high voltage device. It can be made in small sizes for many small power applications. It has the advantage of greater simplicity of control circuits and the disadvantages of (1) the continuous use of energy for heating the cathode when it is not in use and (2) the likelihood of damage from overload and overvoltage.

The ignitron is essentially a large current and a low or medium voltage device. It is suitable for those applications having high peak current and high power requirements when the cost of the complicated ignition system does not form an excessive percentage of the total cost. The ignitron has the advantage of exceptional sturdiness, and it will withstand temporary heavy overloads and even short circuits which would ruin a thyratron. The ignitron does not require any energy for operating the cathode except that used for the ignitor when the tube is supplying rectified current. The energy for operating the ignitor is very small since the actual firing current flows for a few microseconds.

Capacitron

Another method of "firing" a mercury-pool rectifier uses an insulated conductor placed above the mercury pool. Either a high-frequency field or a high voltage surge impressed on this conductor will serve to control the time and firing of a pool tube. A device using this principle is called the *capacitron*. The device has found little application to date.

Cold-Cathode Tubes

A number of tubes using a cold metal (other than mercury) for cathodes have been developed and employed for useful purposes. These tubes are filled with inert gas under low pressure and operate

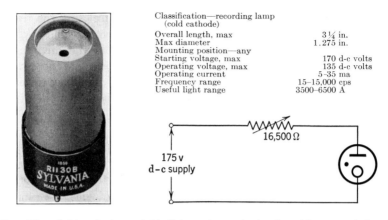

Classification—recording lamp
(cold cathode)

Overall length, max	3 ¼ in.
Max diameter	1.275 in.
Mounting position—any	
Starting voltage, max	170 d-c volts
Operating voltage, max	135 d-c volts
Operating current	5–35 ma
Frequency range	15–15,000 cps
Useful light range	3500–6500 A

Fig. 28. Cold-cathode variable-light tube and circuit. (Courtesy Sylvania Electric Products Inc.)

on the principle of the glow discharge. They serve (1) as sources of light, (2) for voltage regulation, (3) for rectification, and (4) as "trigger" or control tubes. The *glow tube* has two cold electrodes and gives forth light (negative glow) when the breakdown voltage is applied (see Fig. 11, page 181). If a direct voltage is applied, the glow appears on the surface of the cathode, but if alternating voltage is impressed, the glow appears at both electrodes since each serves alternately as a cathode. With simple electrodes and with a constant source of potential the tube serves as a constant source of light and may be used as a signal light, pilot light, and test light. The source of light between two electrodes may be varied by changing the geometry of the electrode construction. Thus if the cathode is a small solid cylinder closely surrounded by a hollow cylinder, the light appears at the ends of the electrodes. The intensity of the light produced will vary as the value of the current conduction. Thus with proper construction a glow tube may become a modulated light source. Such tubes have been used for recording sound on film (light on sound track), for early types of television receivers, and for facsimile transmission. They are known as glow modulator tubes. A commercial tube of this type, its rating, and its circuit are illustrated in Fig. 28.

For high-speed photography and stroboscopic work special types of glow tubes have been developed. One of these tubes (Fig. 29) utilizes a double-grid structure which permits quick firing and gives brilliant flashes lasting for only a few microseconds. This tube was developed by Germeshausen and Edgerton. The cathode cup contains a cesium compound that liberates cesium at a relatively low temperature. Breakdown is initiated between two of the electrodes, grid to cathode, or grid to grid.

One important characteristic of the glow-discharge tube is the nearly constant voltage drop for a wide range in current variation. This property is utilized on a form of glow tube known as a *voltage-regulator tube*. A commercial regulator tube of this type is illustrated in Fig. 30. Larger tubes having constant operating voltages up to 150 volts and currents up to 40 ma are available.

Cold-cathode tubes filled with inert gas are also employed as rectifiers and relays. Millions of a three-electrode tube in this class

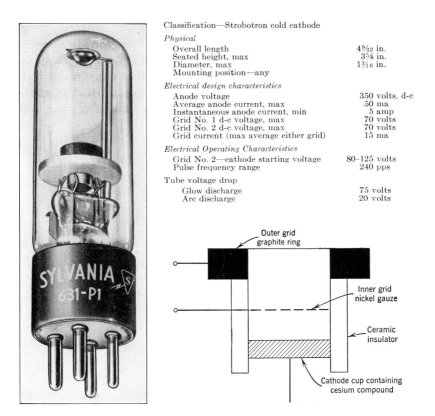

Classification—Strobotron cold cathode

Physical

Overall length	4⁹⁄₃₂ in.
Seated height, max	3⁵⁄₈ in.
Diameter, max	1³⁄₁₆ in.
Mounting position—any	

Electrical design characteristics

Anode voltage	350 volts, d-c
Average anode current, max	50 ma
Instantaneous anode current, min	5 amp
Grid No. 1 d-c voltage, max	70 volts
Grid No. 2 d-c voltage, max	70 volts
Grid current (max average either grid)	15 ma

Electrical Operating Characteristics

Grid No. 2—cathode starting voltage	80–125 volts
Pulse frequency range	240 pps

Tube voltage drop

Glow discharge	75 volts
Arc discharge	20 volts

Outer grid graphite ring

Inner grid nickel gauze

Ceramic insulator

Cathode cup containing cesium compound

Fig. 29. Stroboscopic cold-cathode light source. (Courtesy Sylvania Electric Products Inc.)

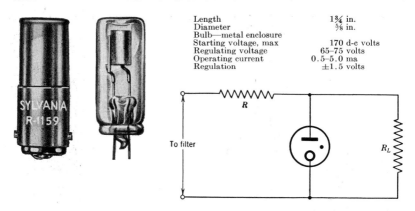

Length	1¾ in.
Diameter	⅝ in.
Bulb—metal enclosure	
Starting voltage, max	170 d-c volts
Regulating voltage	65–75 volts
Operating current	0.5–5.0 ma
Regulation	±1.5 volts

Fig. 30. Miniature voltage-regulator tube, rating, and circuit. (Courtesy Sylvania Electric Products Inc.)

have been used in subscribers' telephone sets to provide selective ringing on four-party telephone lines. The essential parts of this tube are shown in Fig. 31. The tube employs two semicircular bell-shaped disks as cathodes. Between these cathodes is placed an anode consisting of a small circular rod enclosed in a glass tube. The tube

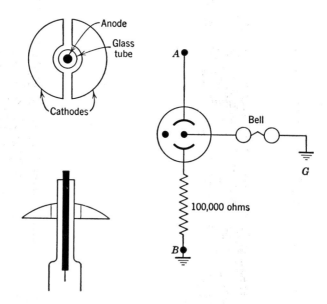

Fig. 31. Construction and circuit of a cold-cathode relay tube.

contains neon gas under low pressure. A nominal breakdown potential of 70 volts is required to create a glow discharge from cathode to cathode, but because of greater spacing a breakdown potential of 175 volts is necessary for a like discharge from either cathode to the anode. However, while a glow discharge exists between cathodes, a potential of only 75 volts positive is necessary for conduction between either cathode and the anode.

This tube is used in the circuit shown on the right of Fig. 31. To ring the bell a pulsating unidirectional potential is impressed between line A and ground. This voltage causes a glow discharge between cathodes with a minute current through the high resistance to the ground. If the ground (and anode) are positive for these pulses, the pulsating ringing current passes through the telephone bell. Individual party ringing is effected because the bells are selective with respect to the direction of current pulses and are properly distributed between the line wires and ground. The commercial relay tube described is illustrated in Fig. 32.

One type of gaseous rectifier starts with a cold cathode and operates on thermionic emission. The tube contains inert gas and has an oxide-coated cathode without a heater. With a minimum peak anode supply potential of 300 volts, a glow discharge takes place and the resulting bombardment of the oxide-coated cathode raises its temperature to the point necessary for satisfactory thermionic emission. After the cathode is heated, the cathode-anode average potential drops to about 24 volts. This voltage is higher than that of a hot-cathode type with heater because the energy for heating the cathode is developed in the cathode-anode circuit. These tubes are known as

Fig. 32. Cold-cathode relay tube. (Courtesy Western Electric Company.)

ionic-heated cathode rectifiers. The output current must be limited by a suitable load impedance, and a minimum cathode-anode current is required to keep the cathode hot. Examples of the ionic-heated cathodes are the OZ4 and the OZ4-G. The principle of the ionic-heated cathode is employed in the operation of some types of fluorescent lamps.

The grid-glow tube is a gas-filled, three-electrode tube having a cold cathode. The tube functions somewhat like the thyratron through the trigger action of its grid. Since it has a cold cathode the tube conduction is of the glow-discharge type involving much higher anode and grid voltages. These higher voltages mean a higher percentage of loss in the tube and lower rectification efficiency. However, the cold cathode does not consume any energy even though the tube is connected in a circuit continuously. The grid-glow tube is constructed much differently from a thyratron, as shown in Fig. 33a. The anode is a wire encased in a glass tube and placed at the center of a much larger cylindrical tube which constitutes the cathode. A metal tubular shield surrounds the glass tube and anode. The grid is a small ring surrounding the projecting top of the anode. The anode is usually operated at a voltage above the breakdown voltage for the glow discharge of the gas from anode to cathode but below the breakdown for grid-to-anode spacing. If the grid is negative or of low potential, most of the lines of the electrostatic field terminate on the grid and no breakdown from cathode to anode can occur. The usual type of circuit for utilizing the grid-glow tube is shown in Fig. 33b. The shield is connected to the cathode outside the tube by a resistance of the order of 5 to 10 meg. The control grid potential is adjusted by the values of R and C. The load in the anode circuit is usually a relay. Changes in R or C or even in the value of the impressed alternating or direct voltage will serve to fire the tube. Change in the capacity of C may be produced by the capacity of an approaching human hand or some other object. A photocell may be substituted for R or C, whereby a change in light will fire the tube.

The cathode of the grid-glow tube is indestructible, but too high a voltage on the anode will cause the glow discharge to change to an arc and thus burn out the tube.

The grid-glow tube is used where a very sensitive control is desired to operate a relay and where the current delivered by the tube is sufficient to meet the requirements of an application.

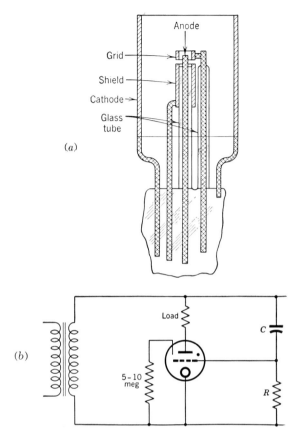

Fig. 33. Construction and circuit of a grid-glow tube.

Gaseous Phototube

The admission of a small amount of inert gas into a vacuum photo-tube will greatly increase the current resulting from light falling upon the cathode. This amplification of current or increase in sensitivity may be tenfold in value, but it is usually limited to the order of three to seven times the current in a vacuum. This increase of current parallels that found in thermionic tubes containing gas, but the cause of the phenomenon is somewhat different. In the thermionic tube the increase is the result of the neutralization of negative space charge near the cathode, whereas space charge is of little consequence in the phototube. The reasons for the current increase in the gaseous tube are (1) the additional ionic current which results as soon as the ionizing potential is reached and (2) an increase in emission of electrons from the cathode due to the bombardment by positive ions. The change in anode current with rise in anode potential is given in Fig. 34 for five different amounts of light flux in lumens falling on the cathode. Obviously, a low anode potential attracts all the primary electrons emitted. At 20 volts (approximately) the ionizing potential is reached and beyond that the current increases with voltage, at first slowly, later becoming accumulative in effect following the theory of the Townsend discharge described in the chapter on gaseous conduction. The potential applied to the gaseous phototube circuit is 90 volts and the actual cathode-anode drop is limited by the load resistance. The trend of the curve will depend on the gas pressure and other factors. The operation of the gaseous tube must be kept below the glow-discharge point or the control of its operation by incident light is lost.

One disadvantage of the gaseous phototube is its poor dynamic response. Dynamic response refers to the speed with which the anode current follows changes in the light incident on the cathode. It is important when there is a high frequency in the light changes. The poor dynamic response is due to the current conduction by ions in this cell. At a given instant the space between the cathode and anode contains a large number of electrons and positive ions. The electrons are swept out of the space instantly by the positive poten-

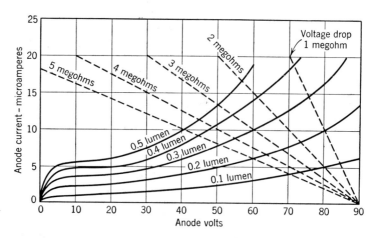

Fig. 34. Anode-current voltage characteristic of a gaseous phototube. (Courtesy Westinghouse Electric Corporation.)

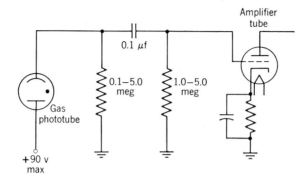

Fig. 35. Typical circuit for sound reproduction.

tial on the anode, but the positive ions, being relatively ponderous, move much more slowly toward the cathode. If the light drops to zero at a given instant, the positive ions take a little interval of time to reach the cathode; when they do reach it they may release a few electrons which then dart to the anode. Thus, although the light goes to zero instantly, the anode current lags in making the change.

A typical circuit illustrating the application of this tube for sound reproduction is given in Fig. 35.

PROBLEMS

1. The mercury-vapor rectifier tube of Fig. 5 is connected in series with a supply of 115 volts a-c and a load resistor. If the arc drop is assumed to be 15 volts and the peak pulse current is 0.5 amp, what is the minimum value of load resistance to protect the tube from overload on continuous service?

2. The phanotron of Fig. 6 is connected for half-wave rectification in series with a load resistor to a 230 volt a-c supply. The rated average load current is 10 amp which is 0.318 times the peak of the current pulse. Assume an arc drop of 15 volts and calculate (a) the magnitude of a load resistor to permit full load continuously.

(b) Now assume that, with the calculated resistor in the circuit and with the cathode only partially heated and giving a saturation emission of only 2 amp, the supply-line switch is closed. What current will flow? What voltage exists across the cathode-anode circuit? What will happen to the phanotron?

3. (a) The thyratron of Fig. 17 is connected in series with a load resistor and 115 volt a-c supply line. What should be the value of the load resistance to limit the current to the rated peak value?

(*b*) Assume that while the thyratron is cold and there are zero volts on the grid the supply line is connected to the cathode-anode circuit followed by a closing of the circuit for heating the filamentary cathode. What will happen?

4. The thyratron of Fig. 17 is in normal operating condition and a direct voltage of 400 volts is to be applied to its anode. What voltage must be applied to its grid to prevent firing? Give the range of grid voltage values necessary to cover the complete range of uncertainty arising from ambient temperatures.

5. Assume that the thyratron of Fig. 17 is to be fired by an alternating voltage which rises to +30 volts maximum and that the arc drop from cathode to grid is 10 volts. What should be the value of a resistor placed in series with the grid to limit the grid current to 0.11 amp?

6. The strobotron of Fig. 29 is flashed by the discharge of a 4 μf condenser (charged to 200 volts) in 100 microseconds. How much power does this represent in watts?

7. The thyratron of Fig. 17 is to be operated in a circuit having an impressed a-c sine-wave voltage of 710 rms. What negative bias voltage should be applied to the grid to cause the tube to fire with a phase-angle lag of 30 degrees, 45 degrees, 60 degrees, 90 degrees?

8. In the phase-shift circuit of Fig. 15, R has a value of 400 ohms and L of 500 millihenries. Calculate the angle of a phase shift on a 60-cycle circuit.

9. In the phase-shift circuit of Fig. 15, R has a value of 4000 ohms and C of 2 μf. Calculate the angle of phase shift on a 60-cycle circuit. (See text for relationship of R and C in shift circuit.)

10. What should be the extreme values of R in Problem 9 to give phase shifts of 20 degrees and 75 degrees?

11. Connect a gaseous phototube into a circuit using a 90 volt battery and a 5 meg resistor. Assume a light flux of 0, 0.1, 0.2, 0.3, 0.4, and 0.5 lumen falling on the cathode of the tube, and determine the voltage drop across the resistor for each case using the curves of Fig. 34. Plot curve of voltage drop versus lumens.

REFERENCES

1. Hull, A. W., "Hot-Cathode Thyratrons," *Gen. Elec. Rev.*, **32** (1929).
2. Winograd, H., "Development of Excitron-Type Rectifier," *Trans. Am. Inst. Elec. Engrs.*, **63** (1944).
3. Slepian, J., and L. R. Ludwig, "A New Method for Initiating the Cathode of and Arc," *Trans. Am. Inst. Elec. Engrs.*, **52**, 693–700 (1933).
4. Germeshausen, K. J., and H. E. Edgerton, "A Cold-Cathode Arc-Discharge Tube," *Elec. Eng.*, **55**, 790 (1936).
5. Coolidge, A. W., Jr., "A High Current Thyratron," *Elec. Eng.*, August 1951.

chapter 8

Rectification
and Inversion

Importance of Rectification

Rectification of alternating current or the conversion of alternating current to direct current is exceedingly important because (1) it is more simple and economical to generate and to distribute electric energy as alternating current, and (2) many applications of electric energy in the field of electric power and communication require the use of unidirectional or direct current. Some of these applications requiring the use of direct current are the power supply to the anodes of electron tubes, electroplating, chemical processes, charging of storage batteries, and operating series railway motors and adjustable-speed d-c motors.

Rectification can be brought about by (1) electronic methods and (2) commutating methods. This textbook is concerned primarily with the electronic methods, but for purposes of comparison some of the commutating methods will be given brief consideration. Inversion, the process of converting a direct current to an alternating current, may likewise be performed by both electronic and commutating means.

Commutating Rectifiers

Commutating rectifiers may be of the vibrating contact, the synchronous motor-driven contact, or the rotary type of commutator. A *vibrating rectifier* consists of an electromagnet which vibrates a spring containing movable contacts. The period of vibration is controlled or tuned by the pulses or alternations of the current, and the movable contacts serve to reverse the direction of current flow so that the outgoing current is rectified or unidirectional. Devices employing this principle were used in earlier years for charging storage batteries and for rectification in telephone-ringing machines. Today the commutating vibrator is widely used as an inverter in portable radio equipment, and in some sets it performs the double function of inversion followed by rectification.

The circuit for a typical vibrating type of inverter is shown in Fig. 1. The closing of switch S energizes the driving coil over a path from the grounded $+$ side of the battery, the driving coil, and the right half of primary winding P to the negative side of the battery. The resulting current energizes the driving magnet and pulls the vibrator V to the right-hand contact. The closing of this contact (1) sends a relatively large d-c pulse of current through the right half of winding P and (2) places a short circuit around the driving coil. The first action induces a voltage in the output side of the transformer, and the second serves to de-energize the driving magnet. The spring of the vibrator now swings the movable member V to the left until it engages the left-hand contact where it sends a pulse of current through the left half of the primary winding P. This new current pulse reverses the flux in the transformer core and reverses

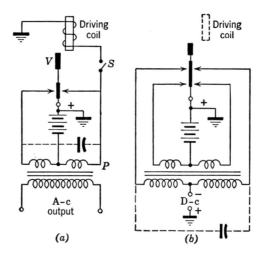

Fig. 1. Vibrator types of inverters and rectifiers. (*a*) Inversion. (*b*) Combined inversion and rectification.

the voltage induced in the output side of the transformer. In the next instant the vibrator V swings again to the right owing to its spring action plus the re-established current through the driving coil. The repetition of the foregoing action produces an alternating voltage at the output terminals of the step-up transformer. This a-c output voltage may be rectified by a vacuum diode, by a small metallic rectifier, or by the addition of two contacts at the vibrator and a mid-tapped secondary to the inverter circuit. The additions are shown in part (b) of Fig. 1. There the driving circuit (not shown) acts in the same manner as before. A study of this circuit will show that the added contacts serve to reverse the voltage between the mid-tap of the output winding of the transformer and ground in such a way as to make the resulting voltage pulses unidirectional, and thus give full-wave rectification. A smoothing filter must be added to give an output suitable for the power supply for radio receiving sets.

The preceding explanation has been an oversimplification of the complete theory of action involved in the vibrator type of inverter and combined inverter and rectifier. Condensers are used in the circuits to reduce arcing at the contacts, but the complete theory of action and design involves a proper balance and tuning of the L and C constants in the circuits.

A new type of mechanical rectifier or *contact converter* was developed by Siemens-Schuckert in Berlin during World War II. This contact converter is capable of rectifying currents as high as 10,000 amp at 400 volts with efficiencies of the order of 97 per cent. The principle of rectifying alternating current by reversing the circuit in step with the alternations is old in the art. In theory it is necessary only to reverse the circuit while the voltage and current pass through the zero point on the cycle. To effect this requirement is difficult because of the short time available for mechanically moving the contacts at the time when the rate of current change is the maximum. Any phase-angle difference between the voltage and the current naturally complicates the problem of commutation. If the wave form of the circuit can be modified to hold the voltage at near zero for a short time interval at the points of voltage and current reversal, it is obvious that the mechanical problem of reversal would be simplified. This important advantage is brought about in the new contact rectifier by inserting saturable inductances or chokes in the a-c leads. These chokes saturate at relatively low values of flux and current, so that they produce a high impedance to current change at low values of current (region when passing through zero) and little impedance at higher current values. The application of the saturable choke gives the necessary delay in the voltage and current change and permits the mechanical reversal of contacts operated by a small synchronous motor. Many mechanical and electrical refinements are necessary to make the contact converter successful. The discussion of these refinements is out of the province of this book. Contact converters are now manufactured in the United States.

Rotary commutating rectifiers have been of three types: simple commutators, motor-generator sets, and rotary converters. The simple commutator device consists of a synchronous motor driving a commutator at such a speed that the polarity is reversed at the proper rate to give a rectified or unidirectional current in the output. This device was widely used in early radio transmitters and X-ray equipment and today has application for rectifying high voltages for precipitation processes in the removal of smoke, dust, and chemical byproducts. The motor-generator rectifier consists of an a-c motor operating from an a-c system which drives a d-c generator. This process is an electrical-mechanical plus a mechanical-electrical conversion process. It has the advantage of good control of the d-c output voltage and the disadvantages of high initial cost, lower efficiency, and the complications of rotating equipment. This system is being replaced by electronic methods of conversion. The rotary converter consists of a single rotating unit which consumes alternating current in motor action and gives forth a d-c output. The output is partly the result of pure rectification and partly of a conversion process. This device has a lower cost and a much higher efficiency than the motor-generator device. Its disadvantage lies in inflexibility in the control of the output (d-c) voltage. This unit once had a wide application in the electric railway field but is being replaced by electronic rectifiers.

All these commutating devices used for conversion of alternating current to direct current may be employed equally well through a reverse process to bring about inversion.

Electrolytic Rectifiers

An electrolytic rectifier consists of two dissimilar electrodes placed in an electrolyte. One type of cell uses an aluminum plate and a lead plate for the electrodes and a solution of ammonium phosphate for the electrolyte. In this cell electrons pass readily from the aluminum electrode to the lead electrode but not vice versa. Thus the cell may be used as a single-wave rectifier. The electrolytic rectifier has been obsolete since 1930.

Electronic Rectifying Devices

The theory and characteristics of the following eight electronic rectifiers have been covered in the preceding chapters.

1. Vacuum diodes
2. Crystal diodes
3. Metallic rectifiers
4. Germanium junction rectifiers

5. Silicon junction rectifiers
6. Gas and vapor diodes
7. Mercury pool devices
8. Gas and vapor triodes

The first five of these rectifiers may be used in a simple circuit like Fig. 2a to produce half-wave rectification. These same five rectifying devices have been shown to possess a forward conducting characteristic of the type indicated by the heavy full line of Fig. 2b. The tangent at any point on this curve represents the internal a-c resistance of the device for this point of operation. In the operation of the rectifying circuit we are primarily interested in the current which results from the applied voltage. Therefore, we should add the iR_L or drop across the load to the drop across the rectifying device. This is shown graphically in Fig. 2b and results in the dotted dynamic curve of operation referred to the applied voltage e. This dynamic curve is approximately linear. Hence for the purpose of analysis on an ideal basis, we may use a straight line as indicated in Fig. 3. This assumes that both the device and load are linear. If a sine wave of voltage is applied to this device, the result will

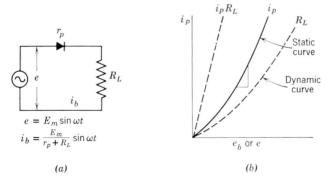

$$e = E_m \sin \omega t$$
$$i_b = \frac{E_m}{r_p + R_L} \sin \omega t$$

(a)   (b)

Fig. 2. Basic load curves of vacuum tube and semiconductor rectifier.

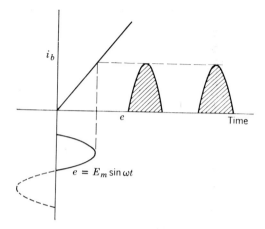

Fig. 3. Half-wave rectification in vacuum tube.

consist of sine-wave pulses of current as shown in Fig. 3. Subsequent analysis of current values will assume this ideal condition.

The last three devices in the preceding list of rectifiers contain gas or vapor and all of them have a nearly constant arc drop while in operation. Accordingly, their typical operating characteristic will be a vertical linear line as shown by the heavy line of Fig. 4a. If, as before, we desire the characteristic referred to the applied voltage,

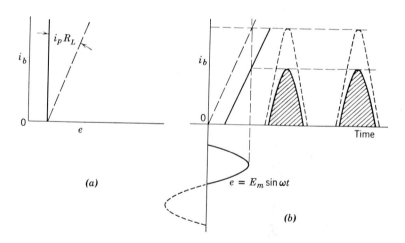

Fig. 4. Half-wave rectification in gaseous tube.

the drop across the load iR_L is added graphically as shown by the dotted dynamic line of Fig. 4a. This dynamic line is plotted as a heavy line in Fig. 4b and a sine wave of voltage is applied as before, giving current pulses of reduced magnitude. The amount of current reduction arising from the arc drop is indicated graphically by dotted lines wherein the operating characteristic has been moved back to the origin.

The mercury pool tubes and the gaseous triodes may have a further reduction in the area of the resultant current pulses if grid control is exercised to delay the time of firing.

Single-Phase Rectifier Circuits

The simplest circuit for rectifying single-phase alternating current gives half-wave rectification. Such a circuit is indicated in Fig. 5a, where the bold-faced arrow represents the rectifying unit and the direction of conventional current flow. When considering this or any other rectifying circuit, the engineer desires to know the magnitude of the direct voltage and current, the regulation of the load voltage, and the efficiency to be expected from the rectifying process. All these values depend upon a number of variables, such as the constants of the supply (transformer), the characteristic of the rectifying unit, and the nature of the load. These variables complicate the analytical solution. However, it is possible to make certain assumptions which reduce the circuit to an ideal basis from which a useful analysis may be made.

Referring to Fig. 5a, assume (1) an ideal source without resistance and having a constant voltage, (2) that the impressed emf is a pure sine wave, (3) that the rectifying unit has zero resistance in the forward direction of current and infinite resistance in the reverse direction, and (4) that the load is a pure ohmic resistance. With these assumptions, let a sine-wave alternating voltage as shown in Fig. 5b be impressed across the rectifying circuit. This will produce a rectified half wave of current as indicated in Fig. 5c. This half wave of current is of a sine form since $i = (E_m/R_L) \sin \omega t$. During the last half of the cycle the rectifier will block the electrons and no current will result. The same loop or half wave of current will flow on both the input (left) and the output (right) sides of the rectifier. This current flowing through the load resistance R_L will produce an iR_L voltage drop which is likewise of a sine-wave form.

Since the function of rectification is to convert alternating current to direct current, we are primarily interested in the equivalent value

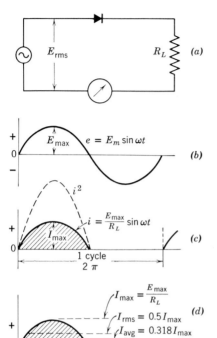

Fig. 5. Circuit and waves for half-wave rectification.

of the direct current. This value will be measured by a d-c ammeter placed in the circuit of Fig. 5a. This d-c value is the average value of the instantaneous rectified current over one cycle, or a period corresponding to 2π radians. This average value may be determined by a graphical and arithmetic process by measuring the instantaneous value of current at a series of equally spaced points along the time axis and then dividing the sum of these values by the total number of points in a cycle. A more accurate solution may be obtained by measuring the area under the rectified current pulse and dividing by 2π. The more direct solution is to apply the method of calculus to the problem, thus:

$$I_{dc} = I_{avg} = \frac{1}{2\pi} \int_0^{\pi} I_m \sin \omega t \, d(\omega t) \tag{1}$$

$$= \frac{2I_m}{2\pi} = 0.318 I_m \tag{2}$$

An a-c ammeter inserted in the rectifying circuit of Fig. 5a gives a different reading from the d-c meter first considered. This difference arises from the fact that the a-c meter registers effective or root-mean square (rms) value rather than average. The heating or effective value of a current varies as the square of the instantaneous current. Hence to determine the effective value of the rectified current graphically, it would be necessary first to plot squared values of the instantaneous current as suggested by the dotted i^2 curve on Fig. 5c. The effective area under the dotted i^2 curve may be obtained by the graphical point method or by calculus thus:

$$\text{Effective area} = \int_0^\pi I_m{}^2 \sin^2 \omega t \, d(\omega t) = I_m{}^2 \left(\frac{\theta}{2} - \frac{\sin 2\omega t}{4}\right)_0^\pi \quad (3)$$

$$\text{Effective current} = I_m \sqrt{\frac{\text{effective area}}{2\pi}} = 0.5 I_m \quad (4)$$

The integrations of equations 1 and 3 are the standard procedures for obtaining the average and effective values of periodic functions.

The average and effective values of rectified current for the half-wave circuit are indicated in Fig. 5d. Summarizing these values:

Input side	*Output side*
E_{rms} = impressed voltage	$E_{\text{dc}} = 0.318 E_m = 0.45 E_{\text{rms}}$
$I_{\text{rms}} = 0.5 I_m$	$I_{\text{dc}} = 0.318 I_m$

The capacity of the input transformer to a rectifier is used inefficiently when supplying power for half-wave rectification because only one-half of the sine wave of current is passed and the secondary winding carries a d-c component of current which magnetizes the iron core and increases the core losses. These factors plus the increased heating losses result in a reduction of the permissible transformer output. This reduction is expressed by the term utility factor. *Utility factor* is the ratio of the permissible rectifier load without overheating to the normal unity power factor load that the transformer will carry.

Two types of circuits are used for full-wave, single-phase rectification. One circuit uses a transformer with a mid-tap in the secondary winding, as shown in parts (a) and (b) of Fig. 6. For one half-cycle of the impressed alternating voltage E_{rms} the upper half of the transformer secondary and the upper diode conducts current, and for the second half-cycle the lower half of the transformer and the lower

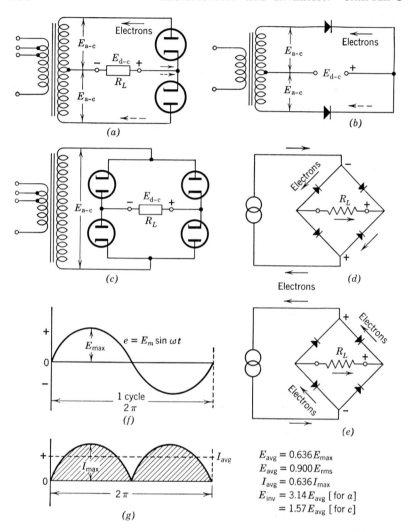

Fig. 6. Circuit and waves for full-wave rectification. (Conventional current flows in direction of boldface arrows.)

diode operates. If a pure sine wave of voltage like part f of Fig. 6 appears across each half of the transformer secondary winding, both halves of the cycle will be rectified as shown in part (g) of this figure. The connection to the midpoint on the secondary of the transformer serves to reverse the polarity on the lower rectifier with respect to the upper one. Since both half-waves of current pass through the transformer (though dividing in the secondary), there is no d-c component of flux in the transformer core to increase core losses, and the current in the primary is normal. The second type of circuit to give full-wave rectification is shown in parts (c), (d), and (e) of Fig. 6. This is known as a bridge circuit since it uses four rectifying units connected in a form similar to the Wheatstone bridge. The rectified currents flow through two diodes in series and the action for the two halves of each cycle is clearly shown in parts (d) and (e) of the figure. The resulting impressed voltage and current waves are the same as for the first full-wave rectifier circuit (Fig. 6, parts f and g).

For the same assumptions made for the preceding half-wave rectifier circuit, the relation between the input and output sides of either full-wave rectifier circuit may be readily calculated. Since both halves of the cycle are rectified, the current and voltage on the input side are normal effective values and those on the d-c or output side are average values. Thus

$$E_{\text{rms}} = \text{applied rms value} = \frac{E_{\text{max}}}{\sqrt{2}}$$

$$I_{\text{rms}} = \frac{E_{\text{rms}}}{R_L} = \frac{E_{\text{max}}}{\sqrt{2}R_L} = 0.707 \frac{E_{\text{max}}}{R_L}$$

$$E_{\text{dc}} = E_{\text{avg}} = 0.636 E_{\text{max}} = 0.9 E_{\text{rms}}$$

$$I_{\text{dc}} = I_{\text{avg}} = 0.636 I_{\text{max}} = 0.9 I_{\text{rms}}$$

Ripple Factor

The rectified voltage and current output of any rectifier consists of a series of unidirectional waves or ripples. For some applications these variations are not objectionable but for others they must be smoothed out by filters. For all cases the relative magnitude of the ripple is important in the comparison of rectifying circuits. The comparison is made in terms of ripple factor. *Ripple factor is the ratio of effective value of the alternating components of the rectified voltage or current to the average value.* In equation form ripple factor is

$$r_f = \frac{\text{effective rectified a-c component } (I_{\text{rms}}')}{\text{average current } (I_{\text{dc}})}$$

The various components of current associated with ripple factor are illustrated in Fig. 7. Here part (a) shows the single current pulse

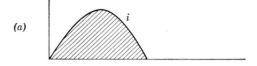

(a)

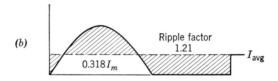

(b)

Ripple factor
1.21

$0.318 I_m$

I_{avg}

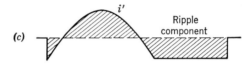

(c)

i'

Ripple
component

(d)

· D–c component

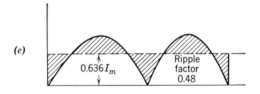

(e)

$0.636 I_m$

Ripple
factor
0.48

Fig. 7. Ripple factors.

of half-wave rectification, part (b) shows the splitting of the pulse into a d-c component and a ripple component. By continuing with Fig. 7, we see that parts (c) and (d) give an actual separation of the components, and part (e) illustrates the components for full-wave rectification.

In accordance with the preceding definition, the ripple factor is the ratio of the effective current represented by i' of Fig. 7c to the d-c component shown in Fig. 7d. This ratio may be computed by following the preceding form of calculation. Thus the instantaneous a-c ripple component i' may be represented as:

$$i' = i - I_{dc} \tag{5}$$

and the total rms value of the ripple component I_{rms}' by the calculus is

$$I_{rms}' = \sqrt{\frac{1}{2\pi} \int_0^{2\pi} (i - I_{dc})^2 \, d\theta}$$

$$= \sqrt{\frac{1}{2\pi} \int_0^{2\pi} (i^2 - 2I_{dc}i + I_{dc}^2) \, d\theta} \tag{6}$$

The first term in this expression is the rms value of the total current I_{rms}. The $\int_0^{2\pi} i \, d\theta$ part of the second term integrates to the average value I_{dc}, and the last term is simply I_{dc}^2 after the limits are applied. Thus

$$I_{rms}' = \sqrt{I_{rms}^2 - 2I_{dc}^2 + I_{dc}^2} = \sqrt{I_{rms}^2 - I_{dc}^2}$$

and

$$r_f = \frac{\sqrt{I_{rms}^2 - I_{dc}^2}}{I_{dc}} = \sqrt{\left(\frac{I_{rms}}{I_{dc}}\right)^2 - 1} \tag{7}$$

Substitution of values from the preceding development into equation 7 gives

$$\text{Half wave } \frac{I_{rms}}{I_{dc}} = \frac{0.5I_{max}}{0.318I_{max}} = 1.57$$

$$r_f \text{ (half wave)} = \sqrt{1.57^2 - 1} = 1.21 \tag{8}$$

$$\text{Full wave } \frac{I_{rms}}{I_{dc}} = \frac{0.707I_{max}}{0.636I_{max}} = 1.11$$

$$r_f \text{ (full wave)} = \sqrt{1.11^2 - 1} = 0.482 \tag{9}$$

The reader may experience some difficulty in obtaining concepts of the components of current discussed in the preceding paragraphs. If so, the circuit diagrams of Fig. 8 may be helpful. In part (a) of this figure, a 1:1 ratio current transformer has been inserted in the

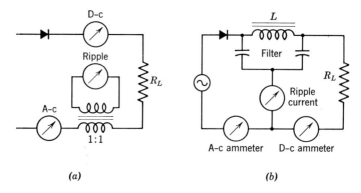

Fig. 8. Circuits for separating components of rectified current.

load circuit and connected to an a-c ammeter. Here, when the ripple component of current represented by Fig. 7c passes through the current transformer, it will induce a change of flux in the core and, in turn, a replica of itself in the central meter. Thus the ripple component will be measured directly. In Fig. 8b, a smoothing filter, with assumed zero energy losses, is inserted in the rectifier load circuit. Now only a true direct current flows in the load resistor R_L and the d-c ammeter reads $0.318 I_m$. The a-c ammeter in the lower line conducts the current pulse shown in Fig. 7a and reads the effective value $0.5 I_m$. Obviously, the remaining current component delivered by the filter to the lower line must be the differential or ripple current which is measured by the a-c ammeter in that circuit.

Rectification Ratios

The preceding discussion of ripple factor leads to the idea that the heating losses $(I^2 R)$ which occur in the various parts of the complete rectifier circuit are increased by the irregular wave forms of current that are inherent in the rectifying process. This may be illustrated by comparing the heating loss produced in the load resistance R_L by a smooth or filtered direct current with that resulting from the actual current waves of Fig. 7a and 7e. The resulting ratio may be termed the *ratio* of rectification. From the preceding calculations

$$\text{Ratio of rectification} \atop \text{(half-wave)} = \frac{(I_{\text{dc}})^2 R_L}{(I_{\text{rms}})^2 R_L} \times 100 = \frac{(0.318 I_m)^2}{(0.5 I_m)^2} \times 100$$

$$= 40.6 \text{ per cent} \tag{10}$$

The ratio of equation 10 is sometimes called the efficiency of rectification. The latter terminology is somewhat misleading since the over-all power efficiency for the assumed conditions (zero losses) must be 100 per cent. The real significance of the ratio of rectification is that it gives a qualitative indication of the increased heat losses that occur wherever a nonsinusoidal and pulsating current flows through resistance elements in the actual rectifier circuit such as the transformer windings and in the load without a filter. A second method of expressing the increased heat losses is by the term current *form factor* which is the ratio of the root-mean-square to the average value.

The actual resistance and power loss of a rectifying unit will alter the voltage and current relations and efficiencies developed in the preceding discussion where an ideal status was assumed. The rectifying units in any of the circuits considered may be high-vacuum diodes, gas or vapor diodes, or semiconductor rectifiers. The differences in the characteristics of each of these units were discussed in earlier sections. It is possible to make some generalization covering these characteristics and thereby make a closer approximation for some factors of rectification. Thus for vacuum diodes and semiconductor units the assumption may be made that the resistance is constant. If the resistances of such a rectifier are represented by the symbol R_R, leaving the load resistance R_L, then for any given set of conditions the rectified current and the rectified voltage will be reduced in the following ratio.

$$\text{Ratio of reduction} \atop \text{(high-vacuum tubes)} = \frac{R_L}{R_L + R_R} = \frac{1}{1 + (R_R/R_L)} \qquad (11)$$

The output voltage E_{dc} of a rectifier using vacuum diodes or semiconductor cells will decrease with load by an amount determined by the reduction factor (equation 11). If it is necessary to hold the value of E_{dc} to a constant value, it is necessary to vary the input voltage E_{rms}. This can be accomplished in steps by changing taps on the primary of the input transformers, or more exactly by some form of input voltage regulator.

The rectified output voltages of the single-phase circuits previously considered are less than the input effective voltages. The output voltage may be raised either by increasing the input voltage, or, if that is fixed, by the use of one of the voltage multiplication circuits shown in Fig. 9. In part (a) of this figure the simple half-wave

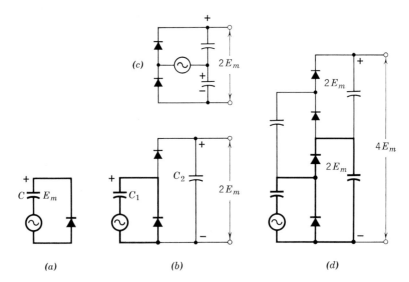

Fig. 9. Voltage multiplication circuits.

rectifier will charge capacitor C up to the peak applied voltage E_m with the top of the condenser at a positive potential. If a second capacitor and rectifying unit is added to part (a) as shown in part (b), the maximum output voltage will be doubled, rising to $2E_m$. This doubling effect results because on the forward conduction or charging of capacitor C_2, the peak applied voltage is the maximum voltage of the source E_m plus the potential of the charged capacitor C. Thus C_2 may be charged to a peak of $E_m + E_m = 2E_m$. Higher output voltages may be obtained by further combinations of the circuits of (a) and (b). If circuit (a) is properly added to circuit (b), the output voltage may be tripled. Again, if circuit (b) is added to itself, the result will be circuit (d) and the output voltage will be quadrupled. Higher multiplication factors are possible but seldom needed or employed. The voltage doubler circuit of Fig. 9c has the advantage that both sides of the power supply circuit are separated from the load circuit. Obviously, the output voltage values just considered are theoretical. The actual values are lower and are determined by the load impedance and other circuit conditions.

In passing, a summary of the relative merits of the three single-phase rectifying circuits is of interest. The half-wave rectifier is simple, uses only one rectifier unit, has a high ripple factor, makes inefficient use of its transformers, and has a low ratio of rectification. The full-wave rectifier circuits have a smaller ripple factor and a much higher ratio of rectification. The full-wave circuit using a mid-tap transformer requires only two rectifying units, but the transformer is special and more costly. Besides the necessity for the mid-tap, the secondary must have twice as many turns of somewhat smaller wire, hence a higher cost. In addition, the distorted wave form of the current in the two secondaries adds to the I^2R losses. When diode rectifying tubes are used, this circuit is standard because tubes have a relatively high initial and maintenance cost. The full-wave bridge circuit uses a simple transformer but four rectifying units. This circuit is standard for metallic rectifiers, crystal diodes, and p-n junction rectifiers. This circuit uses a transformer with a single winding on the secondary and there are no extra theoretical losses arising from rectification.

Effect of Arc Drop in Gas and Vapor Tubes

The effect of arc drop on the characteristic of gaseous and vapor tubes was shown in Fig. 4. Reference to that figure shows that the magnitude of the rectified pulses is reduced in two ways. First, the arc drop reduces the maximum value of the current pulses, and second, it reduces the length of the conduction pulse. The d-c values of the rectified current and voltage for a resistance load R_L may be

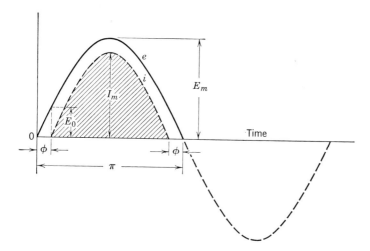

Fig. 10. Rectification in a gaseous tube with a constant arc drop.

determined by the same method of analysis as used in the preceding cases for vacuum tubes and semiconductor rectifying devices. A more detailed picture of the rectifying phenomenon is given in Fig. 10. Here the maximum value of the current pulse for an impressed sine wave of emf is

$$I_m = \frac{E_m - E_0}{R_L} \qquad (12)$$

where E_0 represents the arc drop voltage. The time delay angle for the beginning of the current pulse is shown as ϕ. Conduction starts when the impressed voltage rises to the arc drop E_0. To obtain the value of the delay angle ϕ, first define the ratio α as

$$\alpha = \frac{E_0}{E_m} \qquad (13)$$

Then it follows that

$$\phi = \sin^{-1} \alpha \qquad (14)$$

The instantaneous value of the current is

$$i = \frac{e - E_0}{R_L} = \frac{E_m \sin \theta - E_0}{R_L} \qquad (15)$$

Now the d-c value of the current pulse may be obtained by an integration of the area of the current pulse and by dividing this area by the base 2π. In setting up the integral, it should be noted that the period of the pulse begins at the termination of the delay angle ϕ and ends at a time equivalent of $\pi - \phi$ (Fig. 10).

$$I_{dc} = \frac{1}{2\pi} \int_\phi^{\pi-\phi} i \, d\theta = \frac{1}{2\pi} \int_\phi^{\pi-\phi} \left[\frac{E_m \sin \theta}{R_L} - \left(\frac{E_m}{R_L}\right)\frac{E_0}{E_m} \right] d\theta$$

$$= \frac{E_m}{2\pi R_L} \int_\phi^{\pi-\phi} (\sin \theta - \alpha) \, d\theta \qquad (16)$$

$$= \frac{E_m}{\pi R_L} \left(\cos \phi + \alpha\phi - \frac{\alpha\pi}{2} \right) \qquad (17)$$

Problem

A sine-wave supply voltage of 70.7 volts rms is impressed across a simple half-wave rectifier consisting of a mercury-vapor rectifier tube (15 volts arc drop) and a load resistor R_L of 10 ohms. Calculate the average direct current I_{dc} and the E_{dc} across the load.

Solution (equations 13, 14, and 17):

$$E_m = \frac{70.7}{0.707} = 100 \text{ volts} \qquad \alpha = \frac{15}{100} = 0.15$$

$$\phi = 8.65° = 0.152 \text{ radian}$$

$$I_{dc} = \frac{100}{\pi 10}\left(0.99 + 0.15 \times 0.152 - \frac{0.15\pi}{2}\right)$$

$$= 2.47 \text{ amp}$$

(Note for an ideal rectifier the direct current would be

$$0.318 \times \frac{E_m(100)}{R_L(10)} = 3.18 \text{ amp})$$

$$E_{dc} = I_{dc}R_L = 2.47 \times 10 = 24.7 \text{ volts}$$

In gaseous and vapor triodes, the time of firing or initiating conduction may be controlled by grid action. Here a delay in firing reduces the magnitude of direct current and voltage below those just considered. Calculations for d-c values under these conditions can be made through the use of equation 16 by changing the lower limit of integration ϕ to a new value corresponding to the true firing angle expressed in terms of radians.

Multiphase Rectifier Circuits

Multiphase rectifier circuits are used whenever moderate or large magnitudes of d-c power are applied. Such circuits have the advantage of utilizing the standard three-phase power distribution system and they furnish smoother rectified voltage and current waves at higher efficiencies. A simple three-phase circuit illustrating the principle of multiphase rectification is given in Fig. 11. Power is supplied through a three-phase, delta-wye connected transformer to a three-anode unit rectifier. The rectifying units may consist of vacuum diodes, gaseous diodes, phanotrons, ignitrons, excitrons or semiconductor rectifiers having all cathodes connected together, or a multielectrode tank rectifier having a single-cathode mercury pool may be used. The d-c load is connected to the common cathode terminal (+) and to the neutral of the transformer secondary. All half-wave multiphase circuits require that one load terminal arise from a neutral or common point in the transformer supply secondary. The effective alternating voltage for rectification E_{rms} is always the

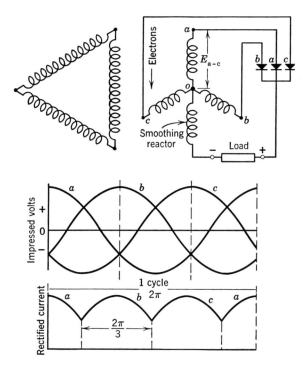

Fig. 11. Half-wave, three-phase rectifier circuit and voltage-current waves (boldface arrows show direction of conventional current).

voltage measured from the transformer neutral to the anodes of the rectifier.

An analysis of the action of multiphase rectification may be made by assuming ideal rectifying units with zero resistance, an ideal transformer, a pure resistance load, and a sine wave of applied voltage. The variation of voltage across the anodes during one cycle is depicted in the middle section of Fig. 11 and the resulting current waves in the lower section of the figure. The direct voltage waves will have the same form as the current waves. The rectified waves have ripples per cycle equal to the number of anodes, but the ripples are lower in magnitude, giving a lower ripple factor and a much smoother wave. Under the ideal theoretical conditions assumed, the rectified current flows to the anode having the highest positive potential and that means that each of three anodes will carry the current for $2\pi/3$ part of each cycle. Since the ripples on the load side of the transformer are equal and continuous, the d-c or average value of the current or voltage will be the average value of a single ripple wave. The peak value of the ripple voltage is the maximum value of the impressed voltage $E_{\max}$. As the number of phases and anodes increase, the number of ripples and the average direct voltage increase and the voltage approaches the maximum value of $E_{\max}$.

One method of obtaining a low ripple from a three-phase circuit and a standard transformer is shown in the circuit of Fig. 12. In practice, this circuit, using a delta-connected transformer, generally employs the blocking-layer rectifier. Six rectifier tubes of any type can be employed though the higher cost of the tubes may make their use uneconomical. The transformer phase voltages and the resulting current output with six ripples per cycle are shown at the right of Fig. 12. Obviously, this three-phase circuit is analogous to the full-wave single-phase bridge type of circuit.

A schematic circuit for six-phase rectification using a special transformer and a rectifier having six anodes is given in Fig. 13. This circuit is called the three-phase diametric (six-phase star). Twelve and occasionally eighteen anodes are used for rectification. The ratio of voltage conversion, that is, volts of direct current to volts of alternating current effective for a few multiphase circuits, is given in Table 1.

The voltage ratios given for the ideal circuit do not hold for the actual circuit because of the voltage regulation of the transformer and the cathode-anode drop in the rectifying unit. Hence the load

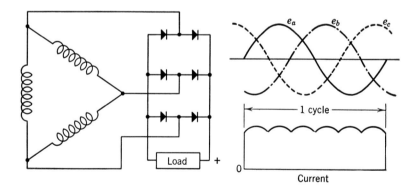

Fig. 12. Full-wave bridge, three-phase rectifier with voltage and current relationship.

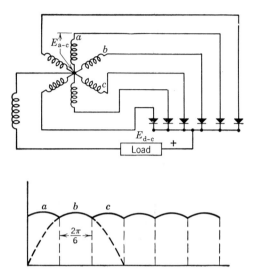

Fig. 13. Schematic six-phase rectifier circuit and wave form.

voltage regulation of the multiphase circuit may be too poor to meet the requirements of an application. Control of the output voltage can be effected in two ways. One method is to control the transformer input voltage by a regulator or by using taps on the primary side of the input transformer. These methods are not well adapted when large amounts of power are involved. The second method is to control the time of firing of the anodes by grid action. A delay in the firing of each anode will change the wave form of the rectified current and voltage and reduce the magnitude of the average value. The application of this method is suggested in Fig. 14. This method of voltage control increases the ripple and the ripple factor.

In the ideal multiphase rectifier circuit the anode at the highest positive potential carries the entire d-c load. As the potential of the conducting anode falls to that of a succeeding anode, the former drops the load and the latter picks it up so that only one anode is

Table 1

Anodes	3	6	12	18
$\dfrac{E_{dc}}{E_{rms}}$	1.17	1.35	1.40	1.41

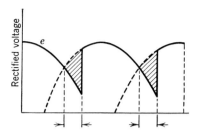

Fig. 14. Voltage control through delay in firing time.

conducting at a time. In the actual rectifier circuit this sudden change of load requiring an infinite rate of change of current for the anodes participating in the action does not take place. The transformer secondary winding that supplies each anode has some leakage reactance which opposes the sudden change of current. Accordingly, the current in the first conducting anode tapers off and the current in the second anode rises as the two anodes pass each other with regard to positive potential. Thus in practice there are periods of transition when two anodes are conducting at the same time. In special cases, such as twelve- or eighteen-anode circuits, there may be three or more anodes conducting simultaneously. A six-phase ignitron rectifying unit is shown in Fig. 26.

In multiphase rectifier circuits, as in single-phase circuits, the part-time rectification of current from each phase produces distorted (non-sine-wave) currents in the transformer secondaries and may produce residual magnetomotive forces and fluxes in the cores of the transformer feeding the rectifier. These things introduce problems in the design and selection of transformer connections to give optimum results and efficiency. An analysis of these problems lies in the realm of the study of power transformers. However, it should be noted that simple multi-phase circuits such as shown in Figs. 11 and 13 are seldom employed. The high peak-to-average demand on the rectifying elements together with poor transformer utilization, efficiency, and regulation dictate the use of multiple-conduction circuits using interphase and other special transformer connections like those illustrated in Fig. 15. Thus a rectifier may sometimes be referred to as a 36- or 72-phase rectifier (common in electrochemical installations), though it is generally made up of a number of three-phase wye groupings properly phased and interconnected with interphase transformers.

The power losses in multiphase rectifiers consist of (1) those in the input transformer, (2) those in the rectifying unit, plus (3) those

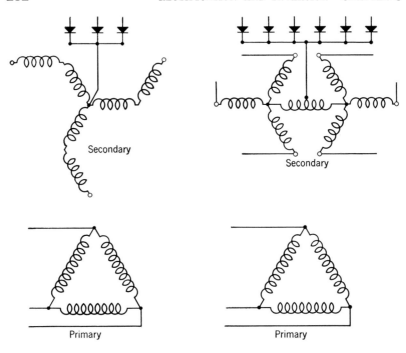

Fig. 15. Delta-zigzag and interphase transformer connections for three- and six-phase rectification.

in auxiliary equipment. Transformer losses under load are relatively low and the full-load efficiency of transformers is very high. In the rectifying units the losses consist of power for producing thermionic emission (if thermionic cathode is employed) plus the loss in the cathode-anode circuit. The cathode-anode fall of potential is of the order of 10 to 20 volts and if the output voltage is 600 volts or higher, the percentage of power lost across the rectifying unit is very low. Thus for 600 volts and an arc drop of 15 volts the power loss in the arc is 2.5 per cent, and for a load voltage of 3000 volts with 15 volts arc drop the power loss is only 0.5 per cent. The over-all efficiency of complete rectifying units of moderate and large size may well be of the order of 95 to 97 per cent.

Summary on Rectifiers

A summary covering some of the important factors and applications of rectifying units is given in Table 2.

Table 2. Summary on Rectifiers

Device	Description	Load Voltage Range	Load Current Range Amperes	Peak Inverse Volts	Applications
Crystal diodes	Semiconductor	40–250	0–0.5	50–1000	Detection, rectification small currents
Copper-oxide	Metallic	3–12 per cell	0.3 amp per sq in.	3–30	Low voltage uses—relay control, electroplating
Selenium	Metallic	18–26–33 per cell	0.3 amp per sq in.	18–45 per cell	Power supplies—radio and TV—misc. low voltage applications
Magnesium copper-sulfide	Metallic	5 per cell	25–50 per sq in.	5 per cell	Low voltage, high current rectification
Germanium power	p-n junction	65–125	600 per sq in.	15–125 per cell	65–250 volt large current applications chemical industry
Silicon power	p-n junction	50–400	35–150 per cell	400 per cell	50–400 volt moderate current applications temperature up to 190° C
Kenotron	Vacuum hot cathode	0–150,000	Usually 0–1	150,000	High voltage supply for X-ray tube, precipitron, radio broadcast tubes, etc.
Gaseous	Gas hot cathode	0–220	0–15	300	Power supplies
Phanotron	Vapor hot cathode	0–2200	0–30	5000	Misc. moderate voltage power supply
Thyratron	Hot cathode gas or vapor	1000–10,000	0–18	25,000	Control functions—resistance welding—controlled rectification
Ignitron	Mercury pool ignitor	250–20,000	30–1000 per tube	1000–20,000	Power rectification—electronic power switching—inversion
Excitron	Mercury pool	0–3000	750 per tube	3000	Power rectification

Smoothing Filters

A smoothing filter is a circuit element or a network designed to reduce the ripples of current and voltage in the output of a rectifier. Some applications of direct current can utilize the pulsating output of a rectifier without modification, but in the majority of cases a smoothing out of the ripples is necessary. The basic elements for smoothing action are capacitors and inductance or choke coils. The former act through their ability to store energy in electric fields and the latter through a similar storage of energy in magnetic fields.

The simplest circuit for a half-wave, single-phase rectifier consists of a capacitor placed in parallel with the load on the output side of the rectifier as shown in part a of Fig. 16. Assuming (1) an impressed voltage having a sine wave, (2) a rectifying unit (low re-

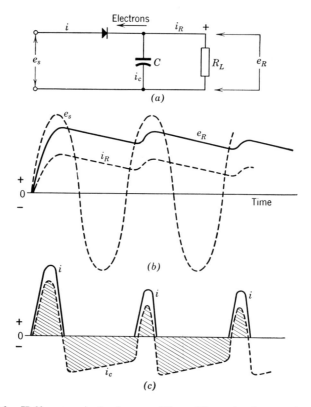

Fig. 16. Half-wave, single-phase rectifier with a simple capacitor filter.

sistance in forward direction), and (3) a high resistance load R_L, the voltage and current values in the circuit will vary as depicted in parts b and c of Fig. 16. First, the impressed voltage follows dotted line e_s which will charge the capacitor C as it rises to the first peak. Then, as the impressed voltage falls below the voltage across the capacitor, the rectifier will cut off and the energy stored in the capacitor will discharge through the resistance R_L in accordance with the transient equation:

$$i = -\frac{E\epsilon^{-t/RC}}{R}$$

The voltage across the capacitor and load will decrease, as shown by the full line e_R, until the next positive loop of impressed voltage rises above e_R and then the capacitor charges again. The current i_R delivered to the load follows the trend of the voltage across the load. The current i flowing through the rectifying unit rises in pulses as shown by the full line in part c, Fig. 16, and the charge and discharge current for the capacitor follows the trend of the dotted line i_c. It should be noted that the pulses of current through the rectifier have a high transient peak and will damage the cathode of a gaseous or vapor-rectifying tube. Obviously, the magnitude of the load current i_R and the magnitude of the voltage and current ripples will be determined by the values of C and R_L. In the actual rectifier the rectifying unit has some resistance which produces a voltage drop and reduces the voltage across the load. As R_L approaches ∞, e_R will approach $E_{\max}$.

A simple capacitor filter connected in a full-wave rectifier circuit as shown in part (a) of Fig. 17 will produce voltage and current waves as illustrated in part (b). In comparison with the half-wave rectifier of the preceding paragraph, this circuit has output ripples of double the frequency but of lower ripple magnitude and gives a smoother output. The pulses of input current i and the capacitor current i_c are indicated in part (c).

A simple choke filter connected in the output of a half-wave single-phase rectifier as shown in part (a), Fig. 18, will produce the current and voltage waves given in part (b). The inductance of the choke will retard the rise of current through the rectifier and, after the impressed voltage reaches its positive peak, the energy stored in the magnetic field will continue the d-c pulse after the applied voltage becomes negative. Thus the conduction period will continue for more than one half-cycle, though the rectified current will be ex-

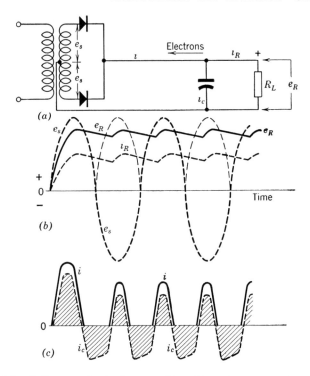

Fig. 17. Full-wave, single-phase rectifier with a simple capacitor filter.

tinguished and appear as pulses. This peculiar action is explained by the induced voltage across the choke as illustrated by the curve e_x. The voltage across the load will have the same pulse wave shape as the current. In a full-wave rectifier without filter the current falls to zero at the end of each half-cycle. Here a simple choke filter will serve to reduce the peaks and prevent the current from falling to zero, as shown in Fig. 19. Likewise, for multiphase rectification where the number of ripples is increased and the ripple factor reduced, the simple inductance filter will be very effective in smoothing out the ripples. The voltage wave form across a resistance load will follow the trend of the current wave.

Filter circuits using combinations of the capacitor and chokes will give more effective smoothing action. One simple circuit combination is shown in Fig. 20. Here the series choke will retard the rise and fall of current input to the shunt capacitor and load. This action will reduce the magnitude of voltage across the capacitor as

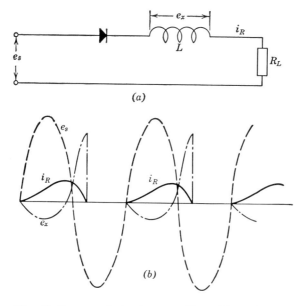

Fig. 18. Half-wave, single-phase rectifier with a choke filter.

well as reduce the change in voltage applied to the capacitor and load. The capacitor, in turn, will absorb energy on the higher voltage inputs and release this energy when the input voltage is low. Both actions tend to maintain a constant voltage across the load and give a good filtering action. The voltage and current relations

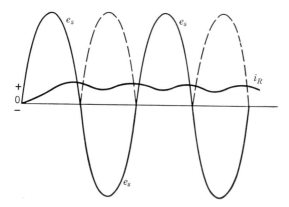

Fig. 19. Full-wave, single-phase rectifier with a choke filter.

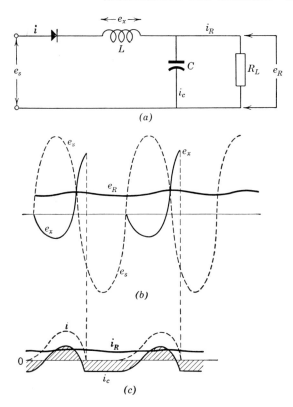

Fig. 20. Voltage and current relations in an L-type filter.

in the choke input L-type of filter are shown in parts (b) and (c) of Fig. 20. A second form of L filter uses a shunt capacitor on the input side as in Fig. 21. In this circuit the capacitor charges rapidly with the rise of rectifier output and to a much higher voltage than in the preceding case. The series choke, in turn, retards the change of current flow to the load and tends to hold constant the voltage at the load. Obviously, the voltage at the load is higher than in the preceding choke input circuit.

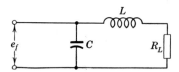

Fig. 21. L-type filter with a capacitor input.

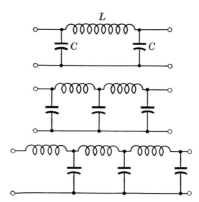

Fig. 22. Combinations of π and T sections to give superior filtering action.

The preceding simple filter sections consisting of capacitors and inductances in "lumps" are frequently called *brute-force filters*. These filters provide satisfactory filter action for many applications at a minimum cost. Better filtering action will be obtained if the capacitance and inductance are broken into smaller units and assembled in π and T sections, as shown in Fig. 22. The cost of the complete filter having multiple units is greater because the cost per unit of capacity or inductance is increased as the capacity of the unit decreases. Hence economy as well as the excellence of filtering action must determine the selection of the filter design. The energy storage per dollar is the most important factor. In applications where the load current is of low magnitude and where cost or weight of apparatus are critical, resistors are sometimes substituted for chokes in smoothing filter circuits.

Comparison of Filter Circuits

The simple capacitor and all other *capacitor input filter circuits cannot be employed with hot-cathode gaseous and vapor rectifier tubes.* This follows because (1) the impedance of a capacitor to its charging current is very low, and (2) gaseous and vapor rectifier tubes will not withstand cathode-anode potential drops above approximately 28 volts during the conduction period without damage to the cathode arising from positive ion bombardment. Vacuum-tube and semiconductor rectifiers can be used satisfactorily with capacitor input filters.

Economy and performance determine the selection of the proper filter circuit. The simple parallel capacitor is low in cost for half-wave rectification. The capacitor input L filter gives a higher load to input-voltage ratio but is likely to give poorer load-voltage regulation. Since the cost of capacitors rises rapidly with voltage rating, the choke input may prove more economical for higher load voltages. The choke input L type gives a lower load to input-voltage ratio but has better inherent voltage regulation. The simple series choke filter is usually satisfactory for filtering with multiphase rectifier circuits.

Precautions on Peak Inverse Voltage

In designing rectifier circuits and the accompanying filters, the engineer must give due consideration to the peak inverse voltage to which the rectifying units will be subjected. The presence of a capacitor filter on a half-wave rectifier may subject the rectifying unit to an inverse peak approaching two times the a-c maximum voltage. Transient voltage surges on supply lines or transients due to transformer switching may increase the peak inverse voltages to which rectifiers are subjected. The peak inverse voltage that a tube will withstand (especially gaseous tubes) varies with the operating temperature and a suitable safety factor should be used for variations of this type.

Inversion Circuits

An inverter is a device for converting direct current to alternating current. The oscillator discussed in Chapter 9 is such a device and is designed for high frequencies and generally for small amounts of power. For low frequencies and larger amounts of power, electronic devices such as the thyratron, the ignitron, and mercury-arc rectifiers are used in inverter circuits. The function of the tubes is to commutate or perform a switching operation. It is essential that the electronic device have grid control and that units of inductance or capacity or both be employed to produce inductive and capacitive storage capacity. Many combinations of these elements may be used for producing inversion.

One simple inverter circuit in which the device determines its own frequency is given in Fig. 23. In this circuit the resistance R_1 is relatively high and R_2 is relatively low. Before the d-c switch S is closed, the anode, grid, and cathode of the thyratron are at the same potential and the capacitor C is discharged. When S is closed the grid is made positive with respect to the cathode, and hence if the direct

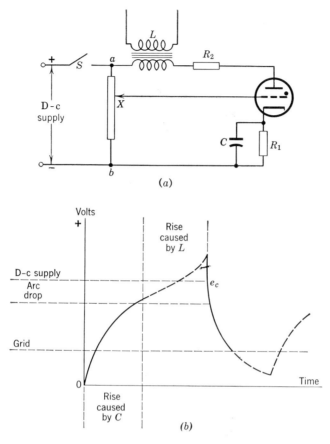

Fig. 23. (*a*) Simple circuit using a thyratron for inversion. (*b*) Analysis of operation.

voltage is higher than the ionization potential, the thyratron will "fire" and current will flow through L, R_2, and C and R_1 in parallel. Since R_1 is large, the capacitor will charge quickly and the potential of the cathode e_c will rise (Fig. 23*b*). The rise of potential of the cathode will tend to lower the potential across the cathode-anode circuit below the ionization potential. At the same time the inertia effect of the inductance L tends to maintain the current and will produce an induced voltage to maintain the current. As a result the capacitor C will continue to charge and the voltage across it will rise above the d-c impressed voltage. When the energy stored in

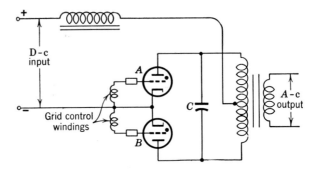

Fig. 24. Single-phase inverter using two thyratrons.

the core of L is expended, the voltage across the thyratron falls, leaving the potential of the cathode higher (owing to capacitor) than the anode and higher than the grid. Hence the current through the thyratron ceases and deionization takes place. In the meantime, the capacitor discharges through the resistance R_1. As the capacitor discharges and lowers its potential and that of the cathode to the point where anode-cathode potential reaches the ionization potential, and when the grid voltage reaches the point where it will fire the thyratron, the thyratron conducts current again, and the cycle is repeated. Obviously, the time of firing and the resulting frequency of the oscillating cycle can be varied by the position of X on the potentiometer ab which controls the grid bias. The frequency can be controlled also by variation of R_1 or C.

A transformer placed in the circuit of the thyratron would deliver alternating current to a suitable load. The wave form of this type of inverter is not sinusoidal.

In most power inverters the frequency is determined by a separate source. A simple schematic circuit for a single-phase inverter of this type is given in Fig. 24. Two thyratrons, A and B, with grids controlled by a separate voltage source are employed in a balanced circuit arrangement wherein both anodes are connected to the positive side of the d-c supply. Assume that the grid supply at the instant of starting is positive for A and negative for B. Tube A fires and conducts electrons from the negative d-c line through the upper half of the transformer primary to the positive d-c terminal. The rise of current through the transformer winding creates an IX drop which lowers the potential of the anode of tube A to the arc drop voltage (above zero). Under this condition the capacitor becomes charged to a voltage of E_{dc} — arc drop with the top plate negative and the lower plate positive. When the grid control potential reverses and makes the grid of tube A negative and B positive, quick action follows. The negative grid on A has no direct effect upon tube conduction, but the positive grid on B causes it to fire and the resulting surge of current through the lower half of the transformer winding lowers the potential of anode B. Simultaneously, electrons are supplied to the lower positive plate of the capacitor C. This permits the unbound electrons on the top plate of C to flow off and lower the potential of the anode of A, thus permitting the now negative grid of A to regain control. At the end of the half-cycle the reverse process will take place with tube A conducting and tube B cut off. Thus the two tubes A and B serve as a reversing switch to cause alternate pulses of current to flow through the primary of the transformer. The resulting flux reversals in the iron core of the transformer gives an a-c output in the secondary having the same frequency as the applied grid potential.

Multiphase rectifiers consisting of thyratrons, excitrons, ignitrons, or multianode tank units may be used for inversion. A schematic diagram for this application is given in Fig. 25. Individual excitron or ignitron tubes may replace the multianodes shown in this figure. The circuit is similar to that for rectification of alternating current but with three fundamental differences. First, the polarity at the d-c source is reversed though the direction of current flow through the rectifier is the same. Second, a reactor has been placed in the cathode lead. Third, the potential across the grid is controlled by a separate a-c source. The key to the inverter action lies in the application of and control of grid potentials. A positive potential on a grid will attract electrons to the grid and cause them to pass through to the anode. Hence if a-c potentials are applied to the multielectrode grids in the proper sequence, the resulting currents will pass through the secondary windings of the transformers connected to the anodes and produce a-c power in the primaries. The reactor in the cathode lead smooths out the power flow from the d-c source and tends to reduce short-circuit current if an occasional short circuit should occur.

Inverters are employed to convert d-c sources of power supply (such as storage batteries) to alternating current. For small magnitudes of power, vibrator types of converter may be used for port-

able equipment. For large magnitudes of inversion, mercury rectifier units may convert power transmitted by high-voltage direct current back to alternating current. Likewise d-c regenerated power
on electrified railroads in mountainous districts may be converted to
a-c power.

Thyratrons have been used for inversion by the General Electric
Company on an experimental d-c transmission line between Me-
chanicville and Schenectady, New York. The inversion unit had a
rating of 5250 kw and took constant current at 28,000 volts at full
load from a d-c transmission line. This inverter installation was
made in 1936 and served to convert millions of kilowatt-hours of
electrical energy.

A modern six-unit, 1000-kilowatt ignitron rectifier installation is
illustrated in Fig. 26. With suitable control circuits, rectifier units
of this general type may be employed as inverters.

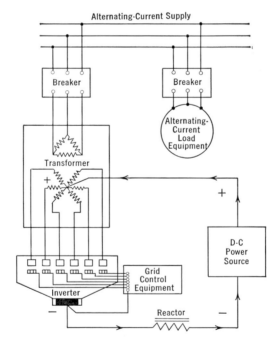

Fig. 25. Circuit using a mercury-arc rectifier for power inversion. (Courtesy
Allis-Chalmers Manufacturing Company.)

Fig. 26. Six-phase ignitron rectifier unit. (Courtesy General Electric Company.)

Transistor Power Supply

A transistor power supply is a combination of circuit components designed to furnish a high direct voltage from a low voltage storage battery. A typical circuit for a 40 watt design is given in Fig. 27. In this circuit a 12 volt battery furnishes d-c power to operate an inverter (oscillator) using two transistors and a transformer. The two transistors operate as switches in the d-c primary circuit and alternately allow current to flow through the transformer, first through one-half the primary and then through the other half. This sets up an a-c square wave in the secondary which is rectified by the silicon diodes in the bridge rectifier circuit. The center-tapped transformer divides the output into two voltages, whereas the capacitors serve to filter the ripple from the output. This combined inverter-rectifier power supply can be assembled into a compact unit. This unit is relatively light, efficient, and trouble free. Its

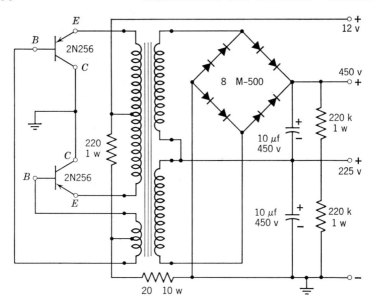

Fig. 27. Circuit for transistor power supply from a 12 volt storage battery. (Courtesy CBS Hytron.)

applications lie in portable communication equipment for automobiles, airplanes, etc.

PROBLEMS

1. In an ideal half-wave rectifier circuit the impressed rms voltage is 65 volts. What is the d-c average voltage? If the peak value of current on the input side is 5 amp, what is the I_{dc}? I_{rms}?

2. In an ideal full-wave rectifier the rms values on the input are 90 volts and 6 amp. Calculate the readings on a d-c voltmeter and ammeter in the load circuit.

3. The unfiltered current from a half-wave rectifier (sine wave applied) is passed through a d-c ammeter and an a-c ammeter. When the d-c meter reads 12 amp, what should be the indication on the a-c meter? Recalculate for full-wave rectification.

4. Recalculate Problem 3 when a current transformer (1/1 ratio) is inserted between the a-c ammeter and the line.

5. The vacuum diode of page 126 supplies a rectified current of 100 ma to a resistance load of 2000 ohms. Calculate the ratio of the reduction of the voltage using d-c plate resistance at 100 ma.

6. A Tungar rectifier tube of page 187 is used for half-wave rectification to charge a 6 volt storage battery for automobiles. If the battery takes 6 amp at 7.5 volts, calculate the impressed alternating voltage when the tube fires. If the transformer has an efficiency of 80 per cent for this load, calculate the over-all efficiency of rectification, taking care to include both cathode and arc losses. (The student should note that a storage battery is not a resistance load and that a new analysis and approach to the problem is required.)

7. Substitute a copper oxide rectifier for the tungar tube and recalculate Problem 6, assuming a peak inverse voltage of 10 volts per plate with a 1 volt drop in the forward direction of current conduction.

8. Two phanotrons of Fig. 6, page 190, are connected in a full-wave rectifier circuit to charge a 110 volt storage battery (125 volts when charging) at 20 amp. Determine the average voltage applied during the conduction period. If the transformer has an efficiency of 90 per cent, what is the over-all efficiency of rectification?

9. In the simple filter circuit of Fig. 16, assume that $C = 1 \mu f$, $R_L = 100,000$ ohms, and e_R falls for 1/80 sec. Determine from Fig. 12, Chapter 10, the per cent of voltage drop from the maximum. Redetermine for $R_L = 10,000$ ohms.

10. What is the ratio of reduction in a half-wave rectifier circuit where the rectifier has a resistance of 100 ohms and the load is a 50 ohm resistor?

11. A sine wave of 120 volts is impressed across a simple half-wave rectifier consisting of a phanotron (tube drop equals 15 volts) and a load resistor of 10 ohms. Calculate the average direct current I_{dc} and the direct current voltage E_{dc} across the load.

REFERENCES

1. Livingston and Lord, "The Single-Tube Thyratron Inverter," *Electronics,* April 1933.
2. Durand, S. R., *A Mercury-Arc Static Inverter,* Allis-Chalmers Mfg. Co., 1939.
3. M.I.T. electrical engineering staff, *Applied Electronics,* John Wiley and Sons, New York, 1943.

chapter 9

Amplifiers
and Oscillators

Amplifiers

The function of an amplifier is to magnify a very weak signal until
it is capable of controlling sufficient electric power for producing
light, sound, or mechanical work. An amplifier does not create
energy but controls sources of electric energy to give outputs that
follow the original input signal with fidelity. The usual signal input
to an amplifier is a varying voltage. An amplifier performs its function in one or in a series of stages or steps. An individual stage of
an amplifier may be designed for (1) voltage amplification or (2)
power amplification. Voltage amplification signifies that the output voltage across the load is greater than the input signal and the
power output is small. Power amplification means that the output
power (volts times amperes) is large compared to the input signal.
Frequently a complete amplifying unit consists of one or more stages
of voltage amplification followed by a final stage of power amplification. The over-all power gain in an amplifier of several stages may
be very large, approaching infinity, because the input to the first
stage of voltage amplification may be near zero, whereas the energy
of the final stage may be large.

Amplifiers may be classified on the basis of (1) range of frequency
handled, (2) the devices used, or (3) the circuit employed. There
is no standardized frequency classification for amplifiers. The following table provides a general picture.

Direct-coupled amplifiers	0–megacycles
Audio-frequency amplifiers	20–20,000 cycles
Radio-frequency amplifiers	Frequencies above the audio range, with each amplifier designed to handle a narrow band of frequencies
Video-frequency amplifiers	0–5,000,000 cycles

The devices used for producing amplification are (1) grid-controlled vacuum tubes, (2) transistors, (3) magnetic amplifiers, and (4) rotary amplifiers.

Vacuum-Tube and Transistor Amplifiers

Vacuum triodes, tetrodes, pentodes, and beam power tubes are employed as amplifiers. The basic circuit (Fig. 1a) and theory of the triode as an amplifier were covered in Chapter 5 and the voltage gain was shown to be

$$\text{Voltage gain} = \mu \frac{R_L}{r_p + R_L} \tag{1}$$

In like manner, the junction transistor as an amplifier was treated in Chapter 3, and its power gain was given as

$$\text{Power gain} = \frac{\alpha^2 R_L}{r_e} \text{ (approx.)} \tag{2}$$

Comparative circuits for these two amplifying units are given in Fig. 1. This figure represents the case for the cathode and the emitter

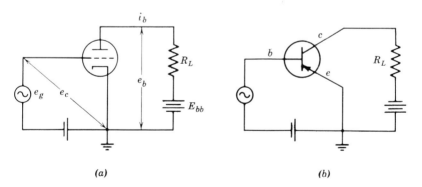

(a)   *(b)*

Fig. 1. Basic amplifier circuit. (*a*) Common or grounded cathode. (*b*) Common or grounded emitter circuit (*n*-point-contact or *p-n-p* junction transistor).

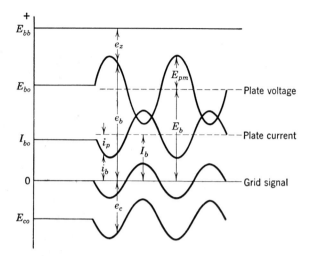

Fig. 2. Amplifier current and voltage relationships.

serving as a common and usually grounded terminal. For vacuum-tube amplifiers the grid is always furnished with a negative bias. However, for the transistor the polarity applied to the emitter depends on the type of transistors, such as point contact (n or p) or junction (n-p-n or p-n-p).

The action taking place within the triode amplifier stage of Fig. 1a can be visualized through the picture of phase relationships of voltages and currents shown in Fig. 2. A sine-wave signal (shown about zero axis) is impressed in series with the negative grid bias,

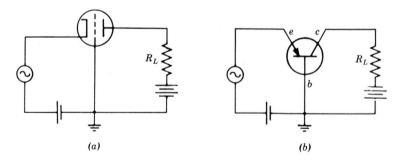

Fig. 3. Basic amplifier circuit. (*a*) Common or grounded grid. (*b*) Common or grounded base (*n*-point contact or *p*-*n*-*p* junction transistor).

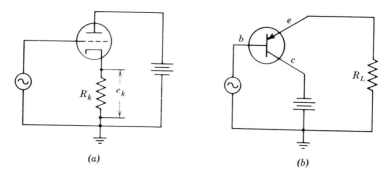

Fig. 4. Basic amplifier circuit. (*a*) Cathode follower. (*b*) Grounded collector circuit (*n*-point-contact or *p-n-p* junction transistor).

giving the net grid voltage shown at the bottom (e_c). The resulting plate current i_p (a-c component) is in phase with the grid voltage, but the varying plate voltage e_b is opposite in phase (180 degrees) to the plate current and grid voltage. Similarly, the load voltage e_z ($e_z = E_{bb} - i_pR_L$) is opposite in phase to the grid input voltage. Thus for resistive loads, *the amplified output voltage is 180 degrees out-of-phase with the impressed signal voltage.*

A second form of basic amplifier circuit is given in Fig. 3. This represents the common or grounded grid and base. In the triode, the grounded grid acts as an electrostatic shield between the input and output circuits. This permits the triode to be used on high fre-quencies because the shielding overcomes the feedback arising from interelectrode capacitances within the triode.

A third form of basic amplifier circuit is given in Fig. 4. These circuits represent the cathode follower for the triode and the grounded collector for the transistor. It should be noted that in the cathode follower circuit, the load resistance R_k is placed in the cathode cir-cuit instead of the plate circuit. Accordingly, the output voltage e_k appears across the cathode load resistor. And the term cathode follower comes from the fact that the cathode rises and falls in po-tential when the grid does—hence the cathode follows the grid. The voltage gain in this cathode follower circuit may be shown to be

$$\text{Voltage gain} = \frac{g_mR_k}{g_mR_k + 1} = \frac{1}{1 + \dfrac{1}{g_mR_k}} \quad \text{(approx.)} \qquad (3)$$

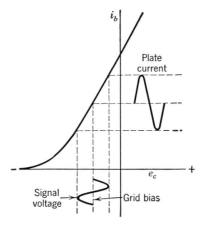

Fig. 5.   Class A amplifier operation.

Inspection of equation 3 shows that the maximum gain of this circuit is 1.0, and hence the circuit is not a voltage amplifier. However, it may serve as a *power* amplifier. The cathode follower circuit has the following important advantages: (1) it may be used to couple a high-impedance source to a low-impedance circuit without distortion, (2) it provides an output circuit with one side at ground potential, and (3) the output voltage is in phase with the input signal. Applications of this circuit are covered later.

Class A, B, and C Amplifiers

A class A amplifier is one in which the grid bias and alternating grid voltages are of such magnitudes that plate current flows throughout the cycle. The class A operation of a tube is illustrated graphically by the dynamic transfer characteristic of Fig. 5. An examination of this graph shows that plate current flows during the positive and negative half-cycles of the a-c signal voltage. Since the i_b–e_c curve is not linear over its entire length, the tube must be biased so that the signal operates over the straight-line section in order to give an exact reproduction of the input wave form. If the grid of the tube is biased incorrectly so that the grid voltage acts over the nonlinear portion of the curve, a distorted plate-current wave form will result. In such a current wave, the positive and negative half cycles are unequal and the result is *amplitude distortion*. If this distorted current is passed through a load resistance, the resulting load voltage will have a like wave form. Some distortion is always present in a

vacuum tube or transistor amplifier, but proper operating conditions
will minimize this.

A *class B amplifier* is one in which the grid bias is approximately
equal to the cutoff value, so that plate current flows for approximately one-half of each cycle of input voltage. The operation of a
class B circuit is illustrated in Fig. 6, showing how only one loop of
the signal wave appears in the plate-current circuit. The signal
voltage applied to the grid of a class B amplifier is usually much
larger than that applied in a class A stage and may be so large that
during part of the positive half-cycle, the grid becomes positive with
respect to the cathode. In the latter case some electrons are attracted
to the grid and constitute a grid current.

A *class C amplifier* is one in which the grid bias is appreciably
larger than the cutoff value so that the plate current flows for less
than one-half cycle of the applied a-c signal voltage. The operation
of a class C amplifier is illustrated in Fig. 7. Here the grid-bias
voltage is twice the cutoff value, which represents common practice
in many type C amplifiers. The plate current flows only during the
positive peaks of the applied signal voltage; hence the signal must
be much larger than the cutoff bias to give a satisfactory value of
plate current.

It is obvious from the preceding discussion and Figs. 6 and 7 that
class B and C amplifiers have high distortion and are unsuited for
audio-frequency amplification except in push-pull circuits to be
explained later. However, they are satisfactory for radio-frequency
amplifier stages. For this use the missing half cycle of plate current
is restored by placing a parallel-tuned LC tank circuit in series with

Fig. 6. Class B operation.

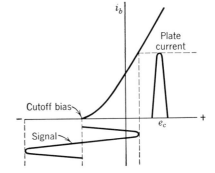

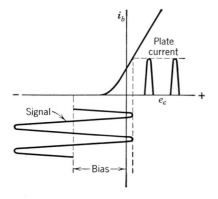

Fig. 7.   Class C operation.

the plate load (see Fig. 12).   This parallel-tuned circuit has the
ability to store and release energy.   Thus during the positive half
cycle of the single-tube stage, the inductance L conducts current and
the capacitor C becomes charged.   Then during the negative half
cycle the capacitor discharges through L with current flowing in the
reverse direction.   Thus the load current flows through L in both
directions and a complete cycle of amplified voltage will be induced
in a second coil coupled to L (transformer action).   This so-called
flywheel effect of the tank circuit occurs only when the resonant
frequency matches the frequency of the signal voltage.

A second method of supplying the missing half cycle in class B
and C amplifier circuits is to employ two tubes in the push-pull
amplifier circuit of Fig. 8.   The two tubes operate from and into
transformers with a center-tapped winding so that each tube oper-

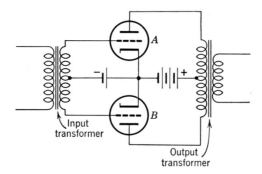

Fig. 8.   Push-pull amplifier circuit.

ates only on alternate half waves and thus furnish an output wave form having reduced distortion. The push-pull circuit, modified in various ways, is widely used with classes A, B, C and AB combinations. Class B push-pull circuits have been used for audio-frequency amplifiers.

Interstage Couplings

The output of each stage of an amplifier must be coupled (connected) to the input of the succeeding stage. Several types of circuit are used for performing this function, with the choice determined by the amplifying device used, the frequency involved, the power transformed, as well as other factors. The simplest coupling circuit is illustrated in Fig. 9 and is known as direct coupling. In this circuit the plate of stage 1 is connected directly to the grid of stage 2, and the cathode of stage 2 is connected to the positive side of the B-supply for the anode of stage 1. This means that the cathode (and tube parts) of each succeeding stage will be maintained at a higher potential above ground and that a separate plate-supply voltage must be provided for each stage. The necessity for separate power supplies can be eliminated by other circuitry (see Fig. 1, Chapter 18). This is the type of coupling used for d-c amplifiers which find applications in control equipment. The d-c amplifier is difficult to operate with a constant gain because any change in cathode emission, grid-bias voltage, or plate voltage of one stage will be amplified in succeeding stages and will produce an effect similar to a change in the original grid signal. This amplifier is costly to construct because of the separate sources of power supply required for each stage. The d-c amplifier is used for applications such as electrocardiography, the study of nerve currents, the use of an oscilloscope to show transient responses relative to a steady component and in analog computers.

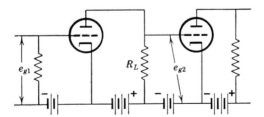

Fig. 9. Direct coupling of an amplifier.

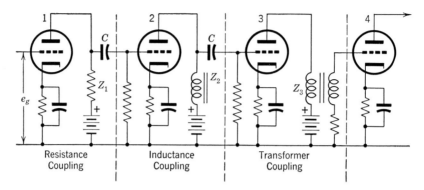

Fig. 10. Types of coupling for amplifiers.

For amplifying a-c signals the individual stages of an audio-frequency amplifier may be separated by a blocking condenser C or a transformer in the coupling network, as shown in Fig. 10. A common plate-power supply may be used. Representative examples of interstage coupling for audio-frequency amplification are given in Fig. 10 for vacuum tubes, and in Fig. 11 for a common emitter circuit using transistors.

For radio-frequency amplification an LC tank circuit may be incorporated in either the grid circuit or the plate circuit or both, as suggested in Fig. 12. The function of the LC resonant tank is to supply the negative loops of rectified current and also to limit the

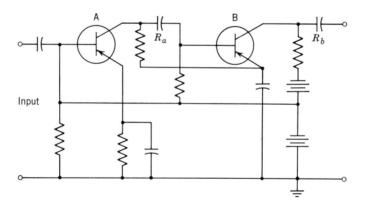

Fig. 11. Transistor coupled amplifier.

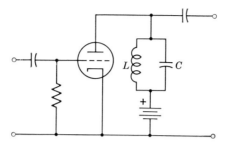

Fig. 12. Tuned LC coupling.

frequency to a narrow band. The LC tank circuit may be added to any of the coupling combinations shown in Fig. 10.

Amplifier Feedback

Feedback exists in an amplifier whenever a portion of the voltage output is combined with the input signal. If the net effect of the feedback is to increase the input signal, the feedback is called positive or regenerative. In like manner when the net effect is to decrease the input, the feedback is called negative or degenerative. Feedback may arise either within the amplifier itself or through an external circuit.

Simple block diagrams of an amplifier without and with external feedback are given in Fig. 13. In part (a) the amplifier voltage gain G is

$$G = \frac{e_z}{e_s} \quad \text{and} \quad e_z = Ge_s \tag{4}$$

In part (b) a fraction of the output voltage β is fed back and combined with the input signal. The resulting input signal to the input amplifier e_s' is

$$e_s' = e_s + \beta e_z \tag{5}$$

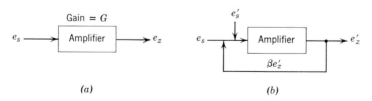

Fig. 13. Block diagram of feedback.

This new input voltage signal produces an output voltage e_z'

$$e_z' = G(e_s + \beta e_z) = Ge_s + G\beta e_z' \qquad (6)$$

and

$$e_z' = \frac{Ge_s}{1 - G\beta} \qquad (7)$$

The resulting gain G' of the amplifier with feedback becomes

$$G' = \frac{\text{output voltage}}{\text{input signal}} = \frac{e_z}{e_s} = \frac{G}{1 - G\beta} \qquad (8)$$

In equation 8 the magnitude of the feedback is represented by $G\beta$. When this feedback is positive, the resulting gain of the amplifier is greater than the initial gain (without feedback) and we say the feedback is positive and regenerative. Conversely, when the effect of the feedback $G\beta$ is negative, the resulting amplifier gain is decreased and the feedback of the amplifier is called negative or degenerative. The negative feedback circuit reduces distortion and improves the stability of the amplifier. This circuit is one of the important inventions of this twentieth century and has wide applications. Positive feedback is important in oscillator circuits and is given subsequent treatment.

The basic theory of the feedback circuit is relatively simple, but the design of the feedback circuit presents difficult problems in avoiding variation in phase and magnitude with changes in frequency.

Gain Control and Stabilization

The amount of gain produced in an amplifier may be controlled in several ways. The simplest manual method to control the gain (or volume) is shown in Fig. 14 wherein a potentiometer form of variable resistance determines the magnitude of signal applied to the grid. A second method of gain control utilizes a variable-mu tube having a high degree of curvature near the cutoff of the i_b–e_c curve. Here a variation of the grid bias determines the point on the curve where the grid signal is applied and thus controls the gain of the tube. In radio-receiver circuits this method of gain control is made automatic, giving automatic volume control to take care of the fading of broadcast waves in space.

The over-all gain in a single or a multistage amplifier may be stabilized and held constant by the use of a negative feedback circuit, shown in the block diagrams of Fig. 13 and discussed in the

Fig. 14. Simple gain-control circuit for an amplifier.

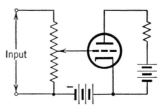

preceding article. In the feedback circuit the phase is shifted so that the feedback voltage has a minus sign. With the feedback circuit open the gain might be 60 db, but with the negative feedback in operation the gain may be reduced to 40 db. With the feedback in operation, the over-all gain has been stabilized. If the cathode emission or power supply potential in the amplifier circuit rises to cause an increase in gain, then the negative feedback signal is increased in proportion, and thus cuts back the net input signal strength. Any tendency for the amplifier gain to decrease has the opposite effect, and hence the over-all gain is stabilized very effectively. This circuit also reduces greatly any distortion arising within the stages of the amplifier itself, because such components of distortion are fed back in the negative sense to the grid, and hence are largely canceled.

Another form of balanced or stabilized amplifier circuit used in industrial control applications is shown in Fig. 15. This circuit carries the names of *cathode-coupled circuit* and the *long-tailed pair*. Two like triodes or other multielectrode amplifier tubes *T*1 and *T*2 (often contained in a single enclosure) are connected to equal load

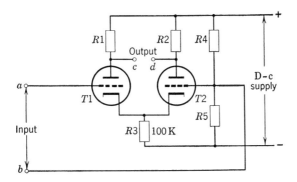

Fig. 15. Long-tailed pair circuit.

resistors $R1$ and $R2$. The common point for their cathodes is fed through a single cathode resistor $R3$ which has a large magnitude (say 100,000 ohms), giving rise to the term a *long-tailed pair*. The grid of tube $T2$ has a potential which is fixed with respect to the d-c supply by the resistors $R4$ and $R5$. The input to the amplifier is applied between the grids at points a and b, and the output appears between the plates of the tubes. If the input voltage is zero, both grids are at the same potential and the tubes will conduct equal currents which will be limited by the rise of potential across the common cathode resistor $R3$ and the drop of potential across equal load resistors $R1$ and $R2$. For balanced conditions both tubes will conduct the same current, and zero potential difference will exist across the output at points c and d. Now if a voltage is introduced into the input which makes a positive with respect to b, tube $T1$ will conduct more current and the rise in current through $R3$ will produce a rise of potential across $R3$, which tends to reduce the difference in potential between the cathode and grid of both tubes. The net result is a rise of current in tube $T1$ and a reduction of current in tube $T2$, which gives a difference in potential across the output cd. A lowering of the grid potential at a will produce an opposite effect. In practice the sum of the currents through the tubes does not change much with variations of the input voltage.

An indicating instrument connected across the output of Fig. 15 converts the circuit into a vacuum-tube voltmeter. The substitution of the d-c windings of saturable reactors for resistors $R1$ and $R2$ makes possible some very useful control applications to be discussed in later chapters.

Principles of Oscillation

Oscillation occurs naturally in the simple parallel LC circuit of Fig. 16. If switch S is thrown to the left, the battery charges the capacitor C by removing electrons from the top plate and storing them on the lower plate. This action stores energy in the electric field of the capacitor. Now turn the switch S to the right and the capacitor will discharge through the inductance L with electrons moving from the lower plate back to the upper. The rising current through L will store energy in the magnetic field surrounding it. When C becomes discharged, the energy of its charge will have been transferred to the magnetic field of L. This stored energy in L will continue the flow of electrons and begin to charge C with a reversed polarity. This process continues until all the energy in the magnetic

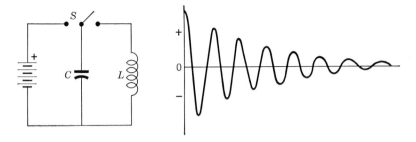

Fig. 16. Elementary oscillatory circuit.

field has been transferred to C. At this point C begins to discharge again with a reversed direction of electron flow. Obviously, when C has released all its stored energy to the inductance L, the latter will have acquired energy to recharge C with the same polarity as originally provided by the battery. Now the circuit is restored to its original condition and is ready to repeat the process. If both the inductance and capacitance were without resistance or any form of loss, the resulting ideal circuit would continue to oscillate indefinitely. Such ideal circuits cannot be realized and some resistance is always present. Such resistance will reduce each swing of current as illustrated in the right view of Fig. 16. The larger the value of circuit resistance, the more rapidly the oscillations will be damped out. A freely swinging pendulum will have its oscillations damped out with time (like right view of Fig. 16). In a clock the pendulum is kept swinging with a uniform stroke by adding enough mechanical energy to each stroke to supply the losses due to friction and windage. In a similar manner, the LC circuit of Fig. 16 may be made to continue oscillations of uniform magnitude by adding the necessary electrical impulse at each swing. The LC circuit has a natural period or frequency which is determined by its resonant frequency f_r, where

$$f_r = \frac{1}{2\pi\sqrt{LC}}$$

and the magnitude of this frequency can be controlled through changes of L and C.

Oscillations may be produced electronically in any amplifying circuit if the input of the amplifier is excited in a suitable manner. Electronic oscillators may be classified on the basis of (1) wave form produced or (2) the principle employed for excitation. The output wave form may be sinusoidal or nonsinusoidal, and the excitation may be self-generated or external. The four common methods of excitation or control which constitute a basis for oscillator classification are: (1) feedback (external), (2) negative resistance (internal feedback), (3) mechanical (crystal vibration), and (4) relaxation.

Vacuum-Tube and Transistor Oscillators

Amplifier circuits are usually designed to reproduce and amplify the signal voltage and frequency applied to the input. If a part of the voltage output is fed back to the input in the proper phase relation, the amplifier will be self-excited and under proper conditions will oscillate. Simple circuits to accomplish this result are shown in Fig. 17. In this circuit, coil L_p in the plate output is coupled inductively to coil L of the tuned LC circuit which, in turn, establishes the signal voltage applied to the grid. When the switch S in the plate circuit is closed, current flows in the plate-cathode circuit through L_p. The rising flux in L_p threads coil L inducing a voltage which charges C. When the plate current reaches its normal value, the energy in the magnetic field of L overruns, charging C to a higher potential. After reaching a peak level, C discharges into L and the LC tuned circuit oscillates at a frequency determined by its resonant frequency. The oscillating grid signal causes the plate current to oscillate which, in turn, feeds back enough energy to overcome the losses in the LC tuned circuit. Thus the circuit of Fig. 17a becomes

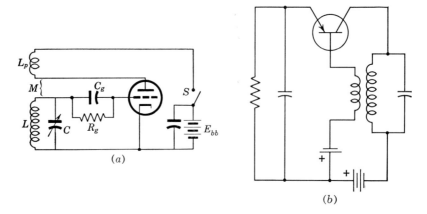

Fig. 17. (a) Tuned grid oscillator. (b) Tuned collector oscillator.

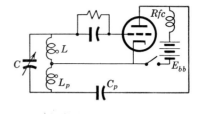

Fig. 18. Hartley oscillator circuit.

a self-excited amplifier. The transistor circuit of Fig. 17b operates in a similar manner.

The conditions necessary for sustained oscillations in a self-excited vacuum-tube oscillator are:

1. The feedback of power from the plate circuit to the grid must have a phase reversal of 180 degrees.

2. The power fed back must be sufficient to supply the losses in the grid input.

3. A tuned circuit LC is generally used in either the output or input or both to establish a resonant frequency. (Exceptions to this statement are given at the end of this section.)

4. Oscillators that are operated Class C (for high frequency) should have all or part of the d-c grid bias furnished by a grid leak. If a fixed bias is used, no initial plate current will flow and oscillations cannot start.

Obviously, many circuits can be designed to produce a vacuum-tube oscillator. Four of the more important ones are now given.

One form of the *Hartley* oscillator circuit is given in Fig. 18. Here the coupling of the load to the input is combined with the tuned LC coil so that the a-c component of the plate current flows through L_p to the cathode. The radio-frequency is kept out of the plate supply by the Rfc choke. The frequency of oscillation is controlled by the variable condenser C, whereas the signal voltage applied to the grid is adjusted by the cathode tap between L and L_p. The capacitor C_p prevents any short circuit of the plate supply through the tuning coil.

The *Colpitts* oscillator circuits of Fig. 19 are similar to the Hartley circuit since a pair of capacitors C_1 and C_2 replace the series inductances L and L_p, giving a capacitive type of feedback. Tuning is accomplished by varying the inductance of L, though it is possible to use a fixed L and to vary C_1 and C_2 by a ganged variable control. In Fig. 19a the grid-bias resistor must be connected directly to the cathode to provide the d-c bias.

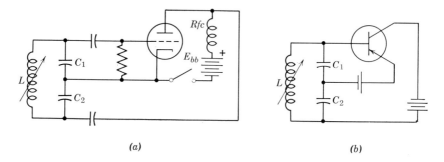

(a)   (b)

Fig. 19. Colpitts oscillator circuits.

An *electron-coupled* oscillator circuit is illustrated in Fig. 20. This circuit uses a tetrode connected so that its cathode, control grid, and screen grid act as an oscillator similar to the Hartley circuit of Fig. 18, and the plate circuit of the tetrode serves in the capacity of an amplifier, thus giving a greater output capacity. The coupling between the two circuits and the two functions is the electron stream within the tube, and hence the term electron-coupled oscillator. In this oscillator a tuned circuit is used in both the input and output circuits. Since the screen grid is held at radio-frequency ground potential and also serves as a shield between the two circuits, this oscillator is very stable and load variations have little effect on frequency change. Another factor that aids the stability of the electron-coupled oscillator is that an increase in screen voltage will decrease the frequency, whereas an increase of plate voltage will increase the frequency. Thus a proper adjustment of the tap on the resistor R will make the frequency independent of supply-voltage variations.

The frequency of oscillations generated by the tickler-coil, Hartley,

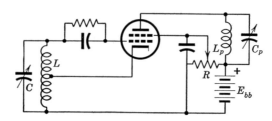

Fig. 20. Electron-coupled oscillator circuit.

and Colpitts oscillator circuits is affected considerably by changes in load, supply voltages, and temperature. Although the variation in frequency is small in electron-coupled oscillators, it is sufficient to be objectionable in broadcast transmitters, telephone carrier systems, and similar applications. Where precision frequency control of a constant frequency is necessary, crystal-controlled oscillator circuits are employed.

Certain crystalline substances such as quartz, Rochelle salts, and tourmaline exhibit mechanical and electrical properties known as the piezoelectric effect. Thus, if a mechanical force is applied to one of these substances, a voltage is developed. Conversely, if a thin slab of the substance is connected to a source of alternating voltage, it changes its physical shape and produces mechanical vibrations. Thin pieces are cut from quartz crystals for use in crystal oscillator circuits. When such a crystal starts vibrating at its resonant frequency, it will take only a small force of the same frequency to obtain vibrations of a large amplitude. The mechanical resonant frequency of a crystal depends chiefly on its thickness. When an alternating voltage is applied to a crystal that has the same mechanical frequency as the applied voltage, it will vibrate, and only a small voltage need be applied to keep it vibrating. In turn, the crystal will generate a relatively large voltage at its resonant frequency. If this crystal is placed between the grid and cathode of a vacuum tube and a small amount of energy is taken from the plate circuit and applied to the crystal to keep it vibrating, the circuit will act as an oscillator. The natural frequency of a crystal is critical (and precise). Thus if the constants of the oscillator circuits are properly adjusted the crystal will assure a precise frequency output.

A crystal-controlled oscillator stage using a tetrode tube is shown in Fig. 21a. It will be noted that this circuit is similar to the electron-coupled oscillator except that the quartz crystal and grid leak have replaced the tuned input circuit. The feedback takes place through the plate-to-grid capacitance within the tube. A crystal controlled oscillator circuit using a transistor as amplifier is given in Fig. 21b.

The power output demanded of vacuum-tube oscillators depends on the application. For the majority of applications the oscillator is used merely as a source of a high-frequency signal which is fed into an amplifier to secure the required power. For such uses a power output from the oscillator of 1 to 5 watts is ample. This low power

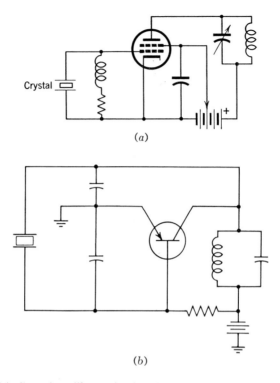

Fig. 21. (a) Crystal oscillator circuit. (b) Crystal controlled transistor oscillator circuit.

output is desirable because larger loads tend to affect the stability and frequency of the Hartley, Colpitts, and similar circuits. The electron-coupled circuit, however, does provide moderate power output with good stability. There are a few applications, such as high-frequency heating (to be covered later), where stability of frequency is unimportant but where a large power output is needed. For such applications circuits of the Colpitts, Hartley, or other types may be used with water-cooled tubes and circuit components of high voltage and current capacity so that a power output of from one to many kilowatts may be attained. In those circuits the load inductor or capacitor for the heating process may constitute all or a part of the tank circuit for the plate of the oscillator tube. For other applications the oscillator is loaded by an inductive or capacitive coupling to the plate circuit of the oscillator tube.

Nonsinusoidal Oscillators

For many applications wave forms are desired that are not sinus-oidal. Such waves are usually rectangular or triangular with respect to the time axis. They are used for control purposes where it is necessary to have a circuit turn on and off periodically for the time base in oscilloscopes, for the sweep circuits in television receivers, for pulse and marker circuits in radar systems, and for many other applications. In the circuits that generate oscillations of this type, the tube operates as an electronic switch which opens and closes to control the current flow through a load resistance. Usually the grid is driven far into the positive region so that the tube operates under Class C conditions, with the operating angle adjusted to give the required wave shape.

The most common nonsinusoidal oscillator is the multivibrator which consists of a two-stage, RC-coupled amplifier whose output is fed directly back to the input, as illustrated in Fig. 22. The frequency of oscillation is determined by the time constant of the coupling condensers and grid resistors, and, if the time constants in the two grid circuits are equal, the wave will be symmetrical. An increase in voltage at plate $T1$ causes grid $T2$ to swing toward the positive, which increases the current in $T2$. This rise of current lowers the plate voltage of tube $T2$ and the grid voltage of $T1$. The reduced grid potential of $T1$ causes the voltage at plate of tube $T1$ to rise even higher, and the action proceeds until grid of $T2$ is driven positively and grid of $T1$ negatively past cutoff. Grid of tube $T1$ will lose its negative charge at a rate determined by its RC circuit. As soon as tube $T1$ begins to draw plate current the action reverses

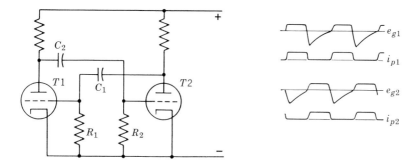

Fig. 22. Multivibrator circuit.

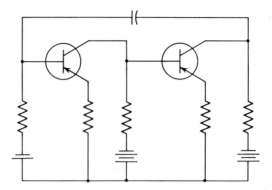

Fig. 23. A transistor multivibrator circuit.

very rapidly until grid of $T1$ is driven positively and $T2$ is negative. The rate at which oscillation occurs is approximately $1/(R_1C_1 + R_2C_2)$ cycles per second. Plate current flows in rectangular pulses, first in one tube and then in the other. The multivibrator circuit may be adjusted for frequencies from less than 1 to 100,000 cycles per second. A similar multivibrator circuit using transistors is given in Fig. 23.

Multivibrators are useful because their output contains harmonics up to several hundred times the fundamental frequency. Also, they are sensitive to synchronization since their rate of oscillation may be readily increased by the application of a small triggering voltage. Under these conditions the multivibrator frequency will be the synchronizing frequency divided by an integer. When the integer is greater than unity, the circuit acts as a frequency divider. Stability decreases as the rate of division increases but is satisfactory up to ratios of ten or more.

A simple relaxation oscillator circuit and its wave form are illustrated in Fig. 24. In this circuit a resistor and capacitor in series are connected across a source of d-c supply and a glow tube is placed in parallel with the condenser. When the direct voltage is first applied, current flows through the resistor R into the condenser and begins to charge it. The voltage across the condenser ($e_c = $ charge$/C$) rises until it reaches the "firing" or discharge value of the glow tube. When the glow tube fires, it takes whatever current is passed by R plus a heavy discharge current from the capacitor. The voltage e_c across the capacitor falls very rapidly until it reaches the extinction

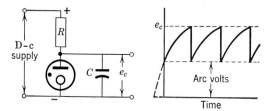

Fig. 24. Simple relaxation oscillator circuit.

point—the minimum ionizing potential across the glow tube. Now the glow tube ceases to conduct and the capacitor starts to charge again. When the capacitor voltage reaches the tube firing potential, the process is repeated. Thus this simple circuit, known as a relaxation oscillator, will produce a series of sawtooth voltage timing waves (Fig. 24, right) which are useful in oscilloscopes and similar devices. A thyratron can be substituted for the glow tube in the relaxation oscillator circuit to give more power and a wider range of control.

Another special circuit for producing sharp current pulses is the blocking oscillator shown in Fig. 25, which uses an iron-cored transformer connected for positive feedback. Increase in the plate current of the tube induces a voltage in the grid winding of the transformer which drives the grid far into the positive region; thus a large grid current is caused to flow and charge the coupling condenser. Plate current increases until the tube reaches saturation. At this point the large negative grid voltage which has been developed across C_g begins to fall as C_g discharges through R_g. Plate current cannot flow again until the charge on the capacitor leaks off through the grid resistor. The duration of the plate-current pulses depends mainly upon the natural resonance of the feedback transformer, whereas the

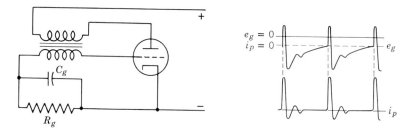

Fig. 25. Blocking oscillator circuit.

rate at which these pulses occur is determined by the RC constant of the grid circuit. Blocking oscillators can be readily synchronized and may be used as frequency dividers. They may be followed by a discharge tube and condenser to provide a sawtooth wave form. Blocking oscillators can also be used to advantage in radar equipment to establish the pulse repetition rate and to generate marker "pips."

Magnetic Amplifier Devices

The magnetic amplifier is a variable inductance device that magnifies and controls the power delivered to a load. It differs from a vacuum-tube and transistor amplifiers which are variable resistance devices, in that its operation depends on the nonlinear magnetization of ferromagnetic materials.

The magnetic amplifier is not new. Some forms of this device have been well understood in America throughout the twentieth century. E. F. W. Alexanderson applied the device for radio telegraphy as early as 1916. In the electric power field the saturable reactor form of amplifier has been used for many years. The rapid development and application of the vacuum-tube amplifier led American engineers to overlook the possibilities of the saturable magnetic device. Meanwhile, the German scientists made marked improvements in the magnetic amplifier which came to our attention during and after World War II. The basic improvement lay in converting the magnetic amplifier to a self-exciting or self-saturating device through the addition of rectifiers in the load circuit.

The three basic elements in any magnetic amplifying device are a closed magnetic circuit, an output or load circuit, and an input or signal circuit, as suggested in Fig. 27a. The *power applied* to the load circuit is *always* alternating current and the power applied for the input or signal circuit is usually a varying direct current. The key to the operation of the device lies in the magnetization curves and hysteresis loops of the magnetic cores, as depicted in Fig. 26. As the direct current or magnetizing force (ampere-turns) is increased in Fig. 26a, the resulting flux ϕ rises along the heavy line *oabc*. Upon reaching the point b on the magnetization curve, the iron core becomes saturated and no further change takes place except what would occur in an air-cored coil. Now if we were to apply an alternating current (instead of direct current) about the vertical ordinate through the origin, a flux change would take place along the line $a'a$. Here the flux change would be large and the self-inductance of the coil would be very large, thus limiting the resulting

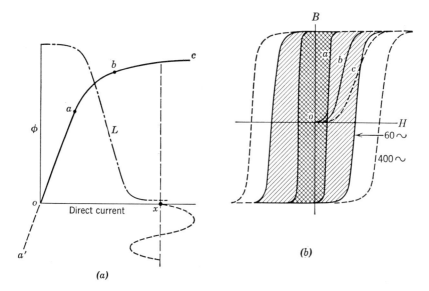

Fig. 26. Magnetization curves and hysteresis loops of magnetic materials.

current. Again, if the alternating current were superimposed upon a direct current of value ox, there would be little flux change and a small self-inductance. Thus the self-inductance of a coil wound on a magnetic core would follow the dot-dash curve labeled L on Fig. 26a.

Several special magnetic materials have been developed with superior properties of high permeability, steep magnetization curves, and low-hysteresis and eddy-current losses. These materials are known under trade names such as Deltamax, Mo-Permalloy, Supermalloy, Hipernik, and Mu-Metal. These materials have characteristics of the general form shown in Fig. 26b. Curve (a) shows the static or d-c magnetization characteristic. When subject to frequency changes, these characteristics change to a dynamic characteristic as shown by curves (b), for 60 cycles, and (c), for 400 cycles. The complete hysteresis loop for the material is indicated by the double crosshatch area for the d-c or static change, single cross for 60-cycle, and the total area for 400-cycle. These characteristics are very important in determining the design and efficiency of magnetic amplifiers.

There are two general classes of magnetic amplifiers for which no distinctive names have been adopted. For the purposes of this text the terms saturable reactor amplifier and self-excited magnetic amplifier are being used.

Saturable Reactor Amplifier

The circuit and operating wave forms for an elementary saturable reactor amplifier are shown in Fig. 27. If an a-c voltage is applied to the load circuit and if the d-c input is zero (voltage and current), the magnetic core operates along the line $a'a$ in Fig. 26a. For this region of flux variation, the inductance of the coil is high and only a small current (exciting) flows in the load circuit. This current is alternating and indicated as i_0 in Fig. 27b. Now if the d-c input circuit is closed and adjusted to give a current corresponding to x on Fig. 26, the magnetic core is saturated, the self-inductance of the coil is near zero, and the load current is limited only by the resistances of the load and load coil winding. Thus a full wave of alternating current flows in the load. Additional adjustments of the d-c input between o and x will produce variations in the period in the half cycles when saturation is reached with corresponding variation in L and load current waves, as suggested by current waves i, i_1, and i_2 in Fig. 27b. Obviously, for the operating region from a to b on Fig. 26, the positive and negative current waves are not symmetrical and harmonics are introduced into the load circuit.

The two-legged elementary saturable reactor amplifier has the disadvantage that current changes in the load circuit induce high voltages into the d-c input circuit which may cause insulation break-down, and they also interfere with the control by the signal. This disadvantage is overcome by using a magnetic-balanced, three-legged core, as shown in Fig. 28. Here the load windings are placed on the outside legs and the signal winding on the center leg. The load coils

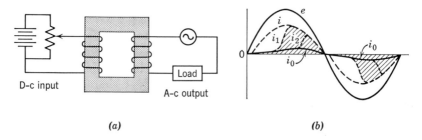

(a)   (b)

Fig. 27. Elementary saturable reactor amplifier and resultant wave forms.

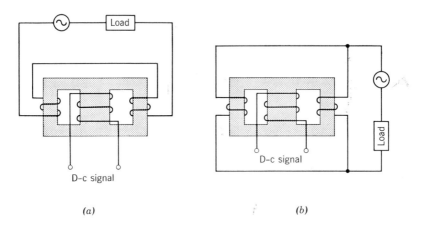

(a)   *(b)*

Fig. 28. Saturable reactor amplifier with (*a*) load coils in series and (*b*) load coils in parallel.

are connected so that their magnetomotive forces are in series (additive) in the magnetic circuit comprising the outside legs but are opposed in the central leg. Therefore, they do not induce any emf in the input winding on the central leg (except for possible reluctance unbalances in the magnetic circuit).

The response time of any magnetic amplifier is the time (usually expressed in cycles of the power frequency) required for the output voltage to reach a major fraction (usually 63 per cent) of its final average value in response to a change of signal voltage. The minimum response time in any magnetic amplifier is inherently of the order of 1 to 3 cycles. When response time is critical, it can be reduced by using higher frequencies such as 400 cycles and higher. It may also be reduced by control of self-inductance of windings, leakage fluxes, etc. However, for the usual applications of saturable reactor amplifiers, response time is usually not critical.

The load winding for the saturable reactor amplifier may be connected in series or parallel, as illustrated in Fig. 28*a* and *b*, respectively. The series connection provides a shorter time response and a higher internal voltage drop. It is generally used for controlling loads of small magnitude. The parallel connection is usually employed for controlling relatively large loads (½ to 300 kva) and when a response time of 1 to 3 sec is not objectionable. The d-c control power varies from a few microwatts up to 50 watts.

Saturable reactors are used to control electric heating devices

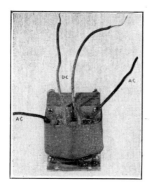

Fig. 29. Saturable reactors: *left,* small size for thyratron phase-shift circuit; *right,* 10-kva and 4-kva units. (Courtesy General Electric Company.)

such as industrial furnaces, superheaters, milk pasteurizers, boilers, etc. In conjunction with temperature control devices, these amplifiers provide proportional or "throttling" power control which is capable of holding temperature within very close limits. Saturable reactors are also used for reduced voltage starting on large capacity a-c motors. They may also be used for voltage regulation. Some commercial saturable reactor amplifiers are shown in Fig. 29.

Self-Excited Magnetic Amplifiers

An elementary self-excited magnetic amplifier and circuit is illustrated in Fig. 30. The commercial forms of the self-excited magnetic amplifier are known by trade names such as Amplistat and Magamp. This unit differs from the elementary saturable reactor amplifier of Fig. 27 in several ways. First, the load circuit contains a blocking rectifier usually consisting of a selenium or silicon diode. This means that the current in the load circuit must be unidirectional for the load winding. Since it is unidirectional, it tends to excite or saturate the iron core and there arises the terms self-exciting and self-saturating. In another sense this unidirectional current may be considered in the light of a positive feedback since it may add ampere-turns to the d-c input signal.

Second, the iron core of Fig. 30 usually differs in two ways from that of Fig. 27. The magnetic material is usually of a special type like that of Fig. 26b, having a very steep magnetization curve. Thus only small changes of magnetizing force are needed to produce large changes in resulting flux. In addition, the cross section of the mag-

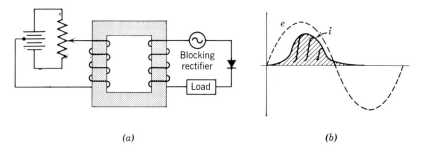

Fig. 30. Elementary self-excited magnetic amplifier.

netic core is reduced so that saturation takes place at lower values of exciting ampere-turns. Third, the d-c input signal may reverse.

The operation of this self-excited magnetic amplifier is shown by the characteristic curve of Fig. 31 and the wave forms of Fig. 30b. First the blocking rectifier causes the load current to be half-wave rectification. If the d-c signal is positive and carries the flux up to near saturation at point a, the applied load voltage e will cause a self-exciting load current i to carry the core flux to saturation, and a nearly complete rectified loop or current will result. If the signal current is zero, the self-exciting load current will produce saturation at some point near midway in the half cycle with a resulting reduced

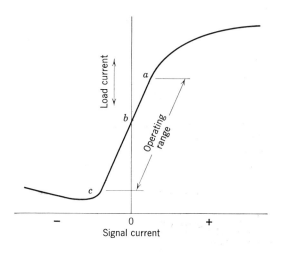

Fig. 31. Operating characteristic of a self-excited magnetic amplifier.

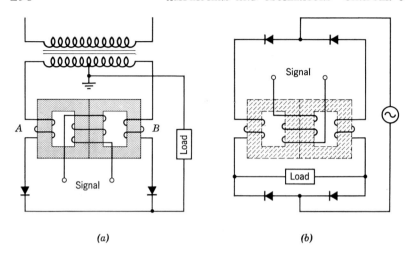

(a)   (b)

Fig. 32. Basic full-wave magnetic amplifier circuits giving d-c output. (*a*) Center-tap transformer. (*b*) Bridge circuit.

current loop. Again, if the d-c signal current is negative, it may bias the normal flux to a point such as *c* and now the rectified load current is unable to carry the core to saturation. Thus if the d-c signal or bias is controlled in the operating range from *a* to *c*, the rectified load current pulses have a wide range in magnitude. It may be noted that the varying rectified current pulses in Fig. 30*b* are analogous to those produced in the output of a thyratron having phase-shift grid control.

The elementary self-excited magnetic amplifier just discussed is undesirable for commercial applications because the load circuit induces voltages in the control circuit and because it uses only one-half wave amplification and is thereby inefficient.

A full-wave self-excited magnetic amplifier may be formed in two ways. First, two separate elementary circuits may be combined electrically by connecting the d-c bias or signal winding in series in such a manner that the induced voltages in them are opposed (see Fig. 33). Second, the magnetic cores of two elementary amplifiers may be placed adjacent and the d-c signal coil wound to encircle both magnetic cores as shown in Fig. 32.

Two full-wave self-excited magnetic amplifier circuits are shown in Fig. 32. Both circuits provide unidirectional or direct current in the load. Both circuits employ one magnetic core for each load winding with the signal coil encircling both cores to give a balanced magnetic effect. Each load coil and its associated blocking rectifier or rectifiers function like the elementary circuit previously described. The circuit of Fig. 32 employs a center-tap transformer and provides a grounded side for the load where this is desirable. The circuit of Fig. 32b is known as the bridge circuit and has the advantage of giving better operation on inductive loads because its two rectifiers connected across the load automatically tend to "snub" any inductive voltage kicks that arise in the load.

A third basic circuit for the self-excited magnetic amplifier is illustrated in Fig. 33. This circuit provides a nonsinusoidal alternating current and voltage output for the load circuit for those applications when alternating current is desired.

The preceding discussion of the magnetic amplifier has assumed a resistive load. An inductive load will produce a delay or phase shift in the rectified load current. Since the load current has a self-excitation effect, the phase shift interferes with the perfect functioning of the control signal. This unfavorable action can be compensated in three different ways as suggested in Fig. 34. First, a capacitor may be connected across the load. This addition raises the power factor and is satisfactory if the load is of low magnitude. Second, a blocking rectifier may be connected across the load to produce a commutating effect in short circuiting or snubbing the induced voltages when the load current pulse is decreasing. This action prevents these induced voltages from being reflected into the signal circuit. Last, a resistance can be placed in series with the load to re-

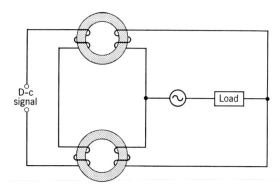

Fig. 33. Basic magnetic amplifier circuit with a-c output.

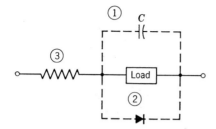

Fig. 34. Compensating circuits for inductive loads.

duce the phase shift. However, the last remedy leads to inefficiency but may be justifiable if the load requirements are light.

Magnetic amplifiers may be treated like vacuum-tube amplifiers in many ways. They may be connected in cascade to provide greater over-all amplification. They may be connected into a push-pull form of circuit. Also, they are often provided with an external feedback. The self-saturation effect may be considered as an intrinsic or internal feedback. The external feedback must be provided by leading the load current through an additional winding which parallels the d-c or input winding. This feedback may be either positive (aiding) or negative, as in the case of vacuum-tube amplifiers. The variable signal input in a magnetic amplifier may be inserted in series with the d-c bias winding as in the grid circuit of vacuum tubes. Again the magnetic amplifier may be provided with one or more input coils wound parallel to the d-c bias winding. Here separate signals may be applied to the magnetic amplifier to give an output which is a composite of the input of several variables.

The magnetic amplifier has a host of applications in the control field. It may be a vital unit for a voltage regulator or a speed regulator. It may control the operation of relays, small motor field and armatures, and heating elements. It has replaced the vacuum tube in many applications in military service in gun fire control, rocket guidance, etc.

The advantages of magnetic amplifiers relative to vacuum-tube amplifiers are:

1. Ruggedness and ability to withstand severe shock and vibration and other adverse environmental conditions.

2. Require no warm-up time.

3. Operate at low cost, require a minimum of maintenance, and have long life.

4. Have high over-all efficiency (better than 50 per cent and may be much higher in larger sizes).

The main disadvantage of the magnetic amplifier is the comparatively slow response time. (Frequencies up to 2000 cycles may be required to reduce the response time in critical applications.)

Dielectric Amplifiers

A dielectric amplifier is an experimental amplifying device which depends upon a variation of a capacitance for its operation. The capacity of a capacitor is

$$C = \frac{KA}{4.45t}$$

where C is in micromicrofarads, A is the area in square inches, t is the thickness of the dielectric in inches, and K is the dielectric constant. Since the capacity is directly proportional to K, any variation of K will control the capacitance of a unit. It is known that some dielectric materials exhibit the property of voltage sensitivity (K varies with impressed voltage) and are called ferroelectric. Accordingly, if a capacitor having a ferroelectric dielectric is placed in a circuit like that of Fig. 35, the circuit will have the properties of an amplifier. Here voltage variation applied as a signal to the capacitor produces large variation in the magnitude of the high-frequency output. This form of amplifier has found little application to date. It is given here to complete the list of devices possible for amplification.

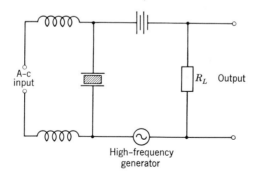

Fig. 35. Proposed circuit for a dielectric amplifier. (Courtesy Aerovox Corporation.)

Rotary Amplifiers

A d-c shunt generator is inherently a power amplifier. Any change in the power input to the shunt field is reflected in a large change in power output from the armature under load conditions. Modifications may be made in the design and circuits of a d-c generator to improve its inherent ability as an amplifier. The *amplidyne* is a widely used rotary amplifier. Its theory of action may be followed in the schematic circuit of Fig. 36. An input or control power is applied to a shunt field winding known as a control field. The excitation of this winding produces the field flux ϕ_{CF} which cuts the inductors of the revolving armature and induces an emf across the brushes cc'. If the brushes cc' are short circuited, a relatively large current will flow in the armature inductors and produce an armature cross field ϕ_{SC} in the direction indicated. This will be a relatively strong cross field (armature reaction) which will be cut by the revolving inductors and thereby furnish an emf across the brushes bb'. The output or load for the generator is taken from brushes bb'. Any load current from bb' flowing through the armature inductors will produce a field ϕ_L that will oppose the control field (demagnetizing action) and tend to weaken the action of the control field. To neutralize this demagnetizing action, a load-compensating field (series) is placed on the same poles as the control field and carries the load current, producing a field ϕ_C in such a direction as to oppose ϕ_L. With this compensation correctly effected, the output of the

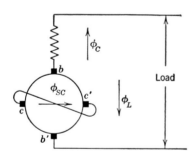

Fig. 36.   Magnetic fields in an amplidyne.

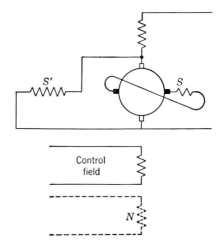

Fig. 37. Series and parallel booster
circuits.

generator should respond to changes of input in the control field and
with a high degree of amplification.

The amplifying action of the amplidyne may be increased further
by the addition of either the field S or S' shown in Fig. 37. These
fields are placed on poles that produce flux along the same direction
as the armature cross field ϕ_{sc}. Field S is a series field in the short-
circuit path and S' is a shunt field connected across brushes bb'.
Although both types of field S and S' could be used on the same machine, there is no need for such combined use. The output of the
amplidyne is controlled by one or more factors. Each factor involved
requires a separate control field and perhaps a separate winding.
One factor may be a constant and the corresponding field is known
as a neutralizing, standard, or reference field. A minimum of two
and a maximum of six control-field windings are used on amplidynes.
A second control or neutralizing field is shown as N on Fig. 37.

Most amplidynes operate as two-pole generators though the actual
machine has four segmental poles, as shown in Fig. 38. Segmental
poles N and N' and similarly S and S' act as one pole. The control
fields are wound on the individual poles and then connected so that N
and N' serve as one north pole structure. The compensating or load
fields may be wound on the individual poles or as a single winding
surrounding two segmental poles. Commutating poles and windings
are provided to give good commutation at the load brushes.

The amplification factor of the amplidyne is defined as the ratio
of the volt-amperes output to the volt-amperes input to the control

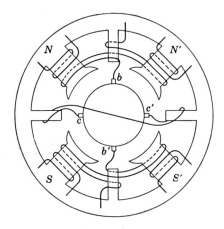

Fig. 38. Field circuits in an amplidyne.

field. The amplification is produced in two stages: first, from the control field to the quadrature field, and, second, from the quadrature field to the output. Amplifications varying from 100 to 100,000 are possible, though the usual practicable range is of the order of 5,000 to 10,000. Amplification can be gained at the expense of time or rate of response. If amplification is carried too far it may be too slow to be useful, especially in the control of sudden changes in machines. The amplification factor increases with the size of the amplidyne because the required control watts do not increase as fast as the output watts. The important things to know in selecting or designing an amplidyne are the amplification factor and the rate of response. The rate of response decreases slightly as the size of the machine increases. The average rate of the rise of voltage in the output is of the order of 2000 volts per second. A commercial amplidyne is illustrated in Fig. 39.

Other machines bearing the classification of the rotary amplifier are certain *multiple-field exciters*. Their theory of operation may be understood through a study of the several field-resistance lines of a typical d-c generator as shown in Fig. 40. For a field resistance of R_2 the no-load generated voltage will rise to R_2, the intersection of the saturation curve and the field-resistance line. For other values of field resistance other steady-state values of generated voltage may be found. There is some value for the field resistance for which the field-resistance line will coincide with and be tangent to the lower linear portion of the saturation curve. In Fig. 40 this is shown by the line OR. Since line OR does not intersect the saturation curve

Fig. 39. One kw amplidyne. (Courtesy General Electric Company.)

at any point where the lines coincide, the generated voltage could lie anywhere along this line of intersection and would not change unless disturbed by some change in field strength produced by some outside factor. But it will be very easy to shift the generated voltage up or down along this line by a change in field produced by a second control or signal winding of a few turns placed on the poles of the generator. Thus the control generator should have at least two separate fields, one designed to produce a field-resistance line coinciding with the linear part of the saturation curve, and the second a light field for receiving the control change or signal.

In order to obtain best results in control, the following points should be observed in the design of the control generator. First, the main field should be designed so that with a suitable external resistor the

Fig. 40. Field-resistance lines of generators.

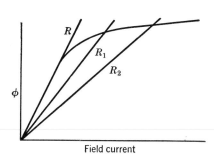

resistance line may be made to coincide with the saturation curve. Second, the cross section of magnetic circuit should be made relatively large so that the saturation curve will be linear throughout the voltage range for which the generator must operate. Third, the iron used for the field should have a low hysteresis loss and the inductance of all parts of the circuit should be low so that a quick response to all current changes may be obtained.

The basic and essential adjustment of the control generator, the coinciding of saturation curve and field-resistance line, is brought about by a self-excited field. This self-excitation may be secured by the use of a series field as shown in part (*a*) of Fig. 41, or a shunt field as in part (*b*) of the same figure. The first basic circuit is used in a commercial machine known as the Rototrol, whereas the latter circuit is used in a similar machine under the name Regulex. In either circuit, the "resistor" is adjusted to give proper operation for the applications involved. In both circuits operation requires the introduction of the signal through the "control" field. For some applications a single control-field winding may suffice, but usually two or more field coils will be needed. When the multifield exciter is used for regulation of voltage, current, or speed, two fields are needed. One field, known as the standard, comparison, reference, or pattern field, is connected to some fixed and constant source of potential. The second field, known as the signal, pilot, or control field, is connected to the varying unit which is to be regulated. These two fields are connected in opposition either in series to one winding or to separate windings so that, when the variable has the desired value, the two fields neutralize each other and the voltage generated by the control generator is stationary. When the varying unit moves up or down, it throws the reference and signal fields out of balance in such a direction as to cause a change in the generated voltage of

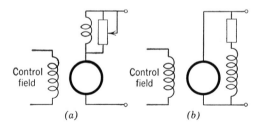

Fig. 41.   Circuits for multiple-field exciters.

the control generator which in turn instantly corrects the shift. In some applications all fields may be of the signal or control type, being connected to different varying factors and giving a composite change in the control generator output. A recent trend is to feed two electrical signals into an electronic amplifier so that their amplified difference operates a control field of the rotary amplifier.

Numerous applications of the multiple-field exciters are made on Ward Leonard systems for controlling speed, acceleration, deceleration, or torque of large motors. They may also be used where control is based on tension (paper, wire, etc.) or the "position" of some unit in an industrial application. These machines, like the amplidyne, can be used to control anything that is convertible into volts, amperes, or watts.

REFERENCES

1. Storm, H. F., *Magnetic Amplifiers,* John Wiley and Sons, New York, 1955.
2. Vincent, A. M., "Dielectric Amplifier Fundamentals," *Electronics,* December 1951.
3. *Dielectric Amplifiers, The Capacitor,* Cornell-Dubilier Electric Corp., July 1954.
4. Alexanderson, E. F. W., M. A. Edwards, and K. K. Bowman, "The Amplidyne Generator—A Dynamoelectric Amplifier for Power Control," *Gen. Elec. Rev.,* March 1940.

chapter 10

Components and Circuits for Control

Components and Circuits for Control

The marvelous achievements in the field of industrial electronics and control are made possible by the use of many components and devices. Several of these components are usually employed in combination to achieve the desired result. An understanding of any complete control system is simplified by a study and classification of the individual component circuits and devices. The complete equipment may be divided and classified in numerous ways. For the purpose of this textbook, the following classification of twelve items is made. The first three items on the list have been treated in the two preceding chapters; the others are to be covered in sequence before passing to the important applications in the industrial field.

1. Amplifiers
2. Oscillators
3. Rectifiers
4. Contactors
5. Voltage components
6. Phase-shift circuits
7. Time-control devices
8. Series impedance transformer
9. Peaking transformer
10. Nonlinear devices
11. Sensors
12. Transducers

Contactors

One of the basic functions in electric control operation is the closing of a circuit. Manual control is effected by the operation of a simple switch which may be push-button, snap, or thermal-overload. The latter has a built-in circuit breaker which opens the switch automatically when the load current exceeds the rated capacity. A pressure switch automatically controls gas or liquid pressure by starting or stopping the electric motor that operates an air compressor or a water pump on a home water supply system.

The mercury switch and the micro switch shown in Fig. 1 are automatic position-control or limit switches. The *mercury switch* consists of a small quantity of mercury sealed in a glass tube containing two contacts. The switch is a make-and-break type and is operated by a small (differential) angle of tilt. These switches are available in voltage ratings up to 250 volts and current ratings up to a maximum of 45 amp. The applications of the mercury switch are too numerous to mention. In a typical application, three mercury switches are located in the cover (lid) of an electric washing machine. When the lid is lifted, one switch tilts and stops the machine; actuated by a trigger, it also shuts off power if the spin-drying basket becomes unbalanced. A float actuates another switch to control proper water level, and the third switch then starts the washer agitator and begins the washing cycle.

The *micro switch* is a make-and-break quick-acting snap switch which is actuated by a small travel of $\frac{1}{16}$ in. or less (see Fig. 1b). This switch is built in ratings of 110 to 250 volts, and currents from 5 to 15 amp. As a limit switch it is employed to shut off the power that drives a traveling mechanism when the traveling unit reaches

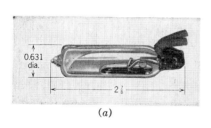

(a)

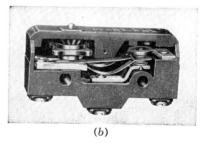

(b)

Fig. 1. (a) Mercury switch and (b) micro switch.

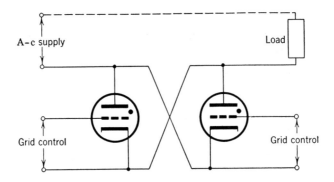

Fig. 2. Circuit contactor using thyratrons.

a predetermined point (such as the end of a lathe bed). In control applications this switch is operated either manually or mechanically as a part of a sequence or cycle in automatic equipment. In many machine tool operations it is used as a safety switch to protect operators, equipment, or material from injury or loss.

Magnetic relays are perhaps the oldest contacting devices in electrical engineering. Telephone switching systems have been built around the magnetic relay for three-quarters of a century. Relays are operated by small amounts of power but may control power involving thousands of amperes when applied as power line contactors. Naturally, magnetic relays play vital parts in all types of control systems.

Electron tubes are often used as electronic contactors. Any of the vacuum tubes, such as the triode, tetrode, or pentode, will block a current flow in the plate-cathode circuit when the grid is biased to cutoff. A positive shift of the grid potential will permit a flow of current for "off" and "on" switching operations. In a similar manner, the so-called trigger tubes, the thyratron, ignitron, and grid-glow tube, can be used as an electronic switch via grid control. The thyratron is adapted to control a moderate amount of power in an "on" and "off" switching operation. When it is desired to pass complete cycles of alternating current, two thyratrons may be employed as in the circuit of Fig. 2. Each thyratron serves to pass alternate half-cycles subject to individual grid control. The ignitron is used to control a large amount of power involving up to hundreds of amperes. One circuit for switching a heavy a-c load is shown in Fig. 3. Two ignitrons, *A* and *B*, are employed so that one or the other is

available for conduction in each direction. The igniters are fired by
separate gaseous diodes, a and b, for the "on" and "off" control
through the switch S. Operation may be traced as follows. With S
open, line voltage cannot be impressed across either diode a or b and
the ignitrons cannot be fired. Close switch S and assume that the
line voltage (sine curve) is rising in positive direction on the anodes
for tubes A and a. Then the cathodes of A and a will be negative so
that, when the voltage equals the ionization potential of tube a, it
conducts electrons from the lower side of the load through the mercury pool and the igniter of ignitron A to the cathode of a, and thence
back to the line. This "shot" of current passing through the igniter
of A fires ignitron A which then conducts a full wave of current having a magnitude determined by the load. When the voltage reverses
on the succeeding half-cycle, the anodes of tubes B and b become
positive and the cathodes negative so that b conducts and, in turn,
fires B for the reversed wave of current. Thus the circuit of Fig. 3
will act as a closed switch to conduct alternating current as long as S

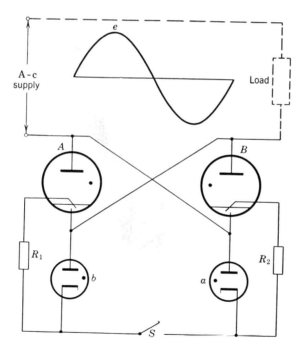

Fig. 3.   Ignitron contactor using gaseous diode firing.

is closed. When S is opened the main line will be opened the first time the a-c impressed voltage passes through zero. The substitution of some automatic control circuit in the place of switch S will give automatic control.

The gaseous diodes (phanotrons) of Fig. 3 may be replaced by blocking-layer rectifiers such as copper oxide or selenium. In some applications it is desirable to control the magnitude of the current as well as to provide "on" and "off" switch operation. This action can be secured by firing the ignitrons via thyratrons instead of phanotrons or blocking-layer rectifiers. A circuit for performing this function and another using copper oxide rectifiers are shown in Fig. 14, page 374. A commercial electronic switch employing ignitrons is shown in Fig. 15, page 375. The self-excited magnetic amplifier also belongs in the class of contactors. A modified form of the magnetic amplifier known as a static control unit is a contactor. It is treated in Chapter 15.

Voltage Components

The *source* of voltage for most stationary equipment is the a-c power supply. On heavy transportation equipment and some air-

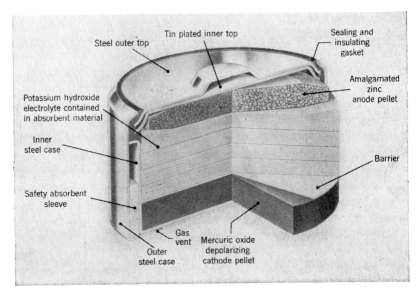

Fig. 4. Mercury cell. (Courtesy P. R. Mallory & Co., Inc.)

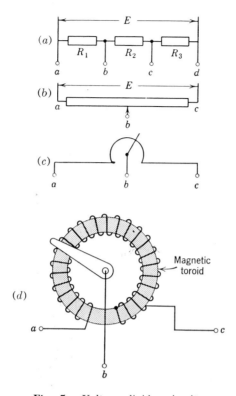

Fig. 5.   Voltage divider circuits.

planes, the voltage source is likely to be a d-c generator and a storage battery.   On lightweight portable equipment, the voltage source is likely to be dry cells or mercury cells.   The mercury cell (Fig. 4) has an emf of 1.345 volts, a long shelf life, and a high ratio of energy to volume and weight.   It is particularly suited for transistor applications requiring constant-current, low drain, and a long service life.

A *voltage divider* is a device for dividing a given voltage into two or more parts.   A fixed division is attained by impressing a potential across a number of resistors in series, as shown at the top of Fig. 5. Since the same current must flow through the series group, the drop in volts across each resistor IR is proportional to its resistance in ohms.   If in Fig. 5a, E is 100 volts, R_1 is 4 ohms, R_2 is 6 ohms, and R_3 is 10 ohms, the respective voltages appearing across the resistors are 20, 30, and 50 volts.   A wide range of voltage can be obtained by using a moving contact b on a long linear wire-wound resistor, as

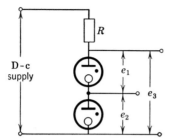

Fig. 6.   Circuit for providing constant voltages.

shown in Fig. 5*b*. The linear resistor may be produced in a circular form (Fig. 5*c*) to permit a rotary travel of the pointer *b*. These latter forms of voltage dividers are called potentiometers, or in electronic slang "pots." It should be noted that the voltage ratios in the preceding devices are accurate only if no current is drawn from the taps. A variable voltage power supply for alternating current is commonly known as a variac. It is a variable auto transformer consisting of a single-layer coil wound on a toroidal magnet core (Fig. 5*d*). Power supply voltage such as 115 volts a-c is impressed across points *a* and *c*. Contact *b* slides over uninsulated spots on the coil. The variable voltage between points *a* and *b* is proportional to the number of turns between these points.

Control circuits frequently require a constant direct voltage which is independent of the supply line potential. These constant voltage circuits supply a *reference potential* which is attained by connecting a voltage regulator or glow tube in series with a high resistance, as shown in Fig. 6. A Zener diode (silicon crystal semiconductor) may be used in place of the glow tube. Two or more potentials may be secured by placing two or more tubes or diodes in series.

Phase-Shift Circuits

The phase shift of voltages on single-phase circuits is readily controlled by the use of an a-c bridge. Such a circuit (Fig. 7) uses a transformer with a mid-tapped secondary to form two bridge arms *AO* and *OB* having equal induced voltages. The other two arms are made up of an inductance and a resistance as in *a* or a capacitor and a resistance as in *b*. A voltage phase shift from coil *AB* exists across the bridge points *O* and *G*. The variation in phase shift is produced by a variation of *R*, *L*, or *C*. The explanation of the shift is shown in the vector diagrams of Fig. 8. The voltage drop across *AB* must be equal to the vector sum of the drops across the arms *L* and *R*

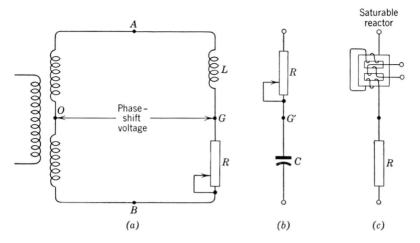

Fig. 7. A-c bridge circuits for producing phase shift.

(or R and C) in series. In each case the IR drop and IX drop will be at right angles to each other. A reduction of resistance R will reduce the IR drop and through some increase of the current will increase IX. A change of L or C will have a similar result. Thus a

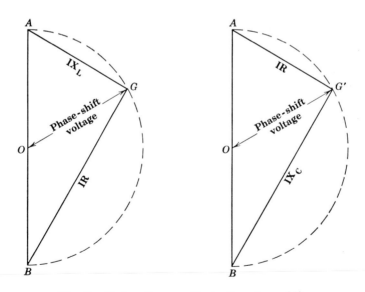

Fig. 8. Vector diagrams illustrating phase shift.

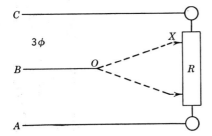

Fig. 9. Phase shift from a three-phase circuit.

variation of the magnitude of IR and IX arms of the impedance triangle will cause the point G or G' to swing on the arc of a circle AGB or $AG'B$. Since the midpoint of the transformer O is fixed, the voltage across OG is constant in magnitude but varies in phase with respect to AB as G or G' swings around the arc. Theoretically, the maximum phase shift is 180 degrees, but the full value cannot be realized in a practical circuit.

The phase shift in the a-c bridge may be controlled manually through a variable resistor R or through a variable inductance (variometer). For some industrial applications the inductance L is varied by sliding an iron core within a solenoid. For electronic control the variation in the inductance is generally secured by replacing L with a saturable reactor (part c of Fig. 7). A variation in phase shift can be secured also by varying the capacitance C, although this method has little practical use.

Voltage phase shift for three-phase and multiphase circuits can be secured by the same principle as described for single-phase circuits though other methods are to be preferred. The simplest and cheapest method is to place a potentiometer (resistance) across one phase of a three-phase circuit as illustrated in Fig. 9. The phase of the

Fig. 10. Hand-operated selsyn transmitter and phase shifter. (Courtesy General Electric Company.)

voltage between C and X can be varied through a range of 60 degrees by moving point X along the resistor R. Phase shift can be secured by manual control of a phase shifter (similar to Fig. 10). This device consists of an a-c motor stator having a three-phase winding and a rotor wound with a similar three-phase winding. The phase of the voltage induced in the rotor relative to the stator will be determined by the fixed position of the rotor.

Time-Control Devices

The timing of operations in industrial control may be performed by electric circuits, magnetic devices, and mechanical devices. The time required for transient current and voltage changes in inductances and capacitors is very useful in timing operations. Four common combinations of RC and RL are shown in Fig. 11 together with the equations and curves of transient currents and voltages. It is recommended that the student review these relations carefully. Combinations of R and C are the most useful circuit groupings. If, for example, a d-c source is used to charge a capacitor in parallel with a resistor (Fig. 11b) and the switch to the supply is opened, the capacitor will discharge at a definite rate. The rate of discharge is determined by the time constant RC of the circuit (see Fig. 12). After an elapsed time equal to the time constant RC, the voltage will fall to 37 per cent of its initial value. Similarly, after a second interval equal to RC, the voltage across the condenser will decay to 37 per cent of the value held at the end of the first period. Since this rate of voltage decay is exact and reliable, this form of timing circuit is very useful. A simple formula for this circuit is time (seconds) = resistance (megohms) $\times$ capacity (microfarads), for decay to 37 per cent initial value. Thus, in Fig. 12, if R is 1 meg, C is 1 μf, and E is 100 volts, the voltage will fall from 100 to 37 in 1 sec. Doubling the value of either R or C will double the time required for the same voltage change, thus giving simple timing control.

The shape of the voltage decay curve with time can be controlled by the substitution of some nonlinear device in the place of a resistance. For example, a pentode tube properly used in place of R will give a linear decay curve.

The rise and decay of transient currents and voltages in series and parallel circuits containing R and L are similar to those in the RC circuits, as shown in parts c and d of Fig. 11. The time constant for the RL circuit is L/R, and the time required for a rise or drop to the 37 per cent value can be increased by increasing L or decreasing R.

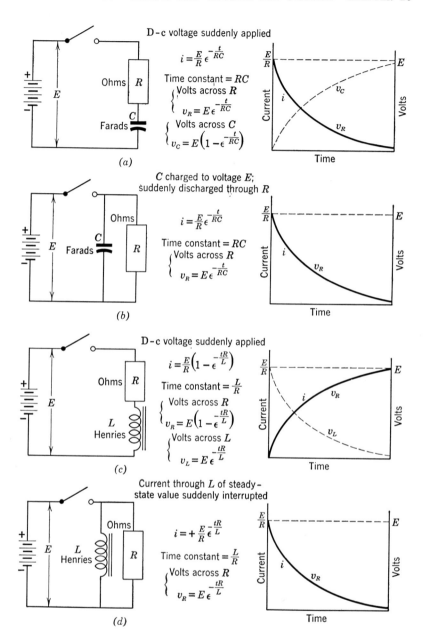

D-c voltage suddenly applied

$$i = \frac{E}{R}\,\epsilon^{-\frac{t}{RC}}$$

Time constant $= RC$

$\begin{cases}\text{Volts across } R \\ v_R = E\,\epsilon^{-\frac{t}{RC}}\end{cases}$

$\begin{cases}\text{Volts across } C \\ v_C = E\left(1 - \epsilon^{-\frac{t}{RC}}\right)\end{cases}$

(a)

C charged to voltage E; suddenly discharged through R

$$i = \frac{E}{R}\,\epsilon^{-\frac{t}{RC}}$$

Time constant $= RC$

$\begin{cases}\text{Volts across } R \\ v_R = E\,\epsilon^{-\frac{t}{RC}}\end{cases}$

(b)

D-c voltage suddenly applied

$$i = \frac{E}{R}\left(1 - \epsilon^{-\frac{tR}{L}}\right)$$

Time constant $= \frac{L}{R}$

$\begin{cases}\text{Volts across } R \\ v_R = E\left(1 - \epsilon^{-\frac{tR}{L}}\right)\end{cases}$

$\begin{cases}\text{Volts across } L \\ v_L = E\,\epsilon^{-\frac{tR}{L}}\end{cases}$

(c)

Current through L of steady-state value suddenly interrupted

$$i = +\frac{E}{R}\,\epsilon^{-\frac{tR}{L}}$$

Time constant $= \frac{L}{R}$

$\begin{cases}\text{Volts across } R \\ v_R = E\,\epsilon^{-\frac{tR}{L}}\end{cases}$

(d)

Fig. 11. Assemblies of timing circuits.

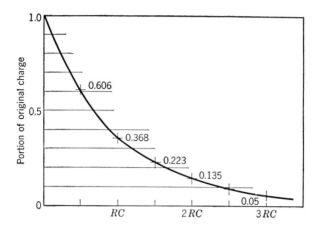

Fig. 12. *RC* time delay curve.

One useful application of the *RL* circuit is made in the construction
of slow-acting relays. In Fig. 13, left, a relay is shown which consists of a d-c coil and a heavy copper ring or "slug" placed on an
iron core. When the d-c coil is excited, the core becomes magnetized
and attracts the armature *A* and closes a circuit. When the d-c circuit to the coil is opened, the flux in the core begins to decay, but
the decrease of flux within the copper ring gives a change in the flux
linkages, causing an emf and resulting current which opposes the
change in flux. The *L/R* time constant of the copper ring determines
the rate of decay of flux. Since only a small amount of flux is necessary to hold up the armature when in contact with the iron core,
there will be some delay before the armature is released. The length
of time delay can be controlled in a fixed design by the axial length

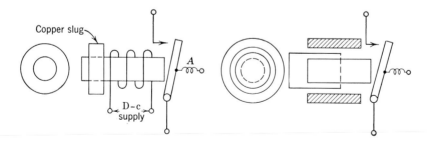

Fig. 13. Types of slow-acting relays.

and position of the copper ring. The time delay can be made variable by the use of movable copper sleeve (tube) placed between the iron core and coil as shown in Fig. 13 (right).

Many mechanical devices are used for timing operations. The clock (both spring type and electric) has uses for "on" and "off" operation. Small electric motors with contacts operated through reduction gearing offer good control for timing intervals from 30 sec to several minutes. Electrically heated bimetallic strips will give a slow motion suitable for timing operations. The oil-filled dashpot is a hydraulic device which will give a controllable time delay as well as serve as a damper for antihunting.

The time-delay properties of LR and RC circuit combinations are often employed in association with inductive loads such as magnetic relays. Inductive loads effectively limit fast current changes from half-wave rectifying sources. One circuit for overcoming this limitation is shown in Fig. 14a where an inverted diode is connected across the inductance coil. The action of this circuit is pictured in part (c) of the figure. Without the diode the current passed by the thyratron is limited to small pulses, as shown by curves marked i. With the addition of the diode, the energy stored in the magnetic field of L causes the current to continue flowing in the same direction through L by virtue of the circulating path provided by the diode and L. On the next positive wave of impressed voltage e, the current rises to a higher value as shown by the full-line curve i_f. Within a few cycles the rectified half-wave pulses rise to a relatively high average magnitude. Since the current "coasts" through the diode on the negative half waves, the circuit is sometimes called the *free-wheeling circuit*.

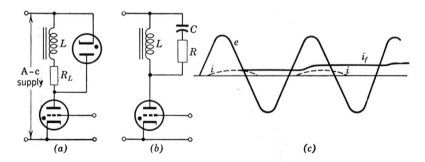

Fig. 14.   Free-wheeling circuit.

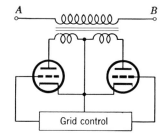

Fig. 15. Series impedance transformer control.

A second useful circuit which performs a similar function is shown in Fig. 14b. This circuit may be used for relays operated by vacuum amplifier tubes or small thyratrons. In this circuit the voltage drop across the relay charges the capacitor on the positive half waves, and the capacitor discharges through the relay (in the same direction) during the negative half cycle. This action serves to hold the relay up and prevent it from chattering on the "off" half cycles. The resistor R protects the cathode of a gaseous tube from the peak current surges into the capacitor but may be omitted with vacuum tubes.

Series Impedance Transformers

The series impedance transformer varies the reactance in a series circuit like the saturated-core reactor but operates on the principle of reducing the flux in an iron core instead of forcing it to saturation. In any typical transformer on open circuit the reactance of the primary is very high. If the secondary coil is short circuited, the resulting current produces a magnetomotive force which opposes the flux in the core and reduces the primary reactance to near zero. For intermediate loads and currents in the secondary the reactance of the primary will vary between maximum and minimum values. This principle of control may be utilized electronically by the circuit of Fig. 15. Here the current permitted in the secondary of a transformer placed in *series* with an a-c line is controlled by a triode (vacuum or gaseous) full-wave rectifier. A suitable grid control applied to the triodes either manually or automatically will vary the series impedance throughout the desired range.

Peaking Transformers

A peaking transformer is a low capacity transformer operated with an oversaturated iron core for the purpose of producing peaked voltage waves in its secondary. The primary of this transformer is con-

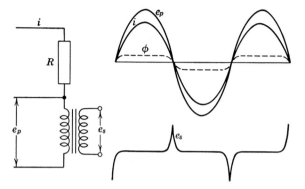

Fig. 16.   Voltage and flux waves in a peaking transformer.

nected in series with a resistor (or inductance) across an a-c supply as indicated in Fig. 16 (left). The resulting wave forms of voltages, current, and flux are depicted on the right of the figure. With a limited amount of iron in the transformer core, saturation comes early in the current wave, giving a long flat-topped flux wave. The flux changes in the iron core occur in a short interval of time in the current reversal zone, thus giving the peaked secondary voltage waves e_s. Peaking transformers are used for firing trigger tubes such as thyratrons and ignitrons.

Nonlinear Devices

Many substances have a nonlinear resistance under changes of temperature, current, and voltage. Some of the substances are employed in devices for protecting electronic equipment. A *ballast*

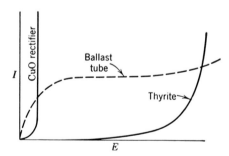

Fig. 17.   Nonlinear resistance characteristics.

or current regulator tube contains a helical coil of wire having a very high positive temperature coefficient of resistance. The rise in resistance with temperature is great enough to hold the current through it nearly constant over a fairly wide range of impressed voltage, as suggested in Fig. 17. Ballast tubes may be used to protect cathode heaters and other circuit parts from excessive currents and the variations of voltage supply.

Silicon carbide (trade name Thyrite) offers a very high resistance to a low impressed voltage but decreases its resistance with rise in voltage (Fig. 17). It is widely used for protecting tubes and circuit parts from insulation breakdown arising from high inductive transient voltages. For further details, see Chapter 3.

Semiconductor diodes have a low resistance to current flow in the forward direction but a high resistance in the reverse direction. In addition to their use as rectifiers, they are employed to block current in certain paths. They may be used in connection with an alarm circuit to indicate an accidental reversal of polarity in a d-c circuit.

Sensors

A sensor is a sensing or detecting device for measuring the magnitude of some variable quantity such as temperature, speed, light, etc. The sensor is an important link in the chain of control that is treated in the following chapter. A list of some important sensing devices and the quantity which they measure is given in Table 1. Some of these devices have been treated in earlier sections of this text, and others are familiar to the reader. Hence the following brief description is given for those which may deserve some explanation.

A *tachometer-generator* is a small d-c generator having a permanent magnet field. Since its field flux is constant, its generated emf is directly proportional to its speed. A *thermocouple* is a junction of copper-constantin which gives a variation of emf with temperature change following the Seebeck effect. The junction and leads are encased in a sealed metal tube. A *bimetal strip* consists of flat sheets of brass and invar steel welded together. The difference in expansion of the two metals causes the strip to bend with changes of temperature. A *resistance-thermometer* may consist of two resistance coils (one nickel—one manganin) insulated and sealed in a metal tube. The nickel has a positive temperature coefficient of resistance and the manganin zero. The ends of the coils in series and the center junction are brought out to a Wheatstone bridge to determine changes in resistance drop across the nickel. A *strain gage* consists

Table 1. Sensors

Quantity	Sensor
Voltage	Voltmeter
Speed	Tachometer-generator
Light	Phototube
	Photovoltaic cell
	Photoconductive cell— selenium—CdS—PbS
Temperature	Thermocouple
	Bimetal strip
	Thermistor
	Resistance thermometer
Pressure	Bellows
Tension	Strain gage
Humidity	Human hair, etc.
Position	Potentiometer
	Selsyn systems
	Micro switch and mercury switch
	Mechanical differential

of a section of fine copper-nickel alloy wire (1/1000 in. diameter and 1 to 6 in. long) formed into loops and bonded firmly to paper or plastic little larger than a postage stamp. This unit is cemented to the sample being tested for strain. The strain on this unit under test lengthens the wire and decreases its cross section, which increases the resistance and permits suitable RI drop measurements.

A *selsyn* system is a combination of rotary units designed to interconnect electrically two remote points and provide indication or control of mechanical displacement between them. The unit at one point acts as the sender or transmitter, and that at the other point as receiver. Either direct or alternating current may serve as the basis of the selsyn system.

The d-c selsyn principle which is widely used on aircraft and some ships is illustrated in Fig. 18. The sender is a circular rheostat to which a d-c voltage is fed by a double slider. The receiver is a steel ring on which three coils are placed, each to span 120 degrees. For every position of the rheostat the current in the coils is so distributed

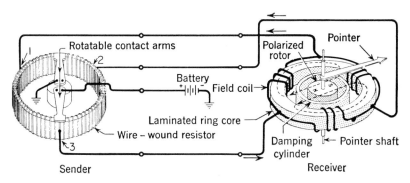

Fig. 18. Circuit for a d-c selsyn system.

that the flux cuts across the diameter of the steel ring at the same angle as the slider on the rheostat is placed. A magnetized vane pivoted at the center of the steel ring lines up with the flux, thus following any motion given to the sender shaft.

The a-c selsyn system (also called synchro system) for transmitting motion electrically consists of two self-synchronous motors. The two motors are connected together by three wires as indicated by the circuit of Fig. 19a. These motors have a three-phase, wye-type of winding on their stator but have a two-pole, shuttle-wound rotor with its coil connected through collector rings to a single-phase, a-c source of excitation (Fig. 19b). In this system one machine is operated as a generator or transmitter and the other as a motor or receiver. When the rotor excitation circuit is closed, the a-c field of each rotor induces voltages in the three-phase winding on the surrounding stator. The three voltages induced in these phases are unequal in magnitude and are determined by the position (of rotation) of the rotor field. When the two rotors are in exactly corresponding positions, the voltages induced in the transmitter stator are equal and opposite to those induced in the receiver stator; that is, they are balanced, so that no current flows in the winding of either stator. If, however, the transmitter rotor is moved from the original position, the induced voltages are unbalanced, current flows in the stator winding, and a torque is set up in both rotors. Since the transmitter rotor is held in position, the receiver rotor moves under the developed torque until it occupies a position corresponding to the new position of the transmitter.

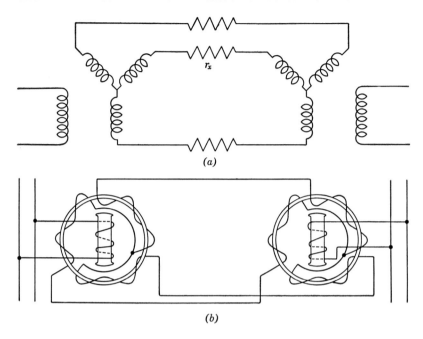

Fig. 19. Circuit for an a-c selsyn system.

Transducers

A transducer is a device for transforming a signal picked up by a sensor into another form that is adapted to the control system being used. For example, most automatic electrical control systems require a voltage signal to carry out their control function. Now if a

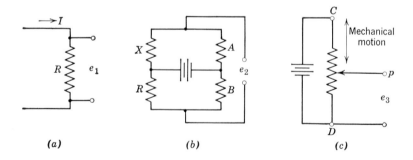

Fig. 20. Simple circuits for transducers.

certain sensor produces a current signal, this current may be passed through a fixed resistor, as shown in Fig. 20a, to provide the desired voltage variation e_1. Again, a nickel-manganin resistance thermometer may be connected to a Wheatstone bridge, as in Fig. 20b. The sensed temperature change will vary the resistance of the nickel coil X and the resulting unbalance in the bridge develops a difference voltage e_2. A sensor measuring mechanical motion can actuate a movable contact p along a potentiometer CD and produce a varying output voltage e_3, Fig. 20c. By these and other ways the transducer converts or transforms various sensed signals into a usable form.

A transducer may also be a device employed to transform the output of an amplifier into a useful form for error correction.

chapter 11 _____

Principles
of Control and
Servomechanisms

The chief difference between man and other forms of animal life is that the animals rely upon muscular strength to satisfy the needs of existence, whereas man utilizes many forces of nature to accomplish his desires. Primitive man domesticated some animals to aid in his work. Later centuries saw the utilization by man of the forces of the wind and water in crude windmills, water wheels, and the sailing of ships. The nineteenth century witnessed the harnessing of the energy in steam and the beginning of the internal combustion engine. The first quarter of the twentieth century brought the development of electricity as the flexible source of energy for light, power, and communication. The second quarter of a century (1925–1950) witnessed a great advance in the automatic control of machines through the medium of electronics and other new electrical and mechanical devices.

Open-Cycle Control System

The open cycle (open loop) is the most common form of control system. The term open cycle implies that the controlling device operates entirely independent of the load which it controls. The simplest examples of open-cycle control are illustrated in Fig. 1. In Fig. 1a, the manual operation of a switch controls the starting and stopping of the motor M. This is a *discontinuous* form of control

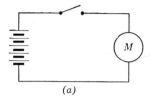

Fig. 1. Simple control systems.

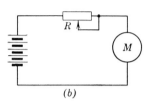

(on and off) wherein the speed and load on the motor do not influence the control in any way. In Fig. 1*b*, an adjustment of the resistor *R* varies the speed of the motor but the circuit is always closed, and hence it represents a *continuous* form of control. Here again the operation of the control does not depend on the response of the motor.

Many of our open-cycle control systems employ automatic controls. The push-button motor starter, the clock alarm radio, and the traffic control system at the street intersection are in this category. In the latter example, it should be noted that the automatic timing of the lights is independent of the volume of traffic. The lights may turn red with cars lined up for a mile and with no cars in sight to use the green light.

Closed-Cycle Control Systems

In a closed-cycle (closed loop) control system the output or load is linked by a feedback to the control unit. Such a system is suggested in the block diagram of Fig. 2. Here the controlled unit is not free or floating but it is tied back (through a feedback) to the control. If the controlled unit deviates from the *reference* or directive unit, this deviation is signaled back to the control unit and permits a corrective action to take place. A very simple closed-cycle control system is illustrated in the schematic electric oven of Fig. 3. Here the oven is heated by an electric resistance heating element. A make-and-break contact operated by a bimetallic thermal unit (sensor) is placed in the oven and connected in series with the heating element. The contact is adjusted by the setting of the tempera-

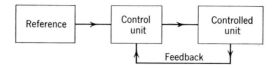

Fig. 2. Block diagram for a simple control circuit.

ture dial (reference) to give the desired oven temperature. When the temperature of the oven rises above the dial setting, the thermostat opens the electric circuit and permits the oven to cool slowly. After the temperature inside of the oven falls to the dial setting, the thermostat recloses. In this example the closed circuit or cycle is very simple and all active elements are located within the oven itself. The controlled factor is temperature and the primary controlling unit is the thermostatically operated contactor.

In most closed-cycle or feedback systems, several components are required in the complete system. These components and their functions are illustrated in the typical home heating system with which we are familiar. Such a system is suggested in Fig. 4. Here the quantity to be controlled is room temperature and the *reference* is represented by the specific setting of the thermostat. This thermostat is a bimetallic strip with contacts located in the room where the temperature is to be controlled. It acts as an error-detecting device. When the room temperature falls below the desired standard (reference), the thermostat closes a low voltage circuit which in-

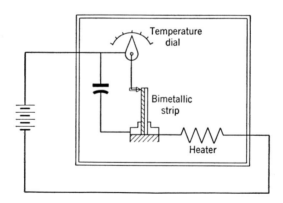

Fig. 3. Simple closed-cycle control system.

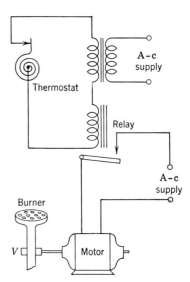

Fig. 4. Furnace-control servomechanism.

cludes a relay. When the relay is actuated it closes a second circuit to a motor or to a powerful electromagnet (amplifier). In a coal-burning furnace the motor feeds coal to the burner and furnishes a blast of air for rapid combustion. In an oil furnace a motor pumps fuel oil and air to the burner. For a gas-burning furnace an electromagnetic valve admits gas to the burner. In each of these furnaces the heat produced by the burner is transferred from the furnace to the space being heated (either by gravity or air-blower action). Thus the furnace is an *error-corrector* device which feeds its heat output to the desired space and maintains a nearly constant temperature. When the space temperature rises above the *reference* temperature, the thermostat (error detector) opens its circuit and stops the motor and the error-corrector furnace.

There are three distinguishing characteristics to the preceding examples of closed-cycle control systems for temperature. First, the errors or swings in temperature may be rather wide because of the lag in operation of the components. Second, the time or period of the temperature cycles is rather large. And, lastly, the control is of an "on" and "off" type, and hence is *discontinuous* in operation.

Servomechanisms and Regulators

For greater refinement in the operation of closed-cycle control systems, the system components are arranged as shown in the block

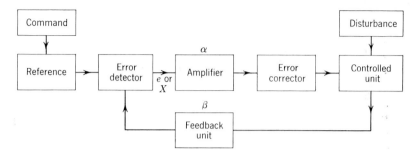

Fig. 5. Block diagram of a servomechanism.

diagram of Fig. 5. Here a command signal, which may be fixed or continuously variable, controls a reference value (usually a voltage). The reference value is fed into an error detector or comparator. Simultaneously, a like value or quantity is picked up by a feedback unit associated with the controlled unit (or load) and fed back to the error detector. The feedback unit may be a sensor and transducer which transforms the signal to a usable quantity and also controls its magnitude by a potential divider element. The incoming reference signal and the feedback signal are fed into the error detector in *series opposition,* and thus produce an output difference or error signal (*e* or *X*). This error signal is then fed into an *amplifier* which, in turn, produces an output of sufficient magnitude to operate an *error corrector* which functions to reduce the deviation of the controlled unit from the value called for by the command unit. Last, the *disturbance* which produces the deviation of the controlled unit may be one of several things—temperature, wind, friction, load, line voltage or frequency variation, etc.

Any of the sensors described in Chapter 10 may find use in the closed-circuit control system under discussion. Likewise, any of the amplifiers described in Chapter 9 may find application in these systems. Error correctors are usually electric motors, magnetic solenoids, relays, valves, combustion units, etc.

The closed-cycle control system illustrated in Fig. 5 and described in the preceding two paragraphs is a *servomechanism.* A servomechanism is continuously sensitive to any error, it is a follow-up system, and it has an amplifier which permits a wide range of input command that is remotely located from the element being controlled. A good example of a servomechanism is given in the gun-fire control system shown in Fig. 6. This diagram represents control about the vertical axis alone and a duplicate system is needed for control about the axis lying within the horizontal plane. The gun turret is located outside a bomber plane. The gunsight is located at a convenient point within the plane. The gun and gunsight are initially aligned and tied to servomotors which are also aligned to give a zero position signal. When the gunsight is turned manually, an error (voltage) is created in the error detector which excites the control field of the amplidyne. The amplidyne gives *power* amplification to the error signal and drives the motor which, through worm and gear action, causes the gun turret to follow any rotation of the gunsight about the vertical axis. The movement of the turret tied to its servomotor, signals its position constantly back to the error detector.

In many servomechanisms, the command or reference is constant or is changed slightly at wide intervals of time. Servomechanisms of this type are usually called regulators. Regulators are used to maintain motor speeds, generated voltage, frequency, temperature, position, strain, humidity, etc. The term servomechanism arises from the word servo, or slave. Since the controlled unit is a slave to the command or input, we use the term servo system or servomechanism.

The control functions of a servomechanism may be combined in many ways. A very simple example covering voltage regulation of a d-c generator is illustrated in Fig. 7. The reference unit is represented by a d-c battery and a potential divider P. Here the functions of error detection, amplification, and error correction are all contained in the circuits of a triode. The generated voltage of the tachometer is applied in series with the reference voltage to the grid

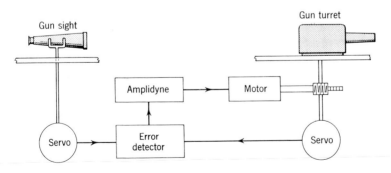

Fig. 6. Servomechanism for gun-fire control.

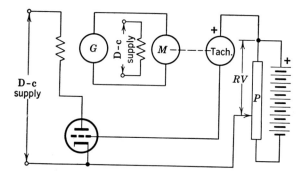

Fig. 7. Schematic circuit for motor-speed regulation.

and cathode of the triode. The difference or error voltage *e* applied between the grid and cathode controls the amplified power output (error correction) fed to the generator field. In this case the feedback is direct without any requirement for a sensor, transducer, or potential divider.

A servomechanism circuit for regulating the speed of a d-c motor by the use of a rotary amplifier is shown in Fig. 8. The reference is a constant field (voltage) applied to the standard field of multifield exciter *A* (Amplidyne, Rototrol). The feedback consists of the output of a tachometer-generator to the control field of the exciter. The interaction between the standard and the control fields constitutes the error detection. The amplified output of the exciter supplies the field of a d-c generator *G*. This generator is the error corrector and its output controls the speed of the motor *M* (controlled unit).

A more complicated servo system for controlling theater lighting is given in Fig. 9. In this system the controlled unit is the group of lamps in the upper right-hand corner. The number of lamps may

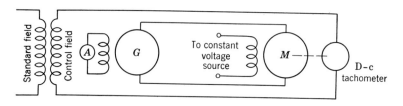

Fig. 8. Motor-speed-control servomechanism using a multifield exciter.

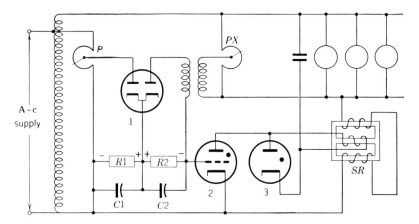

Fig. 9. Circuit for a theater lighting control.

change but the voltage across those remaining will be held constant. The amplifier is the magnetic amplifier SR in the lower right-hand corner. The error detection is the voltage difference across the resistors $R1$ and $R2$ in the cathode grid circuit of the thyratron tube 2. The reference is a command type to control the light output of the lamps and is represented by the a-c potential drop across the lower part of the potential divider or potentiometer P. The operation of this lighting control unit is as follows. Power is fed from an auto transformer on the left to the saturable reactor and lamp load on the right. The auto transformer steps up the voltage to compensate for the voltage drop in the reactor and to give full rated voltage across the lamps. The d-c winding of the saturable reactor is fed by a free-wheeling circuit. The firing of thyratron 2 is controlled by a d-c bias voltage applied to its grid. This bias voltage is the difference in voltage drops across resistors $R1$ and $R2$. The drop across $R2$ is determined by the lamp voltage and that across $R1$ is controlled by the setting of the arm on potentiometer P. With potentiometer P set full on (up), PX is adjusted to give the normal voltage of the lamps. As the arm of P is moved down, the voltage drop across $R1$ lowers, the thyratron grid becomes more negative, tube 2 fires later in the cycle, less current passes through the d-c winding of SR, and the voltage across the lamps falls. As the lamp voltage falls, less current is rectified by right diode tube 1, which gives a reduced drop across $R2$ and permits a new balance of circuit conditions. The placing of PX across the lamp group (lamp voltage) instead of across the a-c line assures the same lamp voltage for a given setting of P regardless of the number of lamps in a group. This permits the use of the same equipment for lamp groupings having different loads in watts.

A smooth phase control of the thyratron is effected in Fig. 9 by adjustment of the time constant of $R1C1$ so that an appreciable ripple exists. With correct phase relations and adjustment this ripple will intercept the critical grid-voltage curve (firing) so as to give a smooth control from "full on" to "full off."

An example of position control by a servo system is illustrated by the automatic stopping or leveling of an elevator car. One method of automatic floor leveling uses a simple oscillator relay unit with the circuit of Fig. 10. This is a tickler oscillator circuit wherein the necessary feedback is provided by the transformer action between coils $L1$ and $L2$. With the proper selection of component constants and in the absence of the vane shown in the figure, the circuit oscillates continuously. While it is in oscillation, the reactance arising from the a-c frequency limits the current through the relay CR (a-c plus a small d-c) so that it does not energize and its contact remains closed. Whenever the magnetic vane is interposed between coils $L1$ and $L2$, the coupling is broken, feedback stops, and the circuit ceases to oscillate. When oscillation stops, a large value of direct current flows through the cathode-anode of the triode and the winding of relay CR. Since CR offers little opposition to direct current, the current rises quickly to a value that energizes relay CR and opens the contact to the elevator motor control.

In the application of this oscillator relay control several units employing the circuits of Fig. 10 are mounted on top of the elevator car. These units are mounted so that as the car moves vertically the space

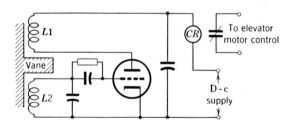

Fig. 10.   Oscillator circuit for elevator-car leveling.

Fig. 11. Automatic elevator-car-leveling apparatus with vacuum tubes mounted on the elevator car and vanes mounted in the hatchway.

between coils $L1$ and $L2$ is intercepted by fixed vanes mounted along the walls of the elevator shaft. A suitable vertical location of these vanes will control the operation of the oscillator relays in steps so that the resulting signals to the control circuits for the elevator drive will decelerate the elevator car at the proper rate and bring the car to rest at the exact floor level. An illustration of the car-leveling oscillator unit is given in Fig. 11.

Problems in the Design of Servo Systems

The design of a servo system depends on the following considerations: (1) magnitude of the permissible error, (2) rate of response and correction of error, and (3) the stability of the system. The simple furnace heating control system of Fig. 4 may have a thermostat design which operates for a change of only 2° F, but there is a lag of two degrees between the lower limit of the thermostat setting and the actual room temperature. A similar difference exists between the room temperature and the upper limit of the thermostat setting. Moreover, the actual room temperature may overshoot after the thermostat cuts off because of the heat energy stored in the heating system. As a composite of these temperature lags, the actual variation of the room temperature may be as much as seven degrees although the thermostat design calls for a variation of only two degrees. This form of error deviation is likely to exist in any on-and-off (discontinuous) form of control. One obvious solution is to provide for a continuous control system which begins to function as soon as any error is present.

The rate of response and correction in a servo system depends on two factors—the over-all amplification of the closed circuit (feedback, error detector, amplifier) and the mechanical inertia and the time constants of the various components of that circuit. The amplifier employed in a servo closed circuit has an amplification factor which may be designated as α. Similarly, the feedback from the controlled unit to the error detector has some transfer factor β (usually much less than one). The resulting over-all amplification of the closed circuit becomes α times β. The various components in any closed circuit servo usually contain a number of inductive and capacitive elements. The RC and LR combinations in these complete closed circuits have individual time constants which serve to produce time delays for any signal being passed through the loop.

The natural tendency of any closed-cycle servo system is to be unstable. When a disturbance causes the controlled unit to fall behind the command, an error signal is created and the error-detector and amplifier tend to correct this error. If the over-all amplification factor is high, the error corrector actuates the controlled unit quickly to restore it to normal. Unfortunately, the inertia of the system will tend to carry the correction too far and cause the controlled unit to overshoot. This leads to the formation of a positive error and a new reversed error, and corrective effort causes the controlled unit to revert to the former negative error. In this manner the entire control system will oscillate between positive and negative error values. If the period of this oscillation should coincide with the natural period of the closed-cycle system, the oscillation can become violent.

There are a number of ways to reduce the tendency of a system to oscillate (instability). First, if the mechanical or the electrical inertia of the closed loop can be reduced, the magnitude of the overshoot, and hence the oscillation, is lowered. Second, if the over-all amplification factor is reduced, the time period for correction is lengthened and the inertia of the system will slow down the corrective effort and avoid overshoot. If the amplification factor is too small, the error will not be completely corrected and the system will underride the command. The third method of controlling instability is to introduce networks between the error detector and the amplifier. Without the use of any network the error signal and the resulting corrective effort are proportional to the error. This is termed *proportional control*. In some cases it is desired to have a corrective action which depends on the rate of change of the error and this is a *derivative control*. The derivative control effect can be approximated by the insertion of a network like Fig. 12a in the error-detector amplifier circuit. Here a rapid rise in error will pass the capacitor C with little opposition, and hence tend to produce an error correction proportional to the rate of change or derivative. A decreasing value of error produces the opposite result, and hence reduces the tendency to overshoot. This system of control is known as the *proportional plus derivative control*.

As suggested previously, some servo systems may fail to produce a correction sufficient to overcome the error (reduce to zero). For such cases a control which gives a corrective effort approaching the integral of the error may be desirable. This integral corrective effect may be approximated by the network shown in Fig. 12b. Here the capacitor C stores a charge proportional to the maximum error voltage. Hence when the error has been corrected to near zero by the control system, the discharge of this capacitor is giving a final kick which reduces the error to zero. This form of control is desired where the inertia or drag of the system tends to prevent a return to zero error for the existing command. This type of error control is termed the *proportional plus integral control*.

In some servo systems it is desirable to combine into a single network the three different systems of error control—*proportional, derivative,* and *integral*. This combination should provide a maximum

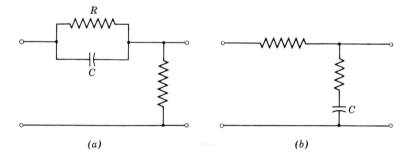

Fig. 12. Network to modify control action.

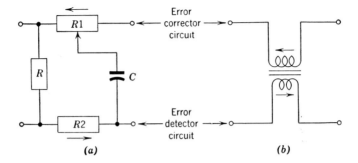

Fig. 13.   Antihunt circuits for servomechanisms.

corrective effort when the error is changing rapidly and later provide the needed final corrective kick to reduce the error to zero.

Antihunt Circuits

In some servo systems the tendency to overshoot or hunt can be restrained by *special* feedback or antihunt circuits. These consist of an inductive or an *RC* coupling between the *error corrector* and the *error detector* circuit as illustrated in Fig. 13. Here the rise of current in the error corrector circuit induces a voltage which tends to oppose the current in the error detector circuit. Since the feedback action is negative and proportional to the rate of change, it has a damping action on rapid changes in the system and prevents hunting.

Approach to Theoretical Servo Design

Early servo systems were built by the experimental approach in the laboratory. Today it is possible to predict and calculate the operation of proposed servo systems on a mathematical basis. The approach to a theoretical design is twofold. First, from known or proposed characteristics of the components of the system, an equation for the operation of the system under steady state may be prepared and solved for time constants. Second, from a knowledge of the time constants and other properties, it is possible to establish and study equations for the dynamic operation of the proposed system. The solution to the dynamic operation gives the period and magnitude of the oscillations, hunting, etc. The information gained from these solutions suggests changes in the circuits and components and permits a final satisfactory design. A complete understanding of the

theory and design of servomechanisms requires an extended treatment of the subject which lies beyond the scope of this text. The
reader who desires further information is advised to consult the
references given at the end of this chapter.

PROBLEMS

1. A gas burner, automatic controls (Fig. 4), and an automatic blower
are installed in a used cast-iron coal furnace in a basement.
(*a*) Disregarding any change in thermal efficiency, what will be the effect
of the cast-iron furnace upon the operation of the automatic control?
(*b*) Will the resulting room temperature variation be more comfortable
or less than that produced by a new gas furnace having lightweight steel
construction? (The answer is not easy.)

2. Is it possible to design closed-cycle continuous error-control heating
systems for a home? What are the difficulties in producing such a design?

3. Some modern home washing machines provide (*a*) complete time-con-
trolled washing and wringing cycles, (*b*) control of correct quantity of water
regardless of water pressure, (*c*) correct hot water temperature. What kind
of control systems and components would you use to perform each of these
functions?

4. If you were given a cadmium sulfide cell, a relay, an electric motor,
and some micro switches, show how you would develop an automatic garage
door-opening system.

5. Can you devise a control for traffic lights which will vary the timing
to accommodate the traffic in both directions?

6. Explain the operation of the antihunt circuit in Fig. 13*a*.

REFERENCES

1. Brown, Gordon S., and Donald P. Campbell, *Principles of Servomechanisms,*
   John Wiley and Sons, New York, 1948.
2. Murphy, Gordon J., *Basic Automatic Control Theory,* D. Van Nostrand
   Company, New York, 1957.

chapter 12

Electronic
Operation of
Direct-Current
Motors

A-C Versus D-C Systems

The a-c system presents well-known advantages for the generation, transmission, and distribution of electric energy which has caused its universal adoption throughout the world. Most a-c motors are rugged and simple in construction, cost relatively little, and require little maintenance. These motors are inherently of the constant-speed type; they have low starting torque, high starting current, and a low power factor. Direct-current motors are more costly and require more maintenance, but they do possess excellent characteristics of speed and torque. The d-c shunt motor can be operated over a wide range of speed with good regulation at all speeds and it possesses good torque characteristics. The d-c series motor develops high starting torque with a variable speed and a nearly constant energy input, which are desirable characteristics for certain types of loads. These desirable characteristics of d-c motors have caused an increase in the use of d-c machinery in industry since 1935 with the result that during World War II approximately one-half the kilowatt capacity of all machinery manufactured above one horsepower was direct current. The use of d-c motors on the a-c distribution system requires the use of some form of a-c to d-c conversion equipment.

The design of conversion equipment for d-c motor drives depends on the factors which govern the starting and speed control of d-c shunt motors. A brief review of these factors will be helpful. The fundamental equation of a d-c motor is

$$\underset{\substack{\text{impressed} \\ \text{voltage}}}{V} = \underset{\substack{\text{back-emf}}}{K\phi n} + \underset{\substack{\text{armature} \\ \text{resistance} \\ \text{drop}}}{I_a R_a} \tag{1}$$

where K is a constant which accounts for the number of armature conductors, paths, and poles, ϕ represents the flux per pole and n the speed in revolutions per minute. Equation 1 may be rewritten in the form

$$I_a = \frac{V - K\phi n}{R_a} \tag{2}$$

which shows that when the armature is at rest ($n = 0$), the only limitation to the current is the applied voltage and the armature resistance.

The torque developed by a d-c motor is proportional to the armature current and the flux ϕ.

$$\text{Torque} = P I_a \phi \tag{3}$$

The motor speed equation results from a rewriting of equation 1, thus:

$$\underset{n}{(\text{speed})} = \frac{V - I_a R_a}{K\phi} \tag{4}$$

Equation 4 indicates that the two basic methods of controlling the speed of d-c shunt motor are (1) vary the numerator (applied voltage) with the denominator (ϕ) held constant and (2) hold the numerator (applied voltage) constant and vary the denominator (ϕ).

The action for starting and speed control for d-c motors expressed in the preceding equations is also shown in the schematic circuit of Fig. 1. For starting, a full field (field volts and current) and a reduced voltage across the armature are required to give maximum torque and a limited current through the armature. The armature current may be limited (for zero or low counter emf) by a series resistor on constant-potential systems or by application of a low

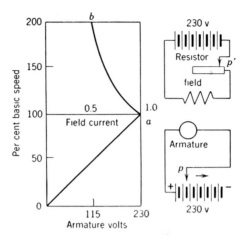

Fig. 1. Speed control of a shunt motor by varying the armature volts and field current.

voltage. This can be accomplished by the setting of p and p' in the schematic circuit of Fig. 1. As p is advanced to the right, the voltage impressed across the armature will rise and the speed will increase linearly from 0 to a as the impressed armature voltage rises to its normal value of 230. This will give the basic or 100 per cent speed. Now the speed can be raised further by reducing the field flux and current through a movement of the point p' to the left along the field resistor. The rise in speed is inversely proportional to the field flux and will follow along the line ab. By this sequence of adjustments any speed from zero up to the upper limit of motor design may be attained and the speed regulation for any given setting will be good.

The conversion of alternating current to direct current may be designed to produce (1) constant voltage or (2) variable voltage. Both of these systems may be produced by motor-generator sets or by electronic rectifiers. The constant-voltage system is used in industries where many d-c motors are required to have a moderate range of speed control but operate normally at a constant speed. It is also applied where the excellent torque characteristics of series motors are required for elevator or hoist service. The M-G sets for constant-voltage service employ a-c motors (induction or synchronous) to drive d-c generators. Electronic rectifiers for constant-voltage service employ the equipment discussed in Chapter 8 on rectification and inversion.

Conversion equipment of the variable voltage type is complicated and rather costly. It is designed to give a *wide range of speed control for a single motor*. Its cost is justified when wide variations in speed are necessary for operating machine tools and for various steps in manufacture on production lines, etc. All early forms of conversion equipment for motor drives consisted of motor-generator sets, as shown in Fig. 2a. Here an a-c motor driving a d-c generator and a d-c exciter comprise the variable voltage unit for driving the motor M. The principle of operation is that of the Ward Leonard speed-control system. The d-c exciter provides a constant potential for exciting the fields of the d-c generator and the motor M. Referring to the shunt motor characteristics of Fig. 1, we note the motor M will be started by applying full or normal field to the motor M and, beginning with zero field on the generator, its field current will be raised uniformly to raise the voltage impressed across the armature and to obtain any desired speed between 0 and normal for the motor. After normal speed is reached, higher values are at-

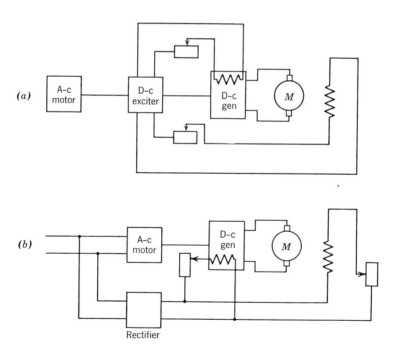

Fig. 2. M-G variable voltage d-c motor speed control.

tained by weakening the field of the motor. The speed variation of the motor is attained by manual control of field rheostats, or it may be attained by some form of automatic electronic control. The development of electronic devices permitted the substitution of an electronic rectifier for the d-c exciter, as suggested in Fig. 2b. This substitution reduces the weight and cost of the complete unit and is employed on all current designs. The complete M-G motor drive is assembled as a compact package unit.

Electronic Motor Drives

The many discoveries and improvements in electronic devices since 1930 have led to the application of electronic drives and controls for d-c shunt motors. A basic diagram for single-phase electronic operation of d-c motors is suggested in Fig. 3. The a-c supply voltage is transformed to a suitable value to power the motor armature and shunt field. Full-wave grid-controlled rectifying units furnish the necessary voltage to the armature for starting and for speeds from zero to normal. The shunt field is supplied by a full-wave rectifier using semiconductor rectifying units or ionic rectifiers. If speeds above normal are required, a manual-controlled resistor may be inserted in the field circuit. For automatic control the semiconductor rectifiers (or phanatrons) may be replaced by grid-controlled rectifiers.

There are many methods and types of control which may be applied to the basic diagram of Fig. 3. All such controls are effected

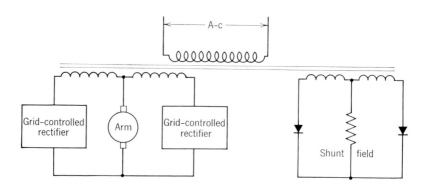

Fig. 3. Basic diagram for electronic operation of d-c motors.

through the grids of rectifying devices and are designed to limit the *speed regulation*. These controls may be classified as follows:

Methods of Speed Control.
1. Manual.
2. Automatic (closed circuit servo with feedback).
   (*a*) Regulated output voltage.
   (*b*) Compensation for armature *IR* drop.
   (*c*) Tachometer feedback.
   (*d*) Acceleration and deceleration control.
   (*e*) Process control (external variable).

In method 2(*a*) the output voltage is matched against a reference voltage. Method 2(*b*) will provide a regulation within a range of 2 to 5 per cent. The tachometer feedback is capable of precise speed control with a regulation in the range of 0.5 per cent to 0.1 per cent. Since electronic controls operate very rapidly, it is sometimes necessary to introduce slight time delays to control acceleration and deceleration and avoid power surges or damage to equipment.

There are many types of grid-controlled rectifiers which may be employed in the basic diagram of Fig. 3.

Grid-Controlled Rectifiers.
1. Ionic rectifiers.
   (*a*) Thyratrons.
   (*b*) Ignitrons.
   (*c*) Excitrons.
2. Magnetic amplifiers.
3. Solid-state thyratrons.

The thyratron is used exclusively for small motor drives. The ignitron and excitron are adapted for large motor drives (50 hp and up). Magnetic amplifiers are just entering the field (1959). The solid-state thyratron will become important in the motor drive field as soon as production rises and lower development costs permit its use.

A simple schematic circuit illustrating the use of thyratrons for electronic starting and speed control of shunt motors from single phase a-c circuits is given in Fig. 4. Here the armature is fed by thyratrons *a* and *b* and the shunt field by thyratrons *c* and *d*. The phase shifters 1 and 2 and similarly 3 and 4 are mechanically locked together. Thus, to operate the motor after the necessary preheating

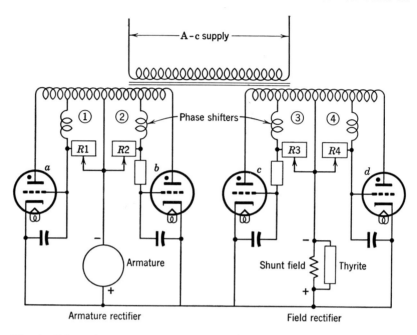

Fig. 4. Schematic electronic starting and speed control for a shunt motor using thyratrons with phase-shifting control.

of the tubes, phase shift 3–4 should be set for full field current (normal ϕ) and the phase shift of 1–2 should be 180 degrees, so that tubes a and b are inoperative. Then phase shifts 1–2 can be advanced to raise the voltage across the armature and bring up the speed. For speeds less than basic armature phase shift is applied, whereas for speeds above basic the field phase shift is adjusted after the armature is adjusted to full normal voltage. This control of speed can be visualized by reference to the speed characteristic curve in Fig. 1 and equation 4. The simple circuit of Fig. 4 illustrates the basic principle of electronic motor drives. However, since it assumes manual control, other and more complicated circuits are employed to give the necessary protective, automatic, and "electronic brain" features of control.

The complete electronic operation of a d-c motor will embody the features of wide range of speed adjustment, constant speed for any adjustment, current limit for armature current, automatic starting, motor reversing, motor jogging, and dynamic or regenerative braking.

Some applications will not require all these features, but the complete control unit will require the use of the majority of the circuit and equipment components previously discussed in Chapters 8 and 10. The exact circuit, equipment, and arrangement used may vary with the equipment manufacturer. Hence the following discussion should be considered as typical for this form of electronic control.

The speed of a d-c shunt motor is governed by the voltage impressed across the armature. This voltage may be supplied and controlled by the simple circuit of Fig. 5. Here the phase shift is produced by the bridge circuit having as one arm a saturable reactor *SR*. (See pages 292 and 313.) The complete control from "full off" to "full on" is accomplished in a stepless manner and with a small current in the d-c winding which is supplied by a triode amplifier. Before discussing the amplifier circuit another component circuit should be recalled. Since the applied alternating voltage may vary with the motor load and with other load and line conditions, it is necessary to provide a constant or reference source of voltage if speed and other desired characteristics are to be maintained constant. Such a constant source may be provided through the use of the constant-voltage circuit explained on page 312. The three-wire constant-voltage source of Fig. 6 now becomes a basic part of the circuits which follow. An amplifier triode *D* is connected to the constant-voltage system and to the saturable reactor *SR*, as shown in Fig. 7

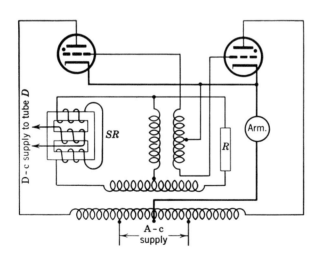

Fig. 5. Phase-shifter circuit applied to motor armature voltage supply.

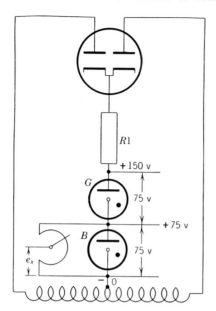

Fig. 6. Constant-voltage supply.

(right).   The cathode-to-plate plus *SR* circuit is across 75 volts (constant) and the grid of triode *D* is tapped to a potential divider circuit between *R3* and *R4* so that normally it is sufficiently positive so that tube *D* conducts fully and *SR* advances the thyratrons to

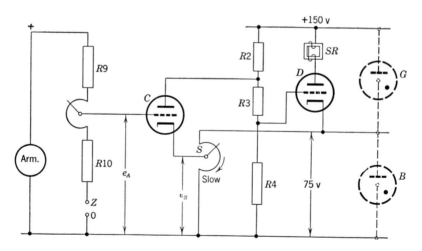

Fig. 7. Circuits for controlling the speed of an armature.

"full on." In order to control tube D it will be necessary to vary the potential of its grid in some manner. Such control is accomplished by a second triode C. To understand the action of the remainder of the circuit it should be recalled that under stable operation the speed of the rotating armature is proportional to its counter emf and approximately proportional to the impressed emf. The armature voltage is impressed across the potential divider circuit consisting of resistance $R9$ and $R10$ (plus a small adjustable vernier resistance) having values such that the voltage drop e_A will be equal to 75 volts for the basic speed of the armature and full shunt field. The voltage e_A is to be compared with a standard (constant) voltage e_S obtained from a potentiometer resistance S. These two comparison voltages are applied to the grid and cathode of tube C which, in turn, controls the grid potential of tube D. To follow the action of the complete circuit, assume that the armature is at rest with e_A equal to zero and that a speed of $\frac{2}{3}$ of basic is desired. Potentiometer S will be advanced (CW) to raise e_S to 50 volts. Now, with the cathode of C at $+50$ volts and the grid at zero or -50 volts with respect to the cathode, tube C is biased below cutoff and does not conduct. Under these conditions the grid of tube D is positive, the tube conducts, and the SR bridge holds the thyratron rectifiers "full on." The rectified current flowing through the armature causes it to accelerate and, as it does so, its counter emf and e_A rise. As e_A approaches e_S in value, the grid of C becomes less negative and at a suitable value tube C begins to conduct electrons from cathode to plate. This electron current passes from the lower zero- or negative-voltage line through S, tube C, and resistor $R2$, to the 150 constant-voltage line. This new current through $R2$ increases the voltage drop over $R2$ and lowers the potential of the grid of tube D because the sum of the drops across $R2$, $R3$, and $R4$ are held constant at 150 volts. The lowering of the grid potential of triode D reduces the current output to the saturable reactor and shifts the phase of the thyratron grid voltages, thus reducing the rectified current and voltage to the armature. With proper adjustments of resistors and tubes, the armature speed is stabilized when e_A equals e_S. Should the mechanical load on the armature be reduced, the speed would tend to rise carrying e_A with it and increasing current output of tube C, which would make the grid of D more negative with subsequent retarding shift of phase of thyratron grid supply. It is obvious from this discussion that any motor speed from zero to basic can be attained by the setting of po-

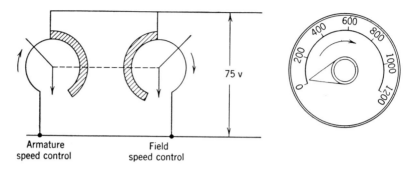

Fig. 8. Speed-control potentiometers mechanically locked together.

tentiometer resistor S. Thus S becomes the basic-speed adjuster control.

In the electronic control unit the excitation of the d-c shunt field will be obtained by a rectifier system. Speeds from basic up may be obtained by reducing the field flux and current by using a circuit identical with Fig. 7 except that the armature is replaced by the shunt field. In the new circuit the speed control (rise) will be secured by advancing S in the clockwise direction (instead of counterclockwise). Since the armature-voltage speed control is made with full field and since field control is accomplished with normal armature voltage, the control and equipment can be simplified by "ganging" or mounting both controls on one shaft and with one dial, as suggested in Fig. 8. Conductor segments are necessary on each control for the sectors in which the particular control is inactive.

In the preceding discussion it was assumed that the voltage drop across the armature was approximately proportional to the speed and counter emf. Actually, the impressed voltage is equal to the counter emf plus the IR drop and the speed is proportionately lower than the impressed voltage (see equation 4). This means that the speed will be allowed to fall as the motor is loaded, the same as operation on a constant-voltage system. This drop in speed can be avoided if a voltage of the proper sign and equal to the IR drop in the armature were introduced into the circuit of Fig. 7 between points O and Z. The desired voltage can be secured from the rectifier circuit of Fig. 9. The primary P of the current transformer consists of two current coils connected into the anode circuits of the thyratrons which feed the armature. These coils are connected so that the rectified pulses of current flow in opposite directions and thus induce an alternating

voltage across the secondary S. This secondary of the current transformer is loaded by a resistor R_Y to control its approximate voltage
value. The transformer is also loaded by a double-anode diode and
an adjustable voltage drop is taken from the rectifier load resistance.
The latter voltage drop which is proportional to thyratron load current is applied between points O and Z on Fig. 7. The rectifier circuit
of Fig. 9 is also used to supply a voltage for current-limitation functions.

The preceding discussion and circuits show how a constant adjustable range of speed may be attained but omits the current-limitation
function of electronic operation. A d-c motor armature during acceleration or during overload will take an excessive current unless
protective measures are provided. An addition of one triode and
circuit to the preceding circuit may be employed to give such protection. This current-limiter circuit is illustrated by tube E and its
circuit in heavy lines on Fig. 10. The grid of tube E is fed from the
same rectifier circuit that provided armature RI drop compensation.
The circuit adjustment is such that the grid of tube E is biased negative for all armature-load currents up to, say, 150 per cent of normal
load (other percentage values may be chosen). Then as the armature-load current rises above 150 per cent, the grid of tube E moves

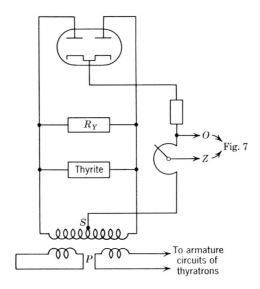

Fig. 9. Circuit for compensating for the IR drop in an armature.

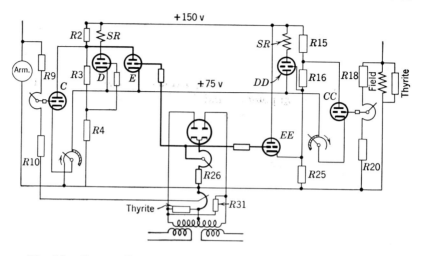

Fig. 10. Current limiter added to armature and field control circuits.

rapidly from slightly negative to positive and tube E conducts via resistor $R2$. The electron current through $R2$ lowers the grid voltage of tube D (like conduction of tube C) which, in turn, shifts the phase of the grids on the thyratrons. It should be noted that tube C functions through voltage comparison and at normal load values, whereas limiter tube E comes into action only for overload current values. Obviously, tube E functions equally well during armature acceleration and at all speeds and loads. The current-limiter action is also applied to the field circuit as a protective measure but in a reversed manner. Here the grid of tube EE is connected to the same source as tube E but the rise of grid potential causes E to conduct and raise the potential of the grid of tube DD (increased drop across $R25$). The increased conduction of tube DD shifts the thyratron grids toward "full on." This action strengthens the field, raises the torque, and reduces the motor speed. It is customary to adjust the current-limiter circuits so that the field action precedes somewhat the armature current-limiter action, thus making it possible for the motor to carry temporary overloads without shutdown.

The circuit of Fig. 10 will give satisfactory current limitation for a motor in operation but may fail to give the necessary protection to all circuits and parts at the instant power is applied. One satisfactory method of overcoming this initial instantaneous condition is to apply a preset grid voltage to tubes E and EE via the starting contacts on the push-button or magnetic starter. This measure assures that the initial current will be limited to, say, 150 per cent normal for the fraction of time it takes for all circuit elements to become conditioned for action.

To complete the details of the electronic control circuit for d-c motors, thyrite resistors are employed at all points where high transient voltage may be encountered. Since the action of circuits employing electron tubes is very rapid, it is possible for oscillating or hunting conditions to develop. Such hunting may be prevented by the use of filter circuits, which usually consist of a series circuit of a resistor and condenser (RC circuit). Such circuits are frequently placed between grid and cathode where they effect a time delay in tube action. The potentiometer type of resistor between $R9$ and $R10$ (Fig. 10) offers a fine adjustment so that the normal voltage applied to the armature equals the rated value. Similarly, the variable resistor between $R18$ and $R20$ serves to give the proper field-current adjustment for normal or basic speed.

The reversing of d-c motors under electronic operation may be brought about in two ways. In one case the rectified power to the armature is removed and the armature is connected to a resistor to effect dynamic braking. After the armature comes to rest a magnetic starter may apply reversed potential to the armature to give the desired reversed direction of rotation. In case a more rapid deceleration is desired, circuits may be employed to give regenerative braking (i.e., to use the kinetic energy stored in the rotating armature to pump electric power back into the a-c system). Regeneration is not easy to accomplish under the electronic system because of the unilateral conduction of the rectifier tube. Suppose, for example, an electronic motor drive is operating a motor at three times basic speed and the field is suddenly increased to normal value. The armature counter emf will rise to nearly three times normal value and will be much higher than the rectified voltage of the driving thyratrons. Since the direction of electron flow cannot reverse, there is no regenerative action and the motor coasts as if the armature circuit were open. Hence in order to obtain regeneration or inverter action, the polarity of the applied voltage must be reversed by magnetic contactors. Along with this reversal the phase shifting of the grids on the thyratrons must be changed so that the regenerating action of the armature may be utilized to pump energy back into the a-c system during that short period while the motor armature is being brought to rest.

Fig. 11. Schematic assembly of the four equipment units in an electronic drive for a d-c motor. (Courtesy General Electric Company.)

An illustration of the equipment which employs the preceding circuits for a single-phase control for a d-c motor is given in Fig. 11.

The preceding single-phase electronic motor drive employed the *diametric* rectifier circuit. This circuit requires a transformer with a center-tapped secondary and two rectifying units. The full-wave bridge rectifying circuit is also employed. The use of the bridge circuit eliminates the weight of the transformers and generally reduces the cost since two additional diode rectifiers cost less than a transformer. However, it should be noted that the omission of the transformer takes away the voltage ratio control for operating the motor. In other words, if a standard line voltage of 230 volts is employed, the conversion ratio, the rectifier RI drops, and the allowance for voltage regulation may reduce the rated voltage for the motor to 140 volts. Since this is not a standard voltage, a special motor having a line voltage rating of 140 volts may be required. Accordingly, electronic motor drives employing the single-phase bridge are likely to be furnished as a package including the d-c motor.

A bridge circuit for a single-phase d-c motor drive is shown in Fig. 12. This is a simple low cost design for fractional and low horsepower motors. Four points of difference from the preceding diametric design should be noted. First, the transformer is omitted. Second, the two controlled rectifiers and the two semiconductor diodes serve for both the armature and the field. Third, the shunt field is supplied with half-wave rectification through diode $S1$ wherein the shunt field and diode $S2$ act as a free-wheeling circuit during the negative half cycle (see page 318). Fourth, the grid control for rectifiers $T1$ and $T2$ employs a *constant phase shift* of 90 degrees plus a

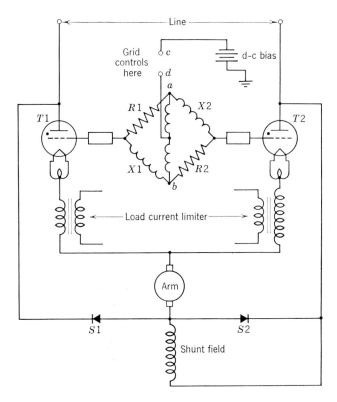

Fig. 12. A bridge circuit for a single-phase d-c motor drive.

variable d-c bias for control. The phase shift is produced in the bridge circuit $R1$, $R2$, $X1$, and $X2$. An in-phase fraction of line voltage is induced across coil ab with mid-tap (see page 199). The operation of this drive is controlled like the preceding diametric circuit by error or deviation voltages introduced into the grid circuit. These control voltages for speed, IR compensation, load current limitation, etc., are introduced between points c and d of the grid circuit.

Polyphase Electronic Motor Drives

The single-phase electronic motor drive for d-c motors is employed for ratings up to approximately 5 hp. Single phase has the advantage of simplicity of control circuits and lower cost in this horsepower range. However, it has the disadvantage of high ripple factor and high form factor. This means that higher peak voltages are impressed across the rectifiers and the motor armature and that greater heating (loss) results in the armature. The greater heating lowers the over-all efficiency and requires a motor of higher normal rating (and cost) to carry the load. For example, a nominal 1 hp motor will carry approximately a three-fourths horsepower load when operating on a single-phase conversion system. Motor derating is not necessary on the three-phase full-wave systems described in succeeding paragraphs.

For electronic motor drives above 5 hp, the three-phase full-wave rectifying circuit is generally employed. A few two-phase systems with Scott transformer connection have been employed for drives in the range of 5 to 15 hp. The basic three-phase full-wave circuit for electronic drive is suggested in Fig. 13. The grid-controlled rectifying units may be thyratrons, excitrons, or ignitrons. Thyratrons are universally used for horsepower ratings in the range 7.5 to 15 hp. The load current rating of approximately 18 amp for the larger thyratrons limits their use to the region of 15 hp. One manufacturer has employed a special design of excitron called the Xatron for use in electronic drives in the range 20 to 50 hp. For horsepower ratings above 50 and up to 10,000, the ignitron has excellent characteristics and gives high efficiencies.

The general system of control for three-phase electronic drives is the same as that employed for single phase with suitable multiplication of control circuitry to cover three phases instead of one. Where ignitrons or excitrons are employed, special circuitry for firing these devices must be used. These circuits follow the theory for firing

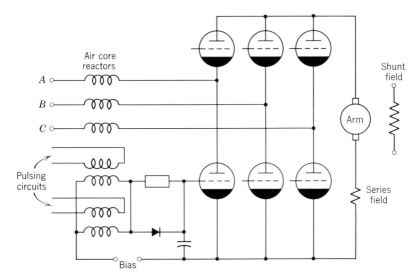

Fig. 13. Basic three-phase full-wave electronic motor drive using ignitrons or excitrons. (Courtesy Reliance Electric and Engineering Company.)

such devices as contained in Chapter 7. Since the response time of electronic circuits is very short, it is necessary to introduce some delay in the operating cycle of large motors. Otherwise, large transient currents may overload the rectifiers and the supply line. One form of delay may be accomplished by the inductance of the air core reactors in the supply line as shown in Fig. 13. Other delays may be built into the control circuitry in the form of RC circuits.

Magnetic Amplifier D-C Motor Drives

The improvements in design and the wide application of magnetic amplifiers since 1945 have suggested their application for d-c motor operation from a-c power lines. At the time these lines were written new designs for magnetic amplifier motor drives were on the drafting boards and in the assembly stage of American manufacturers. The basic circuit of three-phase magnetic amplifier motor drive is suggested in Fig. 14. The circuit parallels the three-phase full-wave electronic circuit previously covered. The rectifying units are Amplistats or Magamps employing silicon rectifiers, feedback, and both bias and control windings. Their general theory of operation follows that given for magnetic amplifiers in Chapter 9. Regulation of rectified current for speed, IR compensation, etc., is effected

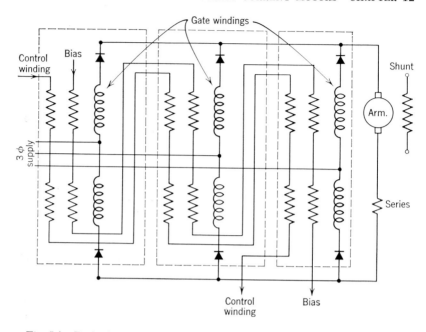

Fig. 14. Basic three-phase full-wave motor drive using magnetic amplifiers.

through the control windings which are connected in series. An example illustrating speed control via a servo system is given in Fig. 15. The setting of potentiometer P determines the rectified terminal voltage (and approximate motor speed). With the armature at rest, the difference voltage e produces current through the control winding which bucks the rectified voltage to a low value. As the armature speed and counter emf rise, the difference voltage decreases and the rectified voltage rises.

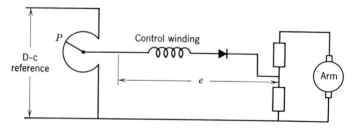

Fig. 15. Basic circuit for speed control with drive using magnetic amplifiers.

Since magnetic amplifier motor drives have not been field tested at this writing, experience data cannot be given. Experience on these devices in other applications has shown that they are reliable, rugged, and require a minimum of maintenance. These characteristics are welcomed by operators in the electric utility and industrial fields. It would appear that the magnetic amplifier drive may find early application for fractional and small power motors. In the matter of cost it is probable that the cost of these units will lie between the high cost M-G drives and the low cost electronic (ionic) drives.

Controlled Semiconductor Rectifier Motor Drive

The solid-state thyratron is superior to the ionic thyratron in having a lower forward voltage drop, a high switching speed, greater ruggedness, longer life, and greater power carrying ability. These important advantages suggest that this currently new device will supplant the gaseous thyratron for d-c motor drives in a few years (1965 or earlier).

Comparison of Operating Systems for D-C Motors

A general comparison of the characteristics, advantages, and disadvantages of the operating systems covered in this chapter is given in the following chart.

M-G set	Simple
	Rugged
	Permits dynamic braking
	Heavy
	Requires large space
	D-c machine maintenance
	Rather low efficiency
	High initial cost
Electronic (ionic)	Rapid response
	Precise control
	Light weight
	Small space
	High efficiency
	Little voltage surge on starting
	Lowest in initial cost
Magnetic amplifier	Rugged
	Small space
	Minimum maintenance

| Controlled semi-conductor rectifier | Future development promises to produce very light, compact, and highly efficient units |

REFERENCE

1. Moyer, E. E., "Electronic Control of D-C Motors," *Electronics,* May, June, July, September, and October 1943.
2. Humphrey, A. J., "The Xatron—A Variable Speed Electronic Drive for Process Control," IRE Transactions on Industrial Electronics, March, 1957.

chapter **13** _____

Resistance Welding

Resistance Welding

Resistance welding is produced by a concentrated electric current
flowing across the contact resistance between two metallic pieces held
under pressure. The heating effect is represented by the equation
I^2RT where I is the current in amperes, R is the contact and load
resistance, and T is the time during which the current flows. In this
process, the resistance R is a very important factor which is determined by nature of material, surface condition of material, and the
pressure employed. The process is classified as pressure welding by
the American Welding Society.

The principle of resistance welding was patented by Professor
Elihu Thompson in 1886. The application of the principle is indi-

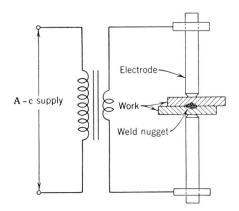

Fig. 1. Schematic circuit for resistance welding.

361

Metals	Aluminum	Ascoloy	Brass	Copper	Galvanized iron	Iron	Lead	Monel	Nickel	Nichrome	Tin plate	Zinc	Phos. bronze	Nickel silver
Aluminum	●										●	●		
Ascoloy		●	●	●	●	●		●	●	●			●	●
Brass		●	●	●	●	●		●	●	●	●		●	●
Copper		●	●	●	●	●		●	●	●	●		●	●
Galvanized iron		●	●	●	●	●	●	●	●	●	●		●	●
Iron		●	●	●	●	●		●	●	●	●		●	●
Lead						●		●			●	●		●
Monel		●	●	●	●	●		●	●	●			●	●
Nickel		●	●	●	●	●		●	●	●			●	●
Nichrome		●	●	●	●	●		●	●	●			●	●
Tin plate	●	●	●	●	●	●	●	●	●	●			●	●
Zinc	●		●	●			●				●			
Phos. bronze		●	●	●	●	●		●	●	●			●	●
Nickel silver		●	●	●	●	●	●	●	●	●			●	●

Fig. 2. Combinations of materials that may be welded satisfactorily. (Courtesy General Electric Company.)

cated in Fig. 1. Two pieces of metal are held under pressure between two electrodes having high conductivity while a heavy alternating current from the secondary of a transformer is passed through the small contact area between the pieces. Since most of the resistance in the secondary circuit exists at the contact between the pieces in the immediately surrounding metal, the energy developed in this circuit is transformed into heat I^2RT at and close to the point of contact. The metal at the point of contact quickly reaches the fusion point and the pressure of the electrodes brings about a molecular union which on cooling results in a welded joint. The voltage employed in the secondary circuit is relatively low, of the order of 2 to 10 volts. The current producing the weld is relatively large but depends on the thickness and size of the parts to be welded, the area of contact, and the material being fabricated. For welding small wires the current may be less than 100 amp, whereas in fabricating heavy structural-steel parts the current may reach hundreds of thousands of amperes. Most applications of resistance welding employ alternating current and the power factor averages approximately 0.5. In special cases the power factor may be as low as 0.1 or as high as 0.9. During the first quarter of this century resistance welding was confined largely to the fabrication of the ferrous metals, but with the improvement in techniques of the method, and particularly with the introduction of electronic controls covered in later sections of this chapter, it has become possible to weld successfully nearly all metals and alloys. A chart showing the combinations of metals that may be welded satisfactorily is given in Fig. 2.

Divisions of Resistance Welding

Resistance welding may be subdivided into (1) spot, (2) projection, (3) seam, and (4) butt welding as shown in the chart of Fig. 3. These forms of welding all follow the principle previously outlined, differing only in the specific method of application. Spot welding is the most common form. Here the welds are made by localizing the welding current through a small area in the parts being welded by the use of points or electrodes of proper shape as suggested in Fig. 1. This method is used for fabricating sheet-metal structures where mechanical strength only is required and not an air- or watertight seal. This includes such structures as metal furniture, metal cases, automobile body work, toys, refrigerator parts, and kitchen utensils. Some common forms of sheet-metal joints suitable for the spot weld process are shown in Fig. 4 and a modern heavy-duty spot welder is illustrated in Fig. 5. The time during which the current is applied is a very important element in satisfactory spot welding. As an example, when stainless steel is spot welded, the metal must be heated for a minimum period of time to prevent carbide precipitation. Usually this time should not exceed 3 cycles on 60-cycle current, or

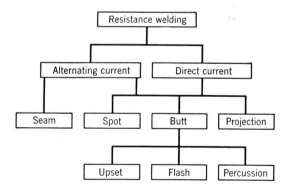

Fig. 3. Chart of the divisions of resistance welding.

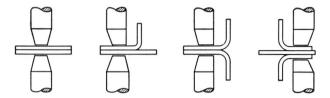

Fig. 4. Forms of sheet-metal joints.

$\frac{1}{20}$ of a second. If the heating time varies 1 cycle, the heating effect would vary $33\frac{1}{3}$ per cent, which is usually fatal to the quality of the weld. A photomicrograph of a weld of stainless steel 0.037 in. thick, made in 1 cycle ($\frac{1}{60}$ sec), is shown in Fig. 6. Copper is one of the most difficult metals to weld. It can be welded and its weldability can be increased if it has a tinned surface.

A modification of spot welding, known as *pulsation spot welding,* makes practical the welding of two pieces of material 1 in. thick and sandwich combinations such as a $\frac{1}{2}$ in. plate between two thicker plates. The procedure for pulsation spot welding is to employ a spot-

Fig. 5. Air-operated heavy-duty press-type spot welder for general purpose use with built-in electronic control. (Courtesy General Electric Company.)

Fig. 6. Photomicrograph of spot-welded joint of two pieces of 18-8 stainless steel, 0.037 in. thick. Heat zone approximately one-half way through the weld made in $\frac{1}{60}$ sec, 50 times. (Courtesy General Electric Company.)

welding press of high capacity, capable of applying heavy pressure, and then through the use of electronic control to apply the power intermittently. For example, the power may be applied for 20 cycles "on" and 10 cycles "off" for ten impulses to weld two pieces of 1-in. stock. The "off" time in this process permits the water-cooled electrodes to retain their temperature below the point where they are upset excessively.

Projection welding is a modification of spot welding in which current is localized by the use of projections on the work parts instead of the use of electrodes having a small diameter or contact area. Where projection welding can be employed it is preferable to regular

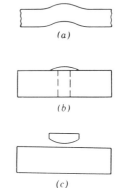

Fig. 7. Forms of projections for projection welding.

spot welding because the electrode maintenance is much lower and
several welds may be made simultaneously by using large flat electrodes. The projection used on the work should have a rounded or
dome shape as shown in Fig. 7, parts (a) and (b), so that the weld
will start with a point contact and have a continuously increasing
cross section to finish the weld. The projections should be made on
the heavier piece when materials of different thickness are being
welded. Silver contacts are welded to various mountings by the projection method shown in Fig. 8. These contacts are prepared for
welding either by forming a projection directly on the back of the
silver (Fig. 7c) or by using silver steel contacts with the steel back
forming a dome. Projection welding should be performed in a time
period of 5 to 30 cycles.

Seam welding consists of a series of overlapping spot welds. Such
welds could be made on a spot welder but are produced more conveniently by two wheel electrodes, or by one wheel and a bar electrode with the work moving between them. On some seam welders
the wheels are driven; on others, they are idle. A typical seam welder
is illustrated in Fig. 9. The current for making seam welds is interrupted so that the metal may chill under pressure, giving a weld
which simulates a continuous spot weld. In this way a pressure-
tight seam weld is made. The current interruption requires the use
of an electronic control to give the same "on" and "off" time to each
interruption and weld. Current interruptions may be as high as 450
per minute. Seam welds are usually made under water to keep the
heating of the work and welding wheels to a minimum. Such cooling
reduces both the distortion of the work and the maintenance cost
of the welding wheels. Seam welding is used in the fabrication of
oil tanks, transformers, refrigerator evaporators, gas tanks, steam
radiators, all-metal vacuum bottles, and various other products.

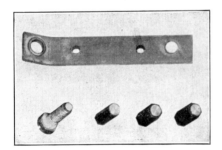

Fig. 8.   Projection-welded silver
contacts. (Courtesy General Electric Company.)

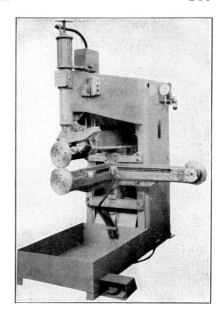

Fig. 9. Special seam-welding machine for both circular and longitudinal seam welding. (Courtesy General Electric Company.)

Butt welding is a process in which two pieces of metal stock or tubes are placed end to end and welded into one piece. In the resistance-welding process two types of butt welding are employed—upset and flash. In the upset type the parts to be welded are clamped in a welding machine (see Fig. 10) in the proper alignment and are brought together with the required amount of pressure. The current is applied, heating the metal by the resistance method until the welding temperature is reached. At this point a pressure is applied which forges the parts together. The required pressure is applied manually by lever and toggle, or automatically by some hydraulic or spring system. Upset butt welding is used principally on nonferrous materials for welding bars, rods, and tubing.

In flash butt welding, the parts to be welded are clamped as in the upset process and the procedure is similar except that the circuit is closed before the parts are brought together. As the parts move into contact at the correct speed, an arc is established which continues as long as this speed continues. This arc burns away a portion of the material from each piece until the welding temperature is reached. At this point the speed of travel is increased, the power switched off, and the weld upset.

Flash welding is used on steel and other ferrous alloys because it

Fig. 10. Butt welder, 200 kva. (Courtesy General Electric Company.)

gives a better weld than the upset process. The superior weld results because the surfaces to be welded are burned away, producing a weld of clean virgin metal. Flash welding is used extensively in automobile construction on body, axles, wheels, frame, and other parts. It is also used for welding motor frames, transformer tanks, sheet metal containers, and it is applicable for steel structures of many kinds. Flash welds may be made on circular sections as small as 0.010-in. diameter and on flat sections of an area of 60 sq in.

Percussion welding is a form of resistance butt welding which uses the discharge from a capacitor for the source of energy. This process is used in factories for welding lead-in wires for incandescent lamps and electron tubes at the rate of 200 per minute. The actual duration of the capacitor discharge is approximately $\frac{1}{3000}$ of a second.

Miscellaneous Application of Resistance Heating

The principle of resistance heating may be employed for other heating processes such as annealing, punching holes, soldering, and brazing. Spot welders may be used for spot annealing. Butt welders are used for annealing hardened shafts and may be used for straightening tubing and other structural shapes. They may be used also to heat pipes and angles for bending. By using a tungsten punch and a copper die in spot welders, holes can be burned in hardened steel parts such as saws, thin milling cutters, and flat spring stock. These holes are not so accurate as drilled stock but they are clean, they do not start cracks in the adjacent material, and the annealing action does not extend far from the hole. The use of carbon, graphite, or tungsten as the top electrode in a welder permits soldering and brazing operations. Here the heat is produced in the electrode rather than in the work. Portable tongs with carbon electrodes utilizing the resistance method are satisfactory for brazing electrical connections in transformers, motors, and other types of electrical equipment. Through the use of silver solder a stronger joint and one that will withstand a higher temperature is obtained at a lower cost.

Welding Equipment

Welding machines must perform the following functions in the resistance-welding process.

1. Support the work and apply the pressure or squeeze.
2. Pass current for the weld.
3. Hold (with current off) for the weld to set.
4. Release work-off.

The work is held and current is applied through the use of electrodes which may be points, rods, wheels, or flat surfaces. These electrodes should have high conductivity (except for soldering and brazing). Originally only copper was used for electrodes. It has the disadvantage of (1) low compressive strength and (2) a low annealing temperature causing it to misform very rapidly. Several types of electrode materials have been developed that are more suitable than copper. Many alloys of copper with cadmium and other elements have been developed with varying degrees of conductivity and strength so that satisfactory electrodes for welding all classes of materials are available. In general, low-conductivity material should be welded with a relatively high-conductivity electrode; high-conductivity materials with low-conductivity electrodes.

The pressure on the work before and during the welding process is produced manually by foot pressure, by spring-mounted electrodes, or by hydraulic operation. Air pressure in piston-type chambers is frequently employed. Pressure may be actuated by electromagnetic solenoids, or by motor-operated cams.

The current supply to the work is furnished by a transformer (except for percussion welding) which is built as an integral part of the welding machine.

The control for the various functions in the welding process is the key to satisfactory resistance welding and will be treated in the remainder of this chapter.

Steps in Welding Control

The process of making a typical weld can be divided into the four steps illustrated in the welding time and duty cycle of Fig. 11. First, the work pieces must be pressed together or squeezed in preparation for the welding current. Second, the welding circuit should be closed and the proper value of current applied for the correct interval of time. Third, the current should be turned off and the work held for a suitable time interval to permit the weld to set. Fourth, the pressure on electrodes should be released and the work removed during the "off" period. The important factors in this welding cycle are: (1) the pressure on work, (2) the current that flows, and (3) the time that the current flows.

Methods of Control

The four steps in a resistance welding operation outlined in the preceding paragraph may be performed (1) by manual operation, (2) by semiautomatic means, or (3) by fully automatic equipment. The duty cycle on the early spot and butt welders was controlled manually and mechanically. On the spot welder a foot-operated lever was designed so that the first part of a downstroke closed the electrodes on the work and applied spring pressure (squeeze), the second continuing part of the stroke closed the circuit of the primary of the transformer (weld), the third part of the downstroke opened

Fig. 11. Typical duty cycle of a resistance welding operation.

the electric circuit but maintained pressure on the work (hold), and the fourth or upstroke of the foot lever released the pressure and the work, thus completing the welding cycle. In the semiautomatic method of control, some one or two of the factors such as pressure, circuit closing, current magnitude, or timing may be performed automatically while other steps in the cycle are controlled by the operator. For example, the pressure on the work may be produced by a motor-controlled or magnet-controlled spring, by a solenoid-operated piston in a cylinder under air, or by hydraulic pressure. The circuit may be closed by a magnetic contactor, a motor and cam action, or an electronic switch. Similarly, the timing may be accomplished by a motor-operated timing device, a magnetic delay device, or an electronic timing circuit. In the fully automatic method of control, all steps in the complete duty cycle are performed automatically in sequence leaving nothing to the operator except the initiation of the cycle through push-button control. Under the automatic method the individual steps may be mechanical or electronic though nearly all present-day welders use electronic controls.

The magnitude of the current used in the welding process may be controlled by varying the voltage applied to the welding transformer or by varying the tap connection on the primary of the transformer. These methods give rather coarse steps of variation. A smooth and stepless control can be obtained by a phase-shift timing for firing the electron trigger tubes in the primary circuit of the welding transformer. This method is covered in a later section on heat control.

The magnitude of the heat, developed in the load by the secondary current of the welding transformer, depends upon the instant in the impressed voltage cycle that the primary circuit is closed. This follows because for some conditions a transient current is produced in the secondary which increases the magnitude of the resultant current for one or more cycles. Accordingly, the amount of heat will vary even though the time of current flow measured in cycles remains the same. This variation in the amount of heat is important in welding materials that are critical as to welding temperature. Also the transient current surges tend to burn electrodes and increase the maintenance cost on the welder.

The phenomenon of transient current suggested above is illustrated in Fig. 12. These oscillograms show that the transient can be avoided by closing the primary circuit at the power factor angle. An exact timing of the circuit can be obtained by using a phase-shift control on a thyratron to fire an electronic switch. The use of this method

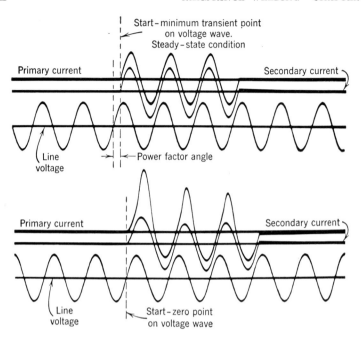

Fig. 12. Oscillogram illustrating the power factor angle. (Courtesy General Electric Company.)

is known as *synchronous timing*. Synchronous timing requires special electronic controls and an additional cost of equipment which is justified in many applications. All mechanical circuit-closing devices and some electronic controls give nonsynchronous switching (i.e., the heat energy developed may vary with different welds).

Block Diagram of Control

The various functions in the welding cycle are usually performed by different units of equipment. These units and their interrelationship are illustrated in the block diagram of Fig. 13. Pressure is applied to the work by some mechanical unit shown at (1). The circuit for the primary of the transformer is closed by the contactor (2). The time that the circuit is closed is controlled by a timer (3), and, if special control of the magnitude of the current for the heating is necessary, it may be provided by another unit known as the heat control (4). It will be noted that the timer may act as a master control for the function of the other units. A welding installation may employ all or a part of the individual units shown in Fig. 13, depending on the refinement needed in the welding process.

Electronic Contactors

Electronic contactors consist of two trigger tubes connected in an inverse parallel arrangement to function as a single-pole switch. Either thyratrons or ignitrons may be employed. Most welders use ignitrons as shown in Fig. 14a. Here the ignitrons are excited by copper oxide (or selenium) rectifiers. The arrows indicate the direction of electron flow and, with the gap from X to Y closed by some switching arrangement, the operation is obvious (see page 309 for ignitron firing). A commercial electronic contactor (Weld-O-Trol) using this circuit is shown in Fig. 15 with the rectifiers appearing on the left and the water-cooled ignitrons on the right. A thermostatic device in the water-circulating system controls the water-flow switch (Fig. 14a) so that the ignitrons are protected (shut off) from overheating which may result from a stoppage of water flow or inadequate circulation in the cooling system. The function of the electronic switch is to open or close the primary circuit subject to the firing and timing control which resides in a separate device connected to points X and Y. The operation of the welder may be synchronous or nonsynchronous, depending on the characteristics of the timing device.

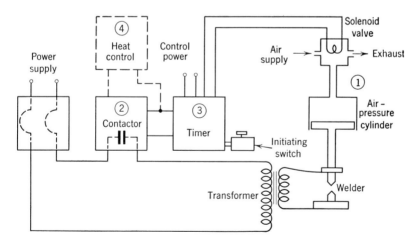

Fig. 13. Block diagram of electronic controls applied to welding processes.

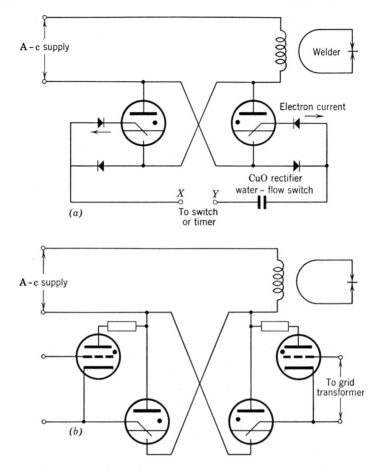

Fig. 14. Inverse parallel trigger circuits for contactors in welding control.

Another type of electronic contactor (switch) for welders uses thyratrons instead of copper oxide rectifiers for firing the ignitrons (see Fig. 14b). Here the instant of firing the ignitrons is controlled by the voltage on the grid of the thyratron which fires the thyratron and in turn the ignitron. This circuit gives a superior control because (1) the actual instant of firing is very precise, permitting synchronous timing and (2) the time angle for firing may be adjusted to control the magnitude of the current loops (half-cycles) and thus control the rate of heat application. Both of these advantages are important in welding materials having critical welding characteristics. Thyratrons may be used directly for switching the power on low-capacity welders. The simple switching circuit for such application is shown on page 308, Fig. 2. Obviously, excellent timing and current control can be obtained through the use of suitable timing control applied to the grids of the thyratrons.

Electronic Timers

Many circuits may be used for electronic timing of the steps in the welding process. A simple and widely used circuit for measuring a definite time interval is given in Fig. 16. The key to the operation of this circuit lies in the *RC* circuit shown within the dotted rectangle. The starting of the time interval is produced by the closing of the initiating switch, and the ending of the time interval is effected by the operation of the telephone-type magnetic relay *TD*. To understand the action taking place note (1) that 115 volts a-c supply is impressed across points *a* and *b* which are the terminals of the potential divider circuit consisting of resistances *R1*, *R2*, and *P*. The potentiometer *P* permits a variation of the a-c potential between

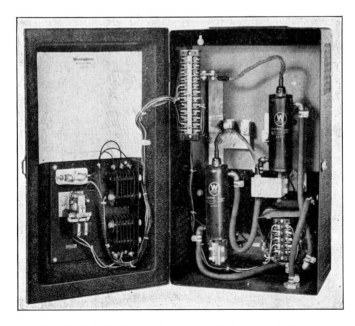

Fig. 15. The Weld-O-Trol—an electronic switch using ignitron and copper oxide rectifiers for welding. (Courtesy Westinghouse Electric Corporation.)

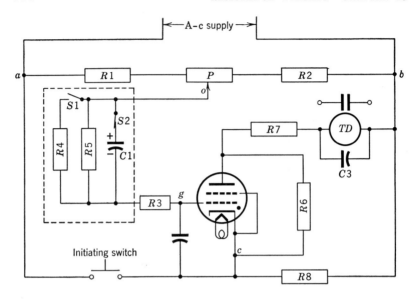

Fig. 16. Simple timer circuit using a shield-grid thyratron and a magnetic relay

points a and o and b and o. Note (2) that, as long as the initiating switch is open, both the cathode and anode of the shield-grid thyratron are connected to the right side of the a-c supply line b and hence are at approximately the same potential so that no conduction can take place. Note (3) that, as long as the initiating switch is open, the cathode and control grid g of the thyratron are connected to a circuit having an applied potential equal to o-b. Hence on the half-cycles when the cathode is negative, grid rectification takes place and electrons pass from b through $R8$, through cathode to grid, and thence through $R3$ and $R5$. After a few cycles of grid rectification the potential across the capacitor $C1$ (drop across $R5$) rises to a nearly constant value determined by the a-c potential across o-b.

The timing cycle is started by closing the initiating switch which connects the cathode of the thyratron to the supply line at a. This action permits the a-c line potential to be applied across the cathode-anode circuit (c, tube, $R7$, and relay TD). On the half-cycle, when the anode is positive the thyratron is ready to conduct (cathode to anode) but is prevented from doing so by the negative d-c grid potential which has been built up on the lower side of the timer capacitor $C1$. Now to understand what happens next, note that the closing of the initiation switch has *shifted the a-c potential applied between the cathode and grid from the value across* o-b *to the value across* a-o, that when point *b* is negative the cathode on the other side of *R8* is positive instead of negative as previously indicated, and that for this condition the alternating voltage applied to the grid (across *a-o*) is negative with respect to the cathode so that grid rectification does not take place as before. Now the value of resistance *R1* and *R2* are selected so that the *IR* drop across *R2* (plus part of *P*) will be sufficiently larger than that across *a-o* (plus part of *P*) so that the negative potential built up on the lower side of capacitor *C1* will keep the thyratron from conducting when the initiating switch is closed. The timing action is illustrated in the graph of Fig. 17. Since the alternating voltage across *a-o* applied to the grid and cathode after closing the initiating switch is lower than before, condenser *C1* discharges slowly and the d-c voltage across it decays as shown. In the meantime the new a-c component applied from *a-o* is superimposed in series with the d-c capacitor voltage and the resulting voltage approaches the critical firing point for the thyratron which depends on the characteristic of the tube employed. This critical point is in the region of zero resultant voltage or equal cath-

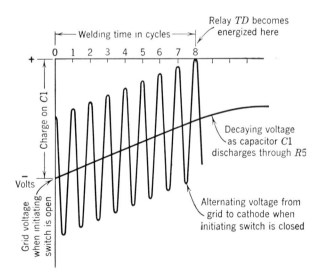

Fig. 17. Graphical illustration of the operating principle of the timing circuit of Fig. 16.

ode and grid potentials. When the decay of the potential across $C1$ permits the thyratron to conduct, relay TD is energized and opens (or closes) contacts which complete the timing cycle.

Capacitor $C3$ serves to hold relay TD and prevent chattering during the half-cycles when the tube does not conduct. Resistor $R7$ protects the tube from "transient" rush of current into $C3$ when the tube conducts. Resistor $R6$ permits a small a-c current to flow through relay TD and keep it from being sluggish in action.

The timing interval is controlled by the setting on the potentiometer which determines the initial negative potential built up on the timing capacitor $C1$. Another and larger range of timing can be secured by closing switch $S1$ which will increase the rate of decay of the d-c voltage across $C1$. The time delay can be made ineffective by opening the timing capacitor circuit at switch $S2$. The usual range of timing for this type of circuit is from 3 to 60 cycles on a 60-cycle circuit.

The timing circuit of Fig. 16 with a slight modification may be combined with an ignitron electronic switch (Fig. 14) to serve as a semiautomatic timer to measure weld time only. The timing circuit of Fig. 16 may be employed also for automatic spot welding wherein all steps in the welding cycle are controlled in the proper sequence. A complete sequence timer employs four circuits like that of Fig. 16 plus relay contacts, an electronic switch, and a foot-operated initiating switch. A schematic circuit for the multiple-timer operation is given in Fig. 18 and the sequence of operation is as follows: the closing of the foot switch causes relay $CR1$ to operate and close three contacts. Contact $CR1b$ places a shunt circuit around the foot switch, $CR1$ energizes the top (squeeze) timing circuit, contact $CR1a$ energizes the solenoid valve (see bottom), and air pressure applies the squeeze. When the "squeeze" timing circuit completes its cycle, relay $TD1$ closes two contacts. Contact $TD1b$ energizes the "weld" timing circuit and $TD1a$ closes the circuit to the Weld-O-Trol (contacts X and Y, Fig. 14a). Energy now flows into the weld for the period determined by the "weld" timing circuit. At the close of this period relay $TD4$ operates three contacts. Contact $TD4b$ places a shunt around $TD1b$, $TD4c$ energizes the "hold" timing circuit, and the opening of contact $TD4a$ de-energizes the "squeeze" timing circuit, which action, in turn, de-energizes relay $TD1$ and opens all its contacts. The opening of $TD1a$ opens the power circuit through the Weld-O-Trol electronic switch. Next assume that switch $S2$ is closed

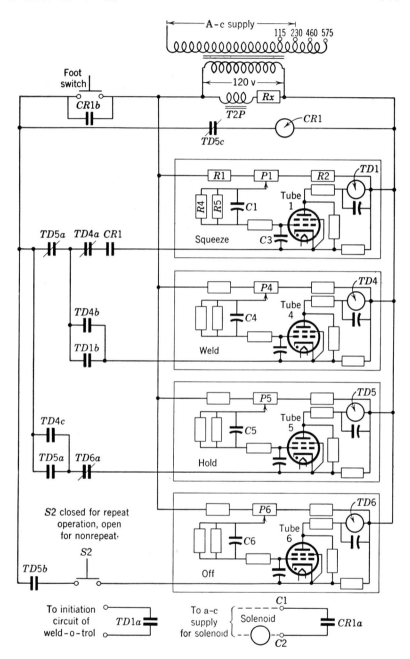

Fig. 18. Schematic circuit of a sequence timer.

for repeat operation. Now when the "hold" timing circuit completes its period, relay $TD5$ operates four contacts. Contact $TD5b$ energizes the "off" timing circuit, $TD5a$ (opens) de-energizes the "weld" timing circuit, and $TD5c$ (opens) de-energizes relay $CR1$, which in turn opens $CR1a$ controlling the solenoid pressure valve. If continuous-sequence cycles are desired the foot switch is held closed, and, when the "off" timing circuit completes its period, relay $TD6$ operates, de-energizing the "hold" timer at contact $TD6a$. The de-energizing of relay $TD5$ releases all its contacts which results in the complete restoration of the circuits to the initial condition ready for a repeat cycle of operation.

Precision timing requires circuits employing more tubes and the omission of magnetic relays. One important part of precision timers is the trailing-tube circuit shown in Fig. 19. This circuit, consisting of two thyratrons and three transformers, constitutes an intermediate link in a precision control circuit. In operation, tube 1 is "fired" by a timing or signal voltage applied to its grid; then, after tube 1 has conducted for a half-cycle, tube 2 is caused to "fire" and conduct for the next half-cycle. Thus, tube 2 always trails tube 1 in action. To understand this operation it should be noted that the grid of tube 2 is excited by alternating voltages from two transformers. The a-c exciting voltage from transformer T is 180 degrees out of phase with the a-c supply from the left. Thus, whenever the anode of tube 2 is made positive, the alternating voltage applied to its grid from transformer T is negative which tends to hold the tube from conducting. Hence as long as tube 1 does not conduct, tube 2 will not,

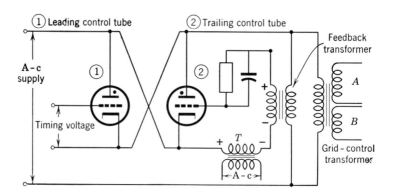

Fig. 19. Trailing-tube circuit.

and the circuits to the right are held open by the inverse parallel connection.

Assume now that a timing signal is applied to tube 1 which makes its grid positive. Tube 1 will now conduct (assuming its anode is positive) for the remainder of that half-cycle and current will flow through the primary windings of both the feedback and grid-control transformers. This current will induce voltages in the secondaries of both transformers. The secondary of the feedback transformer is connected so that its induced voltage "bucks" (180 degrees out of phase) the alternating voltage produced by transformer T. However, during this half-cycle the anode of tube 2 is negative and so it does not conduct. When this half-cycle ends, the applied supply voltages pass through zero and, as they rise on the next half-cycle, the anode of tube 2 becomes positive. During this transition period the primary current and the secondary voltage of the feedback transformer lag (the supply circuit) because of the leakage and other reactance in the parallel-connected primaries of the grid-control and feedback transformers. This lag of voltage in the secondary of the feedback transformer holds a resultant positive potential on the grid of tube 2 for a short interval and causes the tube to conduct for the second half-cycle. In the complete welding-control circuit, the two secondaries of the grid-control transformer, A and B, are used to excite the grids of another pair of thyratrons, which in turn are used to fire a pair of ignitrons in the electronic switch. In some welder-control circuits, the feedback transformer is connected across the primary of the welding transformer and thus causes tube 2 to trail tube 1.

This trailing action of tube 2 assures that any timing device employing this circuit will always give an integral number of cycles (an even number of half-cycles). This feature is important in welding operations because a weld period containing an odd number of half-cycles may leave residual flux in the welding transformer and result in unequal heating for different welding duty cycles.

The trailing-tube circuit of Fig. 19 can be added to Fig. 14a by connecting the two thyratrons 1 and 2 at points X and Y and connecting the primary of the feedback transformer across the welding transformer. A somewhat similar addition can be made to Fig. 14b.

The trailing-tube circuit is utilized in the spot-welder timing-control circuit of Fig. 20. Here direct current is used to produce the timing interval and three thyratrons perform the timing and firing functions. In this circuit the direct current is provided by a double

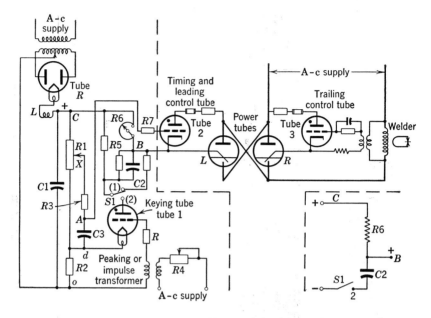

Fig. 20.   Circuit of a spot-welder control without phase control.

diode (two-anode) rectifier at the left with reactor L and capacitor $C1$ serving as the filter. The filtered direct current is applied across the voltage divider formed by resistors $R1$ and $R2$. The voltage drop o-d across resistor $R2$ provides a negative bias for thyratron tube 1 and normally holds it from firing. Tube 1 can be fired at a very definite time in the impressed alternating voltage wave by the peaking or impulse transformer connected in its grid circuit. The student should recall the theory of the peaking transformer explained on page 319. The time of applying heat (impulse) is controlled by an adjustment of variable resistor $R4$.

With $S1$ in position 1, the cathode-anode of tube 1 is open and the tube cannot conduct. When switch $S1$ is moved to position 2, tube 1 will conduct the instant that the next positive "peak" is induced by the peaking transformer. Thus direct current will flow from point d through tube 1, resistor $R5$, and to the point $+C$. Because of the action of a thyratron on direct current, it is obvious that a continuous undisturbed current will flow through tube 1 and $R5$ until the anode circuit is broken at some later time by moving switch $S1$ back to position 1.

The timing of the weld period and the actual firing of the left ignitron is performed by tube 2. To follow this action, note that the grid of tube 2 is held at the potential of point A and that A is at a potential between that of point d and point X on resistor $R1$. Since the potential at A is determined by the charge on the condenser $C3$ and since this charge can be varied only by current flowing through high resistance $R3$, it follows that this potential is quite stable and is influenced little by fluctuations in the supply voltage. Next observe that, with switch $S1$ in position 1, the cathode of tube 2 (point B) is at the same positive potential as point C. Thus tube 2 does not conduct because its grid potential is negative at A. Now when switch $S1$ is moved to position 2, tube 1 conducts at the next peaking voltage surge and the potential on the cathode of tube 2 switches instantly from $+$ to $-$ and fires. To understand this phenomenon, note that an $R6C2$ timing circuit is connected in parallel across resistor $R5$. When tube 1 conducts, direct voltage Cd minus tube 1 arc drop appears across resistor $R5$ and in turn across $R6C2$. From the detailed $R6C2$ circuit (lower right, Fig. 20) it will be observed that, before $S1$ is closed, point B is $+$ like C and both sides of the condenser $C2$ are at the same potential. Now when switch $S1$ is closed, a few electrons rush to the lower plate of $C2$, and simultaneously other electrons are repelled from the upper plate and instantly lower the potential of point B (cathode of tube 2). The number of electrons taking part in the action is relatively small, being limited by the resistance $R6$. However, the phenomenon instantly lowers the potential of the cathode of tube 2 below that of its grid and conduction takes place which fires ignitron tube L. On the succeeding half-cycle, tube 3 trails and fires the other ignitron tube R. Tubes 2 and 3 and the ignitrons continue to fire, while current flowing in resistor $R6$ charges capacitor $C2$ and causes the potential on its top plate (point B) to rise. When the potential of B rises to the potential of the grid of tube 2, tube 2 ceases to conduct and trailing tube 3 stops after completing its half-cycle. The period required for capacitor $C2$ to charge up to the cutoff point depends upon the resistance of $R6$. This period is adjustable from one half-cycle to one half-second or a welding period of 1 to 30 cycles.

The control resulting from a variation of $R4$ permits firing at the power factor angle and gives synchronous timing. The adjustable point on $R1$ permits a slight variation of grid voltage to take care of variations in tube characteristics and variations in the magnitude of the resistor and capacitor components. The trailing-tube circuit assures integral cycles of weld time and still allows for small variations in the timing of the RC circuit.

Heat Control

The term heat control refers to the amount of heat energy delivered to the work in a welding operation. The total heat energy delivered is determined by the expression $H = I^2RT$. Where R is constant, the energy may be controlled by varying the time T or by varying the current I. The preceding discussion has covered the circuits employed for controlling time or the period of application. For some metals the welding time may be varied over fairly wide limits to secure the proper amount of heat energy. However, for other metals the proper welding time may be fixed by the nature of the metal itself, and here it is necessary to control the quantity of heat applied by a control of I. It was suggested earlier that the current flowing in the work may be controlled by using different taps on the

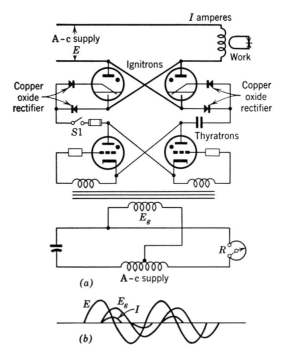

Fig. 21. Electronic contactor with simple phase control added.

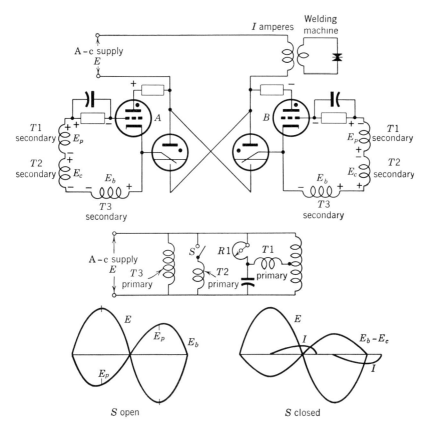

Fig. 22. Phase-shift control for resistance welding.

primary of the welding transformer. This method gives rather large steps of current change and requires some time to effect the change. A nearly stepless control of current can be secured quickly by shifting the phase of the exciting voltage applied to the grid of the firing thyratron. This principle was discussed on page 313 and a simple circuit for applying the principle to a welder control is given in Fig. 21. The phase shift and the firing point of the thyratrons are controlled by the dial on resistor R and may be adjusted to the power angle or a later point in the cycle. In all cases, the current loops for each half-cycle will be equal and synchronous welding will result.

A second circuit for producing a phase shift and firing of ignitrons is shown in Fig. 22. In this circuit three transformers are employed with their secondaries in series in the grid circuit. Transformer $T1$ is a peaking or impulse transformer which provides the peaks for firing tubes A and B and, in turn, the ignitrons. The phase of the peak voltages induced by the impulse transformer is controlled by the setting of resistor $R1$ in the bridge circuit. Transformer $T3$ alone induces a voltage E_b in the grid circuit in opposition (180 degrees out of phase) with the applied a-c E (anode circuit) which has a magnitude sufficient to prevent the thyratrons from being fired by the peaks from transformer $T1$. Transformer $T2$ induces an a-c voltage E_c which is in phase with the applied voltage E and is of such magnitude that when S is closed it bucks the secondary voltage of $T3$ and permits the thyratrons to fire. The opening of switch S permits the voltage of $T3$ to prevent firing. Thus, the period of the weld time is controlled by the operation of switch S.

An excellent welding control can be obtained by combining the features of the circuits in Figs. 19, 20, and 22. Such a combination will utilize the timing control to the left of the dotted line in Fig. 20 with the grid circuit of tube 2 connected to the grid of tube 1 of Fig. 19. Then the secondaries of the grid transformer of Fig. 19 should be substituted for the secondaries of transformer $T2$ in Fig. 22.

Special Electronic Welding Controls

In some applications the quality of the weld depends on factors other than that of the precise timing and the proper phase shift of the firing signal. Such factors are the surface condition of the work (plating, etc.), the pressure applied to the work, and the variation in welding current magnitude caused by changes in welder circuit impedance, welder power factor, or power supply voltage. The resulting variation in welding current (and heating) often requires further refinement in control. Some of these refinements are classified as follows.

1. Preheating and postheating.
2. Voltage and current compensation.
3. Three-phase frequency changer control.
4. Slope control.

In some welding applications it is desirable to preheat the work before applying the welding current; in others it is desirable to reduce the rate of cooling (annealing) after the welding current has ceased. These applications require an extension in the number of steps in the welding cycle. Each added step requires another timing circuit and another current-control unit in the complete sequence control chain.

Any change in line supply voltage produces corresponding changes in the heat input to the welder load. Such changes must be compensated by automatic voltage compensation and current regulation compensators. These compensators utilize the phase-shift method previously explained wherein a peaked triggering voltage is supplied to the grids of the firing thyratrons. The purpose of the voltage compensator is to advance, automatically but arbitrarily, the firing point of a component of control by a definite angle so as to compensate for a given reduction in power supply voltage. One system of compensation is to employ a small "dummy" load in a part of the control circuit. The input to the dummy load varies with the supply voltage and this variation is the basis of the change in phase of the power tube firing for maintaining a constant heating value in the welding current.

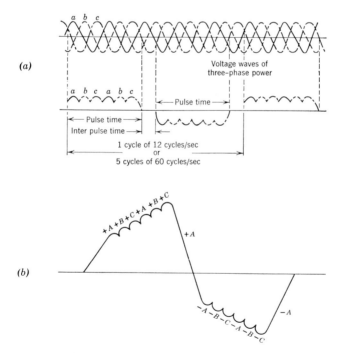

Fig. 23. Wave forms for changing frequency from a three-phase circuit to a single phase. (Courtesy General Electric Company.)

Single-phase resistance welders have the characteristic of requiring a high kilovolt-ampere power supply and at a low power factor. This undesirable characteristic can be overcome by the design of a three-phase frequency changer control and circuit. Three-phase operation employs a special transformer, six firing tubes, and special firing control circuits. The welding transformer is similar to a single-phase transformer having three primary windings. Each primary winding is connected in series with two inversely paralleled ignitrons (similar to single-phase welder). The secondary or pulse frequency is controlled by using a series of positive pulses in one direction and then a like series of positive pulses in the reverse direction. The wave form and method of securing this frequency reduction are shown in Fig. 23. The pulse or welding frequency is controlled by sequence timing circuits. The usual frequency employed lies in the range of 1 to 5 cycles per second. Obviously, such low frequencies reduce the inductive reactance $(2\pi fL)$ of the secondary of the welder transformer, including its long throat. This reduction in reactance improves the power factor of the welder. The use of three phases distributes the welding load over all phases of the power supply and thus balances the required kilovolt-amperes demand.

The basic steps and circuits for welders employing the three-phase frequency changer are similar to those used for the single-phase units. Naturally, these three-phase welders are larger, heavier, and more costly. Their superior characteristics may well justify the additional cost.

Slope control is a system of phase-shift control which varies the magnitude of the welding current during the period of the welding time. Up-slope control increases the magnitude during the early

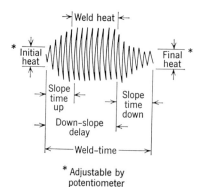

Fig. 24. Weld time with up-down slope control. The start of the down slope or the point where welding current starts to decrease is delayed a number of cycles after the start of the welding current. (Courtesy General Electric Company.)

part of weld time, and down-slope tapers off the magnitude of the welding current at the close of the weld time period. Slope control is illustrated in Fig. 24. Either up-slope or down-slope, or a combination of both, may be employed. It reduces flash and spatter and expulsion in projection welding. It causes the welding current to increase uniformly from a low starting value to the full welding current value. It reduces tip pickup in welding aluminum and its alloys and in welding plated materials, and permits the welding of materials previously possible only with three-phase frequency changers. Slope control can be used with synchronous precision control or nonsynchronous control, which includes heat control.

Seam and Pulsation Welding

Resistance seam welding consists of a series of successive welds between two layers of metal for the purpose of forming either a gastight line weld, or the equivalent of a series of spaced spot welds. Welding current is applied intermittently at definite "heat" and "cool" time intervals as the work progresses between roller-type electrodes. Successive welds are made without breaking the low-resistance secondary circuit of the welding transformer, therefore making it important that the impulses of welding current are free from starting transients. Synchronous firing and a timer giving an integral number of cycles for heating are necessary for seam welding. Circuits for seam-welding control employ the principles previously covered for spot welding. In these circuits a separate dial or potentiometer control is used for the "heat" and "cool" timing. The welding cycle is started by closing an initiating switch and is continuous with alternate heat and cool periods until stopped by opening the initiation switch.

Pulsation welding (interrupted spot welding) consists of making a spot weld by means of a spot welder but using seam-weld timing for a definite number of current impulses. As an example, pulsation welding may use 10 cycles of "heat" time and 4 cycles of "cool" time repeated alternately for five current applications requiring an overall welding time of 66 cycles.

A semimechanical type of seam-welding control consists of a synchronous motor-driven chain having extended link pins for holding removable metallic and nonmetallic buttons. These conducting and nonconducting buttons may contact a set of brushes at the rate of one button per half-cycle or one button per cycle, depending upon the motor-gear-box ratio. The brushes render the firing tubes conductive in accordance with the timing pattern set up on the motor-driven chain. By means of auxiliary link contacts and auxiliary brushes, the timing may be initiated at a definite point on the timing chain to provide special timing patterns. Any special timing pattern can be provided by full electronic control, although there are cases where the additional complications and expense may not be justified, thus making the chain timer preferable.

Bench-Type Spot-Welder Controls

Bench-type spot welders for fabricating small parts may require either a large current for a portion of one half-cycle, or a comparatively small current for several cycles. For a large current, a half-cycle welding control using an ignitron may apply a single unidirectional impulse controlled by phase shift over an angle varying from 20 to 300 degrees. A schematic circuit for a welding control of this type is shown in Fig. 25. This circuit is of interest because it utilizes the discharge of a capacitor for firing the ignitron. A rectifier and filter on the left applies a direct voltage across the potential divider $R2$ and $R3$ with a major part across $R2$. The discharge capacitor $C2$ charges to the voltage of $R2$. The smaller voltage drop across $R3$ and $C3$ is applied to $R4$ and the voltage-regulator tube 4 to hold the shield grid negative, and also across $R6$ and $R7$ to apply a d-c negative bias to the control grid of tube 2. An a-c peak-firing voltage is applied to the control grid of tube 2 through its grid trans-

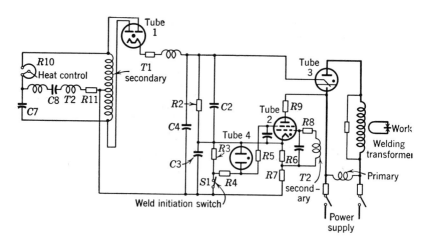

Fig. 25. Circuit for half-cycle welding having heat control.

Fig. 26. Bench-type spot welder operated by half-cycle. (Courtesy General Electric Company.)

former $T2$, which voltage is large enough to overcome the negative d-c bias but not sufficient to overpower the negative bias on the shield grid. The a-c firing peaks are generated in the peaking transformer having its primary in the phase-shift circuit on the left. The peaks are timed by the heat-control resistor $R10$. The weld is made by opening the weld-initiating switch $S1$ which action removes the d-c negative bias on the shield grid and permits tube 2 to conduct on the next voltage peak in transformer $T2$. Capacitor $C2$ discharges through the ignitor of tube 3 and a single half-cycle pulse from the power supply passes the welding transformer. When $C2$ discharges the potential on the anode of tube 2, it drops to a low value so that the tube ceases to conduct. Simultaneously the voltage across $C3$ rises to a high value which also prevents conduction. When the initiating switch is released (closed) the negative d-c bias across the shield grid is restored to prevent conduction of tube 4. Following the release of $S1$, the potential across $R2$ and $R3$ is restored to normal and $C2$ becomes charged and ready for a repeat cycle of operation. The voltage-regulator tube 4 is used to limit the transient negative bias placed across the shield grid when the initiating switch is released. A typical half-cycle bench welder with heat control is illustrated in Fig. 26.

PROBLEM

1. In Fig. 16, capacitor $C1$ and resistor $R5$ are set to give a time delay of 30 cycles in dropping the voltage across the capacitor to 37 per cent. If $C1$ is 1 μf, what is the value of $R5$? Solve the problem for 5 cycles of timing.

REFERENCES

1. Gillette, R. T., "Resistance-Welding Methods and Equipment," *General Electric Bulletin GET*-1189.
2. Palmer, H. L., M. E. Bivens, S. A. Clark, G. L. Rogers, and Barton L. Weller, "Electronic Welding Control," *Gen. Elec. Bulletin GET*-1170. *Electronic Laboratory Manual,* Westinghouse Electric Corporation.

chapter 14

High-Frequency Heating

Electric heating for industrial use may be produced by (1) resistance heating (I^2R), (2) induction heating, or (3) dielectric heating. Each of these methods differs in the theory involved and usually in the preferred applications. The first method is old in the art, the second has been utilized in some measure for half a century, and the third, dielectric heating, is a more recent application.

Most forms of resistance heating are independent of frequency and work equally well with direct current and at low voltages. Induction and dielectric heating require moderate or high values of frequency (also rather high voltages) and are classed as *high-frequency heating*. The higher frequencies require special methods of production in which electronic equipment is generally employed. Since resistance heating supplements the other forms of electric heating, a brief treatment of its theory and application is given here.

Resistance heating is produced by the I^2R or power loss involved when an electric current flows through a heating resistor R. The heating resistor may be (1) a metal conductor, (2) a nonmetallic rod or tube of carbon, or (3) a liquid. Alloys of nickel and chromium are commonly produced in wire or ribbon forms to be wound in helical or coil forms for electric heating units. The heating units may be used in hot plates for heating glue or other compounds or in heat-insulated ovens for laboratory or production processes. Some ovens are furnaces for heat treating metals and other products. Sometimes the heating units are placed in ovens surrounding conveyer systems for drying and baking varnishes, paints, and enamels. For heat

393

treating metals (above 1800° F) one type of furnace consists of carbon or Carborundum tubes (trade name Globar) through which high values of current pass to raise the temperature to red- or white-heat stage. Parts to be heated are placed directly within the heated tube. In other furnaces an insulated oven is heated by current flowing through solid Globar sticks.

Electrolytes and water (not distilled) can be heated by current flowing between electrodes placed in the electrolyte. In this case the resistance of the liquid is the R for the I^2R heating. A similar application is employed in many chemical and metallurgical furnaces. Here the ores and other compounds that make the raw furnace charge are placed in the circular open furnace. Two or more large carbon or graphite cylindrical electrodes are lowered into the charge and current is passed from the electrodes through the charge. Initially, the charge is a solid which slowly fuses to a liquid mass under the action and control of electric currents of large magnitude. These furnaces are called carbon-arc furnaces.

One form of electric heat is produced by infrared (heat) bulbs built like the reflector type of incandescent lamp. These bulbs reflect and concentrate heat rays which may be directed on the work inside a conveyer type of oven. These heat lamps permit the concentration of heat on enamel or painted surfaces and obtain a quick drying action. The concentrated radiant heat penetrates the coating of enamel to a depth sufficient to produce rapid drying without wasting energy in heating the body of the work.

In passing it should be noted that the efficiency of conversion of electric energy into heat via resistance heating is 100 per cent. This means that all the electric energy delivered to the heating resistor is converted into heat energy. Not all this converted energy is delivered to the heating load but, where heat-insulated ovens surround the heating resistor, the ratio of heat delivered to the load to the converted heat energy may be high. Thus the over-all efficiency in using resistance heating is likely to be high. This high over-all efficiency permits resistance heating to be competitive with other methods of heating using fuels as a basis of heat energy.

Induction Heating

Heating by means of low-frequency magnetic fields has been known as far back as 1880. The first practical induction furnace was put into operation in the manufacture of electric light bulbs and electron tubes for many years to fire "getters" and to remove im-

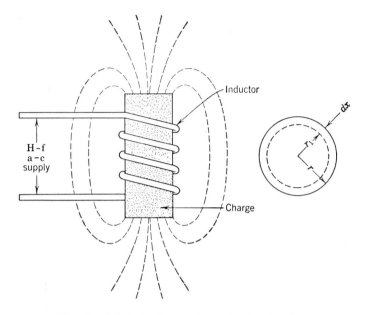

Fig. 1. Method of applying induction heating.

prisoned gas from metal and other parts within the tube. The application of high-frequency induction heating for the heat treatment of metals was a development of World War II.

The elementary theory of induction heating can be studied in Fig. 1. A coil of copper conductor called an inductor surrounds a metal cylinder called a charge or load. If an electric current is passed through the coil, a magnetic field is created which passes through the cylinder. If the current is alternating, the field reverses direction for each cycle and the flux linking the charge or cylinder changes accordingly. Such flux changes will produce heat losses within the charge. The nature and magnitude of these losses depend on the material and temperature of the charge. If the cylinder consists of a magnetic material such as iron, both hysteresis and eddy-current losses may occur. Hysteresis losses are molecular-friction losses which follow the Steinmetz equation for hysteresis loss.

$$W = KB^{1.6}f \text{ (approx.)}$$

where W represents watts, B the flux density, and f the frequency. K is a constant to take care of the parameters involved.

It should be observed that the hysteresis loss varies directly as the frequency and as the 1.6 power of the flux density. Hysteresis losses are of major importance in the heating of iron and magnetic metals at temperatures below the Curie temperature (1420° F for low-carbon steel). Above the Curie temperature magnetic properties effectively disappear and hysteresis loss ceases to exist. Thus it is easier to heat magnetic materials by the induction process, but the limitation of hysteresis loss at higher temperatures and the fact that it does not apply to nonmagnetic metals frequently results in an omission of the effect of hysteresis in the development of some empirical equations for induction heating.

The theory of the production of eddy currents is suggested in Fig. 1. The view on the right is a cross section of the cylindrical charge. An elemental circular conducting ring or shell of thickness dx having an inside diameter r_1 and an outer diameter r may be considered. The changing flux through the charge links this elemental conduction shell and induces an emf in it where

$$e = -N\frac{d\phi}{dt}$$

This emf causes a circulating or eddy current to flow through the elemental shell like the current flow in the secondary of a transformer. The eddy current squared times the resistance of the path represents watts which are transformed into heat loss within the shell. An infinite number of elemental shell-like conductors may be visualized as taking part in the eddy-current heating.

Eddy-current losses can be expressed by the equation

$$W_e = Kf^2B_m{}^2$$

wherein the watt loss is proportional to the square of the *frequency* and the *maximum flux density*. Thus the total heat developed within the load can be controlled through the frequency and the flux density. The frequency employed has an important effect upon the depth of penetration of the heat because of a skin effect which takes place in the load. The distribution of the flux density, the current density, and the heat density varies greatly with the frequency employed, as illustrated in Fig. 2. This figure shows the approximate distribution for a charge consisting of a round stainless-steel bar for two different frequencies. In the upper part of the figure a low frequency is applied to the inductor coil (Fig. 1), so that a uniform flux density B

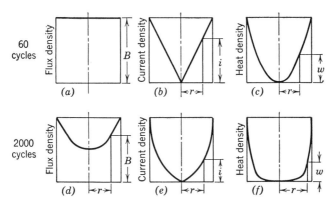

Fig. 2. (Courtesy Allis-Chalmers Manufacturing Company.)

results in the cylindrical charge. The emf induced along the axis of the cylinder by the changing flux will be zero. But, in circular shells surrounding the axis, emf's will be induced that are proportional to the enclosed flux which, in turn, is proportional to the square of the radius of the shell (area $= \pi r^2$). The eddy currents resulting from these emf's will depend on the resistance of the path ($I = E/R$). The resistance of the path is proportional to the length of path ($2\pi r$) and to r. Thus the current density at any point within the cylinder is proportional to emf/resistance or $r^2/r = r$. This gives the linear distribution for the current density as shown in Fig. 2b. The heat produced by the eddy currents is proportional to the square of the current and hence to the square of the distance from the center r. This suggests the parabolic distribution of heat density shown in Fig. 2c. As the frequency of the power applied to the inductor rises, the eddy currents in the incremental shells of the charge produce increasing counter magnetomotive forces which reduce the flux density near the center of the charge. This results in a nonuniform distribution of flux density, as shown in Fig. 2d, and such nonuniform flux density will change the induced emf's and give a resulting current density of the form shown in Fig. 2e. The resulting heat-density distribution will be of the form shown in Fig. 2f. Thus the rise in frequency crowds the flux density and the heating to the surface of the charge or load. Obviously, the depth of heat penetration can be controlled by the applied frequency. The effectiveness of induction heating compared to flame or furnace heating is illustrated in Fig. 3.

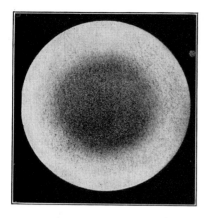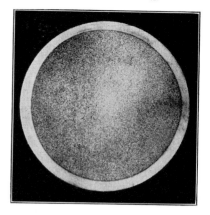

Fig. 3. Comparison of the heating of a shaft with a forge (*left*), and the induction processes (*right*). (Courtesy Allis-Chalmers Manufacturing Company.)

Rigorous equations for eddy-current losses are quite complex and of little general use. Some approximate formulas do serve to show the relationship of the various parameters and hence are useful in analyzing induction heating. Unfortunately, these formulas cannot be applied to many practical problems because of the difficulty in measuring the magnitudes of the quantities involved. The following equation gives the power dissipated as heat in the surface of the charge.

$$\Delta P = \frac{\beta_t{}^2 \sqrt{\rho \mu f}}{8\pi} \tag{1}$$

where ΔP = power dissipated by eddy currents per unit of volume.

β_t = tangential component of magnetic flux density at surface of charge.

ρ = resistivity of the charge.

μ = permeability of charge (unity if nonmagnetic).

f = frequency.

Since the magnetic flux density (β_t) is proportional to the ampere-turns in the coil (for nonmagnetic materials), the factor $\beta_t{}^2$ can be replaced by $I^2 N^2$ (times a constant).

The depth of penetration of the heat may be expressed by the following equation where depth δ refers to the point at which the eddy currents fall to a value equal to $1/e$ (37 per cent) times their magnitude at the surface.

$$\delta = \frac{1}{2\pi} \sqrt{\frac{\rho}{\mu f}} = \text{depth of penetration} \qquad (2)$$

Combining equations 1 and 2 gives

$$\Delta P = \frac{\beta_t^2 \rho}{16\pi^2 \delta} \qquad (3)$$

The following analysis of equations 1, 2, and 3 summarizes some of the salient points in the application of induction heating.

1. For a given flux density, frequency, and resistivity, the heat input per unit volume is proportional to the square root of the permeability (equation 1). Thus magnetic materials will heat more readily than those that are nonmagnetic and have a permeability of one.

2. For a given material, the depth of heat penetration is inversely proportional to the square root of the frequency (equation 2). Thus the depth of penetration may be controlled by the chosen frequency.

3. For a given flux density and depth of penetration, the heat input per unit of volume varies as the resistivity (equation 3). Thus materials with high resistivity can be heated more readily.

4. For a given material and frequency, the heat input per volume is proportional to the square of the flux density (equation 1). Thus the heat input can be controlled by varying the number of turns in the inductor or the current through the inductor or both.

Induction heating is used for melting, annealing, hardening, brazing, and soldering of metals. Some induction furnaces for melting metals have used frequencies as low as 25 to 60 cycles. For heating forgings, for annealing, and for deep surface hardening where larger pieces are involved, frequencies in the range of 500 to 3000 cycles generally give the highest efficiencies. For small pieces, for very thin core hardening of steel, for brazing and for soldering, high frequencies in the range of 100,000 to 1,000,000 cycles are used. Some examples of parts that have been selectively hardened are shown in Fig. 4 and others that are being inductively brazed in Fig. 5.

Some of the methods by which induction heating may be applied to machine parts are shown in Fig. 6. Part (a) shows the method

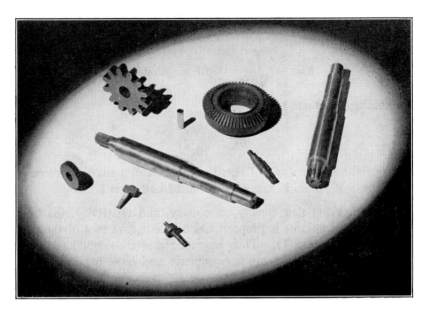

Fig. 4. Parts selectively hardened by electronic heaters. (Courtesy General Electric Company.)

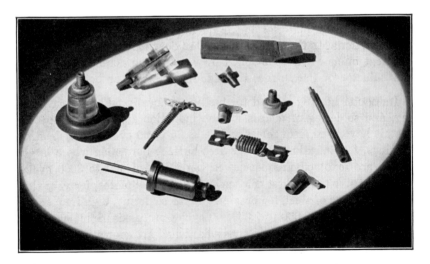

Fig. 5. Parts inductively brazed with a 5 kw electronic heater. (Courtesy General Electric Company.)

of applying surface heating to a shaft. If the coil covers only a short portion of the shaft, that portion may be surface heated and hardened without affecting the interior or surface of the rest of the shaft. The direction of current flow in the charge (cylinder) for an increasing current in the inductor is shown in Fig. 6a. If the charge is moved outside of the inductor as shown in (b) and (c), a current will flow in the charge in the same direction as before, but the magnitude of the current will be smaller because the flux density is much

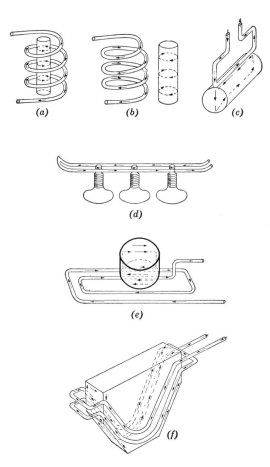

(a)   (b)   (c)

(d)

(e)

(f)

Fig. 6. Sketches showing the instantaneous direction of current flow in the part adjacent to the current in an inductor coil as used in electronic heating. (Courtesy General Electric Company.)

Fig. 7. Induction heating and water quenching for hardening the face of gear teeth. (Courtesy Westinghouse Electric Corporation.)

lower outside the coil than within. Parts (d), (e), and (f) of Fig. 6 and the jig of Fig. 7 illustrate the application of induction heating to actual heating problems. Several methods of applying induction heating for brazing and soldering operations are illustrated in Fig. 8.

A radio-frequency coil surrounding a thin metal plate will induce heat into the surface of that plate. This principle was applied during the war period to melt a very thin layer of tin on tin plate sheets and thus cause it to flow, giving a very thin and complete coverage of the surface. The development of this process in the research laboratories of the Westinghouse Electric Corporation helped to conserve the limited stock pile of tin reserves in the United States.

Some of the advantages of induction heating which have brought about its wide adoption in the metal-working industry are as follows:

1. Speed of heating metals with consequent reduction of oxidation and scaling.

2. Ability to heat limited parts or surfaces of a metal piece instead of an entire piece.

3. Use of power for heating only when desired, without necessity of maintaining furnace temperature continuously.

4. Thorough mixing of alloys when melting due to the "stirring effects."

5. No contamination of the charge by fuel gases.

6. Better working conditions for the operators than with fuel- or gas-fired furnaces.

The over-all efficiency of high-frequency induction heating is the ratio between the heat generated in the charge or load and the energy taken from the supply line. This efficiency is rather low because two factors or efficiencies are involved, neither of which is likely to be high. First, there is the efficiency of conversion from a frequency

of 60 cycles to that required for the heating process. Second, there is
the inductor efficiency or the ratio of the heat generated in the charge
to the input to the inductor. Considering for the moment the inductor efficiency only, it may depend on the frequency and the size or
the diameter of the charge. It may be inferred from equation 1 that
the efficiency would rise with the frequency. This is generally true
for small parts and for small depth of heat penetration, but it is not
true for charges of larger diameter. The effect of an increase in the
diameter of charge can be analyzed as follows. For a given fre-

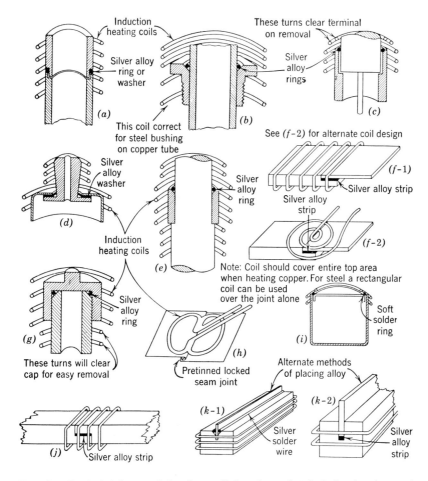

Fig. 8. Typical joints and heating coil locations sketched for brazing and
soldering by induction heating. (Courtesy General Electric Company.)

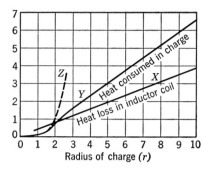

Fig. 9. (Courtesy Allis-Chalmers Manufacturing Company.)

quency and inductor current, let the radius of load be increased. The area of load, the induced flux, and the induced emf's will vary as the square of the radius. The average resistance of the eddy-current path will remain constant because the length and cross section of the path will increase in the same ratio. Since the heat generated is a function of E^2/R, the generated heat will tend to vary as the fourth power of the radius of the charge. However, as the radius of the charge increases, the eddy current will reduce the flux density inside the charge so that the emf's will not rise as the fourth power and the heat loss in charge will tend to become linear. This relationship is illustrated in Fig. 9 where the dotted line is plotted for the fourth power. The actual heat generated (line Y) starts as the fourth power and changes to a linear relationship. Line X gives the heat loss in the inductor which is linear since inductor length varies as r. It is obvious from Fig. 9 that the inductor efficiency is very low for small diameters of charge but rises to a constant value after the heat in the charge becomes linear. This relationship is also shown in Fig. 10 which applies to an aluminum cylinder in which

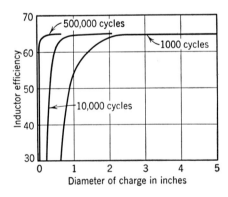

Diameter of charge in inches

Fig. 10. (Courtesy Allis-Chalmers Manufacturing Company.)

the diameter is equal to the height. Two other important considerations are illustrated in Fig. 10. First, the maximum efficiency attained for large diameters of load is the same regardless of the frequency used (65 per cent for the case illustrated). Second, the optimum frequency for a given job depends on the diameter of the charge. For large diameter of charge the lower frequencies of 1000 to 1500 cycles give the same inductor efficiency as a higher frequency with the advantage that the lower frequency can be produced at a lower cost and with a higher efficiency of conversion.

In the design, construction, and use of "inductor" coils for induction heating, the following suggestions will be useful.

1. The heat generated in a part results from the magnetic flux created by the inductor coil. The flux density is greatest at the conductor itself; hence the closer the coil is to the part being heated, the greater will be the heating.

2. The coil should conform to the shape of the part if no sharp corners need be considered.

3. Sharp contours will heat first because of the concentration of flux and lack of mass. Thus the coil should be the farthest from the part at these points.

4. In heating dissimilar metals for brazing, the magnetic flux must be concentrated on the slowest heating metal and the joint should be at the correct temperature before the brazing alloy melts so that it will be drawn into the joint. Thus a concentration of heat on the brazing alloy should be avoided.

5. In hardening, double-bank (double-layer) coils are sometimes necessary because of the current limitations of electronic heaters. (The outside layer of turns is far less efficient and such coils should be used only when necessary.)

6. Uniform heating at the circumference of a disk or bar may be secured by rotating the parts to avoid the heating effects of coil leads.

7. A highly concentrated band of heat on a part or for zones that are not readily accessible may be secured by the use of a single-turn coil carrying a high current. Since it is not economically feasible to construct electronic heaters with a circulating current above 300 amp, it is necessary to use output transformers. Such transformers, being of the air-core type, have a poor coupling and a low over-all efficiency.

Calculations for induction heating to determine the thermal power, input power, and inductor design are very difficult to perform. Equations following the basic theory may not be usable because of the many varying factors entering into the application. Here, as is so often true in electrical design, empirical formulas and curves determined from laboratory experiments and practice must be employed. Hence the industrial user of induction-heating equipment relies upon the recommendations of the design specialists of the equipment manufacturer. For an excellent treatment on calculations for induction heating, the reader is referred to Chapter 14 of the book *Electronics for Industry* by W. I. Bendz and C. A. Scarlott, John Wiley and Sons, New York, 1947.

Dielectric Heating

Dielectric heating is the term applied to the generation of heat in nonconducting materials by their losses when subjected to an *alternating* electric field. This form of heating is applied by placing the nonconductor load between two electrodes across which a high-frequency voltage is impressed as shown in Fig. 11. The load and electrodes constitute a capacitor in effect and a current flows in the circuit in accordance with the equation $I_c = E/X_c$. In an *ideal* capacitor the current leads the impressed voltage by 90 degrees, zero power is absorbed in the capacitor, and the power factor (*pf*) is zero. It is impossible to construct an ideal capacitor and those capacitors which are produced for industrial use do have some losses and some heat is generated. In the dielectric heating or load capacitor (Fig. 11), the losses are much higher and are utilized as the source of heat. The cause of the internal heating is complicated but appears to arise from the following sources. First, a small leakage current flows through the material due to the alternating voltage impressed across it. This current produces a small I^2R heat loss. Second, the alternating potential gradient in the nonconducting material results in a dielectric hysteresis which is a form of molecular friction analogous to the magnetic hysteresis in magnetic materials. Since heating is

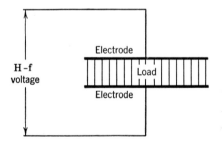

H-f voltage

Electrode
Load
Electrode

Fig. 11. Method of applying dielectric heating.

the desired effect, differentiation as to the cause is not important. The power factor of the material used for a load is the ratio of the heat generated to the volt-amperes input to the load.

$$\underset{\text{Power factor}}{(pf)} = \frac{\overset{(W)}{\text{Heat generated}}}{\underset{(EI)}{\text{Volt-amperes}}}$$

and

$$W = EI \times pf$$

But

$$I = \frac{E}{X_c} = 2\pi f C E 10^{-6} \text{ (approx.)}$$

and

$$W = 2\pi f C E^2 10^{-6} \times pf \tag{4}$$

where C is in microfarads.

Equation 4 shows that, if all other factors are held constant, the heat generated in the load will vary directly as (1) the frequency, (2) the capacity of the heating load, (3) the voltage squared, and (4) the power factor of the load. Obviously, the frequency and the voltage are directly controllable by the operator of the heating process. The capacity of the load will be determined by the geometry of the electrodes and the applied load and by the dielectric constant of the material used in loading. The power factor of the load will depend on the material of the load.

In contrast to induction heating, the heat loss in the insulating or nonconducting material used for dielectric heating may be calculated with a fair degree of accuracy. The calculation for the heat generated follows directly from equation 4. The capacity of the load may be calculated from the following equation:

$$C = \frac{2248AK}{10^{10}d} \text{ (for parallel plates)} \tag{5}$$

where C = capacity in microfarads.
A = area of one electrode in square inches.
d = distance between electrodes in inches.
K = dielectric constant.

The power required to raise the temperature to the desired final temperature within a specified heating time is known as the *thermal power*.

It is an expression for the rate of heating and does not include losses of any kind. Thermal power is calculated from the formula

$$P_T = 17.6Mc\,\Delta T \text{ watts} \tag{6}$$

where M = rate of material heated in pounds per minute.
  c = specific heat of material.
  ΔT = temperature rise in °F.
  P_T = thermal power in watts.

The heat energy required for a given heating load may be determined from equation 6. In applying the above equations to practical problems the following precautions should be observed.

1. The power factor of most materials varies with frequency and temperature. Thus, the power factor should be measured near the operating frequency and at a known temperature.

2. The dielectric constant changes relatively slowly with frequency and temperature and can be taken from published tables with fair accuracy.

3. The equations hold only for uniform electric fields. Since the field at the edges of the electrodes is always distorted, a good approximation is possible only when the minimum dimension of the electrode is large compared to the distance between the plates. The use of plates somewhat larger than the material to be heated will reduce nonuniform heating at the edges.

4. To avoid corona and arcing effects, the maximum voltage applied to the electrodes is approximately 14 to 15 kv rms, with 2 to 3 kv rms per inch of separation as a maximum for smaller spacings.

5. The maximum electrode dimensions must be limited to at least one-eighth of the wavelength to avoid standing waves which result in nonuniform heating. The formula for wavelengths is

$$\text{Wavelength (meters)} = \frac{300}{f \text{ (megacycles)}} \text{ (in air)} \tag{7}$$

6. The charge to be heated must be of uniform analysis throughout and must contact each plate. An air gap between the electrodes and the charge results in a series-capacitor effect and introduces serious errors in the above equations. (It is sometimes desirable to employ electrodes designed to provide an air gap between electrodes and the charge. In such cases the voltages employed must be much higher to provide the same potential gradient across the charge as would exist with contact electrodes.)

The frequency employed for dielectric heating depends on the size of the charge and the power required. For some materials a very high frequency may be desired. The equipment available limits the frequency to approximately 200 mc for power outputs of the order of 100 watts. At 30 mc power up to 40 kw is available and for 15 mc power ratings 200 kw are available.

The dielectric constants for most materials fall in the range of 2 to 6, but they may vary from 1 for gases up to more than 1000 for some ceramics. The power factors found in dielectric heating usually lie between 0.02 and 0.07, but they may be as low as 0.00015 (mica, polystyrene) or as high as 0.15 (asbestos). Gases and pure water have power factors that are essentially zero and cannot be heated.

The important advantage of dielectric heating lies in the fact that the heat is generated inside the material. With a uniform material and a uniform alternating electric field, the heat generation is the same and the rise of temperature is uniform throughout the charge. This uniformity of temperature rise also gives *speed* of heating. Any conventional method of heating will require the application of heat from the sides of the charge. Since nonconducting materials usually have poor heat conductivity or transfer, such heating is necessarily slow and results in nonuniform temperatures.

There have been an increasing number of applications of dielectric heating to nonmetals and nonconducting materials. Some of these applications are:

1. Gluing, drying, and curing of wood.
2. Preheating and curing of plastics.
3. Processing of rubber and synthetic materials.
4. Curing of sand cores in foundries.
5. Sterilization of foods and medical supplies.
6. Drying and heat treatment of textiles such as rayon yarn.
7. Processing of chemicals during manufacture.

An important wartime application was the heating and gluing of plywood panels. A stack of plywood panels 4 ft by 8 ft was placed between the plates of a large hydraulic press. Three conductors or plates are interspaced with the plywood panels (negative plate at top and bottom and positive at center), and the terminals are connected to a high-frequency generator. Upon application of the voltage, every molecule of the plywood becomes stressed by the a-c field and must reverse at the rate of two million to twenty million times per second. With the watts input $W = KE^2 f$, it can be understood how 15,000 to 18,000 volts at 2 mc or 3000 to 4000 volts at 15 to 20 mc will generate the necessary heat. This process of dielectric heating will bring the central parts of the plywood to the desired temperature in 20 to 30 minutes, whereas the older method using steam heat required 6 to 8 hours.

Other applications of dielectric heating concern preheating plastics for molds or curing the plastic within the mold itself. Ceramics may be heated quickly by the dielectric process.

Dielectric heating is being tried for numerous applications in the processing of foods and should have many economical uses. Some of these applications are the "popping" of cereals, the thawing of frozen products (both raw and precooked), the cooking of foods, the killing of molds in bread, and the treatment of dairy products.

Diathermy as applied to man and animals for the treatment of pain and disease is a well-known application of dielectric heating. For this application rubber-insulated coils of a conductor are substituted for the parallel plates of the dielectric heater.

Calculation for Dielectric Heating

For an illustrative problem, assume that eight 24 by 24 by $\frac{1}{4}$-in. maple panels are being glued together in a stack 2 in. high. It is desired to raise the temperature of the stack from 70° F to 200° F in 5 minutes, using a frequency of 1 mc. Calculate the power required at the load and the voltage to be applied on the assumption of a power loss of 20 per cent.

The thermal power from equation 6 is

$$P_T = 17.6 Mc \, \Delta T \text{ watts}$$

$$\text{Volume of maple} = 24 \times 24 \times 2 = 1150 \text{ cu in.}$$

$$\text{Weight of maple from Table 1} \quad = 1150 \times 0.022$$

$$= 25.3 \text{ lb}$$

$$M \text{ (pounds heated per minute)} = \frac{25.3}{5} = 5.06 \text{ lb}$$

$$c \text{ (Table 1)} = 0.42 \text{ Btu per pound per degree F}$$

$$\Delta T = 200 - 70 = 130° \text{ F}$$

$$P_T = 17.6 \times 5.06 \times 0.42 \times 130 = 4870 \text{ watts}$$
Adding 20 per cent for losses $\qquad$ 974 watts

$$\overline{}$$

$$5844 \text{ watts}$$

From equation 5 and Table 1

$$c = \frac{2248AK}{10^{10}d}$$

$$= \frac{2248 \times 24 \times 24 \times 4.4}{10^{10} \times 2}$$

$$= 2.85 \times 10^{-4} \text{ } \mu\text{f}$$

From equation 4

$$w = 2\pi fCE^2 10^{-6} \times pf \text{ watts}$$

$$5844 = 6.28 \times 10^6 \times 2.85 \times 10^{-4} \times E^2 \times 10^{-6} \times 0.0341$$

$$E = 9750 \text{ volts}$$

The required voltage is less than 15,000 and the spacing between electrodes is less than one-eighth of the wavelength.

Equipment for High-Frequency Heating

Several types of conversion units are available for producing the high-frequency power for the heating processes considered in the preceding sections. The frequencies obtainable and the approximate conversion efficiency may be listed as follows:

1. Mercury-arc converters.
   Frequency up to 1500 cycles.
   Approximate conversion efficiency 90 per cent.
2. Motor-generator sets.
   Frequency up to 10,000 cycles.
   Approximate conversion efficiency 65 to 75 per cent.
3. Spark-gap converters.
   Frequency 30,000 to 40,000 cycles.
   Approximate conversion efficiency 50 to 60 per cent.
4. Vacuum-tube oscillators.
   Frequency 100,000 to 100,000,000 cycles.
   Approximate conversion efficiency 50 to 60 per cent.

The units listed under 1, 2, and 3 are used exclusively for induction heating. The vacuum-tube oscillator is the only one used for dielectric heating and it is also used for induction heating where the higher frequencies are required. The mercury-arc converter may be used for melting and heating large charges where a frequency of 1000 to 1500 cycles is satisfactory. Motor-generator sets are available for

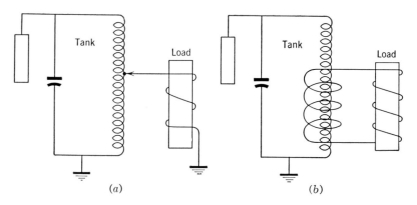

Fig. 12. Circuits for coupling an induction heating load to oscillator.

various fixed frequencies up to 10,000 cycles and for inductive-heating loads. Power output of these units ranges from 7.5 to 1500 kw with initial and maintenance costs lower than such costs for vacuum-tube converters.

Spark-gap converters are available in units for power output from 1 to about 35 kw. They are usually rated in input kilovolt-amperes and not in output kilowatts. In the radio-frequency field they have a slightly lower initial cost per kilowatt output than the vacuum-tube converter and the advantage of relative simplicity. The sparking across the gaps causes corrosion and periodic readjustment of the gaps is necessary. Radio interference is difficult to control.

The vacuum-tube oscillator unit for high-frequency heating may employ any of the oscillator circuits described in Chapter 9. The Colpitts and the tuned-plate circuits are the ones generally employed. The oscillator unit may be connected to the load or charge in a number of ways. Thus, for inductive heating, the inductance of the tank coil may be tapped to supply the inductor as shown in Fig. 12a, or it may be coupled through transformer action as in part (b) of the same figure. For dielectric heating the load or charge capacitance may be substituted for the capacitor of the tank circuit. Since relatively large currents are produced by the oscillator unit, means must be employed to absorb the heat losses within the oscillator circuit. Thus the vacuum tubes employed are usually water cooled and the inductance and inductor coils are copper tubing through which water may be circulated to remove the heat loss. An oscillator unit for high-frequency heating is illustrated in Fig. 13. The tubes used for rectification are of the hot-cathode, mercury-vapor type because they are rugged and can supply the high currents required with little internal voltage drop. The oscillator tubes must be of the high-vacuum type.

All manufacturers incorporate protective devices in the oscillator type of converters to prevent damage to tubes in the event of overload, failure of water supply, and so forth. Some of these devices and their functions are as follows.

1. Thermal element. A bimetallic element connected in the water-return line of the oscillator tube which will shut down the unit when the water reaches too high a temperature owing to insufficient flow or overload.

2. Pressure switch. A bellow-type switch which prevents starting of the unit or opens the switch when the water pressure falls below 40 lb.

3. D-c overload relay. A magnetic solenoid-type relay connected in the negative line of the high-voltage plate supply opens on short circuit, flashover, or overload of the oscillator tube.

4. Time-delay circuit. A circuit to prevent the application of the plate voltage until the cathodes of the rectifier tubes are brought to the proper temperature for emission.

Radio interference from high-frequency generators can be reduced by operation at frequencies differing from local communication chan-

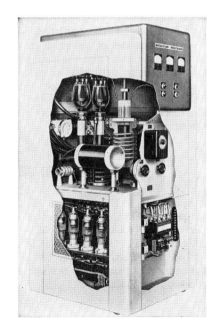

Fig. 13. Construction of a high-frequency induction heating unit. (Courtesy Allis-Chalmers Manufacturing Company.)

Table 1.   **Properties of Nonconductors**

Material	Volume Resistivity (ohm-inches)	Specific Heat (Btu per pound per degree F)	Weight (pounds per cubic inch)	Dielectric Constant		Power Factor		
				1 Mc	30 Mc	1 Mc	10 Mc	30 Mc
Fiber, commercial	2×10^9	0.25	0.038	5.0		0.05		
Glass								
Pyrex "radio"	5×10^{13}	0.20	0.077	4.0	4.0	0.00075	0.001	0.001
Nylon	4×10^{12}	0.55	0.014	3.0	3.0	0.02	0.02	0.02
Phenolic insulation								
Nema grade CE	4×10^{11}	0.42	0.049	5.3	5.0	0.05	0.06	0.066
Resins								
Beetle		0.40	0.054	5.5	5.2	0.027		0.05
Rubber								
Natural gum	10^{13}–10^{15}	0.33	0.041	2.4	2.4	0.002		0.004
Maple	10^{10}	0.42	0.022	4.4		0.0341		
Mahogany	2×10^{13}	0.42	0.024	2.1	2.1	0.03	0.04	0.04

nels or by complete shielding of all high-frequency equipment including the rooms where work is being performed.

PROBLEMS

1. A sheet of commercial fiber 10 by 20 by 0.3 in. is to be heated by the dielectric process using 1-mc power and to have its temperature raised 200° F in 3 minutes. Assuming electrodes of same area as the fiber and a 10 per cent loss of power, calculate the thermal power required, the capacity of the load, and the voltage required.

2. A block of natural gum rubber 1 ft square and 2 in. thick is to be heated by dielectric heat using 30 mc of power. If the temperature is to be raised 200° F in 3 minutes by electrodes of same area as load, calculate the thermal power, voltage required, and total power input to the load, allowing for 20 per cent loss.

REFERENCES

1. Mortenson, S. H., "Induction Heat Works Metal Magic," and H. F. Storm, "Mercury-Arc Converter Masters Metals in Deep Heating," *Allis-Chalmers Electrical Review*, March 1945.
2. Jordan, J. P., "The Theory and Practice of Industrial Electronic Heating," *Gen. Elec. Rev.*, December 1943.
3. Bendz, W. I., and C. A. Scarlott, *Electronics for Industry*, John Wiley and Sons, New York, 1947.

chapter 15

Miscellaneous Electronic Applications

Static Control System

Static control is a new system of control designed to replace magnetic relays. In this system combinations of magnetic devices (similar to magnetic amplifiers) and semiconductor rectifiers perform the functions normally handled by relays. Until recently, the development of *switching* for all types of industrial control and communication systems has utilized the magnetic relay as the basic unit. As switching systems became more complicated, the number of relays required became greater, the need for sensitivity and speed of relays increased, and the reliability of the relay became critical. The performance of relays has been constantly improved over the years. However, the relay has moving parts and one or several contacts. The finest particle of dust may cause a contact failure, and hence the relay has become the weakest link in the chain where reliability is critical. This inherent weakness in the relay is causing a trend toward the employment of control units which do not have moving parts and are not sensitive to dust and other unfavorable environmental conditions. Semiconductor devices and magnetic devices with square hysteresis loop are the logical units to answer the current trend.

The design of a switching system for the starting and operation of any machine or process requires that the control units must govern in a sequence of logical steps. Also the control must exercise logical steps for the protection of the operator, the machine itself, and the work being performed by the machine. Present designs of switching or control systems using relays have provided for the sequence and safeguards suggested. However, in the new designs for static control, a new practice has been adopted. This practice divides control into a few functions termed "logic functions." Specific units or devices are designed to perform each of these functions. Then the requirements for any specific control problem are met by a suitable combination of the logic function devices.

Logic Units

Only four logic functions are required to express any possible condition, set of movements, or specific arrangement of information. These are: AND, OR, NOT, and MEMORY. An additional unit (not logic) for time delay is needed for some control operations. The symbol, relay equivalent, and definition for each of these five units are given in Fig. 1. The AND function unit does not produce an output unless all inputs (that is, A, B, and C for Fig. 1) are energized. AND units are available for two, three, and four inputs. The AND function unit is analogous to a series of open contacts on relays. The OR function unit produces an output when any one (or more) of its inputs is energized. This unit may be designed for two, three, of four inputs. It is analogous to several relay contacts in parallel (Fig. 1). The NOT function unit produces an output when the input is not energized. Conversely, when it has an input there is no output; thus the term NOT. The action of the NOT function unit is analogous to the normally closed contact on a relay—with the relay unenergized the contacts are closed, and with the relay energized the contacts are open. The basic MEMORY unit provides an output with a momentary input at A (see Fig. 1). This output will continue (be remembered) after the A input is removed. A later momentary input at B will turn the output off. There are two variations in memory units. In one type the memory unit will remember its last output condition (on or off) in case of power failure (retentive memory). In the other type the memory unit is always shifted to the "off" condition in case of power failure. The memory unit is analogous to a contactor controlled by relay with a mechanical latching device. Thus in the memory series of Fig. 1, if relay coil c is energized, the contacts are closed and latched closed. Later the energization of coil d releases the latch and permits the contacts to open.

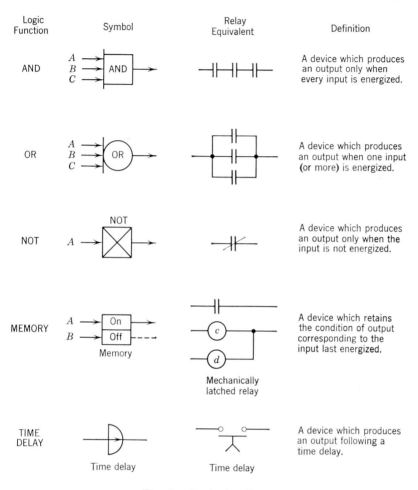

Logic Function	Symbol	Relay Equivalent	Definition

Fig. 1. Logic functions.

Time delay units used in conjunction with logic units may employ the familiar RC timing circuit principle, or they may be based on the time required for a build-up of saturation of flux in special self-saturating magnetic cores and coils.

Circuits for Logic Function Units

The preceding discussion may leave the reader with a hazy concept of the significance and application of logic function units. Perhaps the following humanized version of an application of such units will be helpful. This example is drawn with permission from a tech-

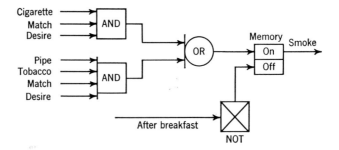

Fig. 2. Logic functions applied to a morning smoke.

nical bulletin of the Westinghouse Electric Corporation. The story of a man who likes to smoke before going to work in the morning is depicted in Fig. 2. If he smokes cigarettes, he requires a cigarette, a match, AND a desire before he can smoke. If he is a pipe smoker, he must have a pipe, tobacco, a match, AND a desire. Assuming he has either the cigarette OR the pipe combination, he has the requisites for a smoke (that is, one input into a memory unit). However, like most men he does NOT consider it desirable to smoke before breakfast. Therefore, a NOT function leads to the "off" input in his memory. Finally, *after breakfast* an input to NOT function removes the "off" input in memory and the morning smoke results.

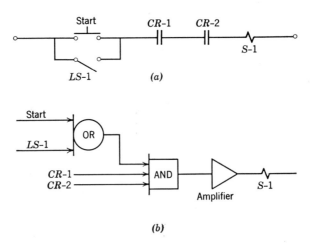

Fig. 3. Conversion of relay control to logic function control.

A direct conversion from a relay system to a logic function control is illustrated in Fig. 3. Here a solenoid S-1 is to be controlled. The first step in operation of the solenoid is the closure of the start push button OR the closing of a limit switch LS-1 (Fig. 3a). This step converts to the 2-input OR logic function of Fig. 3b. Next, it is also necessary that the contactors of control relays CR-1 AND CR-2 be closed to energize the solenoid. In the logic function system of Fig. 3b, this means that the output of the OR function becomes the input to an AND logic function along with inputs corresponding to CR-1 and CR-2. An amplifier is inserted between the output of the AND function and the solenoid because the power handled by the logic functions is not sufficient for operating the solenoid.

An extension of the relay control circuitry of Fig. 3 is given in Fig. 4. Here the solenoid is energized by the relay coil CL-1 and its contactor CL-1 in the lower line of Fig. 4a. Also the solenoid circuit opens (for protection) if limit switch LS-2 is closed and normally

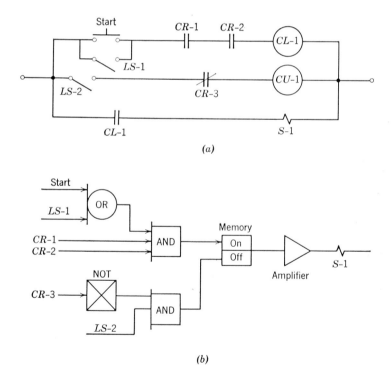

(a)

(b)

Fig. 4. Conversion of relay control to logic function control.

closed CR-3 is also closed. The energization of the latter circuit (LS-2, CR-3, and CU-1) causes CU-1, a drop-out coil, to open the contactor CL-1. The logic function conversion for this extended circuit is the same as given in Fig. 3b plus additional logic units of MEMORY, a NOT, and an AND, as shown. Obviously, the energization of the input LS-2 added to the NOT input turns the MEMORY to off and protects the equipment.

Theory of Logic Function Units

The heart of most logic function units is a small magnetic core of ferromagnetic material having a square hysteresis loop. These cores may be toroidal or rectangular. The cores are wound with several windings and the general theory of action follows that given for magnetic amplifiers in Chapter 9. A basic construction for a unit is shown in Fig. 5a. The *gate* or load (output) winding contains a semiconductor rectifier and is fed by an a-c source or by a pulse power source. It may be considered the primary winding on the unit. If alternating voltage is supplied to this gate circuit, only exciting current flows in pulses in the direction permitted by the rectifying unit and quickly drives the magnetic core to saturation, after which the load or output current flows on each positive pulse. Several secondary windings are usually placed on the magnetic core. One such winding is shown dotted on Fig. 5a. The secondary windings have control functions in that they serve to modify the output in the gate circuit. One control winding is a *bias* winding. It usually carries a direct current which produces an mmf that opposes the flux produced by the gate current. Other secondary windings carry signal currents for controlling the gate output. The amplifier

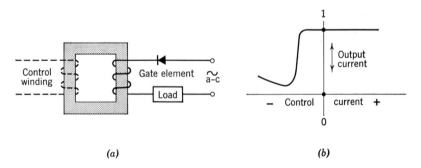

(a)   *(b)*

Fig. 5. Basic construction of a logic unit.

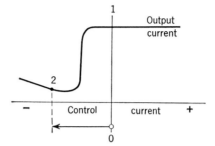

Fig. 6. NOT characteristic.

transfer characteristic for the magnetic core and circuit is given in Fig. 5b. If the gate circuit only is energized, the core is driven to saturation and the output current rises to full conduction at point 1. Next, if a negative biasing current is passed through a secondary or biasing winding, the flux in the core may be driven to zero or completely reversed and the output falls to near zero, as suggested in Fig. 5b.

A NOT logic unit may consist of a magnetic core, a gate winding, and a bias winding. Its action is illustrated in Fig. 6. If no signal is applied on the bias winding, the gate (output) is full on and operates at point 1. If a negative bias is applied to the control circuit, the flux is reversed and the output is at point 2 which is virtually zero.

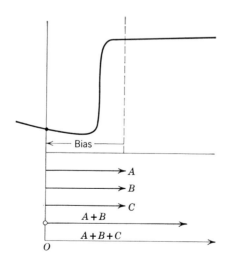

Fig. 7. OR characteristic.

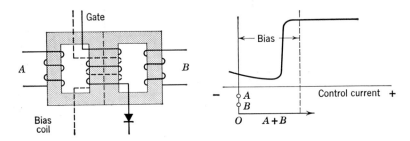

Fig. 8. Two input AND circuit.

The operation of an OR logic unit is illustrated in Fig. 7. Here a fixed or permanent bias (winding) drives the gate output to zero. There are separate secondary windings for all of the inputs such as A, B, and C. A signal on *any input* will neutralize the bias and permit the gate to change to "on." If two or more inputs are energized simultaneously, the result is the same and the output turns to "on."

A second type of OR unit can be constructed of two or more semiconductor crystal rectifiers in parallel. Here, whenever any rectifying unit is energized with the proper d-c polarity for forward conduction, an output results.

A logic AND unit may consist of two adjacent magnetic cores as suggested in Fig. 8. Here the gate winding surrounds both cores. A fixed bias winding drives the cores to negative saturation. Now a signal on either A or B is insufficient to overcome the bias effect and the gate output remains at zero. But if signals are applied simultaneously at both A AND B, the bias is overcome and the gate output conducts. A four-input AND requires four rectangular cores with a common leg at the center for the gate and bias windings.

Assembly of Logic Control Units

The core and coil assembly of logic control units are shown in Figs. 9 and 10. The core assembly and the other components, such as crystal diodes, resistors, and capacitors, are next mounted on a common insulating base which has external plug contacts. The mounted assembly is sealed in a spongy plastic to keep out moisture and dirt and to reduce effects of shock. Last, the logic unit is encased in a metal container which is color coded and marked with the circuit diagram and all necessary information for application. The completed logic units are equipped at one end with the necessary

Fig. 9. Logic element and parts. (Courtesy General Electric Company.)

plug-in terminal for connection to power supplies, and so forth. The completed logic units are plugged into special terminal boards or busses, as suggested in Fig. 10.

Applications of Static Control

The subject of control consists of three parts—information, decision, and action. Information for effecting control comes from sensing devices such as limit switches, push buttons, pressure switches, temperature sensors, etc. Static control with its logic elements makes the decisions and is the "brains" of control. After a decision has been reached, action is produced by a solenoid valve, a contactor or starter, an indicating light, or some other device that performs the

Fig. 10. Logic element. (Courtesy Westinghouse Electric Corporation.)

desired result. The important applications of static control lie in the field of automation. Automation may mean the complete automatic control of a machine that forms, drills, and taps the holes in a unit part. Automation is more likely to consist of the control of a series of machines which function in a continuous cycle for completing a product. Such a process involves the transfer of the product from machine to machine and the interlocking of many functions under logical control. Obviously, the control of such processing becomes very complex and an extreme degree of reliability is necessary. Static logic units without moving parts and contacts are capable of providing such reliability and control.

It should be mentioned that many of the functions of the static control elements are also performed in digital computers.

Photoelectric Controls

Many control devices utilize light as the variable medium for actuating their output. Such devices employ phototubes or photo-semiconductors as detectors and some combinations of circuit elements and tubes or transistors to perform the desired operations. These basic units have been combined in hundreds of different circuits to perform useful functions. Five representative combinations and applications are covered in the following pages.

Most photoelectric controls employ a magnetic relay and contactor in their output which gives rise to the term photoelectric relay circuits. Simple photoelectric relay circuits for operation with d-c or a-c supply are shown in Fig. 11. Under darkness the phototube has infinite resistance and the grid of the tube is biased to cutoff.

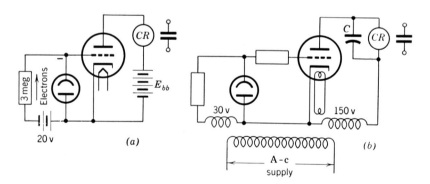

Fig. 11. Simple "on and off" relay circuits operated by light.

When light falls on the phototube, it passes electrons through the 3 meg resistor and varies the potential of the grid (less negative) until the plate current is sufficient to operate the relay CR. When the light decreases sufficiently, relay CR becomes de-energized. Thus this circuit gives "on" and "off" operation of relay CR with variation of light intensity. The sensitivity of the operation of the circuit will be determined by the grid-bias battery voltage, the resistance of the grid resistor, the plate voltage, the relay setting and the characteristics of the phototube and triode. The a-c circuit of Fig. 11 functions in the same manner as explained for part (a). The capacitor around relay CR serves to hold the relay during the half cycles when the triode plate potential is negative.

Automatic Lighting Control

Automatic lighting control is a system using photoelectric relays to turn on artificial lighting whenever daylight wanes and to turn off lighting units when they are not needed. This control may be desirable in library reading rooms, schools, offices, and factories because human beings intent on reading or working fail to notice decreasing illumination and thereby permit eyestrain and inefficiency. This system also has applications indoors for turning on emergency light systems in operating rooms in hospitals and outdoors for turning on yard lights and street lights.

An automatic lighting control system consists of a photoelectric relay unit and a magnetic contactor as illustrated in Fig. 12. The relay unit is placed in the room or location where the lighting is to be controlled, and the magnetic contactor is placed where it is convenient to open and close the lighting circuits.

The simple circuit of Fig. 11b will close a circuit when the illumination falls too low but the resulting rise of illumination from the artificial lighting would cause this circuit to cut out immediately and it would continue to function "on" and "off." To prevent this hunting action the circuit of Fig. 11b must be modified to some other form such as that shown in Fig. 13. The latter circuit will cut in the artificial lighting at a prefixed illumination intensity and later cut out the artificial lighting when daylight rises to another prefixed level. These prefixed levels are set on potentiometers $P1$ and $P2$. In Fig. 13, $CR2$ represents the remote magnetic contactor and $CR1$ is the relay of the photoelectric relay unit.

The key to the action of this room lighting control lies in the changes brought about in the *grid leak* circuit of the triode. This

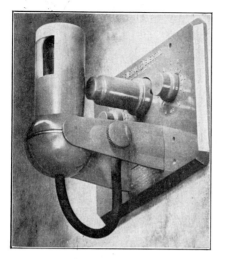 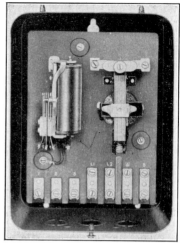

Fig. 12. Photoelectric lighting control unit with the contactor panel on right. (Courtesy General Electric Company.)

grid leak consists of resistor $R1$, the phototube, and differing combinations of resistances in the lower sections of $P1$ and $P2$ and $R2$. To understand the circuit operation assume that the phototube is covered with no light reaching its cathode. Under this condition the grid of the triode will be free (no electron path through either capacitor $C1$ or the phototube), it will be negatively charged to near

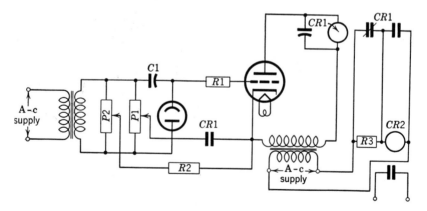

Fig. 13. Circuit for controlling room lighting.

cutoff, and relay $CR1$ will be de-energized. The normally closed contact of $CR1$ short circuits $R3$, magnetic relay $CR2$ is energized, and artificial lights are on. In addition, contact $CR1$ between potentiometer $P1$ and the triode cathode is open. Now assume zero daylight and remove the cover from the phototube. With the proper setting of potentiometer $P2$ the triode plate current will not operate relay $CR1$. Before considering the next step, note that the phototube may be considered as an electron-leak unit for both the triode grid circuit and for the capacitor $C1$. The grid-leak circuit consists of the grid, resistor $R1$, the phototube, the lower section of $P2$ with a small alternating voltage, and resistor $R2$ to cathode. The alternating voltage across $P1$ and $P2$ is also impressed across $C1$ and the phototube in series. When the left side of condenser $C1$ is positive, the right side is negative and electrons are withdrawn from the grid of the triode, making it less negative and permitting more electrons from its cathode to land on it. On the next half-cycle with the anode of the phototube positive, the phototube will conduct electrons from the grid toward the cathode and also will discharge the capacitor $C1$. Now assume an addition of daylight to the room and the phototube. The phototube conducts more electrons from the triode grid and discharges the condenser $C1$ more completely. As the daylight rises in value the point is reached where the triode grid voltage consisting of negative d-c (leak) bias plus the a-c component induced from $P2$ causes the triode to conduct sufficiently to operate relay $CR1$. The energization of $CR1$ de-energizes $CR2$ (artificial lights off) and closes contact $CR1$ between $P1$ and cathode. The closing of contact $CR1$ shifts the grid control of the triode from potentiometer $P2$ to $P1$ so as to prevent relay $CR1$ from dropping back when the artificial lights go out. When daylight wanes later to the preset point of $P1$, relay $CR1$ will drop out and the artificial lighting will be re-established.

Photoelectric Counting and Operational Devices

The most common application of photoelectric relays is for counting passing objects and for initiating the operation of various kinds of equipment. These functions are actuated by the interception of a beam of transmitted light. The beam of light is produced by an enclosed source of artificial light and is directed upon a phototube in a photoelectric relay circuit as illustrated in Fig. 14. Any opaque object passing through the light beam serves to actuate the photoelectric relay and its associated circuits. An inexpensive form of

Fig. 14. Electronic control via a light beam and phototube.

photoelectric relay containing two tubes which is suitable for light interception operation is shown in Fig. 15 and a light-source unit is depicted in Fig. 16. This photo-relay is a relatively insensitive device which requires an illumination of 40 foot-candles or more for operation. It may be used in a location having normal light provided that the illumination on the cathode of the phototube from this source is less than 40 foot-candles. The circuit of the photo-relay is designed to energize its relay coil when the phototube is dark and to de-energize the relay when the phototube is lighted, the predominating condition encountered with simple photoelectric applications. The circuit shown in Fig. 17 employs a gaseous phototube and a shield-grid thyratron. The firing of the thyratron is

Fig. 15. Photoelectric relay. (Courtesy General Electric Company.)

Fig. 16. Light source for photoelectric control. (Courtesy General Electric Company.)

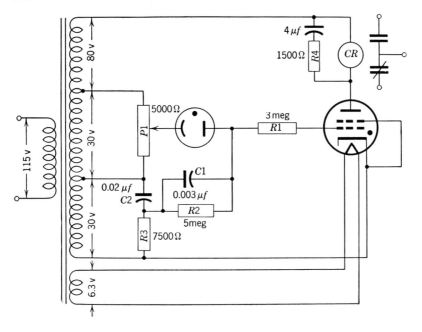

Fig. 17. Circuit for a photoelectric relay.

controlled by two voltages applied in series in its grid circuit. One
of these voltages is an alternating voltage drop across resistor $R3$.
The second of these voltages is a d-c negative bias developed across
resistor $R2$ and capacitor $C1$ by the rectifying action of the circuit
from the pointer on $P1$, the phototube, resistor $R2$, and resistor $R3$.
It should be noted that $R3$ and $C2$ in series across a 30-volt alternating current constitute a phase-shift circuit which shifts the phase of
the a-c drop across $R3$ ahead of the a-c voltage across the anode-
cathode of the thyratron. This shift insures prompt and early firing
of the thyratron. The magnitude of the negative d-c bias across $R2$
is determined by the setting of $P1$ and the illumination on the phototube. For illumination above 40 foot-candles (approximately) the
d-c negative bias will prevent the thyratron from firing. When the
light beam is intercepted, the illumination on the phototube falls
and the negative bias decreases and permits the alternating voltage
across $R3$ to fire the thyratron on half-cycles when its anode is positive. Restoration of light stops the thyratron conduction and de-
energizes the relay CR.

If the contactor on relay CR of Fig. 17 is connected to a magnetic counting device, the system may be used for counting parts on a moving conveyer system, packages on a belt conveyer, automobile traffic on a highway, or customers entering a business establishment. Similar association of the relay contactor with a door-opening mechanism provides automatic opening of garage doors for automobiles, warehouse doors for trucks or trains, and doors for pedestrians. Another application of this system is to open the valve on a drinking fountain when a person bending over to drink intercepts a beam of light.

Sorting and inspection operations by photoelectric relays usually employ *reflected* or *transmitted* light wherein the light-detection mechanism must be sensitive and discriminating. Sensitivity in a photoelectric relay circuit requires the use of an amplifying stage between the phototube and the trigger tube, and light discrimination may require that illumination from external sources be eliminated.

Many photoelectric devices are used to protect human beings, machines, and property. One such device serves to cut off the fuel supply to a burner when the flame in the furnace is extinguished. Dangerous working regions near the jaws of a punch press and moving parts of a machine may be guarded by a beam of light which stops the machine when a human hand is in danger of injury. In like manner, beams of light may serve to prevent the starting of a machine when obstructions are present that would cause damage to the machine itself. Banks, stores, and factories may be guarded at night by beams of invisible light (infrared or ultraviolet), which when intercepted by intruders set off alarms through photoelectric relays.

Photoelectric Register Controls

Photoelectric register controls serve as guides for paper or metal passing rapidly in strip form over rolls. These controls function by scanning the web or edge of the moving strip and thus pick up a signal for correcting the position of the strip. The complete control unit is usually a combination of a light source, one or more phototubes, a suitable optical system, and perhaps a phototube signal amplifier. A commercial web scanner and a light source are illustrated in Fig. 18. The relative positions which these units may occupy when scanning by reflected light and by transmitted light are shown in Fig. 19.

Fig. 18. Photoelectric scanning head. (Courtesy General Electric Company.)

Register controls are divided into two classifications—cutoff and side register. The side register and correction register are illustrated in Fig. 20. In this register the material and roller are of contrasting colors and the control is arranged so that, with the roller under the scanning head, the feed and idler roll are moved to the right. If the material is under the scanning head, the feed and idler rolls move to the left. Thus a balance is reached that will keep the edge of the material under the middle of the light spot. With this equipment it is possible to hold the edge of the material to $+\frac{1}{64}$ in. while it is traveling at 1500 ft per minute.

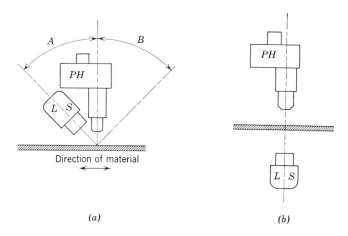

(a)   (b)

Fig. 19. Photoelectric scanning principle. (a) Reflected light. (b) Transmitted light. (Courtesy General Electric Company.)

The cutoff register is operated by a register mark or spot printed on the material being controlled. The passing of this register mark creates an impulse in the phototube circuit as it passes the scanning point. This impulse fires the thyratron and operates a mechanical knife for cutting the material, or it may serve as a corrector of the material speed so as to cut the material in accordance with printed forms on paper used for wrapping.

A form of photoelectric inspection equipment known as a weft straightener control is used in the textile industry. In this application, phototubes scan the cloth as it passes through a machine and detect any skew that is present in the weft threads. When skew is present a difference in the frequency impulse received by two phototubes is noted and this difference in frequency serves as a medium for correcting the skew in the weft threads.

Register control is also used on printing presses for multicolor work to insure the proper alignment or match of the different colors. Normally, alignment is difficult since paper may change its dimensions as much as 1 per cent because of changes in humidity, tension, temperature, and other factors. A schematic drawing of the equipment used is shown in Fig. 21. Two photoelectric scanning heads are used. One scans slits in a ring or disk mounted on the impression or printing cylinder (see lower right of figure); the other scans register marks along the margin of the paper (web) which are printed by the first

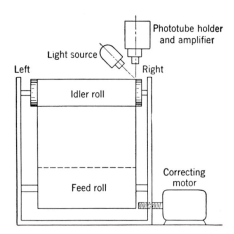

Fig. 20. Diagram showing the scanning and correction method used in a side register control on a paper-handling machine.

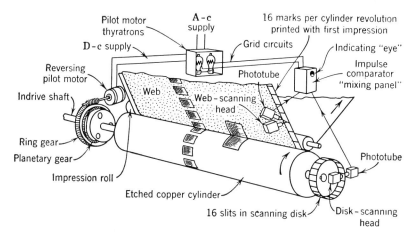

Fig. 21. Automatic register control for rotary web presses showing the general location of parts. (Reprinted from *Printing Equipment Engineer,* August 1941.)

color process (usually yellow). The impulses received by the two photoelectric scanners are fed to a comparator mixing panel and circuit which utilizes any time difference to vary the angle between the indrive shaft and the impression roll so that the successive color design covers properly the first and succeeding color impressions. It is claimed that this equipment will hold the later color impressions within an accuracy of 0.002 to 0.003 in.

Photo-Semiconductor Controls

The photosensitive semiconductors discussed in Chapter 3 have opened several avenues of application for themselves, as suggested in that chapter. It might be expected that some of these devices would replace the phototube in its applications. In general, this has not happened to date (1959) and there are a number of reasons for this. The conservative manufacturer of electronic controls has been testing all kinds of semiconductor devices. He finds a lack of uniformity in commercial samples of some semiconductors. They are often temperature sensitive, and frequently more costly than tubes. These factors combined with a lack of time-tested service data tend to make the designer reluctant to replace the phototube and similar devices.

A recent and important photo-semiconductor application is the use of a photovoltaic cell to provide automatic iris control for 8 mm

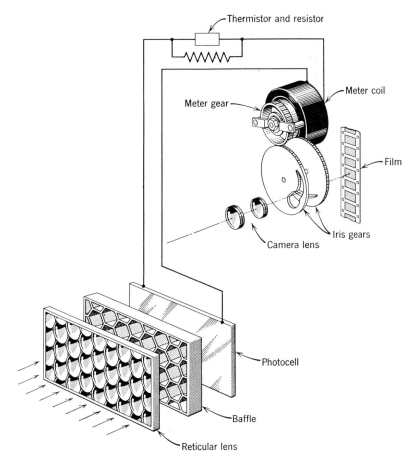

Fig. 22. Automatic iris control on a Bell and Howell 8 mm movie camera. (With permission *Electrical Manufacturing,* January 1958.)

and 16 mm motion picture cameras. The engineers of the Bell and Howell Company have designed very ingenious circuits and mechanisms to bring about this result. It has always been a problem for the amateur and even the professional to obtain the proper iris setting for various light conditions. By the time the operator can read an exposure meter and then set the iris, adjust the shutter timing, and focus on the scene, a good picture may be missed. In order to simplify picture taking on the 8 mm camera, the following steps have been taken. First, a universal focus lens giving good sharpness of focus from 4 to 100 ft was adopted. Second, a single speed of 16 frames per second was accepted. This provided a constant timing of the shutter. With the adoption of these standards, the only variable remaining was that of the light intensity on the subject. The new iris control mechanism consists of three parts—a photovoltaic cell, a sensitive d-c meter element, and a gear-driven iris consisting of two slotted disks. The mechanism is illustrated in Fig. 22. The light pickup unit consists of a reticular lens, a honeycomb baffle, and a rectangular photovoltaic cell. This combination limits the light entry to the angle covered by the camera lens and also provides an average value of light signal.

The meter element has a lightweight gear of aluminum on the shaft normally carrying the pointer. The iris system consists of two gear-driven disks containing teardrop-shaped slots which provide the required variation in light aperture upon rotation. The variation of the output of the photovoltaic cell with change in temperature is compensated by a thermistor-resistor network as depicted in Fig. 22. If it were desired to employ more than one frame speed, automatic

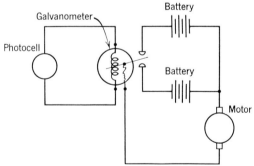

Fig. 23. An 8 mm movie camera with automatic iris control. (Courtesy Bell and Howell.)

Fig. 24. Schematic electric circuit for automatic iris control on a Bell and Howell 16 mm movie camera. (With permission *Journal SMPTE,* July 1957.)

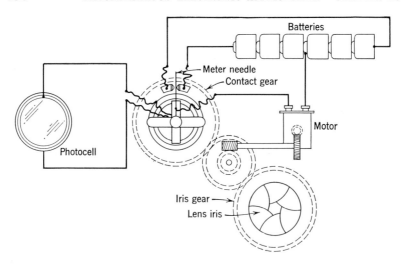

Fig. 25. Automatic iris control mechanism on a Bell and Howell 16 mm movie camera. (With permission *Journal SMPTE*, July 1957.)

compensation for the time of exposure could be accomplished by a mechanical control of the exposed area of the photovoltaic cell. For this purpose the adjustment for the frame speed would control the active area of the photovoltaic cell. An 8 mm motion picture camera which utilizes the automatic iris control is shown in Fig. 23.

A new design of a 16 mm motion picture camera incorporates a self-powered compact automatic iris control. Mechanical power to drive the lens iris originates from a small d-c, permanent-magnet motor driven by mercury batteries. A photovoltaic cell deflects a relay meter according to average scene brightness, and by opening or closing the motor-battery circuit causes the lens iris to be properly positioned. The electrical circuit and the mechanism for this camera control are illustrated schematically in Figs. 24 and 25. The electrical energy developed in a photovoltaic cell is not sufficient to operate the iris mechanism in the 16 mm size of camera. Hence the photovoltaic cell is employed to operate a d-c meter which functions as a relay to open and close contacts. The d-c motor with a fixed permanent-magnet field is reversed by the opposite polarities of the driving mercury cells. A common form of lens iris is employed. The complete operation of the iris control can be followed by a study of Figs. 24 and 25. For further details the reader should consult the references given at the end of the chapter.

Electronic Regulators

Electronic devices and circuits are employed for regulating many different quantities via feedback servo systems. Since the current-carrying capacity of vacuum amplifier tubes is limited, many regulating controls require the use of saturable reactors. An electronic amplifier circuit for regulating the voltage of a d-c generator is shown in Fig. 26. In this circuit the error-detecting triode supplies direct current to a saturable reactor in a phase-shifting unit which, in turn, controls the grids of a full-wave thyratron rectifier. A second method of amplifying the error-detector signal is to apply this signal to the field of a rotary amplifier.

The maintenance of a constant temperature is often necessary in continuous-flow processes. Such temperature regulation is achieved by the principle of servomechanisms. When electrical energy is employed for supplying the heat, a circuit following the block diagram of Fig. 27 is frequently employed. The temperature detecting device may be a thermocouple, a phototube (sensitive to infrared) or a resistance unit which has a high temperature coefficient of resistance. The instrument is usually a device that indicates the temperature and, in addition, has the ability to transfer the temperature-indicating signal into a potential difference for actuating the electronic regulator. The electronic regulator is a thyratron with a

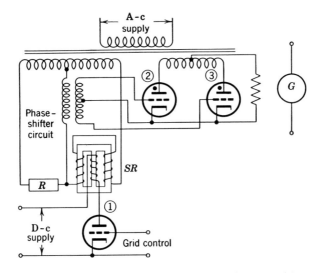

Fig. 26. Voltage regulation using thyratrons and a saturable reactor.

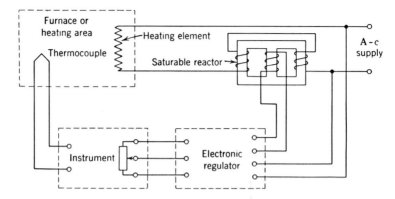

Fig. 27. Block diagram for temperature regulation.

free-wheeling circuit for energizing the d-c winding of the saturable reactor. The saturable reactor controls the current to the electric heating element.

Amplidyne Servos

The amplidyne may be employed to control the voltage of an a-c generator by serving as the exciter for the generator field. A schematic circuit for this application is shown in Fig. 28. Here the alternating voltage is rectified by a bridge-type copper oxide rectifier circuit and impressed across a potential-dividing resistor. Another source of a-c supply is rectified and loaded by a resistor (lower part of Fig. 28). The voltage drops across the two resistors are connected so as to feed in opposition the control field and the standard reference field of the amplidyne. Any voltage difference between these RI drops causes a change in flux in the magnetic field of the amplidyne. This change of flux is in the proper direction to control the amplified voltage output of the amplidyne so that the alternator voltage will be restored to the desired normal value. The output voltage of the alternator may be set for different values by means of the voltage adjustment on the potential divider.

Other applications of voltage control using rotary amplifiers may involve quick changes of voltage or even reversal of voltage in Ward Leonard motor drives in steel mills and the mining industry.

The current in a motor or generator circuit can be held within close limits by the amplidyne regardless of speed, voltage, or load changes. Current control may be desired (1) so that the machine may be operated at peak performance without danger of overload, (2) so that maximum rates of motor acceleration or deceleration may be obtained, or (3) in order to provide a constant tension upon a wire, steel strip, or other material while the motor is in continuous motion. One application falling under class 3 uses the circuit shown in Fig. 29. This diagram illustrates how a large reel motor can be made to operate over a wide range of speed, automatically holding constant the current and tension on the reel. In this application the winding reel for providing tension is driven by a reel motor which has an armature supply from a separate reel generator and a field supply controlled by an amplidyne. The torque and tension are controlled by varying the field strength of the reel motor. The controlling amplidynes employ four separate fields. Field 3–4 is a reference field which tends to increase the torque of the reel motor. Field 5–6 is the control field for the large exciter-amplidyne and is fed by a small control amplidyne. Field 2 of the latter amplidyne is fed by the IR drop in the reel-motor commutating field. Fields 3–4 and 5–6 are

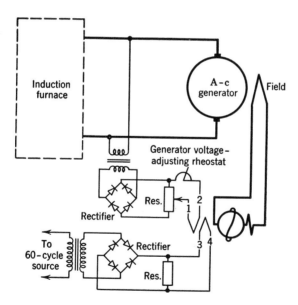

Fig. 28. Circuit for an amplidyne used with a high-frequency generator for induction heating. (Courtesy General Electric Company.)

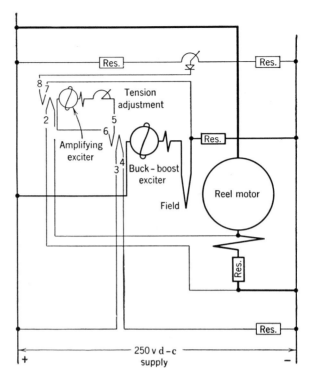

Fig. 29. Circuit for amplidyne control of a reel motor on a cold-strip mill. (Courtesy General Electric Company.)

in opposition and a balance is quickly reached. A limit field (7–8) is normally inactive. Its function is to strengthen the reel-motor field whenever the reel-motor current drops below a minimum value.

Electrostatic Precipitation

Particles of dust, smoke, condensed vapors, and chemical fumes may be removed from gases by mechanical processes and by electrostatic precipitation. The mechanical processes utilize centrifugal devices, simple filters, washers, and viscous-coated devices which depend on impinging the particles upon a coated surface. Electrostatic precipitation is the process of removing suspended particles from gases by the aid of an electrical discharge between electrodes in the gas stream. The cleaning of gases by a corona discharge was suggested by Hohlfield in 1824. In 1906, Dr. Frederick G. Cottrell, a professor in physical chemistry at the University of California, developed a practical electrostatic system which has been very successful in handling difficult cleaning problems that could not be accomplished by other methods.

The fundamental principle of electrostatic precipitation lies in the ionization of the gas by a strong electrical field accompanied by a corona discharge. The ionized gas particles consist of electrons, negatively charged ions, and positively charged ions. The electrons and negatively charged ions become attached to suspended particles in the gas, giving them a negative charge. In the usual form of precipitator, the negative electrode is of comparatively small diameter to give a concentrated field of high gradient, and it is placed at a suitable distance from a large positive electrode which serves as the collector. The negatively charged particles are attracted to the positively charged electrode and collect on its surface. The particles thus collected either drop by gravity into a collecting hopper below, or after interrupting the electric supply the electrodes are rapped manually or automatically to cause the precipitated material to be dislodged and fall into a hopper.

Cottrell Electrical Precipitator

The equipment used in the Cottrell electric precipitation process is shown schematically in Fig. 30. The precipitating chamber at the

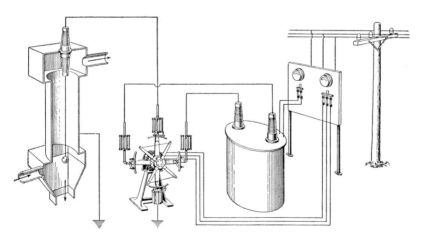

Fig. 30. Schematic diagram of the equipment used in the Cottrell electric precipitator. From left to right: precipitator, rotary rectifier, transformer, switchboard, and supply.

left is supplied with high-voltage direct current through the action of a rotary converter which rectifies the alternating voltage supplied by the transformer. The simplest precipitator unit (pipe type) consists of an insulated wire suspended at the center of a tube or pipe. A high negative potential is supplied to the wire and the grounded positive pipe constitutes the other terminal for the system. Large-capacity precipitators frequently consist of a large number of tubes and wire electrode units placed in parallel. A second general form for the Cottrell precipitators consists of a number of wires suspended between parallel plates which constitute the grounded collecting electrodes. Several designs for the plate collectors are in use and are constructed as follows:

1. *Solid steel,* sometimes corrugated.
2. *Concrete,* also called graded resistance, with conductors imbedded in the center.
3. *Rod curtain,* in which curtains of small rods or pipes are hung close together to form the collecting electrodes.
4. *Perforated plate,* where the collecting electrodes are in the form of narrow boxes with perforated sides.
5. *Pocket type,* in which the precipitated material is trapped in pockets, usually with upward gas flow.

The cross section of a heavy-duty precipitator using parallel plates and vertical flow is shown in Fig. 31.

In order to produce the corona discharge of sufficient magnitude for the Cottrell precipitation process, potentials of the order of 30,000 to 75,000 volts are required. These potentials are obtained by rectifying the output of a high-voltage transformer. Rectification may be accomplished by (1) high-voltage kenotrons, (2) multicell selenium rectifier stacks, or (3) rotary commutating rectifiers. Most early large-scale installations employed rotary rectifiers because of a lower initial cost and a lower cost of maintenance. In the rotary rectifier a synchronous motor drives a Bakelite rotor disk on which are mounted four rotating contact tips connected in pairs by quadrant conductor strips. These tips pass under stationary shoes connected to the transformer and precipitator unit in such a way as to reverse the connections from the transformer to the precipitator in synchronism with the a-c wave and thus produce rectification. Provision must be made for testing the polarity of the rectified wave and for slipping poles to assure correct polarity when starting the motor. Some arcing occurs at the rotary rectifier and within the precipitator

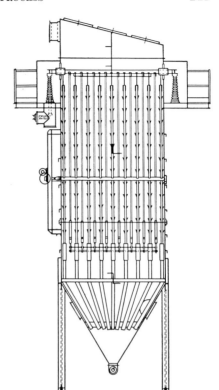

Fig. 31. Vertical-flow high-duty-type precipitator. (Courtesy Western Precipitation Corporation.)

which will cause radio interference unless corrective measures are taken. Improvements in the operating life of kenotrons in recent years have caused a trend toward a greater use of these tubes in rectifiers for precipitators.

Applications of the Cottrell Process

The Cottrell precipitators have been applied in a large number of manufacturing processes. Blast furnaces give forth enormous volumes of gases containing hundreds of tons of dust. Much of the exhaust gas is burned later in stoves, open-hearth furnaces, and gas engines where impurities in the gas may be damaging. Cottrell precipitators are used for preliminary and sometimes for final cleaning of the gas. In smelter operation, precipitators are used for recovering from gases such valuable materials as gold, silver, cadmium, lead, and zinc. The value of such recoveries has amounted to $40,000 to $1,000,000 gross value per year, showing the economic importance of the process. Precipitators are also used to remove the fog and water mist from manufactured gas after it has been scrubbed and cooled. The exhaust gas from cement plants gives a heavy dispersion of dust over the surrounding area. Electric precipitators will remove this dust, making it possible to return the recovered material to the kilns or to separate the potash from the recovery and sell it for fertilizer. In oil refineries precipitators may be used to collect sulfuric acid mist that is carried over in gases. In catalyst-cracking plants for producing high-octane gasoline a costly catalyst may be recovered by the precipitation process to the extent of 99.6 per cent. Power-generating plants using pulverized coal for fuel disperse large quantities of fly ash over the surrounding territory. Electric precipitators are collecting from 90 to 98 per cent of the total fly ash in more than a hundred powdered-fuel plants in the United States and in many hundreds in other parts of the world.

Electrostatic Precipitation for Air Conditioning

A new and valuable method for applying the principle of electrostatic precipitation has been perfected through the research and developmental work of G. W. Penney. This new method makes possible a satisfactory and economical process for purifying air for human consumption as a part of a complete air-conditioning system. The process of electrostatic precipitation described in the preceding discussion is not satisfactory for air conditioning because of the high voltages of 30,000 to 75,000 volts used. Such high voltages result in a high cost of operation because of (1) relatively large power consumption, (2) high initial investment for equipment, and (3) large maintenance expense. Of still greater importance is the fact that the method described produces so much ozone that the cleaned air, although free of dust, is too irritating to the nose and throat to be used where human beings are concerned.

In the new method of precipitation, the functions of charging the particles by corona discharge and the collection of the charged dust particles are performed in two separate stages of equipment. This new method utilizes a lower voltage for the ionization and charging process and a still lower voltage for the collection of charged dust particles. One of the principal advantages of separating the functions is the large reduction in the ionizing current which causes a reduction in ozone generation. The construction for separating these functions is shown in Fig. 32. In the ionizer zone at the left a fine wire electrode carries a d-c positive potential of 13,000 volts and is

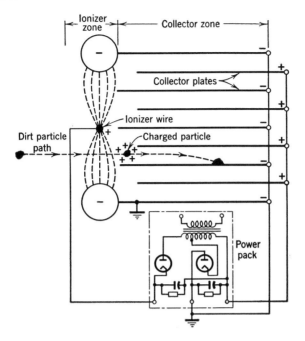

Fig. 32. Construction and action in a Precipitron. (Courtesy Westinghouse Electric Corporation.)

located between grounded cylinders (electrodes). In this zone the gas is ionized and the dust particles are charged while they are being swept into the collector zone. The collector zone consists of many plates disposed edgewise to the air flow. Alternate plates are charged positive to about 6000 volts, with the intervening ones held at zero or ground potential. The positively charged dust particles are collected on the negative or grounded plates where they are held until removal.

The theory of the action taking place is of interest. In the ionizer zone a very high potential gradient exists close to the positively charged ionizer electrode. This potential is sufficient to extract electrons from the surrounding atoms of gas. Having lost electrons the atoms become positive ions and are moved by the existing potential gradient along the lines of the electrostatic field toward the negative electrodes in the ionizer zone. Since dust particles usually have a dielectric constant greater than one, the lines of the electrostatic field will be distorted with more lines passing through the particle. This distortion causes more of the positive ions to collide with and become attached to the dust particles, thus giving them a positive charge very quickly. The charging of the dust particles is also aided by the kinetic or heat motion (random) of the positive ions which results in more collisions and hence in faster charging of the particles. The dust particle will continue to acquire a positive charge from the + ions until the magnitude of its charge exerts a repelling force sufficient to prevent further attachments of charge.

After the dust particles are charged, a few of them along with some unattached + ions may reach the negative electrodes in the ionizer zone. However, most of the dust particles will be carried by the gas stream into the collector zone. In this collector zone there exists between the plates a high potential gradient arising from the 6000 volts applied to alternate plates. This potential gradient E acts upon the charged particles with a force equal to E times the charge Q on the particle. Thus the particle is urged toward the negative plate but is opposed by the air resistance with the resulting motion shown in Fig. 32. Obviously, the magnitude of these factors and the length of the collector plates will determine the maximum permissible velocity of the air stream which will assure that the charged particle reaches the collector plate before emerging from the collector zone. It is well to note that this dual-stage system provides (1) a nonuniform field for ionization which is most efficient for this purpose and (2) a high-magnitude uniform field for collection of charged particles which, in turn, is most rapid and efficient for its function.

When the charged particle reaches the collector plate, it gives up most if not all its charge if it has conducting properties. Hence electrostatic forces cannot be relied upon for retaining the particles. In general, the molecular force that exists between substances in contact offers a form of adhesion which will hold the particles to the collector plate. In special cases the plates may be coated with oil or other material which will cause particles to adhere, although they may adhere so well that cleaning of the plates becomes rather difficult. With some types of dust, the particles may adhere normally, but a jar may loosen agglomerations of dust. This problem may be solved by using a simple mechanical filter beyond the precipitator. The method used for cleaning the plates depends on the nature of the dust collected. Cleaning is usually accomplished by a direct washing process.

The Precipitron

The principle of electrostatic precipitation described is used in commercial assemblies known as the Precipitron. These assemblies are made up of standard sections combined to give the desired air-cleaning capacity. Individual Precipitron units range in capacity from 240 to 350,000 cu ft per minute. A small portable unit is shown in Fig. 33. A simplified circuit for the rectifier which supplies the high voltage for the Precipitron is given in Fig. 34. The transformer steps up the line voltage to 7000 volts and delivers it through a voltage doubling arrangement (see page 244) to two kenotron tubes which rectify it for use in the Precipitron. A part of the necessary indicating and protective equipment for the rectifier is shown at the left of the circuit diagram.

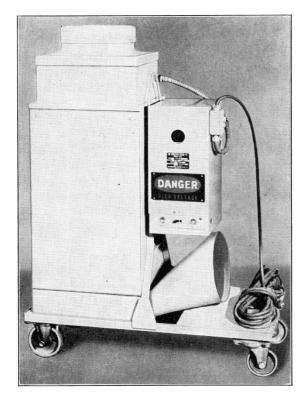

Fig. 33. The Precipitron, a portable precipitation unit. (Courtesy Westinghouse Electric Corporation.)

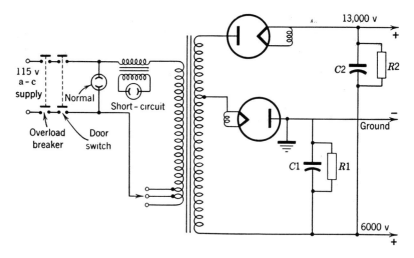

Fig. 34. Basic circuit of a Precipitron.

The Precipitron is particularly adapted to removing light concentrations of fine dust. Some of its principal fields of application are:

1. Removal of industrial dusts which constitute a hazard to the health of employees.

2. Air cleaning to protect delicate apparatus or processes.

3. Air cleaning in homes and offices in soft-coal-burning cities to reduce cleaning of walls and draperies.

4. Air cleaning for the relief of hay fever and asthma.

5. Air cleaning in stores to reduce damage to merchandise.

PROBLEM

1. Construct a diagram of "logic" or static control units to perform the functions illustrated in the relay diagram of Fig. 35.

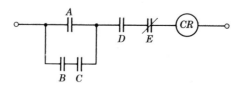

Fig. 35

REFERENCES

1. Kelling, L. U. C., *Photoelectric Scanning for Register Controls,* GET-2411A, General Electric Co.
2. LaRue, Jr., Mervin W., "A New Automatic Iris Control for Motion-Picture Cameras," *Journal of the SMPTE,* July 1957.
3. Bagby, John P., and Mervin W. LaRue, Jr., *Light Energizes Control in Self-Setting Camera, Electrical Man.,* January 1958.
4. Alexanderson, E. F. W., M. A. Edwards, and K. K. Bowman, "The Amplidyne Generator—A Dynamoelectric Amplifier for Power Control," *Gen. Elec. Rev.,* March 1940.
5. *Cottrell Process of Electrical Precipitation,* Research Corporation, and Western Precipitation Corporation, 1940.
6. Schmidt, Walter A., and Evald Anderson, "Electrical Precipitation," *Elec. Eng.,* August 1938.
7. Penney, G. W., "A New Electrostatic Precipitator," *Elec. Eng.,* January 1937.

chapter 16

X-Ray
Applications

X-Ray Tube

In November, 1895, Wilhelm Conrad Roentgen, a German physicist, discovered a mysterious ray which had the power to penetrate flesh, wood, and metal. Since he did not understand the phenomenon, he used the mathematical symbol "X" for the unknown, and called his discovery the X ray. In making his discovery Roentgen was experimenting with a Crooke's tube which consisted of a gas-filled, pear-shaped glass bulb having a cold aluminum disk at one end (cathode) and a similar disk several inches away at the top of the tube. A high potential between the electrodes produced a Townsend discharge. The electrons emitted from the cold cathode by positive ion bombardment hit the glass walls at the opposite end of the tube and produced X rays.

The early form of a gaseous X-ray tube was very inefficient and erratic in its behavior. Many scientists contributed to the development of the characteristics of the modern X-ray tube. Chief among them was Dr. W. D. Coolidge who was the first to build a tube of the hot filament type to operate in a vacuum. He also conducted research which led to a method for producing ductile tungsten. This development made possible the use of tungsten for the hot cathodes and for the anodes. Later he developed the multisection X-ray tube which permitted accelerating potentials of one and two million volts.

A conventional X-ray tube is shown in Fig. 1. Two electrodes are encased in a highly evacuated borosilicate glass envelope. The

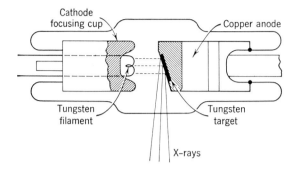

Fig. 1. Conventional X-ray tube.

cathode is a helical coil of tungsten and the anode consists of a tungsten target insert in a copper anode.

The electrons emitted by the cathode are attracted to the anode by a high potential of the order of 10,000 to several million volts. The tremendous impact of the electrons in hitting the target excites the electrons in the atoms of the target so that they send out electromagnetic radiations known as X rays. These emanations are not electrons or particles but wave energy similar to light waves. It will be recalled that the impact of electrons on atoms of gas produces an excitation of the electrons which results in the production of light. In the X-ray tube the impact of the electron is much greater because of the high potential gradients and it acts upon electrons in a solid so that the resulting waves are much shorter (higher frequency) and contain a greater energy. It is probable that the impinging electrons in the X-ray tube penetrate into the inner electron rings and even the nuclei of the atoms constituting the target. The X rays emitted by the tungsten target are a continuous spectrum of electromagnetic radiation. The minimum wavelength is determined by the peak voltage across the X-ray tube according to the equation $Vl = 12.354$, where V is the voltage across the tube measured in kilovolts and l is the minimum wavelength in angstrom units (10^{-8} cm). X rays are propagated with the same speed as light, follow the inverse square law, are unaffected by electric and magnetic fields, and can be reflected, diffracted, and polarized.

X rays have the power of penetration through layers of solids that are opaque to light. These X rays are invisible to the eye but can be detected after passing through solids by their action on a fluorescent screen or on a photographic film. Their ability to blacken sensitized film in a manner proportional to their intensity has been the basis of radiography. Furthermore, their ability to penetrate opaque objects is dependent upon the atomic weight (density) of the object. The penetrating power of X rays is referred to as a degree of hardness; soft rays have small penetrating power, hard rays deep penetrating power. Hardness is proportional to the frequency of radiation and depends on the voltage applied across the cathode-anode circuit. The penetrating power varies approximately as the square of the voltage. Thus in the operation of X-ray devices the hardness is controlled by varying the cathode-anode voltage, the intensity or quantity of X rays is controlled by the voltage across or the current passed through the cathode for heating, and the quantitative effect of the X rays is controlled by the time of exposure.

X-Ray Equipment

An X-ray machine consists of a high-voltage power supply, an X-ray tube, and control equipment. Since X-ray tubes are inherently diode rectifiers, they may be energized by alternating current, by half-wave or full-wave rectifiers, or by direct current. A basic X-ray circuit of the half-wave type is shown in Fig. 2. The intensity of the resulting radiation is controlled by varying the filament current via resistor R. The applied potential and penetrating power of the

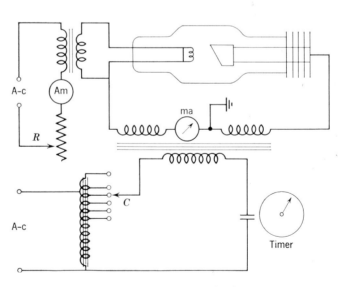

Fig. 2. Basic X-ray circuit.

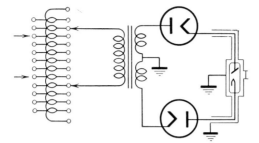

Fig. 3. Two-tube half-wave rectifier with a shockproof X-ray tube.

rays is controlled by selection of a tap on the auto transformer by contactor C. Last, the length of exposure is determined by the setting of the timer device. The equipment and circuit of Fig. 2 are satisfactory for intermittent service and when a low cost is desired, such as in a dentist's office. However, this equipment will fail if overloaded or used above its normal intermittent rating because if the target gets too hot it will become an emitter and a reverse current will flow on the negative half cycle. Commercial equipment covering the circuit of Fig. 2 is usually assembled into a single case and filled with oil. This construction will assist in cooling the unit and give perfect insulation for the equipment and the operator.

The possibility of a destructive reverse current flow in the X-ray tube can be overcome by inserting kenotrons in the circuit, as shown in Fig. 3. Here the transformers and kenotrons are mounted in an insulated stationary unit. The X-ray tube is well shielded and connected to the stationary unit by heavily insulated cables which have a metallic armor or contain an interior metallic braid. Full-wave rectification for the X-ray tube may be secured by the use of a transformer with mid-tap and two kenotron rectifier tubes or by the use of the bridge circuit with four kenotrons, as covered in Chapter 8 on rectification and inversion. The maximum cathode-anode voltage across the X-ray tube for the preceding circuits for power supply is the a-c secondary high-voltage peak. A special power-supply circuit which applies two times the peak voltage across the X-ray tube is shown in Fig. 4. This is known as the Villard circuit and the explanation of its operation is left to the reader.

Since X-ray tubes are operated at the saturation current, the electron current through the tube is determined by the size and temperature of the tungsten filament. The tungsten anode or target may

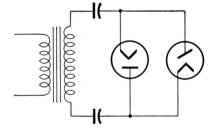

Fig. 4. Villard circuit for X-ray equipment.

be mounted on the end of a molybdenum rod or set in a copper anode. Since only a fraction of one per cent of the electrical power put into the X-ray tube is converted into X rays, nearly all the remainder appears as heat in the target. Therefore, effective means of cooling the target must be provided. Those anodes that consist only of tungsten mounted on molybdenum rods are cooled by radiation. Those targets that are cast in copper rods are cooled by heat conduction along the copper rod to a radiator which permits the heat to be carried away by air or by oil. The anodes of some tubes which are operated continuously at high loads are hollowed out behind the target and cooled by circulating water or oil. The minimum length of an X-ray tube is determined by the spark-over distance for the maximum voltage applied to the tube. Many modern X-ray tubes are made shockproof by being operated inside grounded metal tanks filled with oil. These tubes are shorter than those operated in the open air. A shockproof tube is indicated in Fig. 3.

Applications of X Rays in Medicine

X rays are used in the field of medicine for radiography and therapy. From a knowledge of anatomy and the relative opacities of the various organs of the human body to X rays, it is possible to recognize injuries or diseases by examining the radiograph (shadows upon a photographic film). Broken or dislocated bones, defective teeth, and the presence of bullets or other foreign material are shown by the radiograph. Examples of radiographs of teeth are given in Fig. 5. Lung tissue destroyed by tuberculosis, gallstones, and ulcers of the stomach may be detected on a radiograph by the radiographic specialist. There is an optimum voltage for radiographing each part of the human body, depending on the thickness and density of the part viewed. The maximum voltage required for radiographing the human body is 100,000 volts. X rays are used to treat or destroy

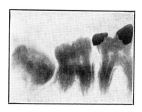

Fig. 5. X-ray photographs of human teeth: *left,* impacted tooth and fillings; *center,* abscessed tooth; *right,* permanent teeth pushing up baby teeth. (Courtesy Dr. C. J. Buster.)

malignant tumors such as cancer. For treating cancers near the surface, tube voltages varying from 10,000 to 140,000 volts are satisfactory, but for deep-seated tumors very hard X rays produced by tubes operating at 200,000 to 1,000,000 volts are required. Since these high voltages also produce soft rays which would burn the surface tissue, these softer rays are filtered out by sheets of copper and aluminum. Radiographic tubes are operated intermittently for comparatively short periods of time, whereas tubes for therapy must be capable of carrying currents of 10 to 25 ma continuously. A deep-therapy X-ray tube is illustrated in Fig. 6.

Industrial Applications of X Rays

In industry X rays are used for fluoroscopy, X-ray diffraction, and radiography of machine parts. *Fluoroscopy* is the visual representation of the construction of opaque objects on a fluorescent screen by the transmission of X rays. This process has wide application in the inspection of foods and packaged devices before distribution. Under small-scale methods the parts to be inspected may be placed under the fluorescent screen manually, whereas under large-scale processes the parts to be inspected move on a conveyer belt so that an operator

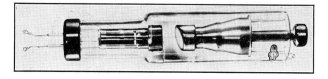

Fig. 6. X-ray tube for deep therapy. (Courtesy Westinghouse Electric Corporation.)

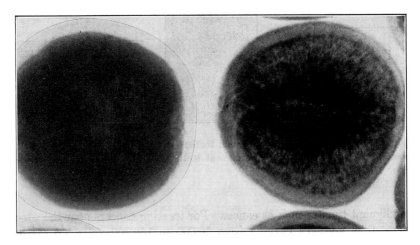

Fig. 7. X-ray photograph of oranges: *left,* good orange; *right,* defective orange. (Courtesy General Electric Company.)

makes a visual inspection as the shadow view passes on the fluorescent screen. A fluoroscopic picture of a good and a defective orange is shown in Fig. 7. Apparatus of the type described is widely used for inspecting all kinds of citrus fruit, and in canning plants for detecting damaged vegetables and foreign bodies, and for checking the fill of packaged containers. Tube voltages somewhat under 100,000 volts are used in fluoroscopy.

The nature and behavior of most substances depend upon the arrangement of atoms and molecules in the crystalline structure. This is true whether the material is a deep drawing steel, a bearing metal, or a tempered steel spring. Every substance such as rolled, forged, or heat-treated metal has a distinct atomic arrangement which determines its properties. Each atomic arrangement controls the diffractive effect produced by X rays. Thus, if a beam of X rays is passed through a crystal, the beam will be bent or redirected in a series of emergent rays whose separation and intensities are characteristic of the material. A radiograph of the diffracted rays constitutes a "fingerprint" of the substance because no two substances have been found to produce identical diffraction patterns. *X-ray diffraction* is used (1) as a laboratory tool in the hands of a trained specialist working on problems of production or product research and (2) as a routine inspection tool in the hands of an operator making repetitive checks on the analysis or condition of a material. Three methods are employed in making analyses by X-ray diffraction. In one method X rays are passed through a very thin section of the substance and the diffraction pattern falls on a vertical film. In a second method the X rays are projected upon a powdered sample at the center of a drum and the film is placed inside the drum. The third application, called a back reflection method, determines the *reflection* pattern from the test specimen. The back reflection method is employed with alloys and combinations of materials that form a substantial solid solution. Examples of X-ray diffraction patterns are given in Fig. 8. Voltages used on X-ray tubes for diffraction studies vary from 10,000 to 50,000 volts.

An important application of X-ray diffraction methods is the determination of the optimum angle for cutting quartz to produce wafers (crystals) for controlling the frequency of crystal oscillators. The orientation or angle requirement for crystals manufactured before the war was met by a trial-and-error performance-selection method. During the war more crystals were required per day of manufacture than in an entire year before. Also it was necessary to produce crystals that would give the same frequency regardless of temperature.

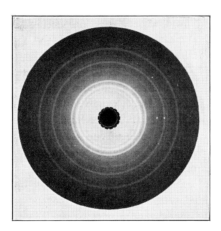

Fig. 8. X-ray diffraction pattern of salt containing 96.12 per cent potassium chloride (*top*) and cold-worked stainless steel. Outer dot shows austenite line; inner dot, ferrite (*bottom*). (Courtesy General Electric Company.)

These requirements were met by the development of an X-ray goniometer which indicates the intensity of X-ray diffraction in the direction characteristic of a certain set of planes. A sample crystal wafer is turned in the X-ray beam until this set of planes diffracts with maximum intensity. At this position the orientation of the diffracting planes is determined and the proper angle for cutting the mother quartz is determined.

Closely allied to X-ray diffraction methods is the process of microradiography. Here radiographs are made of exceedingly thin sections of materials. These radiographs can be greatly enlarged to provide a means of adding depth to the studies of surface conditions with which microphotography is concerned. Radiographs can be applied to solutions so that the process has applications in chemistry as well as in metallurgy. These applications require tube voltages of the order of 6000 to 9000 volts.

X-ray inspection with radiography of castings, machine parts, welding structure, and intricate machinery assemblies provides the design engineer and the production department with a tool of incalculable value. Through the use of X-ray inspection, casting and electric welding techniques may be determined for producing stronger and flawless castings and electric welds. Inspection of castings before machining permits the elimination of parts that would result in inferior or rejected products. X-ray inspection permits a complete study of mechanical parts that are ordinarily obscured. It is important to observe that this method is a nondestructive inspection.

X-ray radiographic inspection utilizes a wide range of applied tube voltage and equipment. For aluminum castings and iron or steel parts up to $\frac{1}{2}$ in. in thickness, a range of 60 to 140 kv may be satisfactory. A 150 kv industrial X-ray unit is illustrated in Fig. 9. The X-ray tube in this unit is of the shockproof, rayproof, oil-immersed design provided with a water-cooling coil. The tube housing is made of cast aluminum and has a bellows arrangement to accommodate all normal expansion of the insulating oil. The expansion bellows are provided with a warning indicator which signifies the approach of unsafe operating temperatures. The interior of the tube housing contains a copper cooling coil which is so terminated that connections to a tap water supply may be made. The X-ray tube head is arranged so that it may be rotated through an angle of 270 degrees around its long axis to give radiation on vertical as well as horizontal planes.

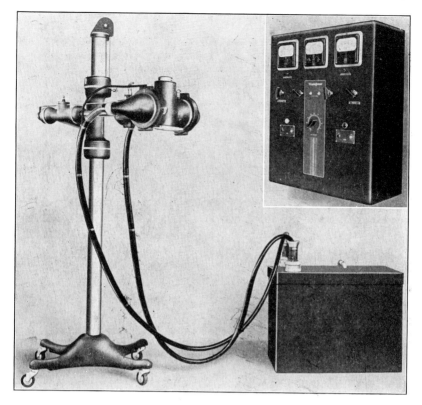

Fig. 9. Industrial X-ray unit and control, 150 kv. (Courtesy Westinghouse Electric Corporation.)

Radiography of steel $1\frac{1}{2}$ in. thick and castings of corresponding size require X-ray tube voltages of the order of 200,000 volts. For heavier and thicker sections, 400,000 volts have been used. The X-ray machines using these higher voltages are often portable and may be mounted on cranes or trucks.

During World War II two new developments were made that have greatly extended the horizon on the application of X radiation. These developments are the one and two million volt X-ray machines and the betatron. These devices have increased the hardness and power of penetration of X radiation and have reduced the required time of exposure for radiography.

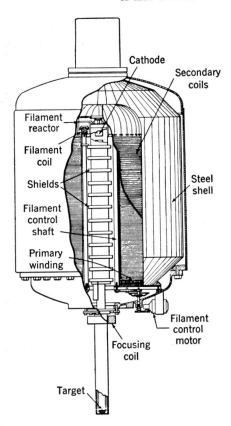

Fig. 10. Sectional drawing of a multisection X-ray tube concentrically mounted within a high-voltage resonance transformer. The unit has a diameter of 3 ft and a total length of 6 ft. (Courtesy General Electric Company.)

The Million Volt X-Ray Tubes

The new million volt X-ray industrial units involve a new type of tube, a new type of transformer, and a new form of assembly. These tubes have a filamentary tungsten cathode, a copper-backed tungsten target at the lower end of the extension chamber, and cylindrical accelerating electrodes in each of the 12 or 24 intermediate sections. The accelerating electrodes serve to distribute the high potential along the length of the tube. The inside walls of the tube are sand blasted to eliminate dangerous field current which might result from the application of increased voltage to each tube section.

The assembly of the unit is shown in Fig. 10. The long X-ray tube is placed at the center of a cylindrical resonance transformer. A cylindrical steel shell encloses the transformer and the main section of the X-ray tube. The space inside the steel shell is filled with freon gas at a pressure of 60 lb per square inch for electrical insulation. The long anode end of the X-ray tube projects from the lower end of the case making it available for insertion into hollow cavities (circular and other shapes) for emitting the high-frequency X radiation.

The method of supporting and applying the million volt X-ray units is illustrated in Fig. 11. The one million volt unit is suitable for radiographing up to an 8-inch thickness of steel and the two million volt unit can be used for steel sections up to 12 in. thick. As to relative speeds, for a focal film distance of 4 ft on an 8-in. steel casting, the two million volt unit is 100 times faster than the one million volt machine. A picture can be taken through steel 12 in. thick in 2 hours at a distance of 3 ft with the two million volt unit.

Fig. 11. One million volt X-ray unit being used to inspect a large casting. (Courtesy General Electric Company.)

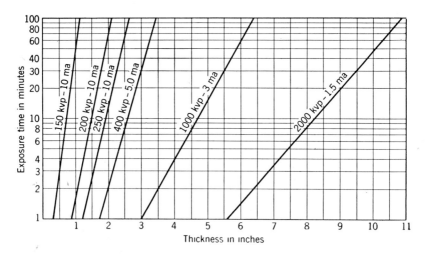

Fig. 12. Comparison of penetrating power of X radiation under different ac-celerating potentials. (Courtesy General Electric Company.)

A comparison of the effectiveness of various voltages in X-ray work is shown in Fig. 12.

Adequate protection must be given to all human beings who work near X-ray equipment. This protection must cover the hazards due to (1) high voltage and (2) the harmful effects of X radiation. The most effective bar to X radiation is sheet lead and it is often used to surround all parts of the X-ray tube except a window for the radi-ation. It is generally used for doors into X-ray exposure chambers and sometimes it is used to surround the entire room where X rays are used. A special form of plaster for the walls of the X-ray cham-ber is often used because of its lower cost. Also thick concrete walls are fairly effective for screening X rays. The advice of experts in the X-radiation field should always be secured before installation of X-ray equipment.

The Betatron

The betatron is an induction electron accelerator wherein elec-trons are accelerated in a magnetic field instead of by direct appli-cation of a high potential. The basic idea of accelerating electrons by magnetic induction was patented by J. Slepian in 1927. In the years following this announcement Wideroe, Walton, and Steenbeck developed equations giving the necessary conditions for an electron accelerator but were not able to produce a machine that would work. It remained for Dr. D. W. Kerst of the Physics Department of the University of Illinois to invent a satisfactory working model of the betatron (announced in 1940). Kerst assisted in the design and development of a 20 million electron volt (mev) commercial betatron in the early forties. A larger 100 mev commercial betatron was completed in 1945.

The basic principle of the betatron is relatively simple. In part (*a*) of Fig. 13 a circular iron core is surrounded by a single turn of wire *t*. If a changing flux is made to pass through the iron an emf will be induced in the turn of wire and, if the wire circuit is closed, a circulating electron current will result. Since a current is a movement of electrons, it is obvious that, if electrons are released in the path shown by *t* while the flux changes in the core, these electrons will be induced to travel around the core in a curved path and will be accelerated as long as the flux is changing in the same direction. One problem in applying this simple principle is to make the electrons follow a constant circular path. The changing flux for the betatron is produced in a three-legged transformer as shown in (*b*) of Fig. 13. A "donut"-shaped accelerating tube is placed around the central leg of the transformer in the plane of *de.*. Exciting coils are placed on the top and bottom sections of the central leg. The transformer is excited by a resonance type of circuit as indicated in part (*c*) of Fig. 13. The resonant circuit on the transformer may be inductively coupled as shown, or a capacitive type of coupler may be employed.

Some of the details of the operation of the betatron are indicated in Fig. 14. The heart of the device is a torus or "donut" of glass which surrounds the changing stream of magnetic flux. The cathode and target are combined into a single unit. A heated tungsten cath-

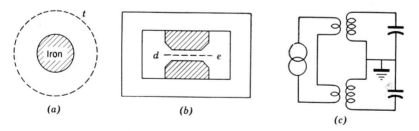

Fig. 13. Schematic construction and circuit of a betatron.

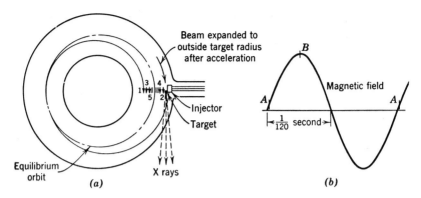

Fig. 14. (*a*) Schematic construction of the X-ray torus in a betatron. (*b*) Sine-wave magnetic field.

ode supplies electrons for an electrostatic gun which fires a stream of electrons tangentially into the central circular path. After arriving in this path, the changing magnetic induction accelerates the flying electron in a circular path. When the desired velocity of the electron has been acquired, a transient current passed through a one-turn coil near each pole face having a diameter slightly less than the optimum orbit serves to force the electron into a circular path of larger diameter (beam expanded) so that it hits the target and produces X rays. The flux change in the transformer follows the sine wave shown at the right of Fig. 14. In operation the electron beam is injected at point *A* (near zero) on the sine curve and the beam is deflected or expanded at any point later (up to *B*), depending on the desired energy in million electron volts.

The problem of maintaining the accelerating electrons in an optimum circular path until they hit the target has been suggested. It is apparent that as the electron stream whirls and accelerates in a curved path the momentum of the electrons increases and they tend to move in a spiral path which would soon carry them outside the "donut." An electron moving at right angles to a magnetic field is acted upon by a constant force which causes it to move in a curved path (circle for constant field *H*). In the present problem the force of the stray field in which the electron stream moves tends to hold the path circular but, since the electron velocity and momentum are constantly increasing, the circular path will be a spiral (increasing diameter) if the field *H* is constant. Therefore, in order to hold the diameter of the electron path constant, it is necessary to have *H* increase at the same rate as the momentum of the electrons. This necessary condition has been secured by the proper shape of the iron pole faces and magnetic disks in the air gap, giving a stray field flux of the necessary value along the optimum circular path of the electrons.

Betatrons in current use range in size from 2 to 300 million volts. A commercial betatron rated at 24 mev is illustrated in Fig. 15. In this unit the electrons circle the orbit about 350,000 times and travel a distance of 260 miles—all in one-fourth of a cycle or in less than 1.4 milliseconds for a frequency of 180 cycles per second. The average gain per electron revolution in its orbit is about 70 ev, and multiplying this figure by 350,000 gives 24 mev.

The 24 mev size of betatron has certain advantages in economy and effectiveness as a generator of X rays. The relative transmission of X rays in steel (ratio of transmission depth of rays to energy in rays) reaches its peak at 22 to 24 mev. This means that for radiography of steel this unit of power is advantageous. In cancer therapy the greatest obstacle to the delivery of a destructive dose of X radiation to a deep-seated tumor is that the skin and intervening tissues may suffer great damage in the process. For radiation energies of less than 1 mev, the skin dose is always higher than the tumor dose. As radiation is increased above two million volts, the dose delivered to the skin is actually less than that delivered to the tumor. For example, at 24 mev the amount of ionization that takes place 4 cm below the skin is many times the amount that occurs at the skin surface. Where the skin dose is high, severe burning will occur and, because of the large amount of X radiation absorbed by

Fig. 15. This 24 mev betatron is constructed to permit angular rotation of the X-ray beam in a vertical plane. (Courtesy Allis-Chalmers Manufacturing Company.)

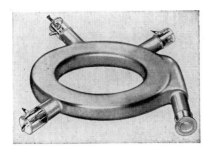

Fig. 16. Twenty-two million volt electron beam donut for the medical betatron. (Courtesy Allis-Chalmers Manufacturing Company.)

the intervening healthy tissue, nausea (radiation sickness) often results.

Many studies are being made in research in the field of biophysics to determine the interaction of radiation with the human body. These studies cover the effects of X rays, beta rays (electron beam), and neutrons on tissue. The donut of the betatron, which can be modified to bring the stream of high energy electrons directly out of the unit, has been effected in the special unit shown in Fig. 16. It has been accomplished by the insertion of a beryllium window 0.02 in. thick and having a diameter of 1 in. The electrons are triggered to the window by a peeling mechanism which consists of a laminated "permendur" magnetic shunt with a longitudinal slot placed tangential to the orbital circumference of the donut.

The design of a betatron makes possible acceleration of electrons to very high energies with low voltage equipment. In the 24 mev unit, electrons are given the same energy they would receive if accelerated by a potential difference of 24 million volts, whereas the voltage required to create the necessary field for their acceleration by magnetic induction is about 100 volts per turn on the magnet coil. The maximum intensity of the X ray is in the direction of the electron stream as it strikes the target. The focal spot of the betatron is very small, about 0.05 in. high by less than 0.005 in. wide. This small focal spot accounts for the sharpness in detail of radiographic work when a betatron is used.

PROBLEMS

1. Explain the operation of the Villard circuit shown in Fig. 4.

2. An X-ray therapy tube operates continuously at 250,000 volts direct current with a current of 10 ma. If 90 per cent of the energy must be con-

ducted away by water cooling, what will be the rate of water flow for a temperature rise (water) of 40° F?

3. If 1,000,000 volts are applied between the cathode and target of an X-ray tube, what would be the velocity of the impinging electron calculated by formula 9 of Chapter 1? How does this compare with the velocity of light? Explain.

4. Assume that the "donut" tube in a betatron has a mean diameter of 1 meter and that an electron in the tube gains energy at the average rate of 200 ev for each revolution. What will be its velocity starting from rest after 0.001 sec?

REFERENCES

1. Slepian, J., United States Patent 1,645,304, October 11, 1927.
2. Kerst, D. W., *Phys. Rev.*, **58,** 841 (1940).
3. Kerst, D. W., and R. Serber, *Phys. Rev.*, **60,** 53 (1941).
4. Girard, J. P., and G. D. Adams, *Elec. Eng.*, May 1946.
5. Westendorp, W. F., and E. E. Charlton, *J. Applied Phys.*, **16:**10, 581–593 (October 1945).

chapter 17

Electronic

Instruments

Cathode-Ray Tubes

A cathrode-ray tube is a device for producing electron beams and for projecting them upon a fluorescent screen to give a picture of some electrical phenomenon. The first device of this type was developed by Braun in 1897. Cathode-ray tubes have used (1) cold electrodes with high potentials in vacuum, (2) hot cathodes with low gas pressure and low voltage between electrodes, and (3) hot cathodes in vacuum with fairly high accelerating potentials. Nearly all the tubes in use today fall in the third class.

There are four functional parts in a cathode-ray tube located as suggested in Fig. 1. The electron gun at the left produces electrons and accelerates them to a high velocity along the line OS. The focus lens overcomes the mutual repulsion of the individual electrons and

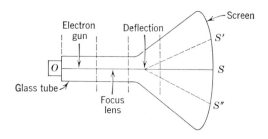

Fig. 1. Parts of a cathode-ray tube.

468

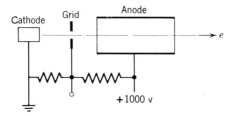

Fig. 2. Elementary electron gun.

causes them to converge to a point on the screen. The deflection section deflects the beam of electrons in the vertical and horizontal planes to bring it to a desired point on the target or screen. The screen consists of a phosphor coating on the inside end of the tube which is capable of transforming the energy of the incident beam of electrons into a spot of light. An elementary electron gun is shown in Fig. 2. Like a vacuum multielectrode tube, it has a cathode, grid(s), and an anode. Electrons are emitted by a cathode with a heater. The grid controls the number of electrons which are permitted to pass. Additional grids are often used for acceleration of electrons or removal of ions. The hollow cylindrical anode operates at a high potential to give the necessary electron velocity for operation of the tube.

Electron beams are focused by electrostatic and electromagnetic lens which are analogous to optical lens. An *electrostatic focusing lens* usually consists of two or three hollow cylinders having different potentials applied to them. A common form of a three-element electrostatic lens is illustrated in Fig. 3. Here the two outside cylinders *A* and *C* are connected electrically to a relatively high potential (that is, 1500 volts). The central focusing cylinder is connected to a variable voltage of the order of 600 to 1000 volts. These poten-

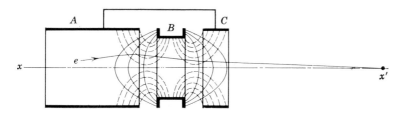

Fig. 3. Three-element electrostatic focusing lens.

tials produce electrostatic fields having the paths shown by the dotted lines leading from B to A and B to C. These fields are really surfaces which may be visualized as formed by rotating the dotted lines about the axis xx'. The equipotential surfaces of the electrostatic field are represented by the solid arcs from top to bottom in Fig. 3. These arcs appear like the surface of double convex optical lens and suggest the theory of convergence. Actually, when an electron e enters an equipotential surface, it is acted upon by a force which tends to move it at right angles to that surface. Thus it may be understood how diverging electrons entering the electrostatic field are redirected along the path shown. The forces acting upon each electron are proportional to the angle of divergence so that it is possible to bring all of them back to the axis at some point x'. The focus of the electrostatic lens is controlled by the shape of the equipotential surfaces which, in turn, is controlled by the difference in potential between the cylinder B and the common potential cylinders A and C.

Magnetic focusing of an electron beam may be produced by the special ferromagnetic core structure shown in Fig. 4a. This structure may be visualized as an armored coil or as the rotation of the magnetic core C about the axis xx'. In crossing the inside air gap, the magnetic flux lines (shown dotted) spread out in diverging paths. The full lines (at right angles to flux paths) represent equimagnetic potential surfaces. These surfaces have an appearance similar to the electrostatic lens systems and the convex optical system. They also do bring the individual diverging electrons to a focus on the axis xx', but the theory of action differs greatly from the other focusing systems. To understand this action consider first a long axial electromagnetic coil (solenoid), as shown in Fig. 4b. Current direction as indicated produces a flux to the right. Electrons e moving parallel to the axis of the coil and parallel to the flux are unaffected by the field. But if electrons enter the magnetic field at an angle θ as shown in Fig. 4c, they are acted upon by a component of force at right angles to B. This component of force tends to cause the electrons to move in an arc of a circle perpendicular to the axis (see page 12). At the same time, the initial component of velocity parallel to the axis carries the electron to the right. The resultant motion is a helical path, as suggested in Fig. 4c.

Returning to Fig. 4a, we note that any electron moving along the axis xx' is always parallel to the lines of the magnetic field and is unaffected in transit. However, any electron e removed from the axis cuts the magnetic field at differing angles with the paths of mag-

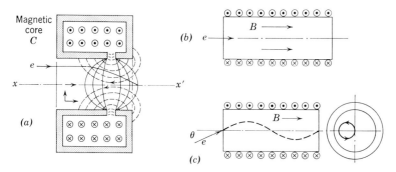

Fig. 4. Principle of magnetic focusing lens.

netic flux. For any component of motion at right angles to the path of the magnetic field, a side thrust is experienced. This thrust is at right angles to the direction of motion and also at right angles to the path of flux. Now that component of force at right angles to the electron motion is like the case of Fig. 4c and causes the electron to go into a helical spin. A second component of force arising from the flux path angle causes the electron to decrease its radius of spin and move toward the axis. Thus the resultant electron motion is a helical one of decreasing radius. The force which accelerates the electron toward the axis is proportional to the distance from the axis. Accordingly, all electrons tend to come to the axis xx'. The focusing or electron convergence may be controlled by a variation of the current in the armored coil. Recent (1958) magnetic focusing lens for TV receivers employs permanent magnet structures. For these late units the exact point of focus is attained by movement of the *PM* unit along the axis of the cathode-ray tube.

The deflection of electron beams in cathode-ray tubes may be produced by electrostatic or magnetic fields according to the principles discussed in Chapter 1. *Electrostatic deflection* is produced by two pairs of plates at right angles to each other, as shown in Fig. 5a. A changing potential across the X-plates provides a horizontal displacement for the beam, whereas a varying potential on the Y-plates gives the vertical deflection. In a similar manner, pairs of electromagnetic coils above and below and at the sides of the tube produce varying magnetic fields which give horizontal and vertical deflections (Fig. 5b). A pair of magnetic focusing coils assembled in the form of a yoke to slide over the neck of the cathode-ray tube is illustrated in Fig. 6.

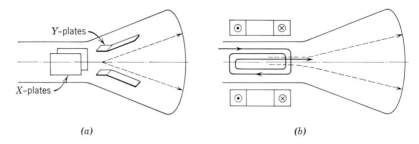

(a)   *(b)*

Fig. 5. Deflection systems in cathode-ray tubes. (*a*) Electrostatic. (*b*) Electromagnetic.

The electron beam impinging on the screen causes it to fluoresce in proportion to the intensity of the beam. Because of the persistence of vision of the eye, a moving beam produces a trace of light, or, in the case of television, a complete image on the fluorescent screen. The fluorescent screen consists of a coating of phosphor. Phosphors consist of compounds such as zinc silicate, cadmium tungstate, zinc sulfide, cadmium sulfide, and calcium tungstate, or a mixture of these compounds together with some substance such as silver or copper. The choice of the phosphor is determined by the color and the persistence time desired. A conducting coating on the inside of the envelope of the tube serves to return the electrons from the fluorescent screen to an anode. The secondary emission due to the impinging electrons removes electrons from the screen and prevents the building up of a negative charge.

The complete assembly of a cathode-ray tube employing electrostatic focusing and electrostatic deflection is shown schematically in Fig. 7. This is the type of tube employed in cathode-ray oscilloscopes. The smaller and lower cost tubes have a single continuous

Fig. 6. Magnetic deflection yoke for cathode-ray tube. (Courtesy Radio Corporation of America.)

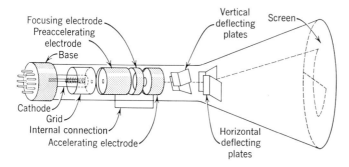

Fig. 7. Schematic of a cathode-ray tube. (Courtesy Allen B. DuMont Laboratories, Inc.)

internal conducting coating extending from the accelerating electrode to the screen. Such tubes use anode-to-cathode potential of the order of 1200 volts with the cathode negative and the anode at ground potential. Other cathode-ray tubes for precision work utilize a second or sometimes multiple ring coatings to produce a postaccelerating field as suggested in Fig. 8. The tube shown in Fig. 8 has its accelerating anodes and first conducting coating at near zero or ground potential. The cathode has a potential near -1200 volts and the postaccelerating coating at $+1800$ volts. This system provides a total accelerating potential of the order of 3000 volts but limits the potential to ground and for insulation of parts to 1200 to 1800 volts.

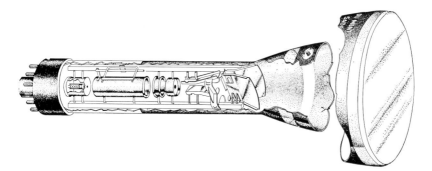

Fig. 8. Cathode-ray oscilloscope tube having electrostatic focusing and deflection. Note rings of conductive coating at right end designed to give a postaccelerating field. (Courtesy Allen B. DuMont Laboratories, Inc.)

The assembly of a cathode-ray tube employing magnetic focusing and magnetic deflection is illustrated schematically in Fig. 9. The theory for the deflection and focusing follows the preceding discussions. However, the electron gun shown contains an ion trap which involves some new and extended theory. Cathode-ray tubes are high-vacuum tubes but do contain some traces of gas atoms. In the early stages of the electron gun a few negatively charged ions may be formed. Magnetic fields produce small deflections on heavy ions compared to large effects upon electrons. The mathematical reason for this will be presented in the next paragraph. Since these heavy negative ions suffer little deflection, they land continuously in a small area near the center of the screen. This bombardment is damaging to the screen and results in a brownish appearance near the center. One method of preventing the formation of the ion spot is illustrated in Fig. 9. Here the first three electrodes or grids of the electron gun are tilted down at a slight angle so that normally the flying particles (electrons or negative ions) would land on grid No. 3. To prevent the useful electrons from being lost in this manner, a small perma-

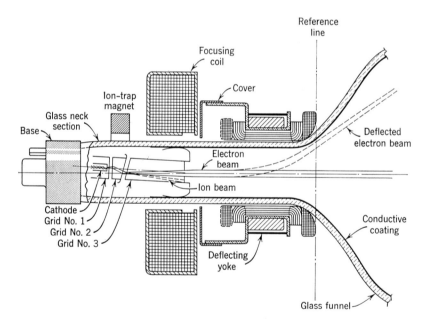

Fig. 9. Cross section of a cathode-ray tube employing magnetic focusing and deflection (one-half actual size). (Courtesy Radio Corporation of America.)

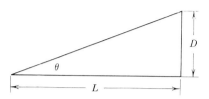

nent magnet called an ion-trap magnet is placed as shown. This little magnet produces a magnetic field at right angles to the electron beam and deflects the electrons up into normal (horizontal) path. However, the heavy negative ions suffer only slight deflection, and hence are trapped on grid No. 3. A second method of preventing the ion spot is to deposit a thin layer of aluminum on the inside of the phosphor on the screen. This thin aluminum layer stops the ions but permits the high-speed electrons to penetrate to the phosphor. The aluminized screen has a second beneficial effect in that it reduces the loss of light back into the tube and reflects it to the face, thus increasing the brilliance of the picture.

The triangle in Fig. 10 represents the deflection of the electron beam in a cathode-ray tube. Here θ is the angle of deflection, D is the actual deflection on the screen, and L is the distance from the center of the deflection system to the screen of the tube. The angle of deflection produced by the electrostatic system from page 10 is

$$\theta = \tan^{-1}\frac{v_y}{v_0} = \tan^{-1}\frac{\sqrt{2E_d(e/m)}}{\sqrt{2E_a(e/m)}} = \tan^{-1}\sqrt{\frac{E_d}{E_a}} \tag{1}$$

and

$$D = L\tan\theta = L\sqrt{\frac{E_d}{E_a}} \tag{2}$$

where E_d is the effective potential on the deflection plates and E_a is the accelerating potential.

The angle of magnetic deflection from page 13 is

$$\theta = \sin^{-1}\frac{l}{r} = \sin^{-1}\frac{l}{mv/Be} = \sin^{-1}\frac{lB}{v}\left(\frac{e}{m}\right)$$

$$= \sin^{-1}\frac{lB(e/m)}{\sqrt{2E_a(e/m)}} = \sin^{-1}\frac{lB}{\sqrt{2E_a}}\sqrt{\frac{e}{m}} \tag{3}$$

$$D = L\tan\theta \tag{4}$$

Equations 1 and 2 prove that for electrostatic deflection both the angle and the deflection are independent of the ratio e/m. Hence both electrons and ions suffer the same deflection although the time of arrival at the screen would be different. Equation 3 shows that the angle of deflection is proportional to the square root of e/m. Accordingly, the heavy negative ion will suffer a deflection inversely proportional to the square root of its mass. This confirms the preceding statements concerning the need of the ion trap.

Electrostatic deflection sensitivity is defined as the deflection of the beam on the screen per volt applied to the deflection plates.

$$\text{Electrostatic sensitivity} = \frac{D}{E_d} \tag{5}$$

Magnetic deflection sensitivity is defined as the deflection of the beam on the screen per unit of flux density B.

$$\text{Magnetic sensitivity} = \frac{D}{B} \tag{6}$$

Oscilloscope *

A cathode-ray oscilloscope is an instrument designed for the analysis of electrical circuits by a study of the wave forms of voltage and currents at various points. The instrument may be employed to study any variable, within the limits of its frequency response characteristic, that can be converted into electrical potentials. Common variables are sound, vibration, light, and all forms of variable impedances such as resistance, inductance, and capacitance.

The basic elements of an oscilloscope are a cathode-ray tube, amplifiers, and a power supply. The frequency limitation of an oscilloscope is determined by the electron transit time across the face of the deflection plates in the cathode-ray tube and by the functioning of the amplifier circuits. In the cathode-ray tube the transit time is of the order of 0.001 microsecond so that little error will be present in frequencies up to 100 mc. Amplifier circuits do have frequency limitations and they become a controlling factor in applying the oscilloscope to many problems.

The basic theory of action of the cathode-ray tube as applied to the oscilloscope may be reviewed by observing the right side of Fig. 11. The electron beam moving perpendicularly to the page passes

---

* The terms oscilloscope and oscillograph are used interchangeably for this device. The contraction "scope" is frequently used.

between the parallel deflection plates HH' and VV' and forms a luminous spot on hitting the fluorescent screen. With zero applied potentials to the deflection plates and the proper adjustment of the tube circuits the luminous spot should fall at the center of the screen. If a varying potential (a-c) is placed across plates HH', the luminous spot will be caused to travel back and forth along the horizontal line hh'. If the frequency of the variation of voltage is 16 cycles or more, the horizontal trace will appear as a solid motionless line because of the persistence of vision of the human eye. In a similar manner, if a variation of voltage is applied only across deflection plates V and V', the moving luminous spot will create a vertical line or trace as indicated by vv'. When varying potentials are placed across both pairs of deflection plates simultaneously, a picture is created on the screen which gives information regarding the wave form of the applied signals. In general, some independent or known signal is applied across the plates HH', whereas an unknown or dependent signal is applied across the plates VV'. The former is called the horizontal signal and the latter the vertical signal. For the determination of wave shapes a synchronized sawtooth signal is used for the horizontal, whereas for the study of frequency and of phase angle a sine-wave a-c signal is used.

The block diagram of a simple oscilloscope is shown in the complete Fig. 11. The circuit is simplified and the cost of the device has

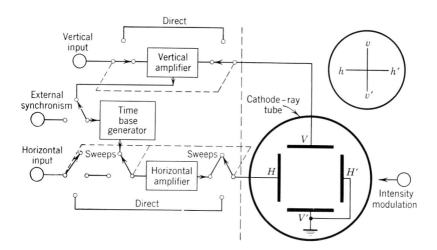

Fig. 11. Block diagram of a simple oscilloscope.

been reduced by grounding H' and V'. The vertical input signal is fed between the post so marked and the ground. If this signal is of sufficient strength it is supplied directly to the deflection plates V and V', but if the magnitude is of insufficient value to produce a satisfactory deflection it may be passed through an amplifier for controlling the final signal strength applied to the plates. In a similar manner, an external horizontal signal may be applied through the lower circuit group to plates direct (lower position of ganged switches) or via an amplifier (middle switch position). For wave analysis it is generally desired to synchronize the "sweep" signal with the applied vertical input signal. This is accomplished by controlling the time based (sawtooth) generator from the vertical input with the connection as shown in Fig. 11. The latter may be considered as an internal horizontal input. For some applications it is desirable to control or modulate the intensity of the luminous spot on the screen by some external signal. This result is accomplished by the intensity modulation indicated on the right of diagram. Intensity modulation in this circuit is effected by feeding a signal into the control grid-cathode circuit of the cathode-ray tube. A better understanding of the oscilloscope may be obtained by expanding the block diagram of Fig. 11 into component schematic circuits.

A cathode-ray tube circuit for a simple oscilloscope, showing the magnitude of the components, is given in Fig. 12. The second anode and the deflection plates are held at or near ground potential by ground connections. The cathode and control grid are maintained at a potential of approximately -1200 volts, giving a maximum electron-accelerating potential of 1200 volts, from potential divider resistors $R1$ through $R6$. Focusing control is attained by connecting the second anode to the variable resistor $R3$. The luminous-spot intensity control is attained by varying the voltage between the cathode and the control grid across a section of resistor $R1$. The position of the focal spot may be centered between the pairs of deflection plates by adjustment of potentiometers $P1$ and $P2$. It will be noted that the potential between the ends of the potentiometer resistances varies from negative (point between $R5$ and $R6$) to $B+$ (above ground).

The amplifier circuits for the vertical and horizontal inputs to the deflection plates use pentodes as indicated in Fig. 13. The time base or sawtooth generator uses the circuit and control as indicated in Fig. 14. This is a relaxation oscillator circuit using a thyratron. The voltage supplied to cathode and anode circuit is determined by

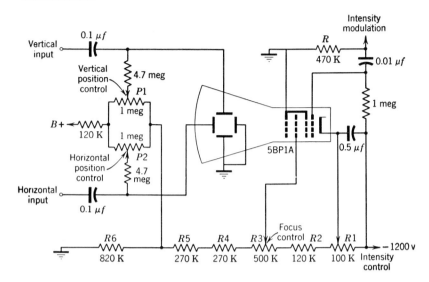

Fig. 12. Simplified schematic of cathode-ray tube circuits.

the voltage drop across the potential divider $R2$ and $R3$. For the setting shown, capacitor $C4$ charges through resistors $R8$ and $R7$ until the thyratron reaches its firing potential. At this point, $C4$ discharges rapidly, lowering the potential across the cathode-anode circuit below the conduction point. Then $C4$ recharges slowly and the process repeats, giving the sawtooth wave form of voltage as shown in the lower left-hand corner of Fig. 14. The instant of firing (trigger action of grid) may be controlled by the connection to vertical amplifier (left) and thus give synchronous timing with the vertical input signal. Again synchronous timing from an external signal

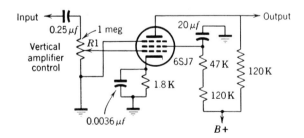

Fig. 13. Simplified circuit of an amplifier for an oscilloscope.

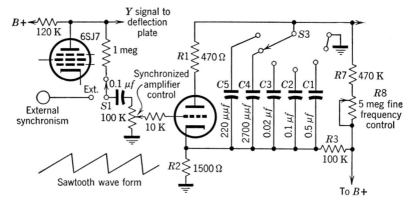

Fig. 14. Simplified schematic of a sweep circuit.

may be attained by movement of switch $S1$ to the left. An excessive synchronizing signal impairs the wave form of the sweep oscillator. Coarse frequency control can be obtained by the capacitor selection of switch $S3$ and fine adjustment of frequency control can be effected by variation of resistor $R8$.

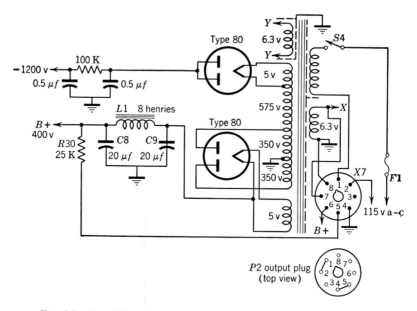

Fig. 15. Simplified circuit of the power supply for an oscilloscope.

The schematic circuit for the power supply of the oscilloscope is given in Fig. 15. The top tube giving half-wave rectification furnishes the high voltage (1200 volts) supply through a resistor and capacitor filter for the electron gun circuit. The lower tube gives full-wave rectification for a 400 volt supply for the tubes and deflection plates in the instrument plus a reserve for operating some electronic equipment accessory to the oscilloscope. The output plug in the lower right corner is for a takeoff of B supply for accessory equipment and serves as a safety "disconnect" of the 115 volt, a-c supply. The safety feature results because this plug must be pulled out to remove the case from the instrument.

A commercial oscilloscope (oscillograph) that uses the cathode-ray tube of Fig. 8 discussed in the preceding pages is illustrated in Fig. 16. This is a precise and versatile oscilloscope which requires three-stage amplifiers and other circuit refinements to give quality performance.

The action of the oscilloscope when studying a wave form plotted against time is illustrated in Fig. 17. A sine wave of voltage is applied to the vertical input (left) and a sawtooth wave of the same frequency is applied across the horizontal input. The magnitude of the vertical and horizontal sweep is governed by respective input

Fig. 16. A commercial oscillograph. (Courtesy Allen B. DuMont Laboratories, Inc.)

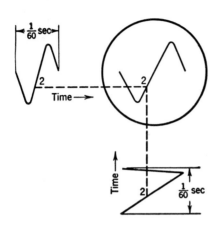

Fig. 17. Projection drawing of a sine wave applied to a vertical axis and a sawtooth wave of the same frequency applied simultaneously on a horizontal axis.

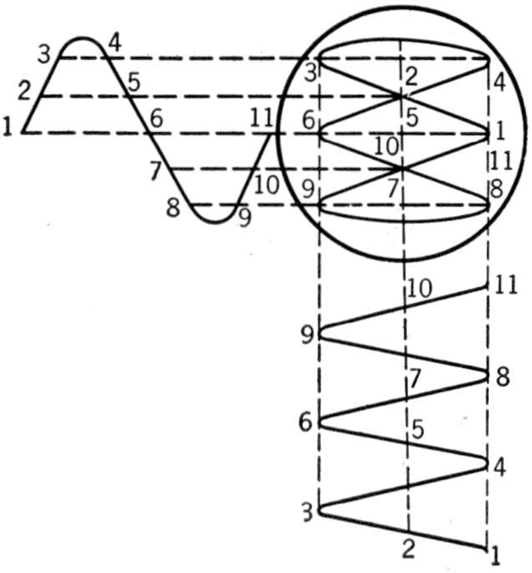

Fig. 18. Projection drawing showing the resultant Lissajous pattern when a sine wave applied to the horizontal axis is three times the frequency applied to the vertical axis.

signal control. For comparative and quantitative measurement of the signals a transparent screen containing cross-section lines is placed on the face of the cathode-ray tube.

When the signal inputs to both the horizontal and the vertical deflection plates are alternating voltages, the resulting action and pattern on the screen are illustrated in Fig. 18. This form of pattern is known as a Lissajous figure, named after the nineteenth-century French scientist. The Lissajous pattern may be traced by joining intersections from like numbered points on the signal. Lissajous figures are used for determining the frequency of unknown signals. Such frequency determination requires the use of one signal of known frequency which is impressed on the horizontal input. If the signals of the same frequency and magnitude and 90 degrees out of phase are impressed across the vertical and horizontal inputs, the trace will be a circle, as shown in part 1 of Fig. 19. Thus the circle becomes the pattern for a frequency ratio of 1/1. A horizontal-to-vertical frequency ratio of 3/1 is illustrated in Fig. 18 and several other ratios in the views of Fig. 19. The frequency relationship is determined by the ratio of the number of loops touching two mutually perpendicular sides such as AB and BC of part 5 of Fig. 19. The algebraic rule for the determination is

$$\frac{\text{Frequency on horizontal axis}}{\text{Frequency on vertical axis}} = \frac{\text{Number of loops intersecting } AB}{\text{Number of loops intersecting } BC}$$

The phase-angle difference between two signals of the same frequency can be determined by the use of Lissajous figures produced by impressing these signals on the horizontal and vertical input to the oscilloscope. In making this determination it is important (1) that the luminous spot be centered on the screen of the cathode-ray tube, (2) that both horizontal and vertical amplifiers have been adjusted to give exactly the same gain, and (3) that the calibrated scale be set to coincide with the displacement of the signal along the vertical axis. The calculation for the angle of phase shift is made by use of the formula

$$\sin \theta = \frac{Y \text{ intercept}}{Y \text{ maximum}}$$

where the Y intercept is the magnitude of the $+Y$ intercept of the trace on the Y axis and the Y maximum is the peak or maximum $+$ value attained by the trace. Several views of patterns and the calculation of the phase-angle difference are illustrated in Fig. 20.

The determination of phase angles, as shown in Fig. 20, is subject to some limitations. First, the amplifiers in the oscilloscopes should

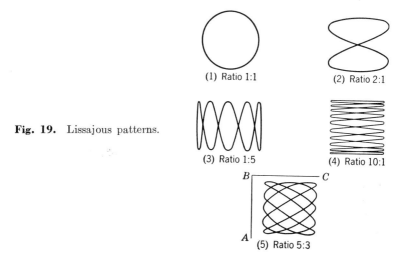

(1) Ratio 1:1

(2) Ratio 2:1

Fig. 19. Lissajous patterns.

(3) Ratio 1:5

(4) Ratio 10:1

(5) Ratio 5:3

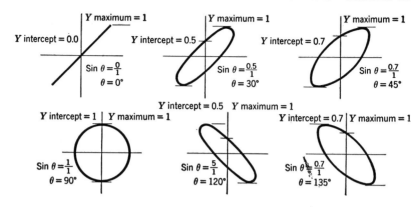

Fig. 20. Examples showing the use of the formula for determination of phase difference.

be free of phase shifts of their own which might give erroneous results. Second, the *quadrant* in which the phase difference is located depends on the inputs to a specific oscilloscope. In other words, a 45 degree pattern on Fig. 20 might turn out to be a 135, 225, or 315 degree on some other oscilloscope or on the same oscilloscope with different input connections. The system of phase shift measurement by Lissajous figures is a method of fairly low precision.

The frequency of a series of pulses and the duration of a single pulse may be determined by impressing the impulse signal upon a known sine wave through intensity modulation. Intensity modulation is the result of applying a signal of varying potential to the control grid of the cathode-ray tube, thereby varying the intensity of the trace at the frequency of the signal applied. The result of such intensity modulation is illustrated in the oscillogram of Fig. 21.

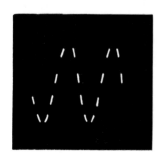

Fig. 21. Example of intensity modulation with a sine-wave signal. (Courtesy Allen B. DuMont Laboratories, Inc.)

Electron Microscope

The electron microscope is a modified and enlarged cathode-ray tube for magnifying minute objects. The optical form of microscope is limited in its effective resolving power by the wavelength of visible light to about 1000 diameters. With ultraviolet light the effective resolving power can be increased to 1500 diameters. Electrons have wave properties which permit them to be used to give resolving power fifty times as great as for light rays.

The first American commercial model of an electron microscope was designed and built by Zworykin and Morton in 1940. The principle of operation of this new device in comparison with an optical microscope is illustrated in Fig. 22. In the light microscope (a of the figure), light rays from a lamp are formed into a parallel beam and directed on a specimen S by the condenser lens L_1. The image of the specimen then falls on the objective lens L_2 which focuses and magnifies it, producing an enlarged image I_1. Part of this enlarged

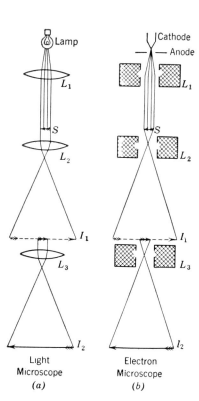

Fig. 22. Comparison of an optical and electron-microscope lens system.

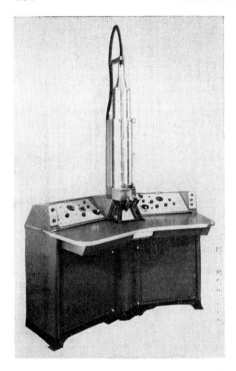

Fig. 23. Electron microscope. (Courtesy Radio Corporation of America.)

image is further magnified by the projector lens L_3. The twice-enlarged image I_2 is seen by the eye.

In the electron microscope (b of Fig. 22), the source of action is a hot cathode which emits electrons. Beneath the cathode there is an electron gun and anode which gives the electrons a high velocity downward. A coil or solenoid L_1 produces a magnetic field which has a focusing action and bends the paths of these electrons into a parallel beam directed on the specimen S. The electrons in the beam are affected in a varying degree, depending on the density of different parts of the specimen. Those that pass through are brought to a focus by the field of a second coil L_2 and form an enlarged image I_1. The electron rays that form a section of this image are in turn deflected and magnified by the field of a third coil L_3 and caused to form a larger image I_2. Since this image I_2 is formed by an electron beam, it is not visible. Accordingly, a fluorescent screen is placed so that the electron beam falling on it produces a visible image. If a directly viewable image is not desired, a photographic film is used in place of the fluorescent screen.

A commercial model of an electron microscope is shown in Fig. 23. It is capable of making magnifications varying from 1400 up to 50,000 diameters via direct viewing. In many cases the picture (negatives) may be given a useful photographic enlargement up to 300,000 diameters. Greater enlargement does not furnish any additional or useful information. A picture taken with the electron microscope showing a total magnification of 94,000 diameters is shown in Fig. 24. The maximum magnification of this latest microscope is such that if we could see an entire dime it would be more than two miles in diameter. Many of the larger molecules are now visible for study.

The cathode-ray chamber of the electron microscope must have a high vacuum when in operation. Since the test specimen and photographic plates and films must be inserted and removed via ports in the chamber, a permanently sealed tube cannot be employed. Therefore the vacuum in the microscope column is created by an oil-diffusion pump. Pumping down to an operating vacuum of approximately 10^{-6} mm of mercury requires from one and one-half to two

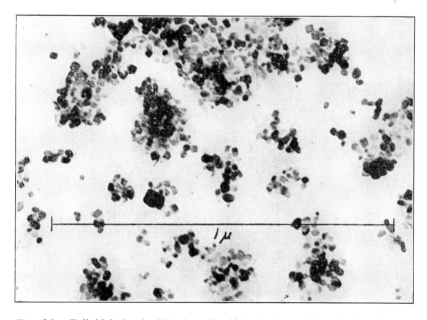

Fig. 24. Colloidal titania (titanium dioxide) photographed with the electron microscope and enlarged to 94,000 diameters. (Courtesy Radio Corporation of America.)

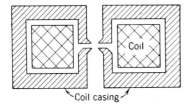

Coil

Coil casing

Fig. 25. Cross section of a magnetic focusing lens.

minutes. The specimen is placed in the vacuum chamber near the top of the column and the cover to this opening is held closed by the vacuum. Since electrons will not penetrate glass, the specimen holder consists of a film of nitrocellulose 1/1,000,000 cm thick held on a fine wire mesh. The photographic film is inserted into the vacuum column by a gate within easy reach of the operator. The microscope column, the oil-diffusion pump, and the power supply are built into a single cabinet as shown in Fig. 23. The voltage regulator and the mechanical first-stage pump are separate and can be located in another room.

The magnetic flux lenses in the electron microscope consist of iron-encased coils. The iron casing for the coils has an air gap on the inside so shaped as to give flux paths at the center of the coil which will deflect the electron in the desired directions (see Fig. 4). A suggestion of the construction is given in Fig. 25. The magnification secured in the electron microscope can be controlled by variation of the current in the magnetic lens coils and by variation of the velocity created by the electron gun.

The electron microscope can be used as an electron diffraction camera. This application requires the removal of the specimen from the upper chamber and its insertion in the lower chamber which is in the position of L_3 in Fig. 22. The diffraction pattern is photographed in the same manner and position as for magnified images.

The introduction of the electron microscope has opened a large field in scientific and industrial research. It has made possible the study of the structure of bacteria and virus not discernible by the optical microscope and the study of minute particles of matter in the fields of chemistry, metallurgy, botany, and food products.

Stroboscope

The stroboscope is an instrument for studying or observing a periodic or varying motion by means of light periodically interrupted. Such an instrument comprises a luminous-arc discharge tube containing gas or vapor which is caused to flash by periodic transient currents. If a rotating shaft, wheel, or gear is given a flash of light once for each revolution it will appear to be at rest, or if the flashes occur at $1/n$th of its revolutions it will appear likewise to be stationary. Again, if the period of the flashes is slightly more than the period of the revolutions, the device will appear to be turning forward slowly at a speed determined by the difference in time of the flashes and period of one revolution. Similarly, a flash period less than a revolution period will give the illusion of a slow backward motion.

This phenomenon of the stroboscope has useful applications, chief among which is the measurement of speed. When the rotating machine appears at rest, the rate of flashing is the same or a submultiple of the speed, and if the flashing rate is adjustable and calibrated the stroboscope becomes a tachometer. A commercial device known as a Strobotac built for speed measurement is shown in Fig. 26. This instrument has a calibrated dial and gives an accuracy of ±1 per cent of the dial for readings above 900 rpm when the Strobotac is standardized in terms of a frequency-controlled power line. The advantages of this type of speed measurement are that (1) no power is absorbed from the mechanism and (2) it can be used to measure the speed of machine elements inaccessible to ordinary tachometers. Thus speeds may be determined for small electric motors and delicate mechanisms which would slow down or stop if minute amounts of power were drawn from them. Likewise, the speeds of inaccessible gears or wheels in a complicated mechanism may be obtained. A

Fig. 26. A commercial form of stroboscope called a Strobotac. (Courtesy General Radio Company.)

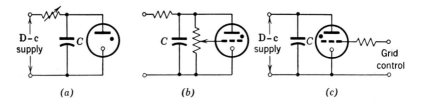

Fig. 27.   Control circuits for flash bulbs.

second important application of the stroboscope is the slow-motion
study of high-speed motion for determining vibration, tension, chattering, whip, and other irregularities that may be present in rotating
and repetitive forms of motion.   Thus mechanical defects and
troubles may be located and remedied in many kinds of industrial
machines.

Several different tubes and circuits may be employed in designing
a stroboscope.   The particular tube or circuit chosen will depend
upon the amount of light desired, the period of the flash, the application, the cost, and other factors.   Theoretically, any cold-cathode
gaseous or vapor tube may be employed.   For low brilliance of light
a small neon glow lamp (see page 181) may suffice or the firing of
a thyratron gives some light.   Long-column gaseous and mercury-
pool and mercury-vapor tubes are often employed.   The most widely
used tube for stroboscopic applications is the strobotron which was
shown in Fig. 29 in Chapter 7.   This tube was developed at the
Massachusetts Institute of Technology by Edgerton and Germeshausen.   The special features of this tube are that it operates at
a relatively low voltage, conducts a very high peak current of short
duration, giving a very brilliant flash, and is easily controlled through
two grid electrodes.

Three simple types of circuits for the operation of a stroboscope
are suggested in Fig. 27.   In all these and other circuits a large capacitor C is needed to supply a heavy discharge current and to give
a brilliant and quick flash.   The circuit of (a) is a relaxation oscillator circuit using a two-electrode gaseous tube.   The flashing period
may be adjusted by the variable resistor which controls the time for
the capacitor to charge up to the breakdown potential of the tube.
Part (b) of Fig. 27 suggests the use of a self-exciting grid control
for initiating the breakdown of the flash tube.   All present-day applications use a flash tube with an internal or external grid for initiating

the firing because of the relatively high breakdown potential between the cold cathode and anode. The circuit of part (*c*), Fig. 27, suggests some form of external grid control. Such grid control may be produced by a mechanical contactor located on the machine which is being studied by stroboscopic light. In other cases the grid control may be effected by an auxiliary oscillator or timing circuit.

High-Speed Photography

High-speed photography is the art of taking pictures of high-speed motion by using brilliant flashes of light of a few microseconds' duration. This new art has been made possible by investigations and developments of Edgerton and Germeshausen. High-speed photography utilizes the general principles discussed under the stroboscope but requires more brilliant flashes of shorter time duration. One commercial form of a flash lamp for high-speed photography is illustrated in Fig. 28. A long flash tube or column is made in a helical form in order to concentrate the light in a smaller area. The helical tube has a small diameter which gives a quick deionization time and short flash. A typical circuit for use in connection with this tube is given in Fig. 29. This circuit embodies a principle frequently employed in stroboscopes for initiating the discharge of the flash tube.

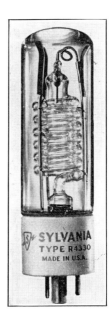

Fig. 28. Flash tube for high-speed photography. Typical operating voltage, 2250 volts; flashing rate, 6 per minute; light output peak, 12,000,000 lumens. (Courtesy Sylvania Electric Products, Inc.)

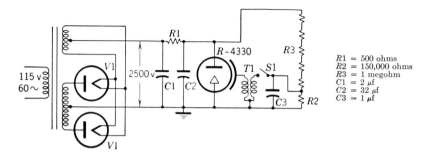

Fig. 29. Circuit for a photoflash operation.

Fig. 30. Multiflash photograph showing the pattern made by a golf club as it moves through the stroke. (Courtesy H. E. Edgerton.)

The principle utilizes an ignition type of transformer for impressing a high transient voltage across the grid. In the lower right-hand corner of Fig. 29 a capacitor $C3$ is charged to the potential across resistor $R2$. The closing of switch $S1$ permits $C3$ to discharge through the primary of transformer $T1$ which, in turn, induces a high voltage (approximately 10,000 volts) between the grid and the cold cathode of the flash tube. This transient initiates cold-cathode emission and capacitor $C2$ discharges through the flash tube.

High-speed photography is employed in research to study the conditions taking place in explosions, destruction of equipment by projectiles, projectiles in flight, and other transient phenomena. In some cases a rapid series of flashes is used to show changes and to determine the velocity of projectiles and other moving objects. An excellent photograph of this type is shown in Fig. 30.

Vacuum-Tube Voltmeters

Commercial voltmeters of the D'Arsonval electrodynamometer and iron vane types are useful for measuring electric potentials on electric power circuits and equipment. For measurements on electronic circuits, communication equipment, and many forms of research apparatus, these instruments require too much power for their operation and are entirely unsatisfactory. For these latter applications a potential measuring instrument is required which (1) takes nearly zero power, (2) has very high sensitivity, and (3) has stable operation (zero drift). Vacuum-tube voltmeters meet these requirements. Essentially, a vacuum-tube voltmeter is an amplifier having one to several stages of amplification and having a very high input impedance. In addition, this instrument should be stable in the sense that its accuracy is little affected by minor variations in power supply voltage, cathode emission, and stray fields.

For direct voltage measurement a balanced-bridge type of circuit such as shown in Fig. 31 is often employed. This circuit is almost identical with the long-tailed pair shown on page 279 and much of the explanation given for that figure applies to this one also. The important features of these balanced bridge circuits are (1) the balanced bridge arms tend to compensate for slight changes in power supply voltage, (2) with the cathode heaters in series emission changes in the two arms are equal, and (3) stray fields are likely to have the same effect on the input of both tubes. The "zero set" on the potentiometer gives the zero adjustment on the meter when zero potential is applied to the input. The RC filter input to the grid

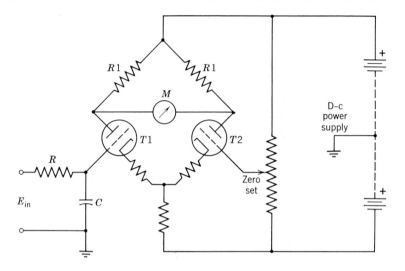

Fig. 31.   D-c vacuum-tube voltmeter bridge circuit.

of tube $T1$ filters out any possible a-c component in the applied
potential.   The grid input impedance to tube $T1$ is very high.

Vacuum-tube voltmeters are usually designed to measure relatively
low voltages in the range of microvolts and millivolts.   To read high
voltages, voltage multipliers must be employed.   These multipliers
are voltage dividers of the types shown in Fig. 32.   They have total
resistances of several megohms in order to meet the requirement of
high input impedances.   The simple potential divider of Fig. 32a is
satisfactory for d-c measurement, but for a-c measurement the circuit

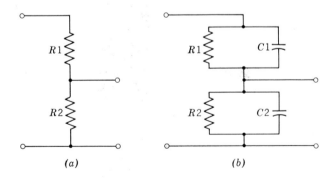

Fig. 32.   Potential dividers for vacuum-tube voltmeters.

of Fig. 32*b* is necessary to compensate for different frequencies of
alternating current being measured. For compensation at all frequencies $R1C1$ should equal $R2C2$.

The vacuum-tube voltmeters for a-c measurement require more
complex circuits to compensate for variations in frequency and wave
form and also require that the amplified voltage be rectified and then
measured by a d-c instrument (a-c meters are relatively insensitive).
The block diagram of one form of a-c vacuum-tube voltmeter is
shown in Fig. 33. Tracing this diagram from left to right, we find
the following steps in operation for the measurement of an a-c potential. The first step is a compensated voltage divider of the type
shown in Fig. 32*b*. The second step is a cathode follower circuit.
The object of this step is to provide a high input impedance for step
one and a constant input impedance for the amplifier stages. The
third or amplifier step consists of four amplifier stages in cascade.
The first three stages are voltage amplifiers and the fourth or last
is a current stage. The fourth step or the load on the current amplifier stage is a bridge rectifier with a d-c indicating meter in the
bridge arm. The over-all gain of this four-stage amplifier is the
product of the gains of the individual stages. One of the important
features of this circuit is the feedback from the last amplifier stage
to the first. This is the stabilizing factor which causes the over-all
gain factor of the cascade amplifier to remain constant. The theory

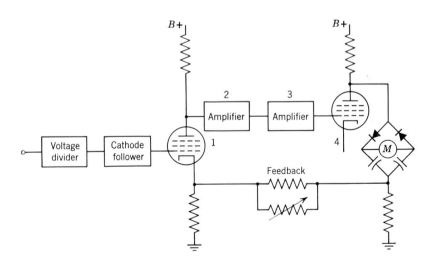

Fig. 33.   Block diagram of a-c vacuum-tube voltmeter.

of the negative feedback was covered in Chapter 9 on amplifiers and oscillators.

Vacuum-tube voltmeters are employed to read direct voltages and alternating voltages of various wave forms, including pulse signals. The wave form to be measured, such as sine, peak, peak-to-peak, and so forth, governs the circuitry employed to obtain the desired result.

Sound-Level Meter

A sound-level meter or noise meter is basically a vacuum-tube voltmeter calibrated to read sound levels. The sensor or pickup for the sound is a microphone plus the necessary auxiliary circuit. Unfortunately, the sensitivity of the human ear to loudness varies with the frequency of sound, being relatively low at both low and high frequencies. Also, the sensitivity of the human ear varies with the degree of loudness present. Since the microphone gives a response proportional to the physical amplitude of the sound waves, it is necessary to introduce compensation in the input circuit to match the characteristic response of the human ear. Such compensation is attained by the use of attenuators which reduce the physical electrical input to the amplifier to match the characteristics of the human ear.

Electronic Electrometer

The true electrometer is inherently an electrostatic instrument of which the gold-leaf electroscope is an example. This type of instrument is an electromechanical device which measures a charge and, with suitable auxiliary circuitry, may be employed to measure other quantities. The electronic electrometer performs the same functions as the gold-leaf model, but in the principle of operation it is similar to the vacuum-tube voltmeter. Inherently the electronic electrometer is a current-measuring device, whereas the vacuum-tube voltmeter is a potential indicating instrument. Both instruments use the vacuum tube as the basic electronic device. The important difference between these instruments lies in their input resistance. The vacuum-tube voltmeter has an input resistance 10 to 20 meg, and the electrometer input resistance may be of the order of 10^{10} meg. This extremely high input resistance permits the measurement of minute currents such as the 10^{-10} μa levels produced in gas ionized by radioactivity. It also permits the measurement of voltages under conditions requiring only the minutest current drain.

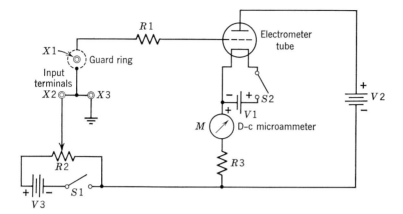

Fig. 34. Typical vacuum-tube electrometer circuit. (Courtesy Aerovox Corporation.)

A typical skeleton circuit for a vacuum-tube electrometer is shown in Fig. 34. The circuit is battery-operated. $V1$ is the filament battery, $V2$ the plate battery, and $V3$ the bucking battery for zero setting. The high input terminal is provided with a guard ring and all other parts of the circuitry are provided with extreme insulation. The indicating d-c microammeter is connected in the cathode return circuit in series with the resistor $R3$ which is kept high in value for maximum degeneration. The instrument is set to zero by means of potentiometer $R2$ and the bucking battery $V3$.

The input terminals are X_1 and X_2. X_1 is connected to $R1$ and the guard ring is grounded at X_3.

A special electrometer amplifying tube must be employed in this circuit since standard tubes have input (grid-cathode) resistance far too low. These special tubes have good evacuation and operate at low plate voltage to prevent ionization of any residual gas. They are also operated at low filament voltage and current, and some types contain an internal shield to isolate the control grid from positive ions. As employed in the electrometer, the tube is darkened to prevent spurious photoelectric effects, its envelope is washed carefully with grease-removing solvent, and the outer surface of the envelope may be coated with a high quality insulating material for additional protection against contamination from accidental touching or from the atmosphere.

The vacuum-tube electrometer usually is provided with several ranges. Range switching is accomplished by changing simultaneously the values of voltages $V1$, $V2$ (and sometimes $V3$), and resistor $R3$. A portion of $R3$ is made adjustable for range calibration. The scale of meter M may be calibrated to read directly in volts. Resistor $R1$ is a current-limiting component, the purpose of which is to limit tube input current when excessive signal voltages are applied.

The applications of the vacuum-tube electrometer lie in the measurement of minute currents and voltages. A very high resistance shunt placed across the input terminals permits the measurement of minute currents in the range of micromicroamperes. Examples of such measurement are (1) the dark current in a phototube, (2) the leakage current in a sample of an insulator, (3) the current in an ion chamber, (4) vacuum-tube grid currents, (5) currents in dimly lighted photocells, and (6) surface leakage on insulators.

Photoelectric Pyrometer

The photoelectric pyrometer is a radiant-energy-responsive device for indicating or recording the temperature of incandescent bodies. The radiant energy from a hot body is directed to a phototube and causes it to pass a current which bears a definite relation to the temperature of the hot body. This current is amplified by an extremely stable vacuum-tube amplifier and the amplified current is passed through an indicating or a recording instrument. The principal feature of this pyrometer is that it provides, without appreciable time lag, a continuous indication or record of the temperature of incandescent bodies.

A heated metal as it approaches its melting point passes through progressive stages in which it has an initial color of red which changes to orange, yellow, and finally white. With an increase in temperature the amount of radiant energy increases exponentially. Phototubes are sensitive to radiant energy throughout the visible spectrum though the response varies as discussed in Chapter 5 (see Fig. 48). The relation between the phototube response and the temperature is a very steep one in the spectrum range for incandescent bodies. For example, the phototube response to a temperature of 2150° F is approximately ten times that for a temperature of 1700° F, or, for a smaller temperature range, a change from 1800° F to 1850° F causes an increase in phototube response of 32.8 per cent. From this relationship it is obvious that a milliammeter could be calibrated to indicate the temperature of an incandescent body provided that a stable circuit and amplifier system is used. A vacuum-type photo-tube with a cesium-oxygen-silver cathode is employed to utilize through a suitable optical system the radiant energy from a specific area of the incandescent body.

A photoelectric pyrometer may employ the schematic circuit shown in the full-line diagram of Fig. 35. A constant voltage applied on the left of the diagram is provided by the conventional power pack plus a voltage-regulator tube circuit. A phototube *PT* and a resistor *R2* act as a potential divider to control the bias on the control grid of the pentode tube 1. The potentiometer *P1* is adjusted to hold the cathode of the pentode at a higher potential than its grid. As the radiant energy from the hot body rises, the phototube conducts an increasing current which raises the drop across *R2* and the potential

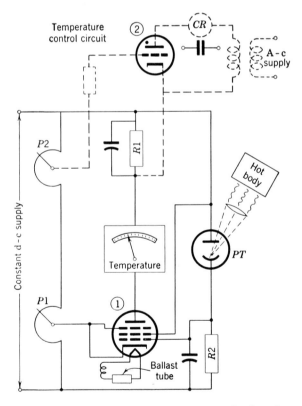

Fig. 35. Schematic diagram of a phototube pyrometer circuit and control equipment.

of the control grid of the pentode. This rise in grid potential controls the cathode-plate current of the pentode which, in turn, operates the temperature-indicating milliammeter. The temperature-indicating meter may be placed at a distance of 50 ft from the control panel. If a record of the temperature is desired, a graphic recording meter may be substituted for the indicating meter.

A production process involving incandescent metals may require an audible signal when a certain temperature is reached or it may require some control of action to take place when one or more temperatures are reached. Such control may be accomplished by the addition of the temperature-control circuit (dotted) of Fig. 35. This additional circuit employs a thyratron 2 and a control relay CR in an a-c supply circuit. The potential of the cathode of the thyratron is determined by the drop of potential across resistor $R1$, and the grid potential is governed by the setting of potentiometer $P2$. Thus $P2$ is set to fire the thyratron at the desired temperature. If control operations are desired at more than one temperature, more control circuits like the dotted lines of Fig. 35 are added and potentiometers corresponding to $P2$ are set for the desired temperatures of action.

Photoelectric pyrometers are used in steel mills to indicate the temperature of steel billets before they enter the process for making seamless tubes, lap welding steel tubes, or rolling structural shapes. The proper temperature of the steel billets coming from different furnaces assures a more uniform product with less spoilage. Similarly, a photoelectric pyrometer control has been used on a spinning machine for making cast-iron pipe by the centrifugal sand-spun process. The pyrometer indicates the temperature inside the pipe and a supplementary control stops the spinning motor when the proper temperature is reached. In another application the temperature of the cement clinker in the kiln of a cement mill is indicated and auxiliary controls regulate the temperature by governing the speed of rotation of the kiln.

Radioactive Measurements

Radioactive materials disintegrate slowly giving off alpha, beta, and gamma rays. Alpha particles are helium ions carrying a double positive charge, beta particles are electrons, and gamma rays are high-frequency electromagnetic waves (not particles). X rays are high-frequency waves produced artificially and lying just below the gamma ray spectrum. All these forms of radiant energy leave a trail of ionized atoms (ions) when they pass through a gas. If these ions are counted, we have a measure of radioactivity. Such measurements are very important today in our search for uranium ores and in our studies of the effects of atomic and hydrogen bomb explosions.

All the forms of radiant energy have the power of penetrating solids and liquids. Measurements of the transmission of beta particles, gamma waves, or X rays may be employed to determine the thickness of solids and the specific gravity of liquids. Gamma and X rays falling on a solid surface are partially reflected and the amount of reflection depends on the material thickness. Thus the determination of the reflection of radiant energy provides another method of measuring thickness of solids. These basic methods of determining thickness of solids by the use of radioactive energy are important because they do not involve any destruction or weakening of the material.

There are two basic forms of detectors or sensors for radiant energy—ionization chambers and photomultiplier tubes having a phosphor-coated input window. The ionization chamber is a small gas-filled tube containing two electrodes. The electrodes may consist of two parallel plates or the envelope may be a thin metal tube (cathode) having a concentric central rod (anode), as shown in Fig. 36. The action taking place within the tube depends on the magnitude of the voltage applied to the electrodes. The radiant energy entering the tube produces primary electrons and + ions. For relatively low potentials of the order of 100 volts, the primary particles are attracted to the electrode of opposite charge and constitute a minute current. This current may be amplified by an electrometer and thus provide a measurement of radiation. When used in this manner, the device is called an ionization chamber and is well adapted for measuring alpha radiation.

If a higher voltage of the order of 800 to 1500 is applied to the tube of Fig. 36, the theory of action is greatly changed and the

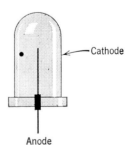

Fig. 36. Construction of an ionization chamber or a Geiger tube.

chamber functions as a Geiger-Muller tube. Now the electrons moving in the strong electric field produce new and cumulative ionizations in accordance with the avalanche effects previously described for the Townsend discharge on page 172. For this situation any radiation, particularly gamma radiation, causes the tube to break down into a self-sustaining discharge. In order to stop this discharge some form of quenching action must be employed. One method is semichemical, wherein an alcohol vapor is introduced into the tube which serves to stop the discharge. The second method is electrical, wherein the rise in current is employed to lower momentarily the anode voltage below the ionizing potential. As a result, the output of the Geiger tube is a series of pulses which is proportional to the incident radiation. These pulses may be counted by amplifying them and passing them directly to a digital counting circuit. A second method of counting (adding) employs an amplifier with a relatively long time RC circuit and a capacitor in the output which permits the integration of the individual pulses and provides a direct reading on a d-c indicating instrument (see Fig. 37).

A scintillation counter is a combination of a special photomultiplier tube, an amplifier, and a count indicator, as suggested in the block diagram of Fig. 38. The photomultiplier tube may have the construction shown in Fig. 53, page 162. Its window consists of a transparent phosphor made of crystals which have the property of fluorescence. These crystals absorb some of the energy of incident electrons, ions, gamma rays, X rays, and so forth, and re-emit as light flashes or scintillations. The energy of the light flashes is transmitted to the photocathode, transformed to photoelectrons, and then multiplied. With the proper choice of phosphors it is possible to encourage the detection of one type of radiation and reject other types. The principle of the scintillation counter is the basis for a

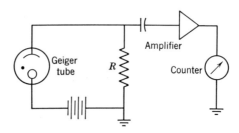

Fig. 37. Simplified Geiger counter circuit.

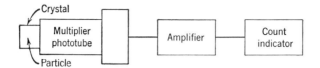

Fig. 38. Block diagram of a scintillation counter. (Courtesy Allen B. DuMont Laboratories, Inc.)

series of instruments used in research and industry. One form of instrument permits aerial surveys for radioactive ores over rugged terrain with large savings in the labor and time that would be needed for ground searches with detection instruments. In transmitting various grades of oil and fuel over a common pipeline, a radioactive chemical is introduced when a change is made in the product being pumped. When this chemical arrives at a distribution station hundreds or thousands of miles away, it is detected immediately by scintillation detection equipment.

An important application of the scintillation counter is the determination of the intensity of X rays in industrial and medical use. With the proper fluorescent screen (for example, activated zinc sulfide or calcium tungate) applied to the photocathode window of the photomultiplier tube and a circuit to measure the output current, the intensity of a variable radiation level can be measured.

Two commercial multiplier phototubes for scintillation counters are shown in Fig. 39. The tube on the left has a large photocathode area and a focusing shield.

In recent years the Atomic Energy Commission has made radioactive isotopes available for commercial application. These small and powerful sources of gamma ray radiation have resulted in many designs of measuring and detection equipment. Two examples will be considered here for illustrative purposes. The principle for measuring the thickness of metal or other plates is shown in Fig. 40. The

Fig. 39. Commercial multiplier phototube for scintillation counting. (Courtesy Allen B. DuMont Laboratories, Inc.)

shaded layers numbered 1, 2, and 3 represent adjacent layers of a homogeneous wall, the thickness of which is to be measured. Penetrating gamma rays emerge from a radioactive source. These rays impinge on the wall and penetrate into it. A portion of the rays passes through the wall and emerges on the opposite side and thus they serve no useful purpose. Another portion of the radiation is scattered by the electrons and atoms which constitute the wall. Some of these scattered rays emerge on the same side of the wall from which they originally entered. This portion of the radiation, termed back-scattered radiation, is utilized for measuring the thickness of the wall. The triangular lead shield prevents any direct radiation from the source in reaching the Geiger tube detector. This detector is also shielded on the outside by a lead sheath which has a window at the bottom to admit the reflected radiation. A preamplifier or first stage of amplification is located at the rear of the detector head. The radiation picked up by the detector creates characteristic current discharges which are amplified and integrated to produce a direct current for measurement by an indicating microammeter.

In order to convert the reading of the microammeter into wall thickness in inches, the instrument is calibrated on specimens of tubing and flat plates having known wall thicknesses, and from these data calibration curves are derived.

A second detector for determining the thickness of the walls of pipe for gas and oil pipelines is shown in Fig. 41. Here the gamma rays from the source are permitted to pass through the wall of the pipe. The principle of detection, amplification, and integration of the transmitted waves is the same as for the preceding illustration.

The liquid level in oil and gasoline tanks may be determined by

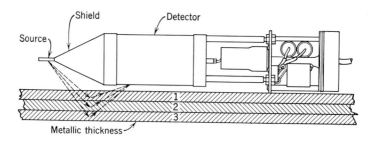

Fig. 40. The Penetron. (Courtesy United Engineers, Inc.)

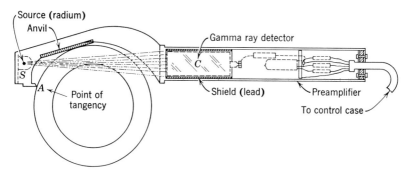

Fig. 41. Principle of measurement-penetron tangential head. (Courtesy United Engineers, Inc.)

placing radioactive material in a guided float near the wall of the tank. Then a detector probe and circuit is moved vertically outside the tank to detect the liquid level.

PROBLEMS

1. In a cathode-ray tube employing electrostatic deflection, the accelerating potential (to deflection plates) is 6000 volts, the effective deflecting potential is 300 volts, and the distance from the center of the deflection plates to the screen is 1 ft. Calculate (a) the angle of deflection, (b) the deflection on the screen in inches, and (c) the sensitivity in inches per volt.

2. In a cathode-ray tube employing electrostatic deflection, the axial length of the deflection plates is 1 in. These plates have a separation of 0.4 in. and their center is 8 in. from the screen. If the accelerating potential is 5000 volts and a continuous potential of 500 volts is applied between the plates, what is the angle of deflection and what is the deflection on the screen in inches?

3. In a cathode-ray tube employing magnetic deflection the accelerating potential is 8000 volts, the distance from the center of the lens to screen is 20 cm, and the assumed flux density is 50 gauss (uniform) over a lens length of 2 cm. Calculate (a) the angle of deflection, (b) the deflection on the screen in centimeters, and (c) the magnetic sensitivity in meters per weber. (Use MKS system.)

4. If the magnetic sensitivity in a cathode-ray tube is 400, the accelerating potential 7000 volts, the distance from lens to screen is 25 cm and the effective length of the lens is 4 cm, what is the value of the uniform flux density B in webers?

REFERENCES

1. Zworykin, V. K., G. A. Morton, E. G. Ramberg, J. Hillier, and A. W. Vance, *Electron Optics and the Electron Microscope,* John Wiley and Sons, New York, 1945.
2. Germeshausen, K. J., and H. E. Edgerton, *Elec. Eng.,* **55,** 709 (1936).
3. "Applications of the Electrometer," *The Aerovox Research Worker,* July–August 1954.
4. Clapp, C. W., and S. Bernstein, "Thickness Gaging by Radiation Absorption Methods," *Gen. Elec. Rev.,* November 1950.
5. Partridge, Gordon R., *Principles of Electronic Instruments,* Prentice-Hall, Englewood Cliffs, N. J., 1958.

chapter 18

Principles of

Electronic

Computers

Introduction

A computer is a combination of devices which serves to make mathematical calculations or to find solutions to various types of problems. Computers may utilize mechanical devices, electrical devices, and components, or electronic devices and circuits. They may also employ combinations of all of them. The conventional adding machine or calculator is a computer with which everyone is familiar. It employs mechanical parts only and is not the type considered in this chapter.

Electronic computers are those which rely upon a multiplicity of electronic devices and circuits for performing their principal functions. They may use electrical and mechanical units for auxiliaries. There are two classes of electronic computers—analog and digital. The direct-current analog computer is best suited for solving problems involving continuous varying quantities and differential equations. It is built around the d-c amplifier as the principal component. The accuracy of its solutions is limited by the degree of precision of its components and the characteristics of its electron tubes and circuits. Its accuracy may lie in the range of 0.1 per cent to 10 per cent. The digital computer employs the principle of counting units or digits, and hence, if properly guided, gives answers which have a high degree of accuracy.

Electronic computers are very complex equipments. A complete discussion of the history, construction, theory, and operation of any one type of electronic computer requires from one to several books. Obviously, it is impossible to condense much of this vast information within the realm of a single chapter. The author aims to present merely a short survey of the functions, electronic components, and applications of the two classes of electronic computers.

Analog Computers

The analog computer may be used to add, subtract, multiply, divide, integrate, and differentiate. Its most useful application lies in the solution of problems involving differential equations. Early analog computers used mechanical systems, but all present-day designs are of the d-c analog type (electronic). Problems are solved on the computer by simulating the magnitudes of physical units by voltages. Thus physical constants or variables are represented by voltages and as such are added, multiplied, integrated, and so forth, via a sequential combination of components on the analog computer. This system of substituting electrical equivalents for variables and physical quantities in the solution of problems gives rise to the term "analog."

The components employed in analog computers are resistors, capacitors, diodes, and d-c amplifiers. The d-c amplifier was discussed on page 275 and two basic circuits for a two-stage unit are shown in Fig. 1. In the circuit of part (a) of this figure, the voltage of the

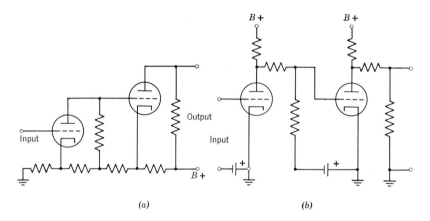

(a)   (b)

Fig. 1. Circuits for a d-c amplifier.

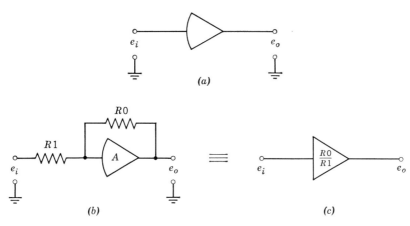

Fig. 2. (*a*) Symbol for d-c amplifier. (*b*) Circuit for multiplication. (*c*) Block diagram of (*b*).

cathode rises above ground as we advance in the stages of a cascade amplifier, so that relatively high potentials are involved if several stages are employed. The disadvantage of such high voltage may be overcome in the alternate circuit of Fig. 1*b*. Here the same plate supply potential may be used for all amplifying tubes. D-c cascade amplifiers are subject to the problem of drift. This is the slow change in the magnitude of the output signal of a cascaded unit. It arises from changes in both emission from cathodes and power supply voltages. These minute changes are amplified in the succeeding stages of the amplifier and may assume large magnitudes. The magnitude of drift is minimized by compensation in the feedback circuit of the amplifier. Checking and resetting for drift are usually necessary at 30 minute intervals.

The basic symbol for any amplifier is shown in Fig. 2*a*. Since a common or ground lead is used in all amplifiers, it is sufficient to show only a one-wire diagram in symbolic and schematic block type circuits. The d-c amplifiers for analog computer circuits are usually of the feedback type. This feedback circuit is indicated by the symbol of Fig. 2*b* where a resistance is inserted in the input and a second resistance in the feedback line. The output voltage of a single-stage amplifier is 180 degrees out of phase with the input signal. Thus any single-stage amplifier is a phase inverter and reverses the sign of the input voltage signal. The equivalent block diagram for Fig. 2*b* is given in Fig. 2*c*.

Multiplication by a constant coefficient greater than one is performed in the analog computer by the basic circuit of Fig. 2b. Here the input voltage e_i is multiplied by some constant A to give the output voltage e_o ($e_o = Ae_i$). The theory of action and the mathematical relationship may be deduced as follows. The d-c amplifier is a very high gain unit (amplification factor μ may be several million). The feedback resistor has a large magnitude of the order of a megohm. The resistor $R1$ also has a large value. Let it be assumed that the grid current input to the amplifier is zero. Also because of the high amplifier gain and the low value of e_o (order of 100 volts) the potential at the grid input to the amplifier may be assumed to be *near* zero volts. With these assumptions, the current input through $R1$ should be $e_i/R1$ and in like manner the current in the feedback $R0$ should be $e_o/R0$. Now, writing Kirchhoff's current law for the point at the grid input to the amplifier and remembering the signs, we have,

$$\frac{e_i}{R1} - \left(-\frac{e_o}{R0}\right) - 0 = 0$$

or

$$\frac{e_o}{e_i} \approx -\frac{R0}{R1} = A \tag{1}$$

and

$$e_o \approx -\frac{R0}{R1}e_i \tag{2}$$

Thus this circuit serves to multiply the input e_i by the constant factor $R0/R1$, and the process requires the proper selection of the magnitudes of the resistors $R1$ and $R0$.

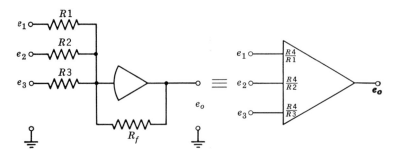

Fig. 3.   Circuit and block diagram for summation.

Fig. 4. Circuit for integration.

The addition or summation of quantities is performed by the circuit of Fig. 3. Here three quantities such as x, y, and z are represented by voltages e_1, e_2, and e_3. Assuming as previously that the current input to the grid is zero, the current in R_f should equal the sum of the currents in $R1$, $R2$, and $R3$. Then the output voltage e_o is the potential across R_f and,

$$e_o = -R_f \sum \left[\frac{e_1}{R1} + \frac{e_2}{R2} + \frac{e_3}{R3} \right] \qquad (3)$$

The integration of a variable voltage is performed by the basic circuit of Fig. 4. Here the feedback is a capacitor and the variable input is fed to a resistor. A simplified proof that the circuit integrates may be shown by the following well-known equations:

$$e_o = \frac{Q_0}{C} \quad \text{and} \quad Q_0 = \int i_0 \, dt$$

$$e_o = \frac{\int i_0 \, dt}{C} = \frac{1}{C} \int \frac{e_i}{R} \, dt = \frac{1}{RC} \int e_i \, dt \qquad (4)$$

The reverse process of differentiation is performed by an interchange of the positions of the resistor and capacitor as shown in Fig. 5. Here the input current i_i into the capacitor is:

$$i_i = \frac{dQ}{dt} = C \frac{de_i}{dt}$$

and

$$e_o = i_R R$$

Fig. 5. Circuit for differentiation.

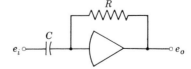

If the current input to the grid is assumed to be zero, it follows from Kirchhoff's current law that

$$i_i = i_R$$

therefore

$$e_o = i_i R \approx RC \frac{de_i}{dt} \tag{5}$$

which shows that the circuit performs differentiation.

In the solution of problems on the analog computer it is often necessary to multiply a variable by a coefficient less than one (instead of greater than one as in Fig. 2). If the coefficient is a constant, the multiplication can be performed by the use of a simple potential divider or potentiometer, as indicated in Fig. 6a. If the coefficient varies with time but always has a positive sign, the operation is implemented by a potentiometer driven by a servo motor, as suggested in Fig. 6b. Here the servo motor is driven and controlled by the incoming variable x_2. Again, if the coefficient varies both in sign and magnitude with time, a special potentiometer connected to a $+$ and $-$ potential (with respect to zero or ground) is employed as shown in Fig. 6c. Oftentimes one input variable may be a sine or cosine function. For handling these functions special potentiometers are built in which the resistance varies in a manner such that the useful voltage drop varies as the trigonometric function desired.

It is possible to build analog computing elements by using passive networks and a few computers use such elements exclusively. Examples of computing networks are shown in Fig. 7. Summation results in Fig. 7a since the voltage e_o across R_o is the result of the currents in R_1, R_2, and R_3, arising from the voltages e_1, e_2, and e_3. In Fig. 7b, the voltage e_o is the integral of the current flowing in capacitor C. And in Fig. 7c the output voltage e_o is the derivative of the input e_i.

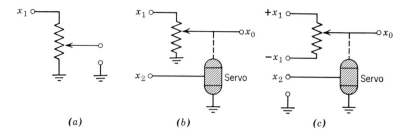

(a)   *(b)*   *(c)*

Fig. 6. Multiplication by constants or variables.

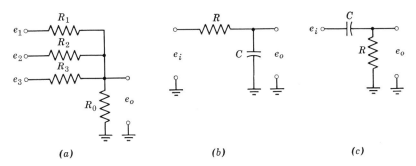

Fig. 7. Passive networks for (*a*) addition, (*b*) integration, and (*c*) differentiation.

The utility of the d-c amplifier and the other analog computer components may be illustrated by their application to the following differential equation.

$$\frac{d^2x}{dt^2} + 0.8\frac{dx}{dt} + x = 0 \tag{6}$$

Separating the highest order of differential gives

$$\frac{d^2x}{dt^2} = -\left(0.8\frac{dx}{dt} + x\right) \tag{7}$$

Equation 7 may be represented by applying the terms on the right-hand side of the equation to a summing amplifier as suggested in Fig. 8*a*. In the figure the unknown x is represented by a voltage e_i. Since the amplifier produces phase inversion as well as addition, the output is d^2e_i/dt^2. The inputs and outputs in all cases are represented by voltages.

Furthermore, if the second derivative is represented by a voltage and is applied to two integrating amplifiers in series (as shown in Fig. 8*b*), the output of the first amplifier will be a voltage representing the first derivative with a negative sign. The corresponding output of the second integrating amplifier is a voltage representing the unknown x with a positive sign. A complete picture of how the computer components may be set up to represent equation 7 is given in Fig. 8*c*. This diagram involves the use of one potentiometer (for multiplication by coefficient 0.8), one summing and integrating amplifier, one integrating amplifier, and one inverting amplifier. Figure 8*c* is suggestive of the type of circuit involved

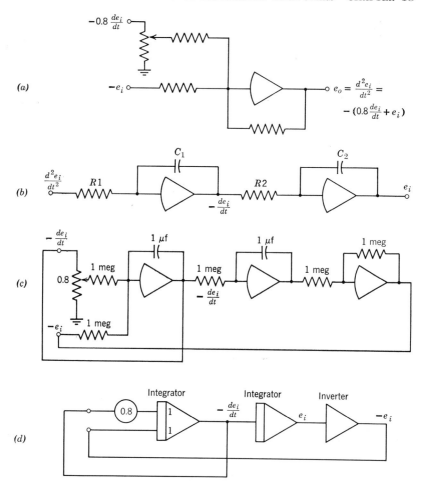

Fig. 8. Partial and complete diagrams for solving differential equations.

in the solution of problems. For actual solutions the initial conditions in a problem for time equals zero, etc., must be applied through voltage magnitudes to grids in the d-c amplifiers in order for the computer to render the proper solution. Figure 8d is the block diagram for the circuit in Fig. 8c.

The diagram of Fig. 8c shows the use of three amplifiers plus other components for the solution of a simple problem. Obviously, the solution of complicated problems will require the availability of many components. Accordingly, analog computers consist of the assembly of large numbers of individual components. For example, a complete computer might have 20 d-c amplifiers, 20 potentiometers with a sine scale, and 5 potentiometers with a cosine scale, a power supply, many resistors, and many capacitors. The d-c amplifiers are all identical and mounted adjacent to each other in panels. In like manner, other components are mounted in banks. The terminals of all components are brought out to jacks. Then the circuits for problem solutions are set up by inserting plug-ended cords in the proper jacks.

The cost and size of an analog computer depend on its usage, complexity, and required accuracy of the problems to be solved. If the computer is to be employed by only one man and for relatively simple problems, it may be built into a small cabinet and placed on a table or desk. Its cost may be a few hundred dollars. A large engineering or research group for an aviation industry where flight problems are solved may require an analog computer which fills a large room and costs hundreds of thousands of dollars.

The time required for a computer to solve a problem is likely to be measured in seconds, but the time required for the operator to set up the circuit with cords and plugs is usually a matter of hours, perhaps days. Accordingly, for large costly computers means must be provided for the computer to be in near constant service. This is accomplished by the use of patch boards which are flat panels with plugs on the under side and jacks on top. These patch boards may be plugged into the permanent jacks on the computer. Then several patch boards are provided so that each engineer or small group of engineers may set up a special circuit on the patch board. When the circuit is ready for test, the patch board is inserted in the computer and the appropriate test is made. When the test is completed, the patch board is removed, leaving the computer available for other operations via the use of setups on other patch boards.

The inputs and outputs of analog computers are frequently voltages which vary with time. These variables may be plotted in the form of curves from performance data. Special equipment is often designed to transform the curve into corresponding voltage variation. In a similar manner, special curve-drawing equipment (output recorders) may be employed to provide the solution to a problem in the form of a curve.

The two most important reasons for using analog computers are (1) to study systems in which nonlinearity plays an important role and (2) to study systems (or equations) which are so complex as to defy solution by standard computing methods.

D-c analog computers are employed in studies of automatic control systems which employ servomechanisms. They are equally useful in the computation of the trajectory of missiles. Similarly, they are employed in the design and testing of autopilots and the solution of aircraft flight equations.

Digital Computers

A digital computer is an automatic machine for solving mathematical problems and for making decisions based on mathematical calculations. The operation of the machine is based on a transfer and handling of *individual digits*. The operation is basically arithmetic and covers addition, subtraction, multiplication, and division. Although the processes of differentiation and integration cannot be handled by direct methods, they can be simulated by arithmetic methods. Some digital computers incorporate a differential analyzer which performs calculus types of solutions.

A general picture of the components and the functions of a typical digital computer is given in the block diagram of Fig. 9. In order to render a solution, all essential information must be fed into the input. This information consists of two important parts: (1) the numerical data involved in the problem and (2) the coded directions of what should be done with the data. These combined data are passed immediately to the central memory unit where each part of the information is stored in separate locations in equipments which

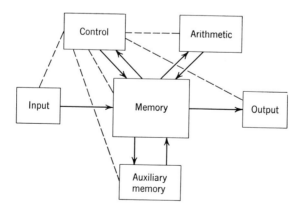

Fig. 9. Functional block diagram of a digital computer.

employ mercury delay tanks, electrostatic storage, or magnetic storage. The memory unit is the heart of the digital computer. It stores the information received initially from the input and later from other functional components and passes this information on at appropriate times during the computing process. After all the necessary information is stored in the memory unit and after the human operator pushes the button for starting the automatic solution of the problem, the control component takes over and directs all further functioning of the computer. The control unit obtains its direction from numerical codes which are stored in the memory. It interprets these codes in the proper sequence and directs the operations for the entire machine.

As a simple illustration, if the interpreted code called for the addition of two numbers, the control unit sends a signal back to the memory unit to pass the stored numbers to the arithmetic component. These numbers will be stored temporarily in registers in the arithmetic unit. Next the control unit signals (dotted line) the arithmetic unit to add the numbers, and after the addition to return the result to the memory unit. If this simple addition constituted the total steps in problem solution, the control unit would then direct the memory component to pass the result to the output. However, the usual computer problem involves many arithmetic solutions before the final result can be passed to the output. Some problems involve the use of more data than can be accommodated in the usual memory unit. Therefore it is common practice to provide an auxiliary storage unit where the data overflow may be placed.

The operation of the digital computer is based on the handling of digits and numbers. The reader is accustomed to work with numbers in the decimal system that uses the digits 0, 1, 2, 3, 4, 5, 6, 7, 8, and 9. In analyzing any number such as 4444, we know that the second 4 from the right has 10 times the value of the same digit (4) to the right of it. Similarly, the third 4 from the right has 10 times the value of the like 4 to its right. Thus each digit in any number has 10 times the value of a like digit on its right, and we say this system of numbering is the decimal system. The number 4444 may also be written

$$4 \times 1000 = 4 \times 10^3$$
$$4 \times 100 \ = 4 \times 10^2$$
$$4 \times 10 \ \ = 4 \times 10^1$$
$$4 \times 1 \ \ \ = 4 \times 10^0$$
$$\qquad\qquad = (4444)_{10}$$

The preceding table emphasizes that our standard numbering system is based on the scale of 10 (the decimal scale). It is probable that man adopted the decimal scale as a base for numbering because he has 10 fingers and 10 toes. Other bases for numbering may be used, however. Let us select 8, 5, 3, and 2 for bases and apply them to the decimal number 433.

$$(433)_{10} = 6 \times 8^2 + 6 \times 8^1 + 1 \times 8^0 = (661)_8 \tag{8}$$

$$= 3 \times 5^3 + 2 \times 5^2 + 1 \times 5^1 + 3 \times 5^0 = (3213)_5 \tag{9}$$

$$= 1 \times 3^5 + 2 \times 3^4 + 1 \times 3^3 + 0 \times 3^2 + 0 \times 3^1$$
$$+ 1 \times 3^0 = (121001)_3 \tag{10}$$

$$= 1 \times 2^8 + 1 \times 2^7 + 0 \times 2^6 + 1 \times 2^5 + 1 \times 2^4 + 0 \times 2^3$$
$$+ 0 \times 2^2 + 0 \times 2^1 + 1 \times 2^0 = (110110001)_2 \tag{11}$$

The last number system used (equation 11) has the base of two and is called the binary number system. It is noted that the resulting number contains only ones and zeros. It also follows that any number whatever can be represented in the binary system by a series of *ones* and *zeros*. Therefore it is apparent that if numbers are converted to the binary base, they may be transmitted or stored by two simple signals to represent a one or a zero. Such signals may be merely positive pulses of voltage sent at regular time intervals. Each binary digit is considered as a "bit." A voltage pulse at one time interval may mean a one and the absence of a pulse at a time interval means a zero. These time generated pulses may be applied to very simple electronic circuits to produce the desired operations for computing purposes. The application of this principle to the transmission of the decimal number 433 is illustrated in Fig. 10. A total of nine time intervals is required to transmit the number. The time intervals for a train of pulses is indicated in the lower part of Fig. 10.

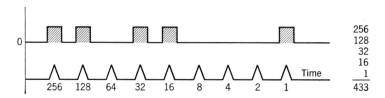

Fig. 10. Pulse wave form to indicate the number 433 in binary.

Table 1

Decimal	Binary	Decimal	Binary
0.0625	0.0001	10.	1010.
0.125	0.001	11.	1011.
0.25	0.01	12.	1100.
0.5	0.1	13.	1101.
1.0	1.0	14.	1110.
2.	10.	15.	1111.
3.	11.	16.	10000.
4.	100.	32.	100000.
5.	101.	64.	1000000.
6.	110.	100.	1100100.
7.	111.	128.	10000000.
8.	1000.	256.	100000000.
9.	1001.		

The decimal magnitude of a pulse at each position in the train is also given. Now if voltage pulses are produced as shown in the upper part of Fig. 10, the equivalent value of these binary pulses is 433 as shown by the additions at the right. A partial list of decimal values and their binary equivalents is given in Table 1.

Electronic Computer Circuits

The arithmetic or computing unit of a digital computer employs large numbers of simple electronic circuits to perform the various steps in its operation. The individual components of these circuits consist of transistors, vacuum triodes and pentodes, crystal diodes, magnetic units, resistors, and capacitors. These components are assembled into simple groupings known as "and" circuits, "or" circuits, flip-flops, inverting circuits, etc. The "AND" and "OR" type of circuits have been discussed in Chapter 15 as applied to industrial control. Schematic AND circuits for computer service are illustrated in Fig. 11. Part (a) shows the common symbol for this type of circuit. If an input signal is applied to A but not to B, there is no output O. Likewise, a signal at B but not at A produces no output. However, when input signals appear simultaneously at both A and B, there is an output signal. This characteristic of output only when all inputs are energized leads to the name of circuit AND.

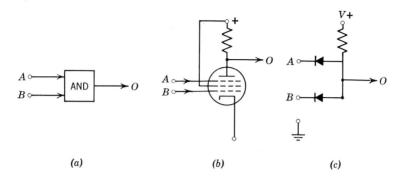

(a)   *(b)*   *(c)*

Fig. 11. Schematic "AND" circuits.

Figure 11*b* illustrates how AND operation may be produced in a simple circuit using a pentode. Normally, both inputs *A* and *B* are negative. A positive pulse applied to either *A* or *B* alone does not produce an output, but simultaneous positive pulses of appropriate magnitude on both *A* and *B* give an output. The same result can be obtained through the use of two diodes and a resistor with the simple circuit of Fig. 11*c*. Here positive pulses of voltage are applied at inputs *A* or *B*, or *A* and *B*. Normally both *A* and *B* are at zero potential and the output *O* is likewise zero. With a positive pulse of voltage at *A* only or *B* only, the output *O* remains at zero. But if a positive pulse is applied at both *A* and *B* simultaneously, the potential of the output *O* rises and the signal is passed. The AND type of circuit may have any number of inputs, two, three, four, etc., but in each case a signal is passed only when all receive a positive input potential at the same time. Circuits using the larger number of inputs require additional vacuum tubes or crystal diodes.

The OR type of computer circuit is illustrated in Fig. 12. In this case a signal is passed whenever the voltage of either *A* or *B* rises; hence the term OR. Normally the grids of both triodes of Fig. 12*b* are held negative to cutoff. Then a positive potential applied at either point *A* or *B*, or both, causes the tube(s) to conduct. A positive pulse of voltage applied at the input *A* or *B* of the crystal diodes in Fig. 12*c* will cause the voltage at *O* to rise correspondingly.

A third type of circuit used in computers is the inverter circuit or unit. It has the property of inverting any signal fed to it (that is, it changes a one to zero or a zero input to a one). This is the same function as performed by the NOT logic unit discussed in Chapter

15. The symbol for the inverter unit is a capital I in a circle. This unit should not be confused with the amplifier inverter described earlier.

A concept of how the preceding AND and OR circuits may be employed for binary addition is given in Fig. 13. Three binary unit pulse signals x, y, and z are fed into the network of AND and OR units plus one inverting unit. The two outputs consist of the SUM and the CARRY binary digits. Since there may be only one of two binary digits (one or zero) in one location at a given time, the addition of binary numbers results as follows:

$$0 + 0 = 0$$
$$0 + 1 = 1$$
$$1 + 0 = 1$$
$$1 + 1 = 0 \text{ and } 1 \text{ to carry}$$

Hence if there is a binary number other than zero in the CARRY output, it is necessary to have a second computing process to add the binary number in the CARRY to that in the SUM. One method of effecting this addition is to provide a feedback from the CARRY to the input of the adding circuit. This feedback must have a time delay of one pulse. This time delay will cause the CARRY digit to be added to the next group of binary input signals, and thereby give the correct output SUM.

The operation of the circuits and components in Fig. 13 may be illustrated by a simple example. Assume inputs x, y, and z are rep-

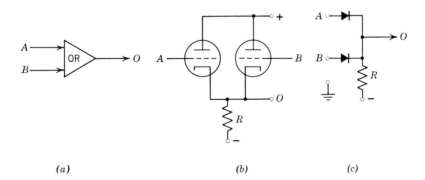

(a)   (b)   (c)

Fig. 12. Schematic "OR" circuits.

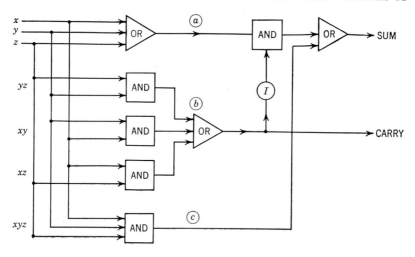

Fig. 13. Schematic of a computer adder circuit.

resented by binary impulses for the decimals 4, 5, and 6. These may
be shown in a table as follows: (Also see Table 1.)

Input	Decimal	Binary		
x	4	1	0	0
y	5	1	0	1
z	6	1	1	0
	15	1	1	1	SUM
		1	0	0	CARRY

SUM		1	1	1
CARRY	1	0	0	
BINARY	1	1	1	1

DECIMAL $= 8 + 4 + 2 + 1$
$= 15$

When the first set of binary impulses (right column in binary table
above) enters the circuit, the y impulse, which is 1, passes the first
OR component in circuit (a). Since none of the AND components
in circuits (b) or (c) are energized, no signal is passed to the CARRY
output or to the I (inverter) component. Accordingly, the input signal from y passes the AND and the second OR components and
registers in the output SUM. When the second set of inputs enters
the adder circuit, only the z input carries a pulse 1 and it registers
in the output SUM (but not in the CARRY) for the same reason
as given for the first set. Now when the third set of input impulses
arrive, all three inputs x, y, and z are energized with positive pulses
(1 s). This situation causes the first OR in circuit (a) and all the

AND components to pass outputs. The outputs of the three AND components in circuit (*b*) pass the OR component. This action registers a positive 1 pulse in the CARRY output and energizes the inverter component *I* to place a block in the AND component so that the pulse coming from the OR in circuit (*a*) does not pass. Finally, the pulse which passes the AND component of circuit (*c*) passes the upper OR component and registers in the SUM.

The preceding action has served to store a binary number 111 in the SUM and 100 in the CARRY. To obtain the total, it is necessary to add the binary numbers in the SUM and CARRY columns. This process involves shifting the CARRY column one line to the left giving the final sum 1111 which corresponds to the decimal 15.

A *flip-flop* is a bistable form of circuit widely used in computer circuits for temporary storage of signals. A simple form of flip-flop circuit and its symbol are shown in Fig. 14. It reminds one of the multivibrator circuit discussed earlier. In Fig. 14, the resistances are chosen so that the circuit is stable when either tube is cut off and the other is conducting. Let it be assumed that tube *A* is conducting. For this stable condition the grid of tube *A* is positive, being determined by the potential divider from $-c$ to the $+$ supply. At the same time the grid of tube *B* is negative because it lies on a potential divider between *a* and $-c$. Point *a* is at a low potential because of the voltage drop across the load resistor of tube *A* when

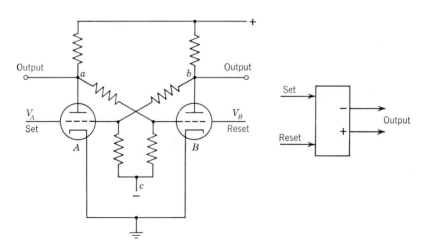

Fig. 14. Flip-flop circuit.

conducting. With the grid of tube A positive and tube B negative, the operation of the flip-flop is stable and the output point a is at a potential slightly above zero and the output potential of point b is high (almost equal to the $+$ supply potential).

Now to cause the flip-flop circuit to change to its other stable condition, a positive pulse of voltage is applied to the grid of tube B at V_B. This pulse causes tube B to conduct and when it does so the potential at point b falls and, in turn, the grid of tube A does likewise. Thus tube A ceases to conduct and with this change the potential of point a rises to the $+$ supply voltage. With this rise of potential at a, the grid of tube B is maintained at a positive potential. This new condition of operation is stable with output a at a positive potential and output b at a near zero potential. This new state of operation can be restored to the original at any time by a positive pulse of voltage applied to the grid of tube A at V_A.

The two states of stable operation of the flip-flop are often called the *set* and *reset*. Ten flip-flops may be connected in a ring to form a scale-of-ten counter. One flip-flop only is in a set condition at any one time. When a pulse is applied to a common reset line, all flip-flops are reset to normal.

Electronic amplifiers are often used in digital computers to increase the magnitude of signal inputs or outputs, and to shape signals, but they are not employed for the computing processes as in analog computers.

Memory Units

The memory unit is the nerve center of the digital computer. Its function is to store approximately 1000 to 30,000 numbers or instructions, and when the binary system is used this means millions of bits of information. These bits of information are fed into the memory at very high rates (that is, each bit may require a time period in the range of 1 to 10 microseconds). In addition to being able to store these huge number of bits at a high speed, the memory must be capable of returning this stored information to other parts of the computer on short notice and again at a high rate of speed.

The three following general systems have been employed for storage in memory: (1) storage in mercury delay tanks, (2) electrostatic storage, and (3) magnetic storage. In the first system supersonic signals are sent through columns of mercury where a short delay in the time of passage occurs. Then these signals are fed back to the input of the column. The feedback contains enough amplification to overcome the attenuation in the column. In the second system the input signals are stored in the form of electrostatic charges on the face of a cathode-ray tube. Most of the later designs of memory units employ magnetic storage. Accordingly, this system will be explained more fully. Magnetic storage may be subdivided into two types—storage on ferromagnetic surfaces (drums and tapes), and static storage in ferrite magnetic cores.

The storage of bits on a magnetic surface follows the same principle as the recording of sound on tape. A magnetic tape moves rapidly past a *writing* or recording head, as shown in Fig. 15a. The current input *bits* shown on the right produce pulses of flux which permeate a small section of the magnetic tape. This pulse of flux leaves a residual of magnetism in the ferromagnetic material on the surface—a magnetic remanence. If the period of the pulse is very short, a tiny dipole of magnetism remains stored in the surface of the tape. Now if this magnetic tape with its stored signals is later passed over the air gap of a similar reading head as shown in Fig. 15b, each dipole induces a small change in flux in the core of the head and results in an induced emf wave as shown at the right. One application of this magnetic storage principle to a system of binary signals, sometimes termed the dipole system, is shown in Fig. 16. The positive pulses are controlled and sent in on a fixed time basis. The presence of a pulse at a time interval indicates a one and the absence of a pulse represents a zero. The wave form produced in the pickup head (reading) consists of alternating emf's occurring at the positive

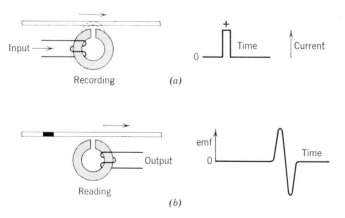

Fig. 15. Storage of signals on a magnetic surface.

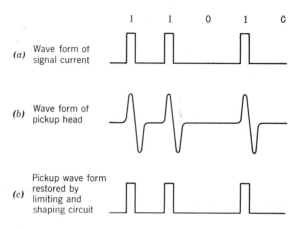

Fig. 16. Wave forms for magnetic storage on surfaces.

pulse intervals (see Fig. 16*b*). This a-c wave form may be restored to one similar to the original by the use of a special circuit which clips the negative pulse and restores the upper positive pulse to the rectangular wave form, as shown in Fig. 16*c*. This magnetic storage of binary bits is more simple and reliable than the magnetic storage of sound on tape. This follows because the sound signal has a non-linear variation which must be recorded with fidelity, whereas the binary signal is an "on" and "off" signal and slight changes in magnitude, and perhaps timing, will not destroy the effectiveness of the signal stored and transferred.

Two modifications of the preceding system of magnetic storage on tape are called the non-return-to-zero and the phase-shift method. Both modifications employ current flow in two directions (+ and −). In the former modification the one bits are produced by positive direction of current and zeros by negative current. If a series of *ones* signals pass, the magnetization remanence does not change until a zero appears (hence the term non-return-to-zero). In the phase-shift modification a current reversal takes place when a bit is passed. A *one* is recorded when the current changes from positive to negative and a zero is recorded when the current changes from negative to positive.

Magnetic storage drums are usually made of brass. They may be nickel-plated or sprayed with a preparation of red or black oxide of iron. The drums are of various sizes (10 in. diameter as an average), and are driven at speeds in the range of 3600 to 12,500 rpm.

The miniature writing and reading heads are placed very close to the drum surface. Heads range in width from $\frac{1}{16}$ to $\frac{1}{10}$ in. They are made by bending strips of high permeability magnetic material about 0.004 in. thick. Their coil frequently consists of only one turn. The "bits" of information are packed on the drum with a density of about 100 per linear inch.

Magnetic tape is made by spraying cellulose acetate or paper tape with a solution containing red or black oxide of iron and a suitable binder. This tape has a large storage capacity. For example, a tape 1200 ft long and $\frac{1}{2}$ in. wide has a theoretical capacity of 360,000 words. This value is based on an assumption of 100 bits stored per channel-inch, 5 channels per half-inch, and 20 bits required per computer word. The solution is as follows:

$$\text{words} = -\frac{\overset{\text{feet}}{1200} \times \overset{\text{inches}}{12} \times \overset{\text{bits/inch}}{100} \times \overset{\text{channels}}{5}}{\underset{\text{bits/word}}{20}} = 360,000 \quad (12)$$

In practice, only a part (perhaps 50 per cent) of the theoretical capacity can be realized. This follows because vacant spaces must be left in the channels to allow for starting and stopping of reels for obtaining access to specific areas of storage. Also space is required for coding and instruction. Obviously, the access time to reach information stored on tape is relatively long.

Static magnetic storage can be produced in a matrix of tiny ferrite magnetic cores having the formation and circuits shown in Fig. 17a. The theory of action follows closely earlier discussions covering magnetic amplifiers and static control devices. Assume that the toroidal core of Fig. 17b is made of a magnetic material having a rectangular hysteresis loop. If a strong positive current is sent through coil A, the magnetic core will be driven to saturation. Now if a second current is passed through coil B, tending to magnetize the core in the same direction, no flux change occurs because the core is in a state of saturation. Thus no output signal (voltage) will occur at winding C. However, if the current through B produces a strong reversing mmf, the flux in the toroid will reverse and an output signal is produced at C.

A more useful application of the toroidal core in Fig. 17b is attained by saturating the core with a strong current in coil C. Then the magnitude of the currents passed through A and B is controlled so that either one alone is unable to reverse the established flux, but

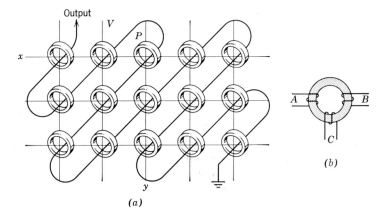

Fig. 17. Static magnetic storage using ferrite cores.

so that the two acting in unison will produce the reversal and give an output in coil C. The latter process is employed in the matrix storage system of Fig. 17a. The ferrite cores used in practice are approximately 2 mm in external diameter and the windings consist of single wires threaded through them. A binary digit is stored in each tiny core. The core represents a 0 when magnetized in one direction and a 1 when magnetized in the other. To read the binary digit stored in core P, currents of one-half magnitude are passed simultaneously through horizontal wire x and vertical wire y. If these current pulses are in the correct direction (additive) to reverse the flux, an output signal is induced in the encircling coil. However, no reversing flux or voltage signal can arise in any other core except P because only one one-half current can flow. The first large scale static matrix constructed stored 1024 words of 16 binary digits each. Static cores and matrix circuits are also employed for switching purposes.

Input Section of Digital Computers

The input to a digital computer may be a keyboard similar to that of a typewriter. It may consist of devices capable of reading punched cards, paper tape, or magnetic tape. Usually it is a combination of two or more of the preceding types of equipment. In the case of large digital computers, the reading of data from punched cards and manual keyboards is usually too slow and represents an uneconomical use of the computer. Such poor economy of the work time of a computer may be avoided through the use of auxiliary equipment which records the input information from keyboards, punched cards, and so forth, on magnetic tape. When all necessary information is recorded in this manner, it may be fed through the normal tape reading input and be transferred to memory at very high speed.

Output Section of Digital Computers

The solution to a problem by a digital computer is ultimately transferred to the output section. At this point the result is recorded on punched cards, printed paper, or on paper or magnetic tape. The numbers given in the solution are usually in binary form and hence must be converted to the decimal system. This conversion could be performed by an operator but in practice is effected by auxiliary electronic conversion equipment, which is incorporated as a part of the computer.

Computers are sometimes used to control the operation of processes or equipment. In such cases the output of the computer is fed directly to external devices instead of being stored.

Programming

Programming is a term which includes all the preparatory steps necessary to present a problem to the input of a computer. Some of these steps are data collection, numerical analysis, and coding. All the numerical data and information bearing on a problem must be collected. Decimal numbers and other information must be converted to the binary system. The numerical analysis of a problem may be difficult because, in a single step, digital computers can perform only simple arithmetic and make simple logical decisions. Most scientific and engineering problems require the use of integrals, trigonometric functions, differential equations, and vectors. Accordingly, numerical methods must be used to translate the preceding mathematical forms into arithmetic processes. If the solution to a problem requires a simple logical answer, the conditions which determine the solution must be set up.

After the data have been assembled in binary form and the numerical analysis completed, instructions for the memory storage and computer procedure must be issued. First, the location of the data and the instructions in the memory must be planned or indexed. Similar types of data or instructions should be located in definite areas on the storage drums or tapes, keeping in mind the importance of quick accessibility to the data. Then the sequence of steps in carrying out the solution of the problem must be prepared and converted to numerical codes for storage in memory. When all this information has been fed from the input into memory, the computer is ready for a trial run.

Applications of Digital Computers

The importance of the digital computer lies in its flexibility and its speed in performing thousands or millions of solutions of a simple basic problem in a very short period of time. During the process the quantities involved may be constant or variable to provide addition or multiplication or to determine averages. Solutions which would require years of human effort may be performed in seconds. Most applications of digital computers arise from the property mentioned. By using multiple solutions the engineer may introduce more variables into problems and obtain more critical results. The engineer may test a new theoretical design by calculations within a computer and determine probable operational results before a test model is constructed. One important application consists in data reduction. Tests on new equipment result in thousands of readings of temperature, pressure, strain, and so forth, which may be reduced to averages and other meaningful answers by computers. In business organizations the processing of payrolls, inventory records, sales records, and so forth can be performed by digital computers instead of the slower processes by hand or ordinary calculating machines. The determination of a prime number may require thousands of arithmetic operations. Some large digital computers can find thousands of prime numbers per hour.

Superconductivity and Cryotrons

Superconductivity (zero resistance) was discovered in 1911 by H. Kammerlingh Onnes. He found that the resistance of mercury drops suddenly to zero at 4.12° K. Since then 21 other elements and many metallic alloys have been found to be superconductive at certain critical low temperatures lying in the range of zero to 17° K. The critical temperature of niobium is 8° K, lead 7.2° K, tantalum 4.4° K, tin 3.7° K, and aluminum 1.2° K. The resistivity of many superconductive materials is relatively high at room temperature. Some poor conductors become superconductive at low temperatures, whereas good conductors such as gold, silver, and copper do not. In an experiment conducted by Professor S. C. Collin at the Massachusetts Institute of Technology, a lead ring held below its transition temperature carried an induced current of several hundred amperes for years without any observable change in magnitude.

In 1916 Silsbee discovered that the critical temperature at which a material becomes superconductive is lowered by the presence of a magnetic field of a suitable value. If the temperature of a superconductor is held below its normal transition temperature, its resistance is zero. It remains at zero when a magnetic field is applied until a critical value is reached, whereupon its resistance is restored. Thus for the region where superconductivity occurs for a given material, its resistance may be varied from zero to normal by the application of a magnetic field. This property suggests the use of this principle for a control device.

The cryotron is a control or switching device which employs the principle of magnetically controlled superconductivity discussed in the preceding paragraph. The basic construction of a cryotron is depicted in Fig. 18. Here a short section of material AB is surrounded by a helical coil CC'. If section AB is held at a temperature just below its critical superconductive temperature, its resistance is zero. Now if a current of sufficient magnitude is passed through coil CC', the magnetic field created along AB causes the resistance of AB to be restored. Thus AB may serve as a gate controlled by the current in coil CC'. As a refinement to the principle involved, both the center core AB and the coil CC' may be constructed of superconductive materials, with CC' having a higher critical temperature. Then for the temperature employed, the control winding remains a superconductor at all times. Hence there is no resistance in the control winding. A magnetic field once established needs no energy for its support and the current continues to flow. Thus the device is very efficient for switching purposes.

The basic cryotron unit of Fig. 18 may be used in many combinations of identical units. Sometimes the core of one unit AB is connected in series with the coil CC' of a second unit. Since the units are small, hundreds of them can be placed in a small space. They are placed in liquid helium and the temperature is controlled by the

Fig. 18. Basic cryotron construction.

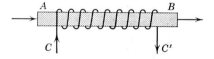

pressure on the liquid helium. At atmospheric pressure liquid helium evaporates at 4.2° K.

Cryotrons have been used experimentally for producing flip-flops and other switching circuits employed in digital computers. The research workers who have been experimenting with them expect that they will find future application in commercial computers.

PROBLEMS

1. A d-c amplifier in an analog computer has an amplification factor of 1000 and a feedback resistor of 1 meg. What is its input resistance?

2. A d-c amplifier is employed to add the expression $2x + y + 0.5z$. Its feedback resistor is 1 meg. Construct the adder circuit, giving resistance values to all inputs.

3. Write the binary numbers for the following decimals: (a) 25; (b) 75; (c) 210; (d) 1250; (e) 23,453.

4. Add the following binary numbers and compute the decimal equivalent:

$$
\begin{array}{r}
1101 \\
11011 \\
1101100 \\
\hline
\end{array}
$$

5. A memory drum is 10 in. in diameter and 1 ft long. If it has 10 channels per inch, 100 bits per channel-inch, 20 bits per word, and 60 per cent of the surface contains information, how many words does it store?

6. If the drum of Problem 5 has a speed of 1250 rpm, what is the reading time and writing time per bit? Ditto for words per second?

7. A roll of memory tape is 2400 ft long and ¾ in. wide. If it has 12 channels per inch and stores 100 bits per channel-inch, how many 20-bit decimals can it store, assuming only 50 per cent of its surface is utilized effectively?

8. If the tape of Problem 7 moves at the rate of 8 ft per second, what is the time required for writing or reading a bit? Also what is the maximum time required to reach a word of information on the reel?

REFERENCES

1. Berkeley, E. C., *Giant Brains,* John Wiley and Sons, New York, 1949.
2. Korn, G. A., and T. M. Korn, *Electronic Analog Computers,* McGraw-Hill Book Co., New York, 1956.
3. Wilkes, M. V., *Automatic Digital Computers,* John Wiley and Sons, New York, 1956.

4. Phister, Montgomery, Jr., *Logical Design of Digital Computers*, John Wiley and Sons, New York, 1958.
5. McCracken, D. D., *Digital Computer Programming*, John Wiley and Sons, New York, 1957.
6. Bremer, J. W., "Cryogenic Devices in Logical Circuitry and Storage," *Elec. Mfg.*, February 1958.
7. Buck, D. A., "The Cryotron—A Superconductive Computer Component," *Proc. IRE,* Vol. 44, p. 482, April 1956.

Index